James Rankin

The first saints

character and church studies in the New Testament

James Rankin

The first saints
character and church studies in the New Testament

ISBN/EAN: 9783741158445

Manufactured in Europe, USA, Canada, Australia, Japa

Cover: Foto ©Andreas Hilbeck / pixelio.de

Manufactured and distributed by brebook publishing software
(www.brebook.com)

James Rankin

The first saints

THE FIRST SAINTS

THE FIRST·SAINTS:

*CHARACTER AND CHURCH STUDIES IN
THE NEW TESTAMENT*

BY

JAMES RANKIN, D.D.

MINISTER OF MUTHILL

WILLIAM BLACKWOOD AND SONS
EDINBURGH AND LONDON
MDCCCXCIII

PREFACE.

HAVING published in 1875 a volume entitled 'Character Studies in the Old Testament,' the idea occurred to me afterwards of a parallel volume for the New Testament. Since then, however, I have been largely engaged in historical study preparing a 'Handbook of the Church of Scotland' in 1879, of which a fourth edition revised and much enlarged appeared in 1888; while the chief portion of it from A.D. 1200-1688 was again revised and enlarged in 1890, as vol. ii. of 'The Church of Scotland, Past and Present,' in five vols., edited by Professor Story. Alongside of these studies in history, I had for many years been engaged on doctrinal subjects, embodied in 1890 in 'The Creed in Scotland.'

After these eighteen years of additional experience, both in professional and literary work, my point of view and method of treatment have been considerably modified compared with my earlier book on the Old Testament, where, indeed, there was less scope for dealing with matters of ritual or Church government. While now,

and always, in practical sympathy with the Church of
Scotland, I have for many years ceased to agree with a
large part of its career which has been shaped by drift
and prejudice, more especially since the Westminster
Standards of 1645 introduced the foreign element of
English Puritanism.   Even beyond that date, declension
had already begun in our Second Book of Discipline,
which is narrow and intolerant compared with the system
set up by Knox in the freshness of the Reformation in
1560.   Alive to the great difference of the principles
recognised by our Church at various periods of her
history since 1560, I make no scruple either to compare
stage with stage of development, or even to criticise the
prudence of certain features and results of the Reformation itself.   Part of these views I have here expressed
under the names of Joseph, Peter, Philip, and Timothy;
part explains the use of ancient Latin hymns as well as
Roman and Anglican Collects; and part I have more
methodically set forth in a concluding chapter intended
as a substitute for a long Preface or Introduction.

JAMES RANKIN.

MUTHILL, PERTHSHIRE,
   February 2, 1893.

CONTENTS.

THE FIRST SAINTS

The Four Evangelists.

Christi perennes nuntii,
Retecta qui cœlestibus
Scriptis Dei mysteria
Totum per orbem spargitis:

Heralds of Jesus through all
   time!
  Who, speaking day by day,
Have scattered wide through every
   clime,   [sublime
Those truths that in the depths
  Of olden Scripture lay !

Olim sub umbris condita
Vates sacri quæ viderant,
Umbris procul cedentibus,
Vidistis hæc pleno die.

          [screen,
What under night's mysterious
  Veiled in a shadowy hue,
Was by the Prophets dimly seen,
'Twas yours, without a veil between,
  In naked day to view !

Humana quæ tulit Deus,
Divina quæ gessit homo,
Seris legenda posteris,
Dictante scripsistis Deo.

What Christ, the Man, divinely
  wrought ;
  The God, as mortal bore ;
Your pens to every age have taught,
In words with inspiration fraught,
  That live for evermore !

Loco remotos, tempore,
Vos rexit idem Spiritus ;
Vestris adhuc in paginis
Nobis loqui non desinit.

By distance severed wide apart,
  Yet by one Spirit swayed,
One were ye all in mind and heart,
And with a more than human art,
  One perfect Christ portrayed.

Da, Christe, nos tecum mori ;
Tecum simul da surgere :
Terrena da contemnere ;
Amare da celestia.
        —*Paris Breviary.*

Wrapt in a voice of mortal mould,
  The Father's secret word
To you His truths eternal told ;—
And still, as we your page unfold
  That self-same voice is heard !
        —E. Caswall.

S. Matthew,

EVANGELIST AND APOSTLE.

DAY, SEPTEMBER 21.

ORATIO.—*Da nobis, quæsumus, omnipotens Deus, ut beati Matthæi apostoli tui et evangelistæ, quam prævenimus, veneranda solennitas : et devotionem nobis augeat et salutem.* (For S. Matthew's Eve.)

Beati Mathei apostoli tui et evangelistæ, Domine, precibus adjuvemur : ut quod possibilitas nostra non obtinet, ejus nobis intercessione donetur. Per Dominum. (For S. Matthew's Day.)

For the Epistle.—Ezek. i. 10-14.
The Gospel.—S. Matt. ix. 9-13.

COLLECT.—*O Almighty God, who by Thy blessed Son didst call Matthew from the receipt of custom to be an apostle and evangelist ; Grant us grace to forsake all covetous desires and inordinate love of riches, and to follow the same Thy Son Jesus Christ, who liveth and reigneth with Thee and the Holy Ghost, one God, world without end.   Amen.*

The Epistle.—2 Cor. iv. 1-6.
The Gospel.—S. Matt. ix. 9-13.

Blessed Lord, who hast caused all Holy Scriptures to be written for our learning ; Grant that we may in such wise hear them, read, mark, learn, and inwardly digest them, that by patience, and comfort of Thy Holy Word, we may embrace, and ever hold fast the blessed hope of everlasting life, which Thou hast given us in our Saviour Jesus Christ.   Amen.[1]

> Dear Lord, on this Thy servant's day,
> Who left for Thee the gold and mart,
> Who heard Thee whisper, "Come away,"
> And followed with a single heart,
>
> Give us amid earth's weary moil,
> And wealth for which men cark and care,
> 'Mid fortune's pride, and need's wild toil,
> And broken hearts in purple rare,
>
> Give us Thy grace to rise above
> The glare of this world's smelting fires ;
> Let God's great love put out the love
> Of gold, and gain, and low desires.
>
> Still, like a breath from scented lime
> Borne into rooms where sick men faint,
> His voice comes floating through all time,
> Thine own evangelist and saint.
>
> Still sweetly rings the Gospel strain
> Of golden store that knows not rust :
> The love of Christ is more than gain,
> And heavenly crowns than yellow dust.
> —Mrs C. F. ALEXANDER.

"And as Jesus passed forth from thence, He saw a man, named Matthew, sitting at the receipt of custom : and He saith unto him, Follow me.   And he arose, and followed Him."—S. MATT. ix. 9.

HERE we are told by the evangelist himself how his connection with Jesus and the Gospel began in a direct personal call, which was at once accepted ; so that henceforth Matthew the publican became first a follower, then an apostle, then a biographer of Christ.

[1] Angl. Collect, 1549.   Second Sunday in Advent.

In the New Testament the name of Matthew occurs only once, in a formal list of the apostles, Acts i. 13, beyond the compass of the four gospels. Within the gospels the name is met only six times—thrice in the record of his call as a disciple, and thrice in the record of his appointment among the twelve as an apostle ; so that he is only twice named in each of the three synoptical gospels. This, added to his own short book in twenty-eight chapters, is not much material from which to form an outline of the life, character, and work of a Christian hero.

The scene of the call of Matthew was Capernaum, a town in the tetrarchy of Herod Antipas ; and his office in the customs or taxes there would not be so offensive to Jewish feelings or prejudices as the same office directly under Roman rule in the procuratorship of Pilate in Judea, for the Herodian family was connected with the Maccabees, who had been patriotic Jewish rulers. When Jesus was born, Herod the Great was still ruling at Jerusalem. When the Holy Family returned from Egypt after Herod's death, they took refuge in the north, at Nazareth, under Herod's son Antipas, who was a milder ruler than the other son, Archelaus, at Jerusalem. It was on the overthrow and banishment of Archelaus that direct Roman rule came in as a procuratorship, to the great irritation and humiliation of patriotic Jews. In his own list of the twelve, it is to the honour of our evangelist that he plainly adds a note of the old occupation, unpopular though it was, " Matthew the publican " coming in as the eighth in order, following the name of Thomas and partly conjoined therewith. In S. Mark's and S. Luke's list Matthew is seventh in order ; but in S. Luke's second list in Acts he is eighth. The original or additional name of Matthew was Levi, but after his call by Christ the old or double name was dropped. Matthew in Hebrew corresponds to the Greek Theodore and Italian Diodati = God's-gift. A like change is observable in the two chief of the apostles, Peter superseding Simon, and Paul superseding Saul.

We are not to suppose that when Matthew was called by
our Lord, this was done entirely off-hand, without acquaintance and intercourse preceding. The manner and amount of
preparation are unrecorded, but the promptness of response to
the call indicates a man whose mind and heart had already
been fully won, and who only needed the formal and solemn
summons in order to take his place decisively among Christ's
disciples. And we may the more confidently take this view
in the case of a man of good business habits, and whose
methodical structure in his gospel-writing shows an orderly
and balanced judgment.

The day of Matthew's call was notable for a series of four
events recorded by the evangelist himself, and also by S.
Luke, from the latter of whom (by observing the conjunctions
which connect the parts of the narrative) we learn that all
belong to the same place and day. The four are,—a feast
given in Matthew's house to Jesus, His disciples, and "many
publicans and sinners"; the visit of the disciples of John
asking why Christ's disciples fast not; the message from
Jairus as to his daughter; and the healing of the woman with
the issue of blood.

The first of these four is of special interest here as being
apparently a farewell feast on the part of Matthew to his
circle of companions on quitting the customs service. The
feast marks a man who stood well with his neighbours, and
who looked with joy and hope on the new way of life he was
entering; and the feast, as S. Luke says, was held in his
own house, which must have been of good extent and well
plenished to admit of such a style of entertainment on short
notice: "And Levi made him a great feast in his own house:
and there was a great company of publicans and of others that
sat down with them."

Touching Matthew's calling in relation to parts of the
Gospel narrative it has been said:[1] "In the list of the
apostles he enters his name as 'Matthew the publican,' and

[1] Dr Frazer, Synoptical Lectures.

he has not written a word to exalt himself or to take away the reproach of the class to which he had belonged. He does not record the story of Zaccheus, chief of the publicans at Jericho, or the parable of the Pharisee and the publican in the Temple. On the other hand, it is he and no other who gives us that saying of the Lord in which the publicans are joined with ' the harlots ' as believing John the Baptist and going into the kingdom of God."

It is in the chapter following the record of the call of Matthew that we have the list of the twelve apostles, and the charge given to them by our Lord. And although no further mention is made of Matthew separately, we require to remember that for the next two or three years, during the whole of our Lord's ministry, he was his Master's daily witness and companion, and shared all the training divinely given by the great Prophet to prepare the apostles for their coming task of founding, rearing, and spreading the Church of the new dispensation. And thus, apart from the mention of his name, we are fully justified in assuming the presence of Matthew, as of the rest of the apostles, man by man, near to Christ, an eye and ear witness of almost everything in the gospels, especially in his own gospel, from chapter ix. to the end. The place of Matthew among the twelve is simple and quiet, even to silence. There was a trio of the twelve specially favoured of the Lord on three marked occasions; but Matthew's place was not so near as that. Many Gospel incidents associate themselves with individual apostles—*e. g.*, Peter, Andrew, James, John, Philip, Thomas, and other three; yet, save the farewell feast to old friends on occasion of his first call, no such incident attaches itself to the name of Matthew. He seems to have been a quiet, unobtrusive, thoughtful, well-conditioned man; a good observer, a faithful recorder, with power of comparison and arrangement, who had had a fine early training in the Old Testament Scriptures, and who entertained a high ideal of how the old Scriptures and the old Church were to receive a vast accession of honour under Jesus the Prophet of Nazareth as the promised Messiah.

What a marvel in the history of Christianity it is that a man so silent and unobtrusive as this should, by God's appointment, blessing, and inspiration, have drawn up for all succeeding ages so admirable a memoir of his Lord and Master as we possess in the opening book of the New Testament! The high merit of the first gospel betokens how great a Teacher Jesus was, and how diligent Matthew was as a disciple of the divine Rabbi in those three years of apostolic education.

In attempting an estimate of S. Matthew's Gospel, commencement may be made by enumerating what things are distinctive to it, as not found elsewhere. These are two miracles, ten parables, nine discourses, and six incidents.

The miracles are the cure of two blind men, and the procuring of the tribute coin from a fish's mouth—both at Capernaum. The parables are—the tares, the hid treasure, the pearl of great price, the draw-net, the unmerciful servant, the labourers in the vineyard, the father with the two sons, the marriage of the king's son, the ten virgins, the talents.

The discourses are—a large part of the Sermon on the Mount; the invitation to the heavy-laden; idle words to be judged; the blessing pronounced on Peter for his confession of Christ; the greater part of chapter xviii. on humility and forgiveness; the rejection of the Jews; denunciation of Scribes and Pharisees in chapter xxiii. as a connected discourse; description in chapter xxv. of the judgment-day; the last commission as to teaching, baptising, and the continual presence of the Lord.

Incidents peculiar to S. Matthew are—the whole of chapter ii. as to the magi and the star, the massacre of the Innocents, the flight of the Holy Family into Egypt and their return to Nazareth; in chapter iii. the coming of the Pharisees and Sadducees to John's baptism; Peter's attempt to walk on the water; three points at the Passion—viz., the covenant of

Judas for thirty pieces of silver, with his remorseful end, the dream of Pilate's wife, and the appearance of resurrection saints in Jerusalem; also three points connected with our Lord's resurrection—viz., the watch placed at the sepulchre, the soldiers bribed to spread a false report, the earthquake. Would not our Christian heritage be greatly curtailed by the withdrawal of all these elements from it?—if one can conceive the possibility of such a loss after eighteen and a half centuries of blessed possession. Yet this is only one item and aspect of our indebtedness to the first evangelist of the four.

A further way of estimating S. Matthew's writing is to consider how many things combine to fit it for its place of honour in the forefront of the New Testament of our Lord and Saviour. Beginning with a genealogy of Jesus that traces Him back through King David to the patriarch Abraham, the foundation of the book is at once and deeply laid in the Old Testament. Moreover, the leading principle and aim of the book join it very closely to the Law and the Prophets and the ancient Church and worship. No New Testament book so frequently makes quotation from or reference to the Old Testament as this of Matthew. Here the fulfilment idea occurs eighty-one times; whereas in the other three gospels the figures are only thirty-two, fifty-six, and thirty respectively.[1]

So strongly Jewish and national was Matthew in his point of view and line of thought, that the first draft of his book was written in Aramaic, the vernacular language of the time and country, as is testified by Papias and Irenæus.[2] The latter says, "Matthew wrote his gospel in Judea while Peter and Paul were founding the Church at Rome. He wrote for the use of Jewish converts, and in their national language. Having formerly preached to the Hebrews, when he was about to go to others also [tradition says in Ethiopia] he committed to writing in his native tongue his gospel, and so

---

[1] The full list is given in 'Aids to the Student of the Holy Bible.'
[2] Quoted in Westcott, Introduction to the Gospels, p. 207.

filled up by his writing that which was lacking in his presence." The first edition in Aramaic, and perhaps also the second edition in Greek, as we now have it, was the earliest written of the four Christian biographies now in our Bible. But the making of the first draft in Aramaic only corresponded to the drift of the book itself, which was to delineate Jesus of Nazareth as in His person the promised Messiah, and in His teaching the great Prophet who carried the old Law to a higher development, and who revived the righteous protests of men like Samuel, Elijah, and Isaiah, aiming at a commonwealth juster, more spiritual and heaven-like, than had as yet flourished in Palestine.

" S. Matthew has treasured up for the Church more fully than the other synoptists the words and discourses of Jesus; such especially as present Him in the character of the great Prophet, who, like the prophets of old time, denounces national sins, and predicts the future of the nation and the Church. Instances of this characteristic are the full report of the Sermon on the Mount in three chapters; the charge to the apostles in chapter x.; the great series of prophetic parables in chapter xiii. peculiar to this gospel; the denunciation of the Scribes and Pharisees in chapter xxiii.; the predictions of the fall of Jerusalem and the parables of the second advent in chapters xxiv. and xxv." [1]

Many of these same features of the first gospel have been noted by Delitzsch as forming a resemblance to the order in the Pentateuch, as if the evangelist's idea had been to show the realisation of the ancient promise of a prophet like unto Moses. Viewed in this light, the genealogy in chapter i., probably copied from the public archives of the Sanhedrim, or got from James, the Lord's brother, would correspond to Genesis, especially to chapter v., which begins, "This is the book of the generations of Adam." The second chapter, recording the slaughter of the infants at Bethlehem and the escape of the holy child Jesus, would correspond to Pharaoh's cruelty to the

[1] Cambridge Bible for Schools, S. Matthew, p. 11.

male children of the Hebrews and the wonderful escape of Moses therefrom. The three chapters of the Sermon on the Mount would correspond to Exodus xx.-xxxi., when Moses was on the Mount forty-days and forty nights communing with God, and received the two tables of the law, with many regulations for the people, and instruction as to the pattern of the tabernacle and the service in it. In chapter viii., in the cleansing of the leper sent to show himself to the priest, according to the law of Moses, we see a recognition of the leading principle which pervades the whole Book of Leviticus. The 10th chapter, recording the names of the twelve, their appointment to office, and the charge full of detailed instructions given to them for guidance in duty as the leaders of the new kingdom, suggests to us the Book of Numbers, which deals with the ordering of the twelve tribes of Israel, beginning with the Levites, and providing for the peace, purity, and obedience of the whole people. Chapter xix., which takes up suddenly our Lord's ministry in "the coasts of Judea," wherein he goes afresh over reproof, exhortation, and prophecy, parallel to what he had already done in the Galilee district, with which the evangelist was most familiar, reminds us not a little of the Book of Deuteronomy, wherein Moses largely does his work in duplicate, a solemn revisal, knowing that the time of his departure is at hand. Then chapters xxvii. and xxviii., narrating the death and resurrection of Jesus, and his directions for the Church's future, have their antetype in the last four chapters of Deuteronomy, which record the dying counsels, death, and mysterious burial of the man of God, the great Hebrew lawgiver.

As a man called in Capernaum of Galilee, and who held public office in the taxes there under the tetrarchy of Herod Antipas, as a man attached to his country's language, and evidently also to its familiar scenery, it must have been peculiarly pleasant to the evangelist to describe the great Prophet, as he has done, in a happy threefold relation to Galilean mountains, each of the occasions forming a great Gospel land-

mark. The Mount of Beatitudes, the type of all sound doctrine, was Galilean. Galilean, too, was the Mount of Transfiguration, the scene of Messiah's glory, and of the blessed
conference touching the decease to be accomplished at Jerusalem. Galilean, yet again, was the Mount of Commission after
the resurrection, where the Church received what Wellington
professionally characterised as its marching orders. "Then
the eleven disciples went away into Galilee, into a mountain where Jesus had appointed them. . . . And Jesus came
and spake unto them, saying, All power is given unto me in
heaven and in earth. Go ye therefore, and teach all nations ;
. . . and, lo, I am with you alway, even unto the end of the
world." Could there have been a grander or more fitting close
to the book than this, wherein the gospel of the kingdom ends
with the victory over death, with the Lord's declaration of His
rule in grace and glory, His headship over civil and ecclesiastical life, His commission to make and baptise disciples, and
His promise of a perpetual world - wide presence for their
strength, guidance, comfort, companionship, courage, defence,
and benediction ?

With overflowing hearts we may thank God for this opening gospel, wherein the most distinctively Jewish of the
evangelists, by God's providence and inspiration, provides a
book specially fitted to stand first in order after the close
of the Old Testament as a transition to the New ; wherein
he gives scope to his patriotic feeling over his fellow-country-
man the Prophet of Galilee ; wherein he exercises his clerkly
and business skill in grouping his material in instructive
order ; and wherein he utilises his various gifts of observation,
memory, retiringness, and reverence, for the commemoration
of Christ and the edification of the faithful.

The apostle's call took place in the first year of our Lord's
public ministry. For three years thereafter Matthew enjoyed
the training common to all the twelve. After Pentecost
he seems to have clung to Palestine for his special sphere
of labour ; and there probably to his own beloved province

of Galilee. Busied in his work among his northern neighbours, the idea seems to have occurred to him of increasing
his usefulness and giving point and permanence to his lessons
touching Christ, by putting down in his mother tongue the
substance of what he taught. And so he wrote, perhaps
within seven or eight years of the crucifixion, his Aramaic
first draft of the divine story of his Master's birth, baptism,
miracles, parables, sayings, journeys, death, and resurrection.
After his writing, as before it, he seems to have busily yet
quietly exercised his apostolic office. And the northern sphere
of his labour among simple people, combined with his special
reverence for the old law, enabled him to do a great deal
without attracting hostile attention. An early tradition represents him as clinging to Palestine for twelve years after
our Lord's death. Then he proceeded to preach the Gospel
"to others," Ethiopia in Arabia being the land traditionally
assigned to him.

"It is a characteristic of this silent unmarked life, in which
the personality of the evangelist is lost in the voice of the
message which he was inspired to utter, that Matthew's name
has been less prominent in the Churches and nations of
Christendom than others of his co-apostles, or even than
many saints, whose services to the Church of Christ have
been infinitely less. None of the great Churches of Christendom have been called by his name; no guild or fraternity,
no college in our great universities, no state or nation, has
chosen him for its patron. Scarcely one famous picture has
taught the lesson of his call. The personal memory, like
the personal life of S. Matthew, withdraws itself from the
observation of men."[1] This is both true and remarkable
when we think of the many dedications to Peter and Paul;
the honour of S. Mark at Venice and Alexandria; the guild
of S. Luke among painters; and the guilds of S. John among
knights and masons. And yet, considering the labour of his
life in steady teaching and preaching, and also considering

[1] Cambridge Bible for Schools, S. Matthew, p. 8.

the solid excellence of his one grand book, let us learn to do justice to this unobtrusive, silent, and ascetic man, whose honourable place at the opening of the New Testament is alike appropriate and well earned.

S. Mark,

THE EVANGELIST.

DAY, APRIL 25.

ORATIO.—*Deus qui beatum Marcum evangelistam tuum evangelicæ prædicationis gratia sublimasti: tribue, quæsumus, ejus nos semper et eruditione proficere et oratione defendi.*
The Epistle.—Eph. iv. 7-16.
The Gospel.—S. John xv. 1-11.

COLLECT.—*O Almighty God, who hast instructed Thy holy Church with the heavenly doctrine of Thy evangelist Saint Mark; Give us grace, that, being not like children carried away with every blast of vain doctrine, we may be established in the truth of Thy holy Gospel; through Jesus Christ our Lord.   Amen.*
The Epistle.—Eph. iv. 7-16.
The Gospel.—S. John xv. 1-11.

From out the cloud of amber light,
Borne on the whirlwind from the north,
Four living creatures, winged and bright,
Before the Prophet's eye came forth.

The voice of God was in the Four
Beneath that awful crystal mist,
And every wondrous sign they wore
Foreshadowed an evangelist.

The lion-faced, he told abroad
The strength of love, the strength of faith;
He showed the Almighty Son of God,
The Man Divine who won by death.

O Lion of the Royal Tribe,
Strong Son of God, and strong to save,
All power and honour we ascribe
To Thee who only makest brave !

For strength to love, for will to speak,
For fiery crowns by martyrs won,
For suffering patience, strong and meek,
We praise Thee, Lord, and Thee alone.

—C. F. ALEXANDER.

Jesu, we praise Thee for his work
  Who hears Thy living word,
Yoked ever in the fourfold car
  Which carries Thee, the Lord.

Taught by Saint Mark, the Morions' land
  Now lifts her hands in prayer :
He bears Thy light to Egypt's gloom,
  And makes a Goshen there.

He sheds Thy Spirit's sevenfold grace
  In evangelic beams ;
Like sevenfold Nile, which cheers the land
  With fertilising streams.

Thy living streams in Afric's sands
  He pours, a holy flood ;
And what the evangelist had preached
  The martyr seals with blood.

We bless Thy Holy Spirit's love
  For all the gifts of grace,
Which cheer the saint and martyr's heart,
  And speed them in their race.

Take from us fear ; give power and love,
  Sound mind and constant soul ;
That we, O Lord, with them may run,
  And with them reach the goal.

—BP. WORDSWORTH, of Lincoln.

"And when Peter had considered the thing, he came to the
house of Mary the mother of John, whose surname was
Mark ; where many were gathered together praying."—
Acts xii. 12.

IN point of historical order this is the earliest Scripture allusion to the author of the second of the four gospels. And
it is also of special value because at once it launches us on the
track best fitted to lead to an accurate estimate of the influences that went to form the man's character and determine
the nature of his Christian work. We see that his home was
in Jerusalem ; that his mother (probably a widow) occupied a
house of some social standing, and was a prominent person
among the first disciples, her house having become a meeting-
place for prayer for many believers. Moreover, the house and
its mistress were so well known and trusted by the apostle
Peter, that on his miraculous escape from prison it was the
place that first suggested itself, both as a safe retreat and
where sympathetic welcome was certain. Both the readiness
of resolving to go there, and the recognition of his voice by
the servant-girl Rhoda, show that the apostle had already
been on intimate terms in the family. The whole scene, in
fact, is a lovely picture of the earnest simple ways of the
early Christians, so helpful to one another, and bound already by common prayer into a sacred brotherhood, even
previous to the organisation of a church service. This
opening intimacy on the part of S. Peter with young Mark
shows the basis of the ancient and universal idea of a close
connection between the second gospel and the chief of the
apostles.

On three occasions when our evangelist is mentioned in the
Acts he is designated "John, whose surname was Mark." Other
twice he is simply called John. In other five places in the
New Testament where he is mentioned it is as Mark simply.
John was the Jewish name of the youth, but his Latin sur-
name of Marcus soon superseded the Jewish name, especially

after his Christian work took him away from Jerusalem, and even from Judea.

In order to understand how Mark was qualified to write an account of the life of our Lord, the simplest method is to trace one by one the passages in which his name occurs, and to observe in connection with each what contribution it makes toward an outline biography.

From Acts xii. 12 we have already seen that his mother's house was a gathering-place for prayer for the first Christians, and that S. Peter had a special acquaintance with the family. The next passage in the last verse of the same chapter is this : "And Barnabas and Saul returned from Jerusalem, when they had fulfilled their ministry, and took with them John, whose surname was Mark." The ministry referred to was a message to Jerusalem from Antioch with alms to help believers in a time of dearth. When the alms had been delivered or distributed, Barnabas and Saul took young Mark back with them to Antioch, in Syria, which was now the scene of their work. This was in 45 A.D., and shows in what circumstances Mark left home to begin to serve Christ in a mission.

In chapter xiii. 4-13, Mark is twice mentioned. "So they [Barnabas and Saul], being sent forth [from Antioch] by the Holy Ghost, departed unto Seleucia [the port of Antioch] ; and from thence they sailed to Cyprus. And when they were at Salamis [on the east side of Cyprus], they preached the Word of God in the synagogues of the Jews : and they had also John to their minister "—*i. e.*, John Mark accompanied Barnabas and Saul as a ministerial assistant. Cyprus was the birthplace of Barnabas, who was a Levite (Acts iv. 36), and was brother of Mary, the mother of Mark (Col. iv. 10). "Now when Paul and his company loosed from Paphos [capital of Cyprus, and at the south end of the island], they came to Perga in Pamphylia : and John departing from them returned to Jerusalem." We are not told the reason of this departure, but we find further on that it was decidedly disapproved of by S. Paul. As Mark returned to Jerusalem, the home of his mother, it may have been on her account; or he may have shrunk from penetrating into Asia beyond the coast, which alone would be familiar and trusted by people connected with Cyprus; or he may have wished to be at Jerusalem to serve under Peter in the Gospel, instead of under Paul and Barnabas. This parting at Perga, whatever its reason, happened in 48 A.D.

Three years later, when Paul, Barnabas, Silas, Jude, and Mark were all at Antioch, delivering and expounding the decree of the first Council at Jerusalem, declaring circumcision obsolete, and inculcating abstinence from idol-meats, strangled flesh, and fornication, it was proposed by Paul to Barnabas, on completion of their special commission from the Council, that now they should start on a general revisitation of the Christian settlements already made. But while the two were at one as to the excellence of the proposal, they fell out on a matter of detail as to the expediency of having Mark as a fellow-worker; Paul saying No, because he was displeased with him for leaving them at Perga, which he interpreted as a deserting of his post. Barnabas, however, interpreted Mark's conduct more leniently, and did not consider it as disqualifying his nephew for further work in the Gospel. So he refused to go with Paul unless Mark was taken also. The result was two missionary parties instead of one; Barnabas taking Mark and going to Cyprus, where they had special acquaintance; and Paul, accompanied by Silas, going to Syria and Cilicia, "confirming the Churches." All this is found in Acts xv. 36-41; and the date of it is 51 A.D.

These are all the references to Mark in the Acts; and there are only other four references in the rest of the New Testament. The earliest of these belongs in date to 61 A.D.—*i.e.*, ten years after the preceding—and at this point we find the breach between Paul and Mark completely healed, because Mark is now at Rome labouring in company with Paul during his first Roman imprisonment of two years, sends a salutation as part of Paul's Epistle to the Colossians (iv. 10, 11), and hints a possible personal visit ere long: "Aristarchus my fellow-prisoner saluteth you, and Marcus, sister's son to Barnabas, (touching whom ye received commandments: if he come unto you, receive him;) and Jesus, which is called Justus, who are of the circumcision. These only are my fellow-workers unto the kingdom of God, which have been a comfort unto me."

Of the same date and place, at least within a month or two of the preceding, is a reference at the end of the Epistle to Philemon: "There salute thee Epaphras, my fellow-prisoner in Christ Jesus; Marcus, Aristarchus, Demas, Lucas, my fellow-labourers."

The latest reference which joins Paul and Mark is 2 Tim. iv. 11, at the very close of S. Paul's life during the second Roman imprisonment in 66 or 67 A.D., when he asks Timothy to come from Ephesus and bring Mark with him: "Do thy diligence to come shortly unto me. . . . Take Mark, and bring him with thee: for he is profitable to me for the ministry." Alluding to the complete restoration of friendship and confidence between S. Paul and S. Mark as manifested in this touching final summons, Keble says on S. Mark's Day:—

> "Companion of the saints! 'twas thine
> To taste that drop of peace divine,
>   When the great soldier of thy Lord
> Called thee to take his last farewell,
> Teaching the Church with joy to tell
>   The story of your love restored.
>
> O then the glory and the bliss,
> When all that pained or seemed amiss
>   Shall melt with earth and sin away!
> When saints beneath their Saviour's eye,
> Filled with each other's company,
>   Shall spend in love th' eternal day!"

The last and most difficult of all the references is one which joins Peter and Mark. "The Church that is at Babylon, elected together with you, saluteth you; and so doth Marcus my son" (1 Peter v. 13). At this date (probably 65 A.D.) Mark was labouring under S. Peter; but *where* is not stated, because the allusion to the Church at Babylon is a very questionable translation, there being no Greek for *church*, but only a feminine pronoun which many interpret to mean that a Christian lady of Babylon sends a salutation in company with that of Marcus. The Revised Version of 1881 renders it, "she that is in Babylon, elect together with you."

Summing up these references, the first of them was in 44 A.D., when Peter was delivered from prison; and the last was in 66 A.D., when Paul (and probably also Peter) suffered martyrdom at Rome. During these twenty-two years Mark was engaged in ministerial work in Jerusalem, Antioch, Cyprus, and Rome; labouring in company with Peter, Barnabas, and Paul, both stating the substance of the Gospel orally in his own teaching and preaching, and hearing frequently similar statements of the oral Gospel in the course of the teaching of these three apostles.

In Acts x. 34-43, and again in xiii. 23-39, we have two specimens of this earliest oral shape of the Gospel; one by S. Peter addressed to Cornelius, and the other by S. Paul spoken at Antioch in Pisidia. In each case the cycle of representative facts which forms the groundwork extends from John the Baptist to the resurrection of Christ. "Then Peter opened his mouth, and said, Of a truth I perceive that God is no respecter of persons: for in every nation he that feareth Him, and worketh righteousness, is accepted with Him. The word which God sent unto the children of Israel, preaching peace by Jesus Christ: (He is Lord of all:) that word, I say, ye know, which was published throughout all Judea, and began from Galilee, after the baptism which John preached; how God anointed Jesus of Nazareth with the Holy Ghost and with power: who went about doing good, and healing all that were oppressed of the devil: for God was with Him. And we are witnesses of all things which He did both in the land of the Jews, and in Jerusalem; whom they slew and hanged on a tree: Him God raised up the third day, and showed Him openly; not to all the people, but unto witnesses chosen before of God, even to us, who did eat and drink with Him after He rose from the dead. And He commanded us to preach unto the people, and to testify that it is He which was ordained of God to be the judge of quick and dead. To Him give all the prophets witness, that through His name whosoever believeth in Him shall receive remission of sins."

It was just this oral Gospel, but in greater fulness, which was committed a little later to writing by certain men who had special means of knowing it and hearing it; as was the case with Mark for these twenty-two years. And this more definite and full form of writing became the more needful as the twelve original apostolic witnesses for Christ were early scattered by persecution, reduced by death, and before the close of the century were to cease entirely; so that thenceforward written and authentic gospels were to be the permanent guides of the Church touching the foundations of Christianity.

From the writer of the second gospel we pass to the writing. That S. Mark's book was written at Rome and for Gentile use, all are practically agreed. He does not lean on the Old Testament as is done by S. Matthew in frequent quotation. At the most there are only three such quotations. Moreover, Hebrew words are explained which to Jews would have been superfluous—*e.g.*, Boanerges, Talitha cumi, Corban, Bartimæus, Abba, Eloi. Further, Jewish usages are explained, which to Jews was needless—*e.g.*, washing of hands before meals; site of Olivet over against the Temple; lamb killed on first day of unleavened bread; preparation day preceding Sabbath. Also use is made of Latin forms—*e.g.*, *speculator, xestes, quadrantes, satisfacere, centurio.*

A very important element in S. Mark's Gospel is its connection with S. Peter already referred to. "The earliest account of the origin of a gospel is that which Papias has given on the authority of the elder John."[1] Papias was himself

---

[1] Westcott, Introd. Gosp., p. 167.

a direct hearer of this John, and John was a disciple of the Lord. "This also then was the statement of the elder. Mark, having become Peter's interpreter, wrote accordingly all that Peter mentioned; though he did not [record] in order that which was either said or done by Christ. For Mark neither heard the Lord nor followed Him; but subsequently, as I said, [attached himself to] Peter, who used to frame his teaching to meet the wants [of his hearers], but not as making a connected narrative of the Lord's discourses. So Mark committed no error, as he wrote down some particulars as he narrated them; for he took heed to one thing, to omit nothing of the things he heard, and to make no false statement in [his account of] them." This Petrine origin of S. Mark's Gospel is confirmed by other very early testimonies. Justin Martyr (100-120 A.D.) quotes it under the name of "the memoirs of Peter." Irenæus (177-202 A.D.) says, "After the decease of Peter and Paul, Mark, the disciple and interpreter of Peter, himself also handed down to us in writing the things which were preached by Peter." Origen (185-254 A.D.) says, "Mark made his gospel as Peter guided him."

The gospel itself has internal proofs and results of its Petrine origin, in that it has passages where Peter is named, although he is omitted by others. Thus it was Peter who followed our Lord in the morning after the miracles at Capernaum; it was he who noted the rapid withering of the fig-tree; it was he who asked our Lord as to the destruction of Jerusalem; and to him the angel directed information to be given of Christ's resurrection.

On other occasions, probably explicable by modesty, Peter's name is omitted in Mark where mentioned by Matthew and Luke. Thus his connection with the question as to meats not defiling a man; his walking on the sea; his talk as to the coin for tribute; his designation as the rock on which the Church was to be built; his being sent to make ready the Passover; his being prayed for by Jesus that his faith might not fail.

A rather common depreciatory view of S. Mark's Gospel, started originally by S. Augustin, is that it is mainly an abridgment of S. Matthew. While it is true that the one has only sixteen chapters, while the other has twenty-eight; and true also that both have a great many passages and even distinctive words in common, thus favouring the abridgment idea; it is no less true that the fundamental lines of each are quite distinct. S. Matthew is remarkable for looking at matters from a Hebrew point of view as the fulfilment of the Old Testament; and remarkable also for presenting Gospel material in classified rather than chronological order—groups of discourses, groups of miracles, groups of parables, groups of questions. But of the thirty-five Gospel parables, S. Mark gives only four in all, and one of his four (iv. 26) occurs nowhere else. He has as many miracles as the other gospels, but two of his miracles occur nowhere else—viz., the healing of the deaf with the impediment of speech (vii. 31), and the healing of the blind who at first saw men as trees walking (viii. 22).

Again, showing that S. Mark is no mere epitomist, all through his gospel occur dozens of minute matters in the course of his descriptions which make his narrative specially lively and graphic, suggesting ever to us at these points a faithful and earnest eyewitness or direct hearer. All the more interesting is this distinctive feature of the second gospel when we know that the eye and ear witness from whom the graphic details proceed is no other than S. Peter writing and speaking through "Marcus my son."

Still another feature of S. Mark's writing can best be presented in the words of the most careful and able of all modern students of the four gospels:[1] "S. Mark, more than any other evangelist, records the effect which was produced on

---

[1] Westcott, Introd., p. 347. In the same book, in a note to p. 344, are given the original Greek and thirty-eight references illustrative of the graphic use of words by S. Mark which introduce original points as above alluded to.

others by the Lord's working. Just as he follows out the details of the acts themselves, he mentions the immediate and wider results which they produced. From the beginning to the end he tells us of the wonder and amazement and fear with which men listened to the teaching of Christ. Everywhere multitudes crowd to hear Him, as well as to receive His blessings. When He was in a house, *the whole city was gathered to the door*, and even then the crowd could find no room. So great at times was the excitement, that *He could no longer openly enter into the city;* and it is said twice that, *as many came and went, He could not even eat*, so that He seemed to His kindred *to be beside Himself*. Those who were healed, in spite of His injunctions proclaimed abroad the tidings of His power. And in His retirement men *from all the cities ran together on foot* to see Him; and wherever *He went, into villages or city or country, they placed their sick* before Him; and *as many as touched Him* were made whole."

Thus marvellous for exactitude and practical directness is this shortest of the gospels, as is apparent even when we put together its opening and closing sentences: "The beginning of the Gospel of Jesus Christ, the Son of God; as it is written in the Prophets, Behold, I send my messenger before thy face, which shall prepare thy way before thee. . . . So then, after the Lord had spoken unto them, He was received up into heaven, and sat on the right hand of God. And they went forth, and preached everywhere, the Lord working with them, and confirming the word with signs following. Amen."

With the year 66, the year of the martyrdom of S. Paul and S. Peter at Rome, we lose all further Scripture trace of S. Mark. Tradition says that he thereafter went to Alexandria, where he suffered martyrdom two years later on 25th April, which is his day in the calendar.

In the year 828, under Doge Giustiniani of Venice, the body of the evangelist was brought as a precious relic from Alexandria to Venice, of which city he became thenceforward the patron saint. His winged lion appears on all coins, flags, and public buildings of Venice, and to him is the glorious marble cathedral of that city, with its priceless mosaics and pillars and veined slabs, dedicated; S. Mark's being to Venice even more than what S. Paul's is to London, S. Peter's to Rome, and S. Andrew's to Scotland. When one glides or walks through the streets of Venice, how frequent is the call to read the legend above, below, or around the winged lion, *Pax tibi, Marce, evangelista meus!* This oft-graven motto is drawn from one of the ancient sections attached to S. Mark's Day in the Roman Breviary, where it is said that on the eve of his servant's martyrdom the Saviour appeared to the faithful evangelist, coming in the same dress He had worn before the Passion, and using to him the comforting words, *Pax tibi, Marce, dilecte meus.*

S. Luke,

THE EVANGELIST.

DAY, OCTOBER 18.

ORATIO.—*Interveniat pro nobis, Domine, quæsumus, sanctus tuus Lucas evangelista : qui crucis mortificationem jugiter in suo corpore pro tui nominis honore portavit.   Per Dominum.*

The Epistle.—2. Cor. viii. 16-24.
The Gospel.—S. Luke x. 1-9.

COLLECT.—*Almighty God, who calledst Luke the physician, whose praise is in the Gospel, to be an evangelist and physician of the soul ; May it please Thee, that, by the wholesome medicines of the doctrine delivered by him, all the diseases of our*

*souls may be healed ; through the merits of Thy Son Jesus
Christ our Lord.*   Amen.
The Epistle.—2 Tim. iv. 5-15.
The Gospel.—S. Luke x. 1-7.

" What thanks and praise to Thee we owe,
O Priest and Sacrifice divine,
For Thy dear saint through whom we know
So many a gracious word of Thine ;

Whom Thou didst choose to tell the tale
Of all Thy manhood's toils and tears,
And for a moment lift the veil
That hides Thy boyhood's spotless years.

How many a soul with guilt oppressed
Has learned to hear the joyful sound
In that sweet tale of sin confessed,
The FATHER'S love, the lost and found !

How many a child of sin and shame
Has refuge found from guilty fears
Through her who to the Saviour came
With costly ointments and with tears !

What countless worshippers have sung,
In lowly fane or lofty choir,
The song that loosed the silent tongue
Of him who was the Baptist's sire !

And still the Church through all her days
Uplifts the strains that never cease,
The Blessèd Virgin's hymn of praise,
The aged Simeon's words of peace.

O happy saint ! whose sacred page,
So rich in words of truth and love,
Pours on the Church from age to age
This healing unction from above ;

The witness of the Saviour's life,
The great apostle's chosen friend
Through weary years of toil and strife,
And still found faithful to the end.

So grant us, Lord, like him to live,
Beloved by man, approved by Thee,
Till Thou at last the summons give,
And we, with him, Thy face shall see.
—ARCHBISHOP MACLAGAN, of York.

"Only Luke is with me."—2 TIMOTHY iv. 11.

THIS being the most honourable of all Scripture allusions to
the evangelist S. Luke, under it as heading may be gathered
together the various notices of him that are scattered over the
New Testament, so that we may learn to appreciate the man
as a spiritual force in the early Church. In the two books
which he has contributed to the New Testament it is note-
worthy that he never once mentions his own name. But his
two dedications to Theophilus imply an acknowledgment as
good as any direct signature; for Theophilus and the whole
circle of his Christian friends would know most openly and
gratefully to whom they were indebted for a carefully written
life of the Lord and a systematic account of the planting of
the Christian Church by the Acts of the Apostles, and we may
be sure that this knowledge would spread with the circulation
of the books themselves.

Only thrice does the name of Luke occur. To the Colos-
sian Christians (iv. 11) S. Paul writes from Rome in his first
imprisonment, which lasted two years, "Luke, the beloved
physician, and Demas, greet you." During the same imprisonment, writing to Philemon, S. Paul says, "There salute thee
Epaphras, my fellow-prisoner in Christ Jesus; Marcus, Aristarchus, Demas, Lucas, my fellow-labourers." After this
imprisonment the apostle was released, and undertook a fourth
great missionary journey, which ended by his arrest at Nicopolis and his being sent to Rome in 66 A.D., and this second
Roman imprisonment ended in martyrdom. In this crisis the
apostle wrote a second Epistle to Timothy, pressing for his
presence, and in these terms telling how he then stood: "Do
thy diligence to come shortly unto me: for Demas hath forsaken

me, having loved this present world, and is departed unto Thessalonica; Crescens to Galatia, Titus unto Dalmatia. Only Luke is with me. Take Mark, and bring him with thee: for he is profitable to me for the ministry. And Tychicus have I sent to Ephesus . . . At my first answer no man stood with me, but all men forsook me. . . . Notwithstanding the Lord stood with me, and strengthened me."

There is a fourth passage in 2 Cor. viii. 18 which falls to be added to these three, for it has always been interpreted of Luke, although his name is not expressly given. When Titus was sent to Jerusalem with the liberality of the Macedonians, he had a companion who is thus described, "And we have sent with him the brother, whose praise is in the Gospel throughout all the Churches; and not that only, but who was also chosen of the Churches to travel with us with this grace." This visit to Jerusalem took place during Paul's third great journey, and previous to his first Roman imprisonment. The very ancient although uninspired colophon at the end of the same epistle gives the name of Luke as the joint bearer of epistle as well as money, for Corinth lay on the route from Philippi to Jerusalem. The colophon is this,—"The second Epistle to the Corinthians was written from Philippi, a city of Macedonia, by Titus and Lucas." In the collect for S. Luke's Day quotation is made of 2 Cor. viii. 18 to the same effect, with the additional point that gospel is taken to mean not merely the glad tidings, but, what it came only afterwards to denote, one of the four biographies of Christ.

A further and very important source of information regarding our evangelist is to mark closely in the book of the Acts those passages in the narrative where the author, the first personal pronoun, *we* or *us*, shows his own presence as an eye-witness at certain points. There are three of these passages.

The first is xvi. 10-17, where *we* or *us* occurs ten times, and wherefrom we learn that Luke joined S. Paul at Troas, and accompanied him in his first preaching and planting the

Gospel in northern Greece, in the province of Macedonia, especially at Philippi.

The second is **xx.** 5-38, where *we* or *us* occurs eight times, and wherefrom we learn that Luke started again for Philippi with S. Paul when he went anew to Troas and Mitylene and Miletus, where took place the tender parting with the elders of Ephesus, whereat Luke was present. This same passage extends into **xxi.** 1-18, where *we* or *us* occurs twenty-six times, and wherefrom we learn that Luke continued the journey from Miletus to Rhodes, to Tyre, to Ptolemais, and to Jerusalem.

The third is chapters **xxvii.** and **xxviii.**, the last two in the book, wherein *we* or *us* occurs twenty and fifteen times, and wherefrom we learn that Luke started with Paul from Cæsarea to go to Rome on appeal from Festus to Cæsar, was with him on the voyage and shipwreck, arrived with him in Rome, and stayed with him there two years, a companion in his imprisonment and a fellow-labourer in the Gospel.

A previous period of two years the evangelist and the apostle had spent together at Cæsarea (Acts xxiv. 27), also in imprisonment; and there, in all probability, it was that Luke wrote his gospel; we may be sure with full knowledge of and help from S. Paul. And if the two years' leisure at Cæsarea enabled Luke to compose his gospel, we may very well consider that the two years' leisure again at Rome enabled him to continue his historical narrative in his second book from the Ascension on to arrival in Rome, with the final verse as to the duration of the stay there without adverting to the issue of S. Paul's appeal, which, according to our supposition, would not yet have come on for hearing. Thus the closing point of the narrative in the Acts gives a clue to the time and place of the composition of the book.

And all the more may this have been a period of literary activity with our evangelist because it was with the apostle himself also a time of literary industry in a different form, but to the same end. It was during this two years' Roman leisure that S. Paul wrote his Epistles to the Colossians, Ephesians, Philippians, and Philemon. Nor need we hesitate to think of the two inspired writers, the younger and the older, talking many a time to each other of their respective occupations, and perhaps also reading to each other their manuscripts. What could be more natural to men so sympathetic with each other, and both so zealous in Christian work, both engaged on Christian literature, together turning to profit a weary seven hundred days of imprisonment and companionship in imprisonment? And they were, moreover, both of them men of professional education and culture in early life—the evangelist trained as a physician, and the apostle trained under Gamaliel to serve in the Jewish Church. It has always been recognised that the writings of the two men dovetail into each other, and are mutually illustrative—the Acts as a historical and geographical basis of the spread of the Gospel, and the Pauline epistles as the authoritative voice deciding disputes, reproving faults, stimulating righteousness, guiding worship, in the various Churches planted throughout Asia and Europe. This interconnection of the writings of S. Paul and S. Luke has been turned to valuable account by Paley and others as a branch or adminicle of the evidences of the truth of Christianity.

In fact we can trace the interconnection of the two men's writings considerably beyond the group of epistles already named. The latest written group of S. Paul's epistles was the three pastoral letters. And the latest of the three in date— viz., 2 Timothy—in the text (iv. 11) at the head of this, expressly mentions Luke's presence during the writing, and the additional fact that he was S. Paul's *only* companion and comforter at this most trying period immediately preceding his martyrdom. This proves S. Luke to have been specially faithful and specially welcome to the apostle. And if with him at Rome in the final imprisonment, there is every reason to suppose him to have been in the apostle's company during the missionary journey preceding, the course of which seems to have been through Macedonia and Asia Minor, places visited again being Philippi, Colosse, Laodicea, Hierapolis, and Ephesus (where Timothy was left). Going to Macedonia again (where 1 Timothy was now written), S. Paul next visits Crete, Miletus, Ephesus, Troas, and Nicopolis (near Actium), where (some think) he was apprehended and sent prisoner to Rome, where in 66 A.D. he died by the sword of the executioner.

The first group of all among the Pauline epistles was 1 and 2 Thessalonians. These belong to the apostle's second journey, recorded in Acts xv. 36–xviii. 28, and of date 53-55 A.D. And in that journey Luke was present, as we have already seen, joining at Troas. And in addition to Luke, Silas and Timothy were also fellow-travellers with the apostle, so that, having had close personal acquaintance with Timothy at this early stage, Luke would have the deeper interest in the epistle sent to him in 66—*i.e.*, eleven years later, and forming S. Paul's last written work.

Then there is a group of S. Paul's epistles which belongs to his third journey, recorded Acts xviii. 23–xxiv. 2, and of date 56-60 A.D. This group embraces 1 Corinthians, 2 Corinthians, Galatians, Romans. Now part of this period, if not the whole of it, Luke spent in S. Paul's company, as part of the *we* and *us* narrative already spoken of proves. Here afresh the author of the Acts is in daily companionship with the author of the Epistles; and can we believe anything else than that their careful writing was subject of conference at their joint presence in many meetings for Christian worship and teaching, organising of congregations and settling of presbyters and deacons? May we not safely as well as boldly go beyond the idea of S. Paul's epistles being matter of conference between him and S. Luke, and even guess that in several cases, especially that of 2 Timothy, S. Luke actually wrote the Epistles to the apostle's dictation?—for through some bodily defect, possibly short-sightedness or the cumbrance of a chained soldier, the apostle did not or could not do his own writing.

Having thus considered *first* the passages in which the

name of Luke is distinctly mentioned ; *second*, the passages in
the Acts wherein *we* or *us* shows his companionship with
S. Paul ; and *third*, traced the result of that companionship
in a wonderful mutual relationship and dovetailing of the
writings of the two men,—next comes a consideration of S.
Luke's own writing.

His name Lucas is. a contraction for Lucanus, as Silas =
Silvanus, and he is called by Eusebius, *c.* 325 A.D., "by race
a native of Antioch." His calling was that of a physician.
We can discern professional terms in his description of
Simon's wife's mother ; in the woman with the issue of blood ;
in Christ's agony in the garden ; in the cripple at the Temple
gate ; in the death of Herod Agrippa ; in the blindness of
Elymas ; and in the sickness of the· father of Publius at
Malta.

The education, partly among books and partly by close
observation and comparison of facts, needful for the medical
profession, seems to show itself in the literary style and
method of the evangelist ; and not least in his very note-
worthy preface to each of his books. These recall to the
classical scholar many an opening paragraph such as we find
in Livy or Sallust.

"Forasmuch as many have taken in hand to set forth in order
a declaration of those things which are most surely believed
among us, even as *they* delivered them unto us, which from
the beginning were eyewitnesses, and ministers of the word ;
it seemed good to me also, having had perfect understanding
of all things from the very first, to write unto thee in order,
most excellent Theophilus, that thou mightest know the
certainty of those things, wherein thou hast been instructed."

· "The former treatise have I made, O Theophilus, of all
that Jesus began both to do and teach, until the day in which
He was taken up, after that He through the Holy Ghost had
given commandments unto the apostles whom He had chosen."

In the way of paraphrase the meaning seems to be : Many
accounts of Jesus Christ have been given by His followers. All

of these, whether written or oral, derive their value from agreeing with the words of those who from the beginning were eyewitnesses and ministers of the Word, as were the twelve apostles and other original disciples. As I have taken special pains and have enjoyed special opportunities accurately to investigate all things from the commencement at the birth of the Baptist on to the ascension of Jesus, I think of composing a fresh narrative more consecutive, proportionately adjusted in its parts, full in details, reliable in sources, and profitable for true doctrine and holy living; with a wish that it may be specially helpful to thee, most worthy Theophilus.

According to this view the many gospels here alluded to by S. Luke do not include, at least not necessarily, those of S. Matthew or S. Mark, but refer to the whole body of floating material familiar on the lips and in the ears of the first generation of Christians within twenty or thirty years of our Lord's death. While all these might be good and true, some would be local, dealing mainly or exclusively with the Galilean or Judean ministry; and others would be sectional, consisting mainly of parables, or miracles, or discourses, or controversies. Further, they would run the risk of perishing, or of being altered, or of losing their proof, if not reduced to a more definite literary shape before the first generation should pass away. This collecting, ordering, narrating, and preserving was the task that Doctor Luke set before himself, probably, as we have seen, to fill his two years' leisure at Cæsarea. And as regards Theophilus—of whom we know nothing certain, but judge from his Græco-Latin name that he was a Gentile, and from the respectful adjective "most excellent" that he occupied a good social and probably official place in Cæsarea itself —the easiest supposition is, that during the two years' stay at Cæsarea he had specially befriended the apostle and the evangelist, and been one of their chief converts.

The first two chapters of the gospel, beginning with the vision of Zacharias in the Temple and ending with the Temple scene among the doctors in the Saviour's twelfth year, would alone justify the high strain employed in the preface. The source of these chapters is almost certainly the Virgin Mary herself, probably in some record in her own hand at her death about twelve years before. In virtue of five poetical pieces interwoven in these chapters S. Luke is entitled to the honour of ranking as the first Christian hymnologist. To him we owe the *Ave Maria*, the *Gloria in Excelsis, Benedictus, Magnificat*, and *Nunc Dimittis*, the inspired forerunners of a countless host of Christian hymns which from that day to this have given expression to the very finest of Christian praise and prayer, and vow and joy, and all variety of devotional feeling. A Scotsman who has long since escaped from the prejudices of his countrymen in certain matters ecclesiastical, may speak somewhat plainly of the pitiable bigotry still partly surviving of those who would confine legitimate sacred song to the Old Testament Psalms, and who are so fiercely set on their own narrow views that they would actually muzzle and explain away those liveliest of the Psalms which speak of instruments of music.

Canon Farrar in Commentary on S. Luke has remarked that there runs through his gospel a joyous strain akin to the five hymns of the two opening chapters. An outburst of glorifying God closes the record of the man healed of palsy ; of the raising of the widow's son of Nain; of the woman bowed together for nineteen years ; of the Samaritan among the ten lepers ; of the blind man healed at Jericho ; and of the centurion at the cross who had devoutly watched the expiring Saviour.

S. Luke's Gospel also gives special prominence to prayer. Besides giving, like S. Matthew, the text of the Lord's Prayer, it alone records prayers of our Lord on six memorable occasions— viz., His own baptism ; after cleansing the leper ; before calling the twelve; at His transfiguration ; on the cross for His murderers ; and on the cross His own commendatory prayer. To which are to be added S. Luke's record of two special prayer-parables—viz., the friend at midnight and the unjust judge.

We see in the selected materials of the third gospel the influence of the best phase and training of a good physician whose aim is to promote health and happiness impartially to all classes of the community, so that he emphasises the openness and equality of the kingdom of God in Christ. He alone joins to the notice of the Baptist's mission the world-wide words of prophecy, "and all flesh shall see the salvation of God." He alone alludes to Elijah sent to heathen Sarepta, and Elisha healing heathen Naaman; just as he alone records the wider mission of the seventy. In the Acts he gives a wonderful development to the same principles: first, in the many languages miraculously spoken at Pentecost; next, in the very full and thrice-repeated record of the calling of Cornelius; and thereafter in the detailed record of the work of the great Apostle of the Gentiles in city after city and province after province of the wide Roman Empire.

Another phase of the same characteristic of Christianity is particularly prominent in S. Luke's Gospel in frequent references to our Lord's favour to the poor, the despised, and the outcast. He records in this line the Beatitudes to the poor and hungry; the parable of Dives and Lazarus; the parable of the rich fool; the parable of the Great Supper, with its invitation to "the poor, the maimed, the halt, and the blind"; the parable of the exaltation of the humble who chose the lowest seats; and the counsel to "sell and give alms." In S. Luke is found a place through repentance for the Samaritan, the publican, the harlot, the prodigal, and the thief. Although there is no ancient evidence that Luke was a painter as well as a physician, yet we can see from his writings that he largely possessed an artistic sense and faculty. Where ever was a shipwreck more graphically presented than in the penultimate chapter of the Acts? In dealing with character great is his skill in the use of light and shade, arising from comparison and contrast. His gospel abounds in this picturesque handling.   We have the slow acceptance of the angel's message by Zacharias, and adjacent thereto the clear firm belief on the part of the blessed Virgin Mary; the coldness of Simon, and the tearful loving penitence of the sinful woman; the anxious housewifery of Martha, and the devout listening of Mary; the Pharisee and the publican in their respective styles of prayer; the good Samaritan over against the heartless priest and Levite; Dives with his purple, fine linen, and daily feast, over against Lazarus, whom the dogs licked at the gentleman's gate.   In S. Luke alone we find Beatitudes and woes in pairs; as also in him the hardened and penitent malefactor confront each other holding dialogue on Calvary.

For pathos as well as picturesqueness the last scene in his gospel may well be compared with the shipwreck chapter at the end of the Acts.   What a wonderful narrative that of the two disciples going to Emmaus—talking sadly and darkly yet sympathetically of the recent crucifixion—joined by the Crucified Himself; guided to truth and comfort by the unknown Traveller's mastery of the Scriptures; the identification at last in the breaking of bread, and only when all was come and gone, the true measure of their own feelings, that their hearts had burned by the way with heaven's own glow!

A vast debtor is the whole Christian world to the physician of Antioch, who under God's holy inspiring Spirit gathered and arranged the materials of these two books, which are so fundamental to the New Testament: the one giving the history of the Christ from the Baptist's birth to our Lord's ascension; the other starting from the same ascension, and tracing the Church of Christ from its commencement in the Pentecostal fire till it had spread over a great deal both of Asia and Europe.

This employment of the two years' prison-leisure at Cæsarea for the gospel-writing, and of the other two years' prison-leisure at Rome for the writing of the Acts, is surely a signal instance of how God overrules persecution and tribulation for the greater good of His Church, and may well furnish a fresh argument for Christian patience, courage, industry, and perseverance.

From the year 66, when the martyrdom of S. Paul gave an end to the long co-operation between him and S. Luke, we lose all definite historic trace of the rest of our evangelist's career. Epiphanius says that thereafter S. Luke preached in Italy, Gaul, Dalmatia, and Macedonia, and died at the age of seventy-four. Hippolytus says he was crucified at Elæa in Peloponnesus, and the modern Greeks add that he suffered on an olive-tree, and at the age of eighty-four.[1]

The Blessed Virgin Mary.

HER PURIFICATION OR PRESENTATION OF CHRIST IN THE TEMPLE.

CANDLEMAS DAY, FEBRUARY 2.

ORATIO.—*Omnipotens sempiterne Deus, majestatem tuam supplices exoramus: ut sicut unigenitus Filius tuus hodierna die cum nostræ carnis substantia in templo est præsentatus, ita nos facias purificatis tibi mentibus præsentari. Per eundem.*

The Epistle.—Mal. iii. 1-4.
The Gospel.—S. Luke ii. 22-32.

COLLECT.—*Almighty and ever-living God, we humbly beseech Thy Majesty, that as Thy only-begotten Son was this day presented in the Temple in substance of our flesh, so we may be presented unto Thee with pure and clean hearts, by the same Thy Son Jesus Christ our Lord. Amen.*

The Epistle.—Mal. iii. 1-5.
The Gospel.—S. Luke ii. 22-40.

[1] Alban Butler, Lives of the Saints under 18th October.

ANNUNCIATION OF THE BLESSED VIRGIN MARY.

LADY-DAY, MARCH 25.

ORATIO.—*Deus qui de beatæ Mariæ semper virginis utero verbum tuum, angelo nunciante, carnem suscipere voluisti: præsta supplicibus tuis, ut qui vere eam genetricem credimus ejus apud te intercessionibus adjuvemur. Per eundem Dominum nostrum.*

The Epistle.—Isaiah vii. 10-15.
The Gospel.—S. Luke i. 26-38.

COLLECT.—*We beseech Thee, O Lord, pour Thy grace into our hearts; that as we have known the incarnation of Thy Son Jesus Christ by the message of an angel, so by His cross and passion we may be brought into the glory of His resurrection; through the same Jesus Christ our Lord.   Amen.*

The Epistle.—Isaiah vii. 10-15.
The Gospel.—S. Luke i. 26-38.

PRESENTATION OF CHRIST IN THE TEMPLE.

O Sion, open wide thy gates,
  Let figures disappear :
A Priest and Victim, both in one,
  The Truth Himself is here.

No more the simple flock shall bleed :
  Behold the Incarnate Son
Himself to His own altar comes,
  For sinners to atone.

Conscious of hidden Deity,
  The lowly Virgin brings
Her new-born Babe, with two young doves,
  Her tender offerings.

The hoary Simeon sees at last
  His Lord so long desired,
And hails, with Anna, Israel's Hope,
  By sudden rapture fired.

But silent knelt the mother blest
  Of Him the silent Word,
And, pondering all things in her heart,
  With speechless praise adored.
                    —E. CASWALL.

ANNUNCIATION OF THE VIRGIN.

Shall we not love thee, Mother dear,
  Whom Jesus loves so well ?
And, to His glory, year by year,
  Thy joy and honour tell ?

Bound with the curse of sin and shame
  We helpless sinners lay,
Until in tender love He came
  To bear the curse away.

And thee He chose from whom to take
  True flesh His Flesh to be ;
In It to suffer for our sake,
  By It to make us free.

Thy Babe He lay upon thy breast,
  To thee He cried for food ;
Thy gentle nursing soothed to rest
  Th' Incarnate Son of God.

O wondrous depth of grace Divine
  That He should bend so low !
And, Mary, oh, what joy was thine
  In His dear love to know !

Joy to be mother of the Lord,
  And thine the truer bliss,
In every thought, and deed, and word,
  To be for ever His.

And as He loved thee, Mother dear,
  We too will love thee well ;
And, to His glory, year by year,
  Thy joy and honour tell.
                    —Sir H. W. BAKER.

"Hail! thou that art highly favoured, the Lord is with thee; blessed art thou among women."—S. LUKE i. 28.

THESE are the words of salutation used by the angel Gabriel to the Virgin Mary of Nazareth, when he appeared by God's command to announce that she had been chosen to be the mother of the Messiah, the Son of the Highest. From these words Mary first learned her high destiny, and from the same words we may fitly consider her whole character and place in the Gospel and in the Church.

The name of the Blessed Virgin has suffered from association with superstition and extravagance to such a degree that it is not quite easy to be respectful and reverent in speaking of her, and to yield her with heartiness that high place to which she is certainly entitled, as affording to all ages a marked example of faith, purity, trial, and humility, joined to her wonderful position as the mother of our adorable Redeemer. Surely as regards these virtues and graces we may look to her in the same way as we do to other servants of God whose lives are also recorded in Scripture for our imitation and encouragement in the various parts and aspects of piety. Such among women are Sarah and Miriam; Deborah and Hannah; Ruth and Esther; Martha and Mary; Magdalene and Dorcas; Priscilla and Lydia; Eunice and Lois. Such among men are the patriarchs and prophets of the Old Testament, and the evangelists and apostles of the New Testament. And surely no man, whose reason and sense of proportion are not marred by ultra-Protestant crazes, would dare to deny to the mother of Jesus a far higher spiritual place than any one of the fourteen good women above named can be supposed to hold.

In pursuance of our plan, we require to bring together into one view the not inconsiderable number of passages of the Bible that touch more or less directly the personal history of the Blessed Virgin. The salutation in Luke i. 28 may be regarded as the earliest direct allusion to the mother of Jesus in the New Testament. In the Old Testament there are two clear prophetic allusions. The first is that contained in the original promise of all, the Protevangelium, which mentions expressly the seed of the *woman.* " I will put enmity between thee [the serpent] and the woman, and between thy seed and her seed." The second is in Isaiah vii. 14 : " Therefore the Lord Himself shall give you a sign : Behold, a virgin shall conceive, and bear a son, and shall call his name Immanuel." Also referring, but less directly, to the mother of Jesus, are those passages of the Old Testament which speak of the Messiah as a child, as a man, to be born, of the seed of Abraham, and son of David. " Unto us a child is born, unto us a son is given." " In thy seed [Abraham's] shall all the nations of the earth be blessed." " Once have I sworn by my holiness that I will not lie unto David. His seed shall endure for ever, and his throne as the sun before me." These and such passages of prophecy animated the common and strong desire of Hebrew women in all grades of life, at the time specified in Daniel, to be the mother of the Prince of Peace that was to be born. And it would be unreasonable to suppose that she for whom this great and unparalleled honour was divinely appointed and reserved, was not a woman pre-eminently endowed with the virtues and graces that go together to constitute the very highest type of true womanhood. We are bound to think thus highly of the earthly mother of the Son of God ; and it is a scandal that lies heavily on the Protestant branch of the Church, that a large part of it is so degraded, or embittered by controversy, that it cannot speak of the Blessed Virgin except with coldness, fear, or even venom.

In the way of practical example and encouragement to the women of all generations, there stands at the very commencement of the history of S. Mary the Virgin the great fact, viz., that this highest possible earthly honour, and this character invested with a singular beauty of holiness, did not belong to one who had been trained in palaces and courts, or gifted with intellectual genius, or brilliant by accomplishments, but to a maiden of common station and very poor condition, whose natural rank, dress, and education were simply those of a peasant or artisan's daughter, wife, or sister. Such and no other was the Blessed Virgin Mary of Nazareth.

Born and bred like a good and ordinary daughter of Zion, the Scripture is entirely silent regarding her until she has come through girlhood to woman's estate and a marriageable age. It is to this point that the text belongs; for Mary of Galilee, at the date of the salutation by the angel, was "a virgin espoused or betrothed to a man whose name was Joseph, of the house of David." Instead of dwelling on the grandeur of the annunciation made by the angel, it is more to our purpose to mark the mode of its reception by the Blessed Virgin. First of all, "she was troubled at his saying, and cast in her mind what manner of salutation this should be." Then, when the message had been further explained by the angel as implying a child, the Son of the Highest, to be born of her, the natural obstacle of her maiden estate suggested itself. "Mary said unto the angel, How shall this be, seeing I know not a man?" Upon the angel meeting this difficulty by the further explanation, "The Holy Ghost shall come upon thee, and the power of the Highest shall overshadow thee;" and when the angel added thereto the somewhat parallel and corroborating token that had already happened to her cousin Elisabeth,—then all of Mary's difficulties disappeared. All that had passed and all that was announced, she accepted in the twofold spirit of faith and meekness. "And Mary said, Behold the handmaid of the Lord; be it unto me according to thy word." Even compared with the behaviour of a good priest like Zacharias, who hesitated and asked a sign, and received one that constituted a temporary punishment (S. Luke i. 18-20), how perfect was the conduct of the Virgin on this critical occasion!

In the next scene in which the Blessed Virgin appears, on her visit to the house of Elisabeth in the hill-country, we find that Elisabeth in the spirit of prophecy specially adverts to the faith and willingness shown by her cousin of Nazareth, probably with a latent reference to the judgment of temporary dumbness then lying on her own husband—"Blessed is she that believed, for there shall be a performance of those things which were told her from the Lord." Immediately previous to this, however, Elisabeth in the same spirit of prophecy had re-echoed the grandeur of the angelic salutation—"Blessed art thou among women, and blessed is the fruit of thy womb. And whence is this to me, that the mother of my Lord should come to me?"

It is to that same occasion of the visit "in haste" to the hill-country (probably near Hebron, about twenty miles from Jerusalem), where dwelt Zacharias and Elisabeth, that we owe the finest song in the New Testament, that peerless *Magnifi cat*, wherein, rivalling the ancient seers and psalmists, the Blessed Virgin, now herself inspired, celebrates what had thus far passed, and anticipates the fulfilment of all that had been miraculously promised. This visit lasted three months, so that possibly before leaving, the Blessed Virgin had the satisfaction of witnessing the birth of that child who was to be the herald of her own.

As the time advanced with Mary, a singular and sore trial awaited her in the suspicion as to her purity that began to cross the mind of Joseph, to whom she stood in the relation of betrothment. This betrothal beforehand was so public and solemn a matter in old Jewish times that it was esteemed nearly as binding as marriage itself. A like custom holds good in Germany to this day, where lists of betrothed couples are inserted in newspapers in the same way as births, marriages, and deaths. It is on this principle that at this stage Joseph is in one place called her husband, although as yet only betrothed. "Then Joseph her husband, being a just man, and not willing to make her a public example, was minded to put her away privily. But while he thought on these things, behold, the angel of the Lord appeared unto him in a dream, saying, Joseph, thou son of David, fear not to take unto thee Mary thy wife ; for that which is conceived in her is of the Holy Ghost." Here, then, in underlying the suspicion of infidelity to the betrothal-vow, was an exceptionally hard trial for a season to the faith and patience of the Blessed Virgin of Nazareth.

When the time for the birth of the Holy Child arrived, how great once more was the trial of Mary's faith by the circumstances of lowliness and destitution in the courtyard and outhouses of the inn, where the manger had to serve as cradle! But again was the balance restored, and faith had both help and reward in the other attendant circumstances. Shepherds soon arrived to render homage and adoration to the Child so humbly and hardly born. These shepherds had a beautiful and wonderful tale to tell of a company of angels appearing and singing in the midnight sky in celebration of the King born in Judea. Farther on, other and higher visitors appeared—men of rank and learning, who had come from afar bearing royal gifts, therewith and also otherwise to render like homage and adoration to that more simply but not less heartily already rendered by the shepherds. Of all these incidents not one would be forgotten, but each would be carefully and reverently marked by the Virgin-Mother,—the angel to Joseph; the song of the heavenly host to the shepherds; the star to the kings.

The first public appearance of Mother and Child in the Temple on occasion of her purification and His presentation was marked by a double incident, which could not fail to impress itself deeply on Mary's memory along with the previous events and words. This incident was that which was connected with the names of Simeon and Anna, which will be taken up separately further on. The song of Simeon, though so short, is one of the finest expressions ever given to the feeling of contentment and peace. We know from two passages of Scripture that it was a characteristic of Mary to lay up in her heart things as they happened, especially things hard and dark, faithfully and hopefully to await clearer light in coming days from the fuller unfolding of the plan of God's providence. "His mother marvelled at those things which were spoken of

Him." Again, "His mother kept all these sayings in her heart."

Regarding the place in the Calendar or Sacred Year of the two chief of the above events that form part of the Virgin's history, it is to be noted that they do not succeed one another as here, because the Purification falls on 2d February, or Candlemas-day, whereas the Annunciation, or Lady-day, is 25th March. The reason of this apparent reversal of order is simple—namely, that in the Virgin's history the annunciation happened in one year in March; the birth then announced fell on 25th December of the same year; and afterwards in the next year came the purification. But when we arrange all the great Gospel events to be commemorated within the course of one year, sometimes the historical order crosses the order of the months. Further, in the case of both of these festivals we are free to speak of them either in their relation to the Saviour Himself or in their relation to His mother. But if we wish with full sincerity to commemorate either event, it is not a little dishonest to minimise the Virgin's share at a point when she had full parental responsibility and authority, and when her Son, although divine, was as yet a babe. Such evasion of respect to the mother is a piece of sneaking Protestantism, at variance with proper Christianity.

Another point at which S. Mary's personal history appears in connection with that of her divine child, is in the flight into Egypt to escape the wrath of Herod the king. This event was the subject of prophecy, and has been also a frequent theme of representation in sacred art, all the more so as being one of the events commemorated separately in the Church Calendar under the name of the Holy Innocents' Day.

But of far more interest and significance is the scene that happened in the Temple when Jesus had grown to twelve years of age, and had remained behind in eager converse with the rabbis, both hearing them and asking them questions. The child having been at last found, on the third day of search, his mother addressed him in words of expostulation for causing herself and her husband all this trouble and anxiety. Instead of simply naming Joseph as her husband, she uses the word "father"—whereupon the answer of Jesus is very striking. "His mother said unto Him, Son, why hast Thou thus dealt with us? behold, Thy father and I have sought Thee sorrowing. And He said unto them, How is it that ye sought me? wist ye not that I must be about my Father's business?" ("I must be in my Father's house?"—R. V.)

This is one of three occasions on which Jesus is recorded to have spoken in peculiar terms to or of His mother, in which the word of Simeon was fulfilled, "Yea, a sword shall pierce through thy own soul also." The second is that which occurred at the marriage at Cana in Galilee, whereat Jesus made His beginning of miracles in changing water into wine. "And when they wanted wine, the mother of Jesus saith unto Him, They have no wine. Jesus saith unto her, Woman, what have I to do with thee? mine hour is not yet come. His mother saith unto the servants, Whatsoever He saith unto you, do it." The third occasion was in connection with His public teaching. "While He yet talked to the people, behold, His mother and His brethren stood without, desiring to speak with Him. Then one said unto Him, Behold, Thy mother and Thy brethren stand without, desiring to speak with Thee. But He answered and said unto him that told Him, Who is my mother? and who are my brethren? And He stretched forth His hand toward His disciples, and said, Behold my mother and my brethren! For whosoever shall do the will of my Father which is in heaven, the same is my brother, and sister, and mother."

These three occasions have this feature in common, that they are instances wherein the Virgin-Mother was putting forward her earthly relationship into competition with or authority over that spiritual and higher element which was joined with the life and work of Jesus. Such interference Jesus guarded Himself against in each case; but it was simple self-defence at the moment, there was no anger concurrent or estrangement following. We see this directly or indirectly in each case. In the first, Jesus protested against the blame attached to Him, and against the name of father as applied to Joseph ; but still we read in the very next words, " He went down with them, and came to Nazareth, and was subject unto them." In the second, notwithstanding the protest made against His mother's suggestion or urgency, the wine was actually provided—soon, plentifully, and of the best quality. In the third, can we doubt that as soon as Jesus had ended His sayings to the crowd, His very first act, and that affectionately and joyfully done, would be to speak, according to desire, with His kindred after the flesh ?

This in fact is the very spirit and attitude of Jesus toward His mother on the last and most affecting of their earthly meetings, the chief verification of Simeon's predicted sword in the soul, as she stood near the foot of the cross an agonised witness of her Son's crucifixion. Among the seven sacred words spoken from the cross, the third in order was that which was addressed, one half to the mother of sorrow, and the other half to the disciple of love, bequeathing that mother unto S. John's care and home. " Now there stood by the cross of Jesus His mother, and His mother's sister, Mary the wife of Cleophas, and Mary Magdalene. When Jesus therefore saw His mother, and the disciple standing by whom He loved, He saith unto His mother, Woman, behold thy son ! Then saith He to the disciple, Behold thy mother ! And from that hour that disciple took her unto his own home." Thus evidently before this date, perhaps a good number of years previously, Joseph had died.

The only other mention of the Virgin, mother and widow, in Scripture is in Acts i. 14, where, after the names of the apostles have been mentioned as returning from Olivet to the upper room in Jerusalem, it is added, " These all continued with one accord in prayer and supplication, with the women, and Mary the mother of Jesus, and with His brethren." To the end doubtless, whenever the end came, the house of her nephew S. John continued to be her home. Such are the facts of the life of the Blessed Virgin, according to the truth of Scripture. And three of these events have a place in the

Calendar of Festivals—viz., Christmas, Candlemas, and Lady-day ; but the first of the three belongs more to Jesus than to His mother ; and perhaps it might have been well to have been content with one festival of commemoration in the case of the Virgin, as in the case of the evangelists and apostles, instead of assigning her two or even more.[1]

But errors of excess on the subject of the Virgin-Mother on the part of others, should not tempt any to errors of defect by leading to speak or think slightingly of her who, on angelic authority, was pre-eminently blessed among women. It is our duty from time to time to refer to her life and example for our guidance ; and the duty will be all the better done if associated with a commemorative and fixed day. The same use is to be made of every godly example in both Old and New Testament biography. And it is consistent, with all caution and proportion of doctrine, to say plainly that there is a stronger plea for so dealing with the mother of our Lord than with any other saint in all Scripture. She who was saluted by the angel as highly favoured of the Lord and blessed among women, was, notwithstanding, of a fallen

---

[1] The amount of doctrinal exaggeration on the subject of the Virgin in the Roman Church, is apparent from a mere list of the festivals in her honour *additional* to Candlemas and Lady-day, viz. :—

1. The Immaculate Conception, 8th December. This, since a papal decree of 8th December 1854, is an article of Catholic faith.
2. The espousals of S. Mary, 23d January.
3. The seven dolours or sorrows of Mary, on Good Friday, and on third Sunday of September. The seven sorrows are—Simeon's prophecy, flight into Egypt, loss of Jesus for three days, carry-ing of the cross, crucifixion, receiving the body from the cross, the burial.
4. The visitation, 2d July, meeting with Elisabeth.
5. The assumption of the Virgin into heaven, 16th August.
6. The nativity of the Virgin, 8th September.
7. Presentation of the Virgin when three years old in the Temple by her parents, 21st November.

To which may be added—
8. S. Anne, the Virgin's mother, 26th July.
9. S. Joachim, her father, 21st August.

nature, just as we are—saved by faith in Christ, just as we are—and had no power to help others to pardon or progress by means different from the help which any ordinary believer can give to a friend. At the same time, there is that of distinction and pre-eminence in the history and character of S. Mary which should lead every careful reader of Holy Scripture to ponder devoutly the events of her career and the features of her disposition, that he may thereby be edified, guided, and encouraged.

The qualities in which she excels are—lowliness, purity, faith, sorrow, patience, and consolation.

The lowliness we see—in her word, "Behold the handmaid of the Lord;" in the poverty that had to be content with the stable and manger of an inn for childbirth; and that had again to be content in the Temple with the simple offering of a pair of doves.

The purity we see in her whole conduct as maid, wife, mother, and widow. Of that great purity the whiteness of the tall Madonna lily has been the suitable emblem to all Christendom.

The faith we see — in her reception of the message of Gabriel; in her creed as expressed in her inspired hymn; in her trustful conduct at the marriage in Cana; in her clinging to the meetings of the Church between Ascension and Pentecost.

The sorrow, foretold by Simeon, was seen—in the flight into Egypt to save the Child's life; in the three days' loss of her Son at the age of twelve; in the rejection of her Son by the rulers of the Jews; and in the sight of His crucifixion.

The patience we see—in her submission to suspicion even by Joseph, her betrothed; in her thirty years of waiting before the miracles that attended her Son's birth bore any public fruit; in witnessing the labours and disappointments of her Son's ministry, who had more enemies than followers.

The consolation we see—in the miracles that she saw or knew her Son work; in her hearing of His wise doctrine; in her daily observation of His faultless life, full of love and devotion; in His resurrection from the dead; in His heavenly gift at Pentecost; and in the wonderful progress of His Church thereafter.

In the whole compass of Scripture there is certainly no higher example of a holy and true woman than we have in the Mother of Jesus. In her joy the Church has ever sympathised by its uniform and great favour shown toward her inspired song, as worthy of a place in the daily worship of Christians, on account of its wonderful fervour of thanksgiving. So also in her sorrow has the Church always and deeply sympathised—a sympathy that centuries ago embodied itself in that most touching hymn—

> " Stabat Mater dolorosa
> Juxta crucem lacrymosa
> Dum pendebat Filius."

Although originally written from the Roman point of view in doctrine, so true and deep is the feeling expressed that, with the change of a few words, objectionable on the ground of intercession of saints, the hymn has commended itself to the great body of Christians. The text may be given of another hymn of the Virgin equally famous with the *Stabat Mater*, and several centuries earlier—in fact, as early as the ninth century—used in the Anglo-Saxon Church in the north of England, and preserved unchanged since then :—

Ave maris stella,	Hail, thou star of ocean !
Dei Mater alma,	Portal of the sky !
Atque semper virgo,	Ever Virgin Mother
Felix cœli porta.	Of the Lord most high !
Sumens illud Ave	Oh ! by Gabriel's Ave,
Gabrielis ore,	Uttered long ago,
Funda nos in pace,	Eva's name reversing,
Mutans Evæ nomen.	Grant us peace below.

Solve vincla reis,
Profer lumen cæcis,
Mala nostra pelle,
Bona cuncta posce.

Break the captive's fetters ;
 Light on blindness pour ;
All our ills expelling,
 Every bliss implore.

Monstra te esse matrem,
Sumat per te preces,
Qui pro nobis natus,
Tulit esse tuus.

Show thyself a mother ;
 Offer Him our sighs,
Who for us incarnate
 Did not thee despise.

Virgo singularis,
Inter omnes mitis,
Nos culpis solutos,
Mites fac et castos.

Virgin of all virgins !
 To thy shelter take us :
Gentlest of the gentle !
 Chaste and gentle make us.

Vitam præsta puram,
Iter para tutum,
Ut videntes Jesum,
Semper collætemur.

Still as on we journey,
 Help our weak endeavour,
Till with thee and Jesus
 We rejoice for ever.

In Longfellow's "Golden Legend" words are put into the mouth of Prince Henry, looking on Italy after crossing the ridge of the Alps, that present what many a traveller has felt on the two sides of this subject, even though his own mind is entirely at one with the doctrine of S. Peter, touching the name of Jesus Christ of Nazareth, that "there is none other name under heaven among men whereby we must be saved."

" This is indeed the blessed Mary's land,
 Virgin and Mother of our dear Redeemer !
All hearts are touched and softened at her name ;
Alike the bandit with the blood-stained hand,
The priest, the prince, the scholar, and the peasant,
The man of deeds, the visionary dreamer,
Pay homage to her as one ever present !
   .   .   .   .
And if our faith had given us nothing more
Than this example of all womanhood,
So mild, so merciful, so strong, so good,
So patient, peaceful, loyal, loving, pure,
This were enough to prove it higher and truer
Than all the creeds the world had known before."

Notwithstanding the extravagance of many both in past and present days, alike safely and profitably may we think of this most blessed among women. Let us think of her as yielding lowly obedience and holy welcome to the angel's annunciation. Let us think of her as previously and especially thereafter reading and pondering diligently what the Old Testament foretells of Messiah. Let us think of her carefully watching over the Holy Child alike in infancy, youth, and manhood; watching His private life, His public teaching, and His persecution by His enemies. Let us think of her as treasuring up day by day and year by year those indications in deed and word that pointed forward to things great and mysterious. Let us think of her as conscientiously observing the laws of Moses in all the feasts and ordinances of the Jewish Church—circumcision, purification, the yearly journey to Jerusalem at Passover-time. Let us think of her as living after her Son's Passion a life of most deep but also hopeful sorrow in the quiet, prayerful, and loving shelter of S. John's house. Let us think of her as joyously watching the gradual extension of her Son's Church in Judea and beyond. And let us think of her as at last peacefully entering into rest in the faith of Christ and in sure hope of everlasting life.

COLLECT.—*O Christ our God Incarnate, whose Virgin-Mother was blessed in bearing Thee, but still more blessed in keeping Thy word; grant us who honour the exaltation of her lowliness, to follow the example of her devotion to Thy will, who livest, &c.*[1]

[1] Bright, Ancient Collects, p. 236.

𝕾. 𝕵𝖔𝖘𝖊𝖕𝖍.

DAY, MARCH 19.

ORATIO.—*Deus qui ineffabili providentia beatum Joseph sanctissimæ Genetricis tuæ sponsum eligere dignatus es: præsta, quæsumus; ut quem protectorem veneramur in terris, intercessorem habere mereamur in cælis.   Qui vivis.*

The Epistle.—Acts iv. 23-30.
The Gospel.—S. Matt. i. 18-25.

Te, Joseph, celebrent agmina cœli-
    tum,   [chori,
Te cuncti resonent Christianum
Qui clarus meritis, junctus es in-
    clytæ
    Casto fœdere Virgini.

Almo cum tumidam germine con-
    jugem
Admirans, dubio tangeris anxius,
Afflatu superi Flaminis Angelus
    Conceptum puerum docet.

Tu natum Dominum stringis, ad
    exteras
Ægypti profugum tu sequeris
    plagas;
Amissum Solymis quæris et invenis,
    Miscens gaudia fletibus.

Post mortem reliquos mors pia
    consecrat,   [it;
Palmamque emeritos gloria suscip-
Tu vivens, superis par, frueris Deo,
    Mira sorte beatior.
        —*Parisian Breviary.*
    (NEWMAN, *Hymni Ecclesiastici.*)

Joseph, pure spouse of that immor-
    tal Bride,   [bright,
Who shines in ever-virgin glory
Through all the Christian climes
    thy praise be sung;
    Through all the realms of light.

Thee, when amazed concern for thy
    betrothed   [dismay,
Had filled thy righteous spirit with
An angel visited, and, with blest
    words,
    Scattered thy fears away.

Thine arms embraced thy Maker
    newly born;   [thou flee;
With him to Egypt's desert didst
Him in Jerusalem didst seek and
    find;
    Oh grief, oh joy for thee!

Not until after death their blissful
    crown   [given,
Others obtain; but unto thee was
In thine own lifetime, to enjoy thy
    God
    As do the blest in heaven.
            —E. CASWALL.

"Joseph her husband, being a just man."—S. MATT. i. 19.

S. JOSEPH is probably the most ill-used man in sacred history ; not that any professing Christians are so profane as directly to assail him, but many shut their eyes as much as possible to his existence, they avoid speaking of him as a saint, they grudge him a day in the Calendar, and they make him to pay the penalty of the over-attention he receives in the Roman Church. This treatment is grossly unfair to the saint, and is despiteful to the inspired gospels, which mention him not unfrequently, and always with honour. The root of this neglect of S. Joseph is that Protestants are carried off their head by the surviving heat of sixteenth-century controversy. In fact it would almost seem as if Protestants deliberately cherished and magnified the Joseph of Genesis for the purpose of overshadowing or forestalling the Joseph of the gospels.

Not only has S. Joseph no day in the Calendar of the Church of England, but he has no day in the Salisbury Breviary, which was the chief Service-book anciently in use both in England and Scotland, and on which, more than any other single book, the Anglican Prayer-book is based ; so that this omission in the use of Sarum may be the reason of there being no S. Joseph's Day in the Anglican sacred year. By some S. Joseph is considered as the special patron saint of the Church of Rome. He is patron of the Order of S. Teresa ; and Gerson, Chancellor of the University of Paris, has a Latin poem on the saint, named Josephina. While the Western Church observes 19th March as his day of commemoration, the Syrians keep 20th July.

Untouched by prejudice, and seeking closely to follow where inspired Scripture leads, let us, as in other cases, gather and compare the New Testament references to our saint, alike in his relation to the Blessed Virgin and her divine Son ; for it is these three who constitute that Holy Family which was a favourite subject in the Christian art of medieval times, before controversy had dulled men's sense of justice, reverence, and beauty. The Scriptural allusions to S. Joseph are of three kinds—relative respectively to his genealogy, his visits from angels, and his connection with incidents in the early life of Jesus.

The genealogy in S. Matt. i. begins and ends thus: "The book of the generation of Jesus Christ, the Son of David, the son of Abraham. Abraham begat Isaac; . . . Matthan begat Jacob; and Jacob begat Joseph the husband of Mary, of whom was born Jesus who is called Christ." Conform to which, four verses further on, is the word of the angel, "Joseph, thou son of David, fear not to take unto thee Mary thy wife." Again, in S. Luke iii., the genealogy is reversed, beginning with Jesus, and going back to Adam. "And Jesus Himself began to be about thirty years of age, being (as was supposed) the son of Joseph, which was the son of Heli, which was the son of Matthat, . . . which was the son of Enos, which was the son of Seth, which was the son of Adam, which was the son of God."

On the surface, each of these genealogies is that of Joseph, and not of Mary as we would have expected. But as Joseph and Mary were both descendants of David, cousins as well as spouses, and having Matthan or Matthat for their common grandfather, the same family-tree will serve for both. At the end of the line it has been proposed to arrange thus in modern way [1] :—

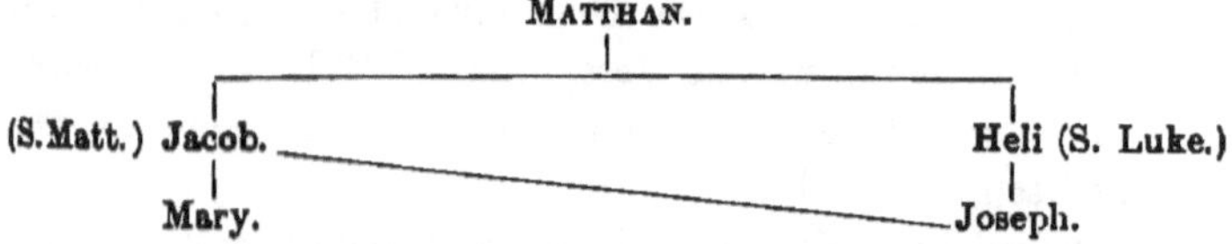

This man (the spouse of Mary), descended from the kings of Judah, was a carpenter by trade, according to allusion in Matt. xiii. 55, Mark vi. 3, John vi. 42, and also by Justin, who says that Joseph and Jesus made ploughs and yokes for oxen. He seems to have been somewhat advanced in life at

---

[1] Farrar on S. Luke, Excursus II.

the time of his betrothal to the Virgin, and (as comes up for discussion under James, the Lord's brother) to have been previously married, and to have had a family almost grown up. This, however, is one of the standing questions of the Gospel history, the final settlement of which is perhaps impossible with our present material, and any decision on which rests on inferences drawn from a variety of small hints—hints which many interpret under prejudices associated with the controversial views of their own branch of the Church.

Here we require to give heed to the adjective used to delineate a leading feature of Joseph's character, "a just man"—*i.e.*, righteous, conscientious, perhaps also ascetic man. This feature in his disposition is mentioned in connection with his perplexity as to how to act in the face of the hard fact of his betrothed kinswoman being about to become a mother independently of him, and in violent contradiction to her own previous reputation. In view of this staring fact it seemed to him that he could not avoid doing a certain extremely unpleasant thing, the breaking off of the betrothal; and yet, regardful of his kinswoman's singularly pure name hitherto before this mystery, he felt it was due to her to make the change in the mildest possible way—*i.e.*, by a secret paper before witnesses, and not by a public action in a law court. "Then Joseph her husband, being a just man, and not willing to make her a public example, was minded to put her away privily." It was a perplexing crisis; he seems not to have dared to name his difficulty to Mary, nor does she seem to have dared to tell her condition even to him who had so strong a claim to her full confidence. Probably this reticence was part of her supreme confidence in God and submission to His will in this case of high mystery. If so, she was right, for God interposed anew by His angel, probably the same Gabriel who had delivered the message to herself, to give the solution of the mystery to her betrothed without straining of her own modesty, and without unduly extending Joseph's painful perplexity.

At this stage of relief and explanation as concerns Joseph we enter on a fresh stage of the development of his character, to which enough of attention is not ordinarily paid. Here his position is pretty much parallel to that of Mary at the point when she said, "Behold the handmaid of the Lord; be it unto me according to thy word." After the angel's communication, "Joseph, being raised from sleep, did as the angel of the Lord had bidden him, and took unto him his wife." In credence given to the angel, Joseph excelled the priest Zacharias on a like occasion and resembled his own saintly betrothed. And a very noticeable feature is, that this is only the first of four visits and communications of angels made to this same "just man," proving surely a high degree of the divine favour, for even in the case of the Blessed Virgin we read of no angelic message but the superlatively grand one of the annunciation. S. Matthew alone records these angel messages for Joseph's guidance—viz., i. 20; ii. 13, 19, 22—and it is well to mark the occasion associated with each of the four.

The first of the occasions is that already described of the original perplexity that seemed hopelessly to break off the betrothal. "But while he thought on these things, behold, the angel of the Lord appeared unto him in a dream, saying, Joseph, thou son of David, fear not to take unto thee Mary thy wife; for that which is conceived in her is of the Holy Ghost. And she shall bring forth a son, and thou shalt call his name Jesus; for He shall save His people from their sins." To this message he was obedient. The second was after the visit and gifts of the Magi, and to this also was Joseph obedient. "And when they were departed, behold, the angel of the Lord appeareth to Joseph in a dream, saying, Arise, and take the young child and His mother, and flee into Egypt, and be thou there until I bring thee word: for Herod will seek the young child to destroy Him. When he arose, he took the young child and His mother by night, and departed into Egypt; and was there until the death of Herod." The third occasion was the fulfilment of the angel's promise associated with the preceding. "But when Herod was dead, behold, an angel of the Lord appeareth in a dream to Joseph in Egypt, saying, Arise, and take the young child and His mother, and go into the land of Israel: for they are dead which sought the young child's life. And he arose, and took the young child and His mother, and came into the land of Israel." The fourth and last of this series of angelic visits to Joseph had for its object to direct him to settle in a safer part of the country than near Jerusalem: "But when he heard that Archelaus did reign in Judea in the room of his father Herod, he was afraid to go thither: notwithstanding, being warned of God in a dream, he turned aside into the parts of Galilee: and he came and dwelt in a city called Nazareth." Nazareth being in the territory of Herod Antipas, another son of Herod the Great, and less associated both with the capital and the priesthood, was a quiet and safe retreat for such a household as Joseph's.

By those who wish to minimise S. Joseph to carry out controversies that have arisen at least ten centuries after the above events, it can be said, and truly, that the object of these angelic messages was really Christ Himself, and that Joseph's relation to the matter was only that of means to an end. This construction, however, is seen to be no better than an evasion when we come to trace the conduct of Joseph in his care from point to point, in his unfailing obedience, in his subordinating his residence and trade and personal comfort for a series of years, so as to subserve what related to the Blessed Virgin and her Son, as these had been made matter of a series of angelic messages to him. Surely it was no light matter for Joseph hastily and secretly to quit Bethlehem on the warning of the angel against Herod's cruelty, and flee into Egypt with an infant child and mother, three days' journey, to take refuge among strangers. The amount of the trial is to be inferred from the way in which the scene has impressed itself on the minds of devout painters, with whom the Flight has been a favourite theme. This flight reveals Joseph as the chief instrument in the hand of God in preserving Jesus from Herod. It may be mere legend, but it is a beautiful and appropriate one, which represents the oracles of the heathen temples as dumb, and the statues of the heathen gods as shaking all over Egypt, when the infant Christ took refuge in the ancient land. The stay of the Holy Family in Egypt is computed to have been for nearly two years.

Here one cannot but think for a moment, in passing, of the ties, both earlier and later, that bound Egypt and Palestine together in the bundle of life. This was evidently in S. Matthew's mind when he quoted the Old Testament, "Out of Egypt have I called my Son." The same idea has guided the choice of lessons from Genesis relative to the first Joseph to illustrate the Gospel as to the husband of Mary. Nor would S. Joseph's stay of two years in Egypt be wholly among heathen, for it was the resort for long of many Jews, as the Septuagint Bible testifies. These Jewish residents early and widely received the Gospel, so that Alexandria especially (joined with the name of S. Mark the evangelist) became a Christian stronghold. In fact all North Africa, as the land of Tertullian, Cyprian, Origen, and Augustin, rivalled Asia Minor itself for its vigorous Churches. No land was at one time more rich in true saints and eremites and monks than Egypt, although its Coptic Church is now so low compared with the rest of modern Christendom.

Joseph's intention, on returning from Egypt to Palestine, was evidently to settle afresh in or near Bethlehem, his ancestral town; but at the suggestion of the angel, and to promote the safety of the child to whom he was a faithful and self-sacrificing foster-father, he returned again to remote Nazareth. And it is at Nazareth we find the Holy Family ten years later, when Jesus accompanied His mother and Joseph to one of the Passovers at Jerusalem, as recorded by S. Luke. That is the latest mention of S. Joseph in Scripture. The exact date of Joseph's death is unknown; but from the absence of his name as a guest at the marriage at Cana, where

the mother of Jesus is so prominent, and from the legacy of
the mother to S. John at the cross, we may be quite sure that
Joseph died before the beginning of our Lord's public ministry.
Doubtless also the good man was tended and comforted on his
deathbed both by Jesus and His mother.   And it is in conformity with the Gospel hint of Jesus being named both as
a carpenter and a carpenter's son, to suppose that, in the interval of His sacred life between the age of twelve and thirty, he
first helped Joseph in the joiner's shop, and then succeeded
him in the trade as a means of earning a plain independent
livelihood, alike for Himself and for His widowed mother.
Joseph's own children by his first marriage seem to have
married and scattered and settled in houses of their own
about Nazareth and Cana, leaving the Virgin alone with her
divine Son.   The brethren of Jesus—*i.e.*, Joseph's family by
a former wife—were not believers in our Lord's mission until
after His resurrection, which finally opened their eyes to the
true nature of their father's foster-child.   And it says not a
little for the respect in which they were held, and the kind of
home-training they had received in early days, that two of
Joseph's sons in succession—James and Simeon—were the
first and second bishops of Jerusalem.   This devout, somewhat stern and ascetic training which they received and
inherited, explains the adjective "just" which characterises
Joseph, and reappears especially in James, whom we know
best from his epistle.   Moreover, a third son of Joseph meets
us in Scripture, and contributes to it one chapter in the Epistle
of Jude, "the brother of James"—an epistle which also bears
the family trait of sternness.   A man who gave three such
sons of his own to the New Testament and the New Testament
Church, and who himself was both husband to the Blessed
Mary and foster-father to her divine Son, would surely have
been universally recognised as a saint, but for the blinding
and embittering influence of dogmatic controversy.   It is a
shame to Protestant Christendom that the Joseph of the

gospels has not a fourth part of the attention that is given to the Joseph of Genesis. What labour of exposition is devoted to the finding of types of Christ in the latter! whereas, probably, twenty years of the life of the former were devoted to supplying food, raiment, and home to Jesus in His infancy, boyhood, and opening manhood! If men are honest in their love of evangelic doctrine, and intelligent in their search for it, there is much more of it surrounding the husband of Mary than the old prime minister of Pharaoh : the one is as the first flow of the vintage ; while the other is the result of pressure, and even bruising, in the wine-press, yielding at most a trickling runlet. But when one-half of a man's creed consists in abusing some other branch of the Christian Church, he must pay for it elsewhere; hence the hydrophobia with which tens of thousands of professing Christians regard S. Joseph, who for twenty years watched and toiled to provide food, clothing, education, and shelter for his divine foster-Son, from the first having knowledge of His divinity on the sure testimony of that angel of God who said : "Joseph, thou son of David, fear not to take unto thee Mary thy wife ; for that which is conceived in her is of the Holy Ghost. And she shall bring forth a son, and thou shalt call His name Jesus; for He shall save His people from their sins." It is thus a simple historic fact that, believing and acting on these words, Joseph was the first of all Christian men, as Mary was the first of all Christian women. The foundation doctrine of their creed, as of ours, was that of our blessed Lord's divinity, and to each of the spouses the doctrine was separately revealed by an angel from heaven ; and, with reverence it may be said, that each had a right to know this grand doctrine, from their relation to each other as husband and wife, and from the fact that this Son of God was to be trained from birth to manhood under their roof, and daily provided for at their table.

And now we come to a point deliberately reserved for the close of what is here said touching S. Mary and S. Joseph. It is the question of the perpetual-virginity of the mother of Jesus. No word of Scripture affirms it directly, but also no word of Scripture is inconsistent with it. Long before the celibacy of the priesthood became a matter of controversy, the voice of the early Christian Church was raised and written on the side of her perpetual virginity. Whether it be called feeling, or instinct, or belief, it seems to the present writer that by far the more reverent course is to accept the early Christian sentiment or judgment. The point is incapable of proof, either Scriptural or historic ; but there need be no difficulty in heartily accepting it as a pious opinion, in view of the high angelic annunciation to each of the spouses of the true fatherhood of the Holy Child ; in view of the firm belief of each in this revelation from heaven ; in view of the deep devoutness of each of the spouses as traced in the whole line of the personal career of each.

Looking at S. Joseph's character in a practical light as a pattern for all Christian men to follow, it may be said that the virtues and graces which distinguish him are — constancy, courage, humility, obedience, and self-denial. He is rich on the firmer side, where is justice, and conscience, and perseverance ; but if there was also a gentler side to the same nature, as is most probable, it is less prominent, unless we trace it in his uniform care year by year, and in journeys to and from Egypt, all in the interest of the divine Child that was so long the hidden treasure of his house, and in whom he himself heartily believed from the first, and surely to his clear faith would add the warmth of love and piety, very genuine though not obtrusive.

Simeon and Anna.

CANDLEMAS DAY.

COLLECTS.—*Almighty and ever-living God, we humbly beseech Thy Majesty, that as Thy only-begotten Son was this day presented in the Temple in substance of our flesh, so we may be presented unto Thee with pure and clean hearts, by the same Thy Son Jesus Christ our Lord.   Amen.*

O almighty and everlasting God, who not only givest every good and perfect gift, but also increasest those gifts Thou hast given; we most humbly beseech Thee to increase in us the gift of faith, that we may truly believe in Thee and in Thy promises; and that neither by our negligence, nor infirmity of the flesh, nor by grievousness of temptation, nor by the subtle crafts and assaults of the devil, we may be driven from faith in our most blessed Lord and Saviour Jesus Christ.   Amen.[1]

The Epistle.—Eph. i. 3-14.
The Gospel.—S. Luke ii. 25-38.

Just and devout old Simeon lived ; to him it was revealed,
That Christ, the Lord, his eyes should see ere death his eyelids sealed.

For this consoling gift of Heav'n to Isr'el's fallen state,
From year to year, with patient hope, the aged saint did wait.

Nor did he wait in vain ; for, lo ! revolving years brought round,
In season due, the happy day, which all his wishes crowned.

When Jesus, to the Temple brought by Mary's pious care,
As Heaven's appointed rites required, to God was offered there,

Simeon into those sacred courts a heav'nly impulse drew ;
He saw the Virgin hold her Son, and straight his Lord he knew.

---

[1] Appendix to Euchologion.

With holy joy upon his face the good old father smiled ;
Then fondly in his withered arms he clasped the promised Child :

And while he held the heav'n-born Babe, ordained to bless mankind,
Thus spoke, with earnest look, and heart exulting, yet resigned :

Now, Lord ! according to Thy word, let me in peace depart ;
Mine eyes have Thy salvation seen, and gladness fills my heart.

At length my arms embrace my Lord, now let their vigour cease ;
At last my eyes my Saviour see, now let them close in peace.

This great salvation, long prepared, and now disclosed to view,
Hath proved Thy love was constant still, and promises were true.

That Sun I now behold, whose light shall heathen darkness chase ;
And rays of brightest glory pour around Thy chosen race.
—*Scottish Paraphrase.*

"Lord, now lettest Thou Thy servant depart in peace."
—S. LUKE ii. 29.

ALL that we know regarding Simeon is contained in S. Luke
ii. 25-35 ; and the first word uttered on the occasion in the
Temple represents in one breath the spirit of the event and
of the man. The occasion was the Purification of the Virgin,
otherwise called the Presentation of Christ in the Temple,
which is commemorated on Candlemas, 2d February, because
by Jewish custom it fell forty days after birth. Taking 25th
December for birthday, and counting it in the Jewish method
as one of the forty, we have in December seven days, in
January thirty-one, and in February two, which make up
the forty. Thus the Collect for Presentation-day may be
associated with Simeon as denoting the date of the occurrence of his famous act of faith and thanksgiving.

Such was Simeon's satisfaction to have lived to that blessed
and promised day, that he is gratefully content to retire from
the completed scene. Surely it is marvellous to behold a
man so entirely satisfied with God's fulfilment to him of
the promise to see the Messiah's coming that, although he

knew all the glories of the Messiah's age to be in immediate nearness, yet he willingly can go away after having seen only the beginning. Far beyond bare willingness, there is positive joy and triumph in the inspired expression of his feeling—

> "Lord, now lettest Thou Thy servant depart
> In peace, according to Thy word:
> For mine eyes have seen Thy salvation,
> Which Thou hast prepared before the face of all people;
> A light to lighten the Gentiles, and the glory of Thy people Israel."

The fact that this hymn has been used daily in Christian worship since at least the fifth century, makes the history or the character of its inspired author all the more interesting. This notable instance of faith in Israel is associated with the sad reflection of how few there are like it. Simeon is in one instance what God had designed in the whole nation. What hindered all the men and women of that time from being so many Simeons and Annas, but their own negligence to acquaint themselves with what God had promised to their fathers, or their personal ungodliness, or of godliness only the formal to the exclusion of the spiritual part? Thus when the men and women of that age did think of a Messiah to come, it was quite a different kind of Messiah from the Lord's Anointed; and accordingly, when the true One came, it was almost without observation.

Simeon is described as "just and devout, waiting for the consolation of Israel." Nothing is directly said as to his age, but great age is implied in several circumstances,—his conjunction with Anna the prophetess who was eighty-four, his waiting attitude, his readiness to depart, and the promise hinting at the extension of his natural course for this end that he should not see death till he had seen the Lord's Anointed. An apocryphal gospel gives his age as 113, and a legend represents him as stumbling at Isaiah vii. 14, "Behold, a virgin shall conceive," and that his hesitation was met by a divine intimation that he should not die till he had seen this fulfilled. "Just and devout" clearly mark Simeon as a man distinguished for righteousness, and probably also for some measure of learning and social standing. Waiting for the consolation of Israel recalls the saying of Dan in Genesis xlix. 18, "I have waited for Thy salvation, O Lord;" also of words in Isaiah, "They shall not be ashamed that wait for me." "Comfort ye, comfort ye, my people, saith your God." Simeon at the beginning of the gospel resembles the honourable councillor Joseph of Arimathea at the crucifixion, who " waited for the kingdom of God, and went in boldly unto Pilate, and craved the body of Jesus."—S. Mark xv. 43.

This expected Consolation was ancient as the grief and misery it was to heal; it had its beginning before David, Moses, or Abraham in the Protevangelium. For many ages it was a vague promise of a deliverer; when or how, God had not defined. But ever narrower was the line marked out whence he was to arise. It was Seth's and not Cain's; it was Judah's and not his brethren's; it was David's and none other of the sons of Jesse. Again, it was by blood and not more easily; for there was sacrifice to foreshadow it. It was by blood, with many more definite adjuncts; a Levitical priesthood, a tabernacle, a temple, and times and seasons, for only once a-year did the high priest enter the Holy of Holies. At length in the days of Daniel the prophet the special date itself was fixed, seventy weeks—*i.e.*, seven times seventy years from a certain point marked. And not only time but also place was fixed, Bethlehem Ephratah of the prophet Micah. Thus point by point was the promised and expected Consolation of Israel defined and brought home to the hearts of the faithful —in family, time, place, nature, effect.

And now, in proportion to the greatness of the blessing, attention was challenged by its acknowledged nearness. With prophecies so many in number and so distinct in substance, no mistake need have been made as to the main facts by those who laid due value on the divine word, pondering with care and prayer what had been thus revealed. The issue was that as the fulness of time drew nigh the Jewish people was in a state of expectancy, and bent with eagerness over the future, over what even a day might bring forth, in such a way as never perhaps before or since any nation did in the entertaining of a great common hope. True, every man shaped the expectation according to his own nature. With the more worldly and those taken up with mere politics it assumed that aspect. With the Pharisee the expected Messiah was to be an exaltation of Pharisaism. With a few more humble and devout men it approached nearer to the Scriptural idea of a spiritual kingdom and blessings for the soul.

Already the Saviour's forerunner had come; and connected with his birth there had been revival of the spirit of prophecy and revelation, which had been dormant in the long centuries since Malachi. God had appeared to Zacharias. And some form of revelation had been vouchsafed to Simeon himself. To a devout Israelite how precious a privilege this would be! and in the case of so aged a believer, the promise could not but be ready for immediate fulfilment, and consequently all the more precious and oft-remembered.

When at length the birth privately foreannounced by Gabriel took place, then God Himself anew proclaimed the event, and from heaven, by the anthem of the angelic host, "Glory to God in the highest, and on earth peace, goodwill toward men." To what extent this became known beyond the immediate circle of the shepherds around Bethlehem we are uncertain; but in all probability it gained some currency, especially in that district. Thus might Simeon, and those like him, patient waiters upon God, be led step by step by influences from without to knowledge of the day and person of the Consoler of Israel. But in Simeon's case there was an internal leading as well. He was visited and instructed directly by the inspiring Spirit of God, through whose afflatus he was enabled at the great moment of realisation to extemporise the fervent prayer-hymn of the *Nunc Dimittis*. And thus came it at length that the aged saint was led into the Temple to be present on that first occasion, when the Son of

God was brought by His Virgin Mother and His foster-father (S. Luke ii. 33) into His heavenly Father's house for presentation to God.

At this point we may well begin afresh. Leaving the region of the older and more scattered predictions of Messiah's advent, we now enter on the contemplation with Simeon of the circumstances under which his first actual beholding of God's fulfilled promise took place. Previously he manifested the general faith to be expected of every son of Abraham; but now he manifests a more special faith in recognising God's promise as present. It was natural for him to think in his heart, Can that which has been so long and oft announced but be of the most imposing nature when it appears? The hopes of a nation, and even of mankind, are suspended thereon, and God's own promise lies underneath. No nation on earth entertained so glorious and honourable ideas of the Creator of all things as did the Jewish people; and this higher estimate of God's nature and character led them all the more to conceive highly of any blessing to which God attached importance, as was clearly done in this case touching the Messiah, who was to come miraculously. For all the evils that oppress man's heart and lot, this was to be one great countervailing blessing; over all enemies, one great conqueror. Simeon has entered once more God's temple, this time conscious through some illumination of the Spirit that he is to find what from his youth he has been taught to regard as the greatest of all hopes fulfilled. How difficult to conceive anything that will satisfy conditions and demands like these! You need power, purity, glory—nothing less or else will suffice for the Hope of Israel.

Among the prophets of old, Moses, Isaiah, and Ezekiel have each recorded and described visions of the divine glory. Moses describes his vision as too dazzling to be seen by the eye of flesh; God's face is too bright to be gazed on by living mortal, and only the train of His glory can be seen by life with life— Exod. xxxiii. In Isaiah vi. we read of the house filled with smoke, and the posts of the door trembling at the voice, the angels hiding their faces with their wings, and the prophet himself filled with consternation and crying out, "Woe is me! for I am undone." In Ezekiel i. we behold in a gorgeous mystery the vision of the living creatures, with the wheels, and the cherubim, and the uplifting, which would take the whole sky for its fitting scene to convey a faint idea of the prophet's conception.

In all these there is nothing more glorious than what is here required to fulfil the hope and consolation of Israel; because now God's Son, the world's Saviour, the everlasting King for the throne of David, is to be met. Yet when Simeon is divinely guided to the Temple on this solemn occasion, he finds earthquake none, fire none, visions or voices of angels none, crowd and excitement none. Only a priest is calmly ministering, and a mother humbly presenting an offering for her purification,—a humble offering, the humblest on the graduated list,—and in her arms a child. Thither the Spirit leads aged Simeon, for *that* Child is Israel's Consolation, and *that* Child is God's Son.

How the identification took place is a deep mystery of inspiration on which the sacred narrative throws no light, but the same narrative is very emphatic and clear on this point, that the identification was made decisively and with the accompaniment of rapture and prophecy and song. In the Arabic gospel of the Infancy an explanation of how Simeon recognised the Messiah is attempted by saying that the Holy Child shone like a pillar of light in his mother's arms, the hint being drawn from Simeon's own expression, "a light to lighten the Gentiles." In view of this problem of identification we think of later helps to faith, the mighty works that began at Cana; the word of resurrection at Lazarus's grave; the word of peace to the storm on the lake; the wise and authoritative teaching at the Mount; the transfiguration at Tabor; the forgiving prayer on the cross; His reappearance after death; His ascension into glory. These all were sublime helps to faith. But for Simeon to see merely the child Jesus, and at the first sight still to believe, to take the infant Saviour into his arms with reverent love, and to improvise the *Nunc Dimittis* with its glorious expression of mingled adoration, gratitude, and contentment—this is so transcendent an act of faith that only God's immediate inspiration can explain it. There is here out of simple elements a grandeur of which secular life and literature have no conception. The most wonderful feature of Simeon's song is its clear recognition of the two provinces of Messiah's kingdom at so early a stage, before the Saviour had emphasised the mission to the lost sheep of the house of Israel; before the baptismal commission to all the world; before Peter and Paul had adjusted terms and labourers as between the Circumcision and the Uncircumcision; and before the first decree of the first Council of 52 A.D.—"A light to lighten the Gentiles, and the glory of Thy people Israel." The effect of Simeon's hymn on the married pair who were devoutly presenting the Divine Child is thus given in the corrected text used in the Revised Version of 1881—"And His father and His mother were marvelling at the things which were spoken concerning Him, and Simeon blessed them." Independently of his holding any priestly office, Simeon's years and inspiration combined would well entitle him to the privilege of bestowing benediction on two saints who stood higher in God's kingdom than himself. Moreover, his blessing had almost a deathbed solemnity about it, coming after such an allusion to his own departure.

But the aged saint has contributed more to Scripture than the *Nunc Dimittis.* "Simeon blessed them, and said unto Mary His mother, Behold, this Child is set for the fall and rising again of many in Israel: and for a sign which shall be spoken against; (yea, a sword shall pierce through thy own soul also,) that the thoughts of many hearts may be revealed."

Here are two verses of prophecy that present germ-wise much of the Saviour's career on earth in its trials, sorrows, difficulties, and successes. "The fall and rising again of many" reminds us that Jesus in His Gospel was then as now the savour to some of life unto life, and to others of death unto death. The "sign to be spoken against" is of course the cross and the atonement doctrine which the cross symbolises. The emblem of salvation has provoked fierce rage and opposition many a time in Church history; sometimes in heathen fury against Christians, as in the ten great persecutions; sometimes in Moslem fanaticism, as in Spain and Syria and North Africa; sometimes in revolutionary and unbelieving intolerance, as in France; sometimes in puritanic bigotry, as against the cross in architecture and as a baptismal sign; sometimes in philosophy falsely so called, which is ever busy with fresh arguments against the Scripture doctrine of sacrifice and atonement. As to the sword that pierced the soul of the Virgin-Mother, then so happy in her offering for her purification, was not that pre-eminently true when at her Son and Saviour's death she stood at the foot of the cross a witness of every pang and mark of shame which His enemies devised? It was in these and kindred ways that "the thoughts of many hearts were revealed;" for no man or cause ever so fully compelled men to develop their deeper selves as the Gospel of Christ. Under the influence of His Word and Spirit, either men were led to God to humble themselves before Him in penitence, receiving grace and working righteousness, or they hardened their hearts the more, and fled from God the farther into darkness.

How edifying to remember that in all this Simeon was not alone, but that a like testimony, more quietly but not less cordially made, was borne on the same happy occasion by a devout and also divinely enlightened woman, who may be taken as representative of her sex, so many of whom afterwards were so kind and bountiful toward the Man of Sorrows! "And there was one Anna, a prophetess, the daughter of Phanuel, of the tribe of Aser: she was of a great age, and had lived with an husband seven years from her virginity; and she was a widow of about fourscore and

four years, which departed not from the temple, but served God
with fastings and prayers night and day. And she coming
in that instant gave thanks likewise unto the Lord, and spake
of Him to all them that looked for redemption in Jerusalem."
This speaking of the Child-Saviour on the part of Anna
to all in Jerusalem who were looking for Messiah, furnishes
a hint of the first spread of the tidings of salvation. Doubtless Simeon would do the same; so too the shepherds with
their part of knowledge; so too the Magi with theirs; so
too the neighbours of Zacharias and Elisabeth.

The one outstanding lesson of the experience of Simeon and
Anna is as to how to attain a peaceful departure through our
own faith and joy in the reception of the Son of God. Still
does the Divine Spirit, even apart from special inspiration as
was granted to Simeon, enable us so to live on earth as that
earth's greatest blessing will come last of all in what has often
been made a special subject of prayer—*mors bona*, a peaceful
end, the death of the righteous.

COLLECTS.—*O God of love and peace, who for the salvation
of mankind didst endure to be hanged on a cross, and didst
pour forth Thy blood for our redemption; favourably and be-
nignantly receive my prayers, and bestow on me Thy mercy;
That when Thou shalt command me to depart from the body,
the enemy may have no power over me, but the angel of peace
may place me among Thy saints and elect, where light abides
and life reigns, world without end.*[1]

*O God, who, condemning us to death, didst conceal the
moment and the hour of it, grant that, walking in the paths of
justice and holiness, we may be able to depart from this world
in Thy holy love, through the merits of our Lord Jesus Christ,
who liveth and reigneth with Thee in the unity of the Holy
Ghost, world without end.   Amen.*[2]

[1] Gallican Sacramentary, Bright, Anc. Coll., p. 94.
[2] Catholic Belief, p. 268.

The Holy Innocents.

DAY, DECEMBER 28.

ORATIO.—*Deus, cujus hodierna die præconium innocentes martyres non loquendo sed moriendo confessi sunt : omnia in nobis vitiorum mala mortifica, ut fidem tuam, quam lingua nostra loquitur, etiam moribus vita fateatur. Qui cum Deo Patre.*

The Epistle.—Rev. xiv. 1-5.
The Gospel.—S. Matt. ii. 13-18.

COLLECT.—*O Almighty God, who out of the mouths of babes and sucklings hast ordained strength, and madest infants to glorify Thee by their deaths ; mortify and kill all vices in us, and so strengthen us by Thy grace, that by the innocency of our lives and constancy of our faith even unto death, we may glorify Thy holy name ; through Jesus Christ our Lord. Amen.*

The Epistle.—Rev. xiv. 1-5.
The Gospel.—S. Matt. ii. 13-18.

Audit tyrannus anxius	When it reached the tyrant's ear,
Adesse regum Principem,	Brooding anxious all alone,
Qui nomen Israel regat,	That the King of kings was near,
Teneatque David regiam.	Who should sit on David's throne ;
Exclamat amens nuntio :	Stung with madness, straight he cries, [sword !
Successor instat, pellimur :	Treason threatens — draw the
Satelles i, ferrum rape :	Rebels all around us rise !
Perfunde cunas sanguine.	Drown the cradles deep in blood !

Quid proficit tantum nefas ?
Quid crimen Herodem juvat ?
Unus tot inter funera
Impune Christus tollitur.
   —PRUDENTIUS, 348-415 A.D.

What is guilty Herod's gain,
  Though a thousand babes he
  slay ?—
Christ, amid a thousand slain,
  Is in safety borne away.
      —E. CASWALL.

Salvete flores martyrum,
In lucis ipso limine
Quos sævus ensis messuit,
Ceu turbo nascentes rosas.

Sweet flowerets of the martyr band,
So early plucked by cruel hand ;
Like rosebuds by a tempest torn,
As breaks the light of summer
  morn.

Vos prima Christi victima,
Grex immolatorum tener,
Aram sub ipsam simplices
Palma et coronis luditis.

First victims offered for the Lord,
Ye little knew your high reward,
As at the very altar, gay   [to play.
With palms and crown ye seemed

Quid proficit tantum nefas ?
Quid crimen Herodem juvat ?
Unus tot inter funera
Impune Christus tollitur.
    —PRUDENTIUS.

Ah ! what availed King Herod's
  wrath ?   [path ;
He could not stay your Saviour's
The Child he sought alone went
  free,
That Child is King eternally.
     —Sir H. W. BAKER.

" In Rama was there a voice heard, lamentation, and weeping, and great mourning, Rachel weeping for her children, and would not be comforted, because they are not."—S. MATT. ii. 18.

THE massacre of the Innocents by Herod, as commemorated three days after the joy of Christmas, vividly suggests to us the sudden changes and alternation of human feeling in the lives of individuals as in the history of peoples. And the change is even more rapid from joy to sorrow than from the 25th to the 28th of December, for the commemoration of S. Stephen the protomartyr is on 26th December. From the very beginning of the Christian Church this awful deed of Herod has touched alike the heart and the imagination of believers, as is shown by its place in the first gospel; by the early memorial festival of the slaughtered infants; by the hymn of Prudentius in the fourth century; by its prominence in Christian art. Herod the Great was by birth an Idumean or Edomite, originally an adventurer or usurper, and made king of Judea through the influence of Mark Antony, but his kingship was after all subordinate to Rome. He reigned from 36 B.C. to 1 B.C.—*i.e.*, the birth of Christ took place really three years previous to the year fixed on as the first of our chronology, and Herod survived our Lord's birth by two years. The narrative of S. Matthew distinctly records the tyrant's alarm at the visit of the Magi, connected with the birth of a King of the Jews, for it was in this alarm that he summoned a meeting of the Sanhedrim, a Church court to which he was no friend; "he demanded of them where Christ should be born." The narrative also exposes the cunning and hypocrisy of Herod in privily calling the wise men and inquiring of them diligently what time the star appeared, and especially in saying, "When ye have found Him, bring me word again, that I may come and worship Him also." His real intention was to prevent worship, by the method of murder. To thwart the tyrant's design against the Holy Child, the angel of God interposed with a message to S. Joseph to flee into Egypt, and a message to the Magi not to return to Herod. "Then Herod, when he saw that he was mocked of the wise men, was exceeding wroth, and sent forth, and slew all the male children that were in Bethlehem, and in all the coasts thereof, from two years old and under, according to the time which he had diligently inquired of the wise men."

It is impossible to tell the number of infants thus sacrificed to Herod's cruel jealousy, because the number depends on not only the population of Bethlehem, but the population also of villages within a radius of perhaps four or five miles. Those who speak of thousands (an Ethiopian liturgy and a Greek Calendar name 14,000) certainly exaggerate; but it might easily be up to or even beyond one hundred. Taking that moderate estimate of one hundred families each desolated by sudden military violence exercised on a helpless speechless boy, what an agony of sorrow must have lain on the stricken population of the district, and especially on the poor nursing mothers! The simultaneous wail of so many childless mothers is put before us by the sympathetic evangelist (formal tax-gatherer though he was) with a wonderful touch of tragic power, borrowed aptly from the book and experience of Jeremiah. The same district six hundred years before had had a bitter sorrow when many or most of its people had been made captive and gathered at Ramah (now El-Rama, five miles north of Jerusalem and in Benjamin territory), previous to being carried into exile to Babylon. "Thus saith the Lord, A voice was heard in Ramah, lamentation, and bitter weeping; Rachel weeping for her children, refused to be comforted for her children, because they were not. Thus saith the Lord, Refrain thy voice from weeping and thine eyes from tears: for thy work shall be rewarded, saith the Lord; and they shall come again from the land of the enemy. And there is hope in thine end, saith the Lord, that thy children shall come again to their own border."—Jer. xxxi. 15. "The word that came to Jeremiah from the Lord, after that Nebuzar-adan the captain of the guard had let him go from Ramah, when he had taken him, being bound in chains among all that were carried away captive of Jerusalem and Judah, which were carried away captive unto Babylon."—xl. 1. Although this old sorrow was partly met by comfort administered through the prophet, yet in its freshness it was an overwhelming woe to see the manhood of the country-side in chains to start for exile for many years, and many to die there by the Euphrates. The woe was so deep as to stir the land to its very graves, and especially as the circle of desolation and sorrow happened to surround that ancient and cherished burial-place of Rachel, the ancestress of the tribe who died and was buried there. "And it came to pass, as her soul was in departing, (for she died), that she called his name Ben-oni: but his father called him Benjamin. And Rachel died, and was buried in the way to Ephrath, which is Bethlehem. And Jacob set a pillar upon her grave : that is the pillar of Rachel's grave unto this day."—Gen. xxxv. 18. The conception is touching and patriotic that the sleeping mother of the tribe, after occupying her grave so long, yet, like a true mother and ever-wakeful patron saint, has her first grief and agony over Benjamin reawakened, when after 1100 years a captive gang of the tribe is marched off to Babylon, and again 600 years later, when a baby company of one hundred tribe-sons are suddenly slaughtered in one day by a monster in the name of king. "Rachel weeping for her children, and would not be comforted," is a grand poem of patriotic imagination. Such recalling of the old heroic dead to take part anew on great national occasions of peril, grief, or joy, betokens alike a nation's feeling and power. On the same principle, in the sphere of Scottish history a legend associated with the eve of the battle of Largs, 3d Oct. 1263, shows how beloved and trusted Queen Margaret (+1093) and her family had been, when it was believed that the sainted queen, her beloved Malcolm, and their three royal sons, Edgar, Alexander, and David, quitted their honoured tombs at Dunfermline and proceeded in full armour to take part in the grand old cause of the land's independence by helping in the fight against Haco and his Norsemen.

As this tragic incident in early Christian history arises so directly from the almost inhumanly reckless character of Herod, part of the picture of that character as given by Canan Farrar in his 'Life of Christ' may be quoted here :—

"Herod had massacred priests and nobles; he had decimated the Sanhedrim; he had caused the high priest, his brother-in-law, the young and noble Aristobulus, to be drowned in pretended sport before his eyes; he had ordered the strangulation of his favourite wife, the beautiful Asmonean princess Mariamne, though she seems to have been the only human being whom he passionately loved. His sons Alexander, Aristobulus, and Antipater—his uncle Joseph—Antigonus and Alexander, the uncle and father of his wife—

his mother-in-law Alexandra — his kinsman Cortobanus — his friends Dositheus and Gadias,—were but a few of the multitudes who fell victims to his sanguinary, suspicious, and guilty terrors. His brother Pheroras and his son Archelaus barely and narrowly escaped execution by his orders. His reign was so cruel that, in the energetic language of the Jewish ambassadors to the Emperor Augustus, 'the survivors during his lifetime were even more miserable than the sufferers.'

"It must have been very shortly after the murder of the Innocents that Herod died. Only five days before his death he had made a frantic attempt at suicide and had ordered the execution of his eldest son Antipater. His deathbed was accompanied by circumstances of peculiar horror, and it has been noticed that the loathsome disease of which he died (eaten of worms) is hardly mentioned in history except in the case of men who have been rendered infamous by an atrocity of persecuting zeal. As he knew that none would shed one tear for *him*, he determined that they should shed many for *themselves*, and issued an order that, under pain of death, the principal families of the kingdom and the chiefs of the tribes should come to Jericho, where he lay in his palace dying. They came, and then, shutting them in the hippodrome, he secretly commanded his sister Salome that at the moment of his death they should all be massacred. And so the soul of Herod passed forth into the night.

"The day of his death was, as he had foreseen, observed as a festival. His will was disputed; his kingdom disintegrated; his last order was disobeyed; his sons died for the most part in infamy and exile; the curse of God was on his house, and though he had nine sons and five daughters, yet within 100 years the family of the *hierodoulos* (his father was temple-warder) of Ascalon had perished by disease or violence, and there was no living descendant to perpetuate his name."

Leaving the character of this truly demoniac king, from

whose power, cruelty, and cunning the infant Saviour escaped only by the special and miraculous providence of God in heaven, there are lessons good and useful in connection with ordinary human life that may reasonably and closely be associated with the commemoration of the holy Innocents. Keble, in poetical manner, has conceived the spirits of these infant martyrs as already bearing palms and garlands, and acting in company with the celestial guard attendant on the new-born King of kings. Still poetical, but more practical, he goes on to trace the Lord's knowledge and remembrance of these early sufferers as during His ministry influencing Him to be the special friend of childhood, blessing the living children for the sake of the holy dead, and declaring that of such was the kingdom of heaven, and that unless men receive His message as little children, they cannot become citizens of His kingdom. Also practically, and in a sphere no less wide, he joins with Innocents' Day a comforting function for all mothers bereaved of children by early death, and would lead the bereaved to think of each child withdrawn as already an ascended saint, the object of the love and care of the Divine Head of the Church.

> " Mindful of these, the first-fruits sweet
> Borne by the suffering Church her Lord to greet ;
> Blessed Jesus ever loved to trace
> The ' innocent brightness ' of an infant's face.
> He raised them in His holy arms,
> He blessed them from the world and all its harms :
> Heirs though they were of sin and shame,
> He blessed them in His own and in His Father's name.
>
> And next to these, Thy gracious word
> Was as a pledge of benediction, stored
> For Christian mothers, while they moan
> Their treasured hopes, just born, baptised, and gone.
> Oh, joy for Rachel's broken heart !
> She and her babes shall meet no more to part ;
> So dear to Christ her pious haste
> To trust them in His arms, for ever safe embraced."

If this application of the Scripture history of the holy Innocents is reasonable—and what Christian with any claim to orthodoxy or human sympathy will dare to challenge it ?—then what a wide field the lamentation in Ramah covers, and how wide the exercise for the ministry of consolation to weeping Rachel now and here as well as there in Benjamin ! A large proportion of the human race is year by year swept away by various causes, preventible and unpreventible, before reaching the period of intelligence and education. And this law of infant and early mortality, let us remember, is potent alike among Christian and heathen children. Keble is right in joining special comfort to mothers with the fact of Christian baptism received by their children who are taken away. But surely it is a rash intrusion into the unseen world which is peculiarly God's kingdom, to associate Christ's blessing of children too exclusively with the mere administration of the baptismal rite, sacrament though it be, or with the Christian profession of parents, as if a child's spiritual future alone and entirely depended on these two. The safe and charitable, as also Scriptural course, is to leave this mystery, and some others besides, with all confidence in the hands of a faithful Creator and a most tender Redeemer and Judge. If we poor men, often too professional and doctrinaire clerics, try our hands at judgment, we may go as wide of the mark as the prophet Elijah did when he made out only one, and that one himself ! where God made 7000.

> " There is no place where earth's sorrows
>   Are more felt than up in heaven ;
> There is no place where earth's failings
>   Have such kindly judgment given.
>
> For the love of God is broader
>   Than the measures of man's mind ;
> And the heart of the Eternal
>   Is most wonderfully kind.
>
> If our love were but more simple,
>   We should take Him at His word,
> And our lives would be all sunshine
>   In the sweetness of our Lord."

Another lesson that may be fitly joined with remembrance of the holy Innocents is, the parental and ecclesiastical duty of the very early Christian instruction of the young. Parents, pastors, and teachers (says Alban Butler in ' Lives of the Saints,' under 28th December) are bound to make it their principal care that children in their innocent age be, by piety and charity, consecrated as pure holocausts to God. This is chiefly to be done by imprinting upon their minds the strongest sentiments of devotion, and by instructing them thoroughly in their catechism. Children must be instructed in prayer and the principal articles of faith as soon as they attain to the use of reason, that they may be able to give their Creator His first-fruits by faith, hope, and love, as by the law of reason and religion they are bound to do. Great art, experience, and earnestness are often required to manage and gradually increase the small rays of childhood's opening intelligence, and to place therein whatever one would have the children comprehend. A good catechist contributes more toward maintaining public peace than all the laws and magistrates, as ties of duty are far more binding than coercive force. Neither can any one think it beneath his parts or dignity. The great S. Augustin, S. Chrysostom, and S. Cyril, and other most learned doctors, popes, and bishops, applied themselves with singular zeal and assiduity to this duty.

S. John the Baptist.

NATIVITY, JUNE 24.

ORATIO.—*Præsta, quæsumus, omnipotens Deus : ut familia tua per viam salutis incedat, et beati Johannis præcursoris hortamenda sectando ad eum quem prædixit secura perveniat Dominum nostrum Jesum Christum Filium tuum.   Qui tecum vivit et regnat in unitate.*

The Epistle.—Isaiah xlix. 1-7.
The Gospel.—S. Luke i. 57-68.

COLLECTS. —*Almighty God, by whose providence Thy servant John Baptist was wonderfully born and sent to prepare the way of Thy Son our Saviour, by preaching of repentance; make us to follow his doctrine and holy life, that we may truly repent according to his preaching; and after his example constantly speak the truth, boldly rebuke vice, and patiently suffer for the truth's sake; through Jesus Christ our Lord. Amen.*

The Epistle.—Isaiah xlix. 1-11.
The Gospel.—S. Luke i. 57-80.

O Lord Jesu Christ, who at Thy first coming didst send Thy messenger to prepare Thy way before Thee ; grant that the ministers and stewards of Thy mysteries may likewise so prepare and make ready Thy way, by turning the hearts of the disobedient to the wisdom of the just, that at Thy second coming to judge the world, we may be found an acceptable people in Thy sight, who livest and reignest with the Father and the Holy Spirit, ever one God, world without end.   Amen.[1]

[1] Third Sunday in Advent.

Ut queant laxis resonare fibris
Mira gestorum famuli tuorum,
Solve polluti labii reatum,
 Sancte Joannes.

Unloose, great Baptist, our sin-
 fettered lips ; [may proclaim
That with enfranchised voice we
The miracles of thy transcendent
 life,
 Thy deeds of mighty fame !

Nuntius celso veniens olympo,
Te patri magnum fore nasciturum ;
Nomen, et vitæ seriem gerendæ
 Omine promit.

Oh lot sublime ! an angel quits the
 skies, [declare
Thy birth, thy name, thy glory to
Unto thy priestly sire ; while to the
 Lord
 He offers Israel's prayer.

Ille promissi dubius superni,
Perdidit promptæ modulos loquelæ :
Sed reformasti genitus peremptæ
 Organa vocis.

Mistrustful of the promise from on
 high,
His speech forsakes him at the
 angel's word ; [re-attune
But thou on thine eighth day dost
 For him a vocal chord.

Ventris obstruso recubans cubili
Senseras Regem thalamo manen-
 tem :
Hinc parens, nati meritis, uterque
• Abdita pandit.
  —PAUL THE DEACON, + c. 799.
  Monk at Monte Cassino.

No marvel ; since yet cloistered in
 the womb, [inspired ;
The presence of thy King had thee
What time Elisabeth and Mary sang,
 With joy prophetic fired.
  —E. CASWALL.

Antra deserti teneris sub annis,
Civium turmas fugiens, petisti;
Ne levi posses maculare vitam
 Crimine linguæ.

In caves of the lone wilderness thy
 youth
Thou hiddest, shunning the rude
 throng of men, [guard
So the pure treasure of thy soul to
 From the least touch of sin.

Præbuit durum tegumen camelus
Artubus sacris, strophium bidentes ;
Cui latex haustum, sociata pastum
 Mella locustis.

There to thy sacred limbs the camel
 gave [supplied ;
A garment ; the hard rock a bed
The stream thy thirst, locusts and
 honey wild
 Thy hunger satisfied.

Ceteri tantum cecinere vatum	Oh, blest beyond the prophets of
Corde præsago jubar affuturum ;	old time ! [to be :
Tu quidem mundi scelus auferentem	They of the Saviour sang that was
Indice prodis.	Him present to announce, and show
	to all,
	Thy God reserved for thee !
Non fuit vasti spatium per orbis	Through the wide earth was never
Sanctior quisquam genitus Joanne,	mortal man
Qui nefas sæcli meruit lavantem	Born holier than John ; to whom
Tingere lymphis.	was given
—PAUL THE DEACON.	The guilty world's Baptiser to
	baptise,
	And ope the door of heaven.
	—E. CASWALL

"He said, I am the voice of one crying in the wilderness,
Make straight the way of the Lord, as said the prophet
Esaias."—S. JOHN i. 23.

A PECULIARITY of the chief festival commemorative of
the Baptist (for there is a commemoration of his beheading or decollation also) is that it fixes on his nativity, whereas
all or nearly all saints' days are the day of death. An exception is made with the Baptist because of the circumstances of
his birth, first as a subject of special prophecy, then at the
time accompanied by prodigies, and (as some hold) distinguished
by special grace of sanctification from birth onwards. This last
point, however, is not quite clear, but only inferred from S.
Luke i. 15, and depends on interpretation.

Another peculiarity of the Baptist is the large amount of Holy
Scripture that is assigned to him in his person and work, com-
pared with most other men of whom the New Testament speaks.
Of none are we told so much save perhaps S. Paul and S. Peter.
The reason of this is that the Baptist occupies a unique position
as a link between the two Testaments and the two economies.
He might have been placed first in the list of New Testament
saints ; but as he precedes the Saviour Himself only by six

months in point of time, both for age and commencement of ministry, and as his work did not begin till he was thirty years of age, it is really more to the point, as concerns the Gospel system, to begin with the Blessed Virgin and her husband Joseph, and after them to take even Simeon and the Innocents, whose main relation is to the Saviour's early years, before the Baptist's real work began at all.

To gain both an orderly and Scriptural basis in setting forth the history and character of the Baptist, commencement may be made with three passages in which he is prophetically mentioned in the Old Testament, and all the more so as these passages are founded on in the New Testament. "The voice of him that crieth in the wilderness, Prepare ye the way of the Lord, make straight in the desert a highway for our God. Every valley shall be exalted, and every mountain and hill shall be made low : and the crooked shall be made straight, and the rough places plain : and the glory of the Lord shall be revealed, and all flesh shall see it together : for the mouth of the Lord hath spoken it."—Isaiah xl. 3-5. "Behold, I will send my messenger, and he shall prepare the way before me : and the Lord, whom ye seek, shall suddenly come to His temple." "Behold, I will send you Elijah the prophet before the coming of the great and dreadful day of the Lord : and he shall turn the heart of the fathers to the children, and the heart of the children to their fathers."—Malachi iii. 1, iv. 5.

To these three passages, preceding what is said of the Baptist in the gospels, may be here added all the references to him that are found following the gospels, and all in the book of the Acts, as follows : I. 5, where it is Jesus who speaks, "For John truly baptised with water ; but ye shall be baptised with the Holy Ghost not many days hence." I. 21, where S. Peter says, "Of these men which have companied with us all the time that the Lord Jesus went in and out among us, beginning from the baptism of John, unto that same day that He was taken up from us, must one be ordained to be a witness with us of His resurrection." XIII. 24, where S. Paul at Antioch in Pisidia says, "When John had first preached before His coming the baptism of repentance to all the people of Israel. And as John fulfilled his course, he said, Whom think ye that I am? I am not He. But, behold, there cometh one after me, whose shoes of His feet I am not worthy to loose." XVIII. 25, xix. 1-7, where, at Ephesus, Apollos, who had hitherto "known only the baptism of John," was taken in hand by Aquila and Priscilla, who "expounded unto him the way of God more perfectly;" whereafter Paul, coming to Ephesus, found certain disciples, to whom he put the question, "Have ye received the Holy Ghost since ye believed? And they said unto him, We have not so much as heard whether there be any Holy Ghost. And he said unto them, Unto what then were ye baptised? And they said, Unto John's baptism. Then said Paul, John verily baptised with the baptism of repentance, saying unto the people, that they should believe on Him which should come after him, that is, on Christ Jesus. When they heard this, they were baptised in the name of the Lord Jesus. And when Paul had laid his hands upon them, the Holy Ghost came on them, and they spake with tongues, and prophesied. And all the men were about twelve." Here, about twenty years after the death both of the Baptist and of the Saviour, we come upon a group at Ephesus of twelve disciples of the Baptist, additional to Apollos of Alexandria, who still occupied their original standpoint of repentance and righteousness, and expectation of Christ and the new kingdom, showing how firm a hold the old work of the Baptist had taken that it survived so long by its own energy, and that those in whom it survived so easily crossed over to the fulness of the Gospel so soon as it was explained to them; doing after twenty years what Andrew and John had done immediately under the Baptist's own guidance and advice, as told in S. John i. 35-40.

The many references to the Baptist that are spread over the four gospels may first be presented in Gospel order, and then in biographic succession and connection. S. Matt. iii. 1-12 records the Baptist's preaching in the wilderness of

Judea, his quotation of Isaiah, his personal habits, the throng of hearers, including Pharisees and Sadducees, who were specially warned. III. 13-17 records the coming of Jesus from Galilee to Jordan for baptism; the argument between the Baptist and Jesus on the subject of need—"I have need to be baptised of Thee, and comest Thou to me?" "Suffer it to be so now: for thus it becometh us to fulfil all righteousness;" the performance of the rite, and the two signs from heaven that followed the great consecration. IV. 12, "Now when Jesus had heard that John was cast into prison, He departed into Galilee; and leaving Nazareth, He came and dwelt in Capernaum." XI. 1-19 tells how the Baptist in prison, hearing of the miracles done by Jesus, sends two disciples to ask, "Art thou He that should come, or do we look for another?" Christ's answer by a list of His works, which ends with the preaching of the Gospel to the poor; Christ's warm praise of the Baptist to the people after the departure of the deputation. XIV. 1-13 tells how the fame of Jesus made Herod think of the Baptist as risen from the dead, and then explains the tyrant's fear by his having imprisoned John for reproving his vices. Herodias, who instigated this, would have had the prophet's life taken, but the king hesitated on account of the people's reverence; but his hesitation was overcome through his own rash promise to Herodias's daughter, who, "instructed of her mother, said, Give me here John Baptist's head in a charger." After the execution John's disciples buried their master's body, then went and told Jesus, who at the heavy tidings retreated for prayer into a desert place.

S. Mark i. 1-11, beginning at once with the Baptist's person and work, repeats most of S. Matt. iii. 1-17. I. 14, 15, "Now after that John was put in prison, Jesus came into Galilee, preaching the gospel of the kingdom of God, and saying, The time is fulfilled, and the kingdom of God is at hand: repent ye, and believe the Gospel." (Parallel to Matt. iv. 12.) VI. 14-29 tells very graphically the alarm of Herod on hearing the fame of Jesus, thinking it was the return of John whom he had beheaded, which leads explanatorily to tell the reason of the imprisonment of John, and its issue in his being beheaded, as already given by S. Matthew.

S. Luke gives the most copious and original information as to the Baptist of all the four, as follows: I. 5-25, immediately after the preface, starts with an account of Zacharias and Elisabeth, the Baptist's parents, both of priestly descent, the latter a cousin of the Blessed Virgin: the angel Gabriel appears to Zacharias in the Temple at the altar with this message, "Fear not, Zacharias: for thy prayer is heard; and thy wife Elisabeth shall bear thee a son, and thou shalt call his name John. And thou shalt have joy and gladness; and many shall rejoice at his birth. For he shall be great in the sight of the Lord, and shall drink neither wine nor strong drink; and he shall be filled with the Holy Ghost, even from his mother's womb. And many of the children of Israel shall he turn to the Lord their God. And he shall go before Him in the spirit and power of Elias, to turn the hearts of the fathers to the children, and the disobedient to the wisdom of the just; to make ready a people prepared for the Lord." Then follows that the priest asks a sign, and that of temporary dumbness is imposed, under which he goes to his home. I. 39-45 records the visit of S. Mary to her cousin Elisabeth in the hill-country, now within three months of the Baptist's birth, and the mutual salutations. I. 57-67 records the Baptist's birth, circumcision, name, in conformity with Gabriel's command, and the removal from Zacharias of the sign of dumbness. I. 68-79 gives the inspired thanksgiving hymn of Zacharias, known ecclesiastically from its first word as the *Benedictus*, and used in public worship since the sixth century, its function being to join the Church of the Jews with the Church of Christ. In iii. 1-9 is told how, at a date elaborately described both by civil and ecclesiastical reckoning, being 27 A.D., when the Baptist was thirty (the real year of Christ's birth being 3 B.C.), "The word of God came unto John the son of Zacharias in the wilderness. And he came into all the country about Jordan, preaching the baptism of repentance for the remission of sins." Also repeating the warning to Pharisees and Sadducees in Matt. iii. 7-12, and adding, iii. 10-14, separate instructions for people, publicans, and soldiers who come asking direction in duty ; while iii. 15-20 guides the people's thoughts as to John's own relation to the Messiah, telling plainly that he was not the Messiah —that the Messiah was to be far mightier, baptising with the Holy Ghost and with fire, and who was to judge the whole world,—the narrative ending with an account of the sudden and complete close of the Baptist's ministry. "And many other things in his exhortation preached he unto the people. But Herod the tetrarch, being reproved by him for Herodias his brother Philip's wife, and for all the evils which Herod had done, added yet this above all, that he shut up John in prison." III. 21, 22, is remarkable as a statement forming an addition to what has gone before, when the record of the Baptist's work seemed ended, and furnishing a preparation for the genealogy of Jesus that follows. Points peculiar here are, that Jesus was baptised *after* "all the people," and that He *Himself prayed* on the occasion. "Now when all the people were baptised, it came to pass, that Jesus also being baptised, and praying, the heaven was opened, and the Holy Ghost descended in a bodily shape like a dove upon Him, and a voice came from heaven, which said, Thou art my beloved Son ; in Thee I am well pleased. And Jesus Himself began to be about thirty years of age, being (as was supposed) the son of Joseph." Then vii. 18-35 records the deputation of two disciples sent from the prison by the Baptist to Jesus to ask, "Art thou He that should come ? or look we for another ?" and giving our Lord's answer, including the splendid eulogy on the Baptist, as already seen in S. Matt. xi. 1-19.

S. John's contribution to the history of the Baptist, while very pointed, is all confined to the opening stage of his ministry, passing over his parents, and circumstances of birth and name and wilderness life, and not, except in an anticipatory allusion in iii. 24, advancing to either the imprisonment or the beheading.   I. 19-28 is of special value as showing that the deputation from Jerusalem was of authorised and official persons—"This is the record, when the Jews sent priests and Levites from Jerusalem to ask him, Who art thou?"   Three separate questions they put to ascertain his exact position— was he Messiah, or Elias, or "that prophet"?—to each of which the Baptist answered No.   Insisting on a positive answer, the Baptist's reply was by quoting Isaiah as to the voice in the wilderness.   This gives judicial definiteness to the vaguer terms of S. Matt. iii. 7 as to Pharisees and Sadducees, and of S. Luke iii. 15 as to the people's "musing in their hearts of John, whether he were Christ, or not."   I. 29-34 records the Baptist's testimony to the people, as part of his regular preaching as distinguished from the previous official testimony to the deputation.   I. 35-37 forms a specimen of the Baptist's individual dealing with men in the noted and most fruitful cases of Andrew and John the Evangelist himself.   III. 22-30, iv. 1-3, carries us forward to a stage immediately preceding the Baptist's imprisonment, "for John was not yet cast into prison;" it shows a change of locality from Bethabara or Bethany to Ænon; it shows (which is important) the administration of baptism as taken up by the disciples of Jesus (iii. 22, iv. 2); above all, it shows a malicious attempt by certain Jews to create and foster jealousy, first by the fact of Christ's disciples baptising at all, and next by their being more popular in this part of their work than John himself.   "Then there arose a question between some of John's disciples and the Jews about purifying. And they came unto John, and said unto him, Rabbi, He that was with thee beyond Jordan, to whom thou barest witness, behold, the same baptizeth, and all men come unto Him."   To this clever and wicked attempt at setting the herald and the King at loggerheads, the Baptist's answer is very noble—the noblest act, perhaps, of his whole life—to accept the position and enshrine it in a proverb,—"He must increase, but I must decrease."

A further and shorter arrangement of the Scriptural material touching the life and character of the Baptist is the presentation of it in biographical succession and connection, after which attention may fitly be drawn to a few cardinal points.

The Baptist's coming was foretold by two prophets.

His birth, name, and office were foreannounced by Gabriel in the Temple.

Zacharias, his father, was stricken dumb for slowness of belief.

Elisabeth, his mother, was inspired in her greeting of the Blessed Virgin Mary.

The dumbness of Zacharias was removed on his obedience as to the name of his son.

Zacharias spoke the hymn *Benedictus* by inspiration.

Consecrated from birth, the Baptist lived in the wilderness from early manhood ; food, dress, and drink regulated by vow.

Called at age of thirty by the word of the Lord, he came to Jordan and began his ministry by a baptism of repentance.

Ministry frequented by crowds, including publicans, soldiers, common people, Pharisees, Sadducees.

An official deputation came from Jerusalem to inquire as to his exact position.

He answers that he is not Messiah, but His herald.

He baptises Jesus at His own desire and plea, and two miracles follow the act of consecration.

He points out Jesus as the Lamb of God that taketh away the sin of the world.

He privately guides two at least of his own disciples to Jesus.

He repels the attempt to make him jealous of the more frequented baptising by Christ's disciples, and bears a fresh testimony to Christ's divine supremacy.

He is imprisoned for reproof of Herod's sin.

His imprisonment forms a marked date in Christ's own
movements, both in preaching and place of residence.
From prison he sends two disciples to Jesus to ask as to His
Messiahship.
He receives a clear answer based on Christ's miracles and
His preaching the Gospel to the poor.
Honoured by warm testimony of Jesus to his character and
office as the Forerunner.
Beheaded in prison after two and a quarter years' ministry,
one year before the death of Christ Himself.
On the tidings of the Baptist's death, Jesus in His grief
withdrew to the desert for solitary prayer.
Twelve of his disciples, twenty years later at Ephesus,
receive Christian baptism and the gift of the Holy
Ghost.

A matter worthy of special attention is the fact that at a
certain point the disciples of Christ began to exercise a ministry of baptism, which of course was the same rite as that
administered by John, and not an earlier form of the full
sacrament of S. Matt. xxviii. 19. The Lord Himself took no
part in this work of His disciples further than silent acquies-
cence. Moreover, there seems to be some close connection between this widening of John's baptism and the impending
imprisonment of the Baptist. Before imprisonment John
makes change of sphere from Bethabara to Ænon (S. John iii.
22-30), and is cunningly tempted to oppose the new and more
popular baptisers, but the base temptation only drew forth
from the man blessed from his birth with a gift of the Holy
Ghost a more effective testimony towards his Divine Master's
greatness, a testimony all the more touching because it was
joined with prophetic knowledge and acknowledgment of His
own vanishing life and work, "He must increase, but I must
decrease." Further, immediately after the record of our Lord's
temptation in the wilderness, S. Matt. iv. 12 says, "Now
when Jesus had heard that John was cast into prison, He de-

parted into Galilee; and leaving Nazareth, He came and dwelt in Capernaum. . . . From that time Jesus began to preach, and to say, Repent; for the kingdom of heaven is at hand." Here Jesus changes His sphere of ministry, partly for a reason connected with the Baptist, and the description of His ministry at this period exactly reproduces the Baptist's message as regards preaching, while His disciples continued the Baptist's work as regards the rite of immersion. This record on the part of S. Matthew is repeated almost verbatim by S. Mark i. 14, 15.

What a trial it was to a man of open-air life in the desert, and for the last two years surrounded by a circle of attached disciples, as also by revering crowds—a man dealing faithfully and boldly with the besetting sins of priests and laymen, and courtiers and kings—to be suddenly shut up in a dungeon by the revenge of an exposed Jezebel; and thus to have the work stopped for which he had undergone so many years of ascetic discipline, at least from the age of fifteen to that of thirty! He could hardly fail to feel like a caged eagle; and it seems under such feeling that from his prison he sent an embassy of two of his disciples to Jesus, after having heard in prison the fame of His miracles—in particular, as appears from S. Luke vii. 18, the miracle of the raising from death of the widow's son of Nain, and the healing at Capernaum of the centurion's servant who was at the point of death. The question put in the Baptist's name by the disciples was, "Art Thou He that should come, or do we look for another?" Three explanations have been offered of the question,—that John's convictions were temporarily shaken in prison; that it was for the satisfaction of his disciples' faith only; that it was John's own, relating, however, not to John's hesitation, but to Christ's delay, and was meant to urge Jesus to declare Himself to the nation and enter on the outward kingdom of the Messiah. In His answer Jesus clearly points to the fulfilment of prophecy, especially Isaiah xxxv. and lxi., to be seen in His works and word; just as the same prophet in xl. 3-5 had foreshown the

Baptist himself. Jesus so joins work and word as to intimate that they are to be interpreted and valued spiritually, for last and greatest is the Gospel preached to the poor. This is the Christ foretold by Isaiah, and to this agrees Jesus of Nazareth. Thus the answer is, I am He that should come; look not for any other. I am He, though I neither claim nor found earthly monarchy. I am He by works of merciful power to the afflicted in body, and by words of spiritual healing to the poor in spirit and to the common people. "And blessed is he, whosoever shall not be offended in me."

Coldly judged, the question thus answered seems to spring from misapprehension and impatience on John's part; charitably judged, it calls forth not disapproval but pity. Such was the train of thought and feeling stirred in the breast of Jesus Himself after having first given a direct and earnest and satisfactory answer to the two disciples. "And as they departed, Jesus began to say unto the multitudes concerning John, What went ye out into the wilderness to see? A reed shaken with the wind? A man clothed in soft raiment? A prophet? yea, I say unto you, and more than a prophet. . . . Verily I say unto you, Among them that are born of women there hath not risen a greater than John the Baptist: notwithstanding he that is least in the kingdom of heaven is greater than he." This most generous eulogy shows how appreciative a Royal Master the Baptist had been serving in his now closed ministry. And can we doubt that the eulogy was intended by the Lord as a special return for that most loyal utterance of John when certain Jews would fain have stirred jealousy, but met only from the Baptist the most lowly estimate of his own place, and a correspondingly exalted estimate of the place of the Messiah as ever to increase? It was a message to the understanding in the list of miracles, and the gift of the Gospel to the poor, which the two disciples bore back to their imprisoned master; but in addition to the sound argumentative reply, here was a message to the heart of the lonely captive awaiting death, for the words of divine approval from God's own Son were as precious and true as those to be spoken hereafter to all who are to be heaven's citizens, "Come, ye blessed of my Father." Receiving such a message, John must have thought, I was in prison, and the Lamb of God came unto me with comfort and peace, and hope and fellowship: mine eyes have seen Thy salvation, O Lord Christ.

The scene of the Baptist's murder was the castle of Machærus, on the east of the Dead Sea, in Arabia Petræa; and the time was Herod's birthday, about a year after the imprisonment began, Herodias watching all the time for her opportunity, which was at once eagerly seized when it came through her daughter. Salome was the daughter of Herodias by Herod Philip, brother of Herod Antipas. The castle of Machærus, improved by Herod the Great, at one time belonged to Aretas, ruler of Petra, and father of the lawful wife of Herod Antipas, who, on her husband's sinful alliance with Herodias, fled first to Machærus, then to Petra. And the scene of the Baptist's murder for reproving the king's sin soon after became the scene of Herod's defeat; for Aretas, avenging in war the insult to his daughter, there gained a decisive victory over Herod, which the people were not slow to interpret as a divine retribution for the martyred prophet.

We gather from a hint in S. Matt. xiv. 12, 13, that the beheading of John very deeply grieved the Saviour, so much so that on reception of the tidings He withdrew into the desert for prayer, and only quitted His retreat under pressure of work and sickness among the people. "And his disciples came, and took up the body, and buried it, and went and told Jesus. When Jesus heard of it, He departed thence [His own country, xiii. 54] by ship into a desert place apart."

A fuller retribution came on Herod a few years after his defeat by Aretas, and also reached him through Herodias. She, seeing the favour of the Emperor Caius, *alias* Caligula, towards Herod Agrippa I., the nephew of Antipas, and the subsequent murderer of S. James, the brother of John, urged

her husband to go to Rome and seek a share. But Agrippa,
averse to his uncle's advancement, sent a freedman to accuse
him of treason, and so successfully, that in 39 A.D., seven
years after the tragedy at Machærus, he was banished to
Lugdunum in Gaul, where he and Herodias died in exile and
obscurity.

The esteem in which the Baptist is held throughout
Christendom is seen not only in the double commemoration
of his nativity and his beheading, but also in the large
number of churches that bear his name by ancient and
solemn act of dedication. In this testimony of high regard
to the martyr the old Church of Scotland has its share. The
chief churches of Perth and Ayr are those of S. John the
Baptist, the old name of Perth being St Johnstoun. Chapels
of S. John the Baptist existed in the Drygate of Glasgow, at
Arboll in Ross-shire, and at Barvas in Lewis. There is a
"St John's Clachan" at Dalry in Kirkcudbright, which gets
its name like old Perth. There are several other old churches
of S. John, but it is S. John the Evangelist. All the above-
named, however, are dedicated distinctly to S. John the Baptist,
and in all probability there would be others besides.

> Where is the lore the Baptist taught,
> The soul unswerving and the fearless tongue?
>   The much enduring wisdom, sought
> By lonely prayer the haunted rocks among?
>   Who counts it gain
>   His light should wane,
> So the whole world to Jesus throng?
>
>   So glorious let our pastors shine,
> That by their speaking lives the world may learn
>   First filial duty, then divine,
> That sons to parents, all to Thee may turn;
>   And ready prove
>   In fires of love,
> At sight of Thee for aye to burn.
>   —KEBLE, *S. John Baptist's Day.*

Nicodemus and Joseph of Arimathea.

COLLECTS.—*O Lord God Almighty, who hast commanded Thy servants to be born again of water and the Holy Ghost, preserve in them the holy baptism which they have received, and be pleased to perfect it unto the hallowing of Thy Name; that Thy grace may ever increase upon them, and that what they have already received by Thy gift they may guard by integrity of life.*[1]

O God, with whom is the well of life, and in whose light we see light; increase in us, we beseech Thee, the brightness of divine knowledge, whereby we may be able to reach Thy plenteous fountain; impart to our thirsting souls the draught of life, and restore to our darkened minds the light of heaven.[2]

"There was a man of the Pharisees, named Nicodemus."
—S. JOHN iii. 1.

ALL that Holy Scripture says of this saint is contained in one book, and in three passages, each marking a decisive point in his spiritual history—S. John iii. 1-21, vii. 45-53, xix. 38-42. Saint is an unfamiliar prefix to his name, and yet he has an indisputable title to it, and is so styled in the Roman Calendar, where his day of commemoration is 3d August, and he is called S. Nicodemus of Caphargamala or St Gamaliel, the name of his country-house.

Not improbably the reason for S. John being the only evangelist who names Nicodemus is, that he was present at this conference, and if he made his acquaintance then, that would further furnish a reason for making the other two allusions to him, especially the last at the taking down from the cross,

---

[1] Gallican Sacramentary, Bright's Collects, p. 161.
[2] Mozarabic Liturgy, Bright's Collects, p. 78.

where the evangelist's mother Salome, and his aunt, the mother of Jesus, were both present, and himself too. And Nicodemus would probably himself tell, to all these three at least, how he had spoken and acted at the meeting of the Sanhedrim in vii. 45-53. Chapters iii. and iv., whose main subjects are respectively our Lord's conferences with Nicodemus in Jerusalem, and with the woman of Samaria at the well of Jacob, are a noted feature of this gospel, and form a pair of companion pictures. In each we have the history of a soul on its way to the knowledge of the truth as it is in Jesus; but though both are sinners, they are of quite different types. Nicodemus has a sense of inward deficiency, but is in the eye of society a man of respectability, and also a high and worthy official in the Church; whereas the woman of Samaria was a sinner flagrantly in her domestic life, and yet in her heart seems to have had little feeling of sin or shame. The first illustrates the principle, "Draw nigh to God, and He will draw nigh to you." The other illustrates a different yet also true principle —"I am found of them that sought me not: I said, Behold me, behold me, unto a nation that was not called by my name." Nicodemus seeking Jesus comes in as a contrast to what is recorded at the close of the chapter preceding,—"Now when He was in Jerusalem at the Passover, in the feast day, many believed in His name, when they saw the miracles which He did. But Jesus did not commit Himself unto them, because He knew all men, and needed not that any should testify of man; for He knew what was in man. But there was a man of the Pharisees, named Nicodemus," unto whom Jesus committed Himself in the circumstances stated in the sequel. The many who believed with a merely outward impression at seeing marvels, Jesus let alone; but Nicodemus, with his sincere words, even although there is the drawback that he requires the shelter of night to screen their sincerity, wins Christ's ear and heart, and goes not away until to him is committed that which is most precious of all things on earth, the revelation of the Messiah in His person and primary doctrine. This different treatment was adopted because Jesus' prophetic sight discerned in the others an evening twilight where darkness would be victor in the struggle with light; while in Nicodemus it was a morning twilight, where darkness would be discomfited and day prevail.

The words are given (the evangelist himself having probably been present (wherewith Nicodemus approached Jesus in this nocturnal conference,—"Rabbi, we know that Thou art a Teacher come from God: for no man can do these miracles that Thou doest, except God be with him." The miracles to which reference is here made are easily traceable in the context: chap. ii. records the miracle at Cana, and calls it "the beginning of miracles"; and the same chap. contains two or three marks of time which connect that first miracle and the conference with Nicodemus. "After this He went down to Capernaum, and continued there not many days. And the Jews' Passover was at hand; and Jesus went up to Jerusalem." That was the visit at which He drove the money-changers out of the Temple; and "then answered the Jews and said unto Him, What sign showest Thou unto us, seeing that Thou doest these things?" His reply being, "Destroy this Temple, and in three days I will raise it up again." The record proceeds—"Now when He was in Jerusalem at the Passover, in the feast day, many believed in His name, when they saw the miracles which He did. But Jesus did not commit Himself unto them." And then comes the case of Nicodemus as an exception where Jesus did commit and reveal Himself.

Thus only a very few weeks can have elapsed since the first miracle; and the "these miracles" are miracles wrought in or near Jerusalem during that first Passover in our Lord's public ministry. Under these circumstances there is a comparative quickness in Nicodemus's coming forward, and he is fairly entitled to have this early date in part set over against the less favourable fact of his coming by night. He is a man of mark among his countrymen, both in a worldly and Church point of view, "a ruler of the Jews;" and to find such a man within the short space of a few weeks voluntarily drawn toward the newly risen Teacher is surely something. Moreover, he comes with full recognition of the reality of Christ's miracles, and with equally full recognition of the fact that these prove a commission from God. The words used are so strong as almost to imply a direct admission that Jesus was the promised Messiah,—"a Teacher come from God;" "except God be with him;" "we know that Thou art." We have here a man who has looked devoutly on the mighty works recently performed, and who has pondered the teaching joined with the works; who has discerned in both clear evidence of God's presence, but not so clear (to him at least) expression of God's meaning; and who now sincerely, but modified and injured by constitutional timidity, seeks to find the meaning through a private conference with the Prophet. Like another Moses, Nicodemus says to himself, "I will turn aside to see this great sight." And like Moses further, he has the blessing of hearing from Jesus a direct statement of His being and mission, so that the issue of the interview is a new "I AM," spoken by Him who dwelt in the bush.

After the opening acknowledgment of Jesus' miracles and mission as from God, Nicodemus seems to have asked some question regarding the nature of the new kingdom and the way of entry to it—or, in speaking of these, he may have betrayed very defective conception of them, for the subsequent words of our Lord are an answer to such a question or correction of such an error, and not a direct reply to the opening words of the conference. "Jesus answered and said unto him, Verily, verily, I say unto thee, Except a man be born again, he cannot see the kingdom of God." And this regeneration, second birth or birth from above, is explained as being "of water and of the Spirit." And further explanation is made by a reference to the common air for the existence of a parallel power that is most real and strong though also invisible. "The wind bloweth where it listeth, and thou hearest the sound thereof, but canst not tell whence it cometh, and whither it goeth : so is every one that is born of the Spirit." Of this famous sentence, however, a different rendering has been coming into favour of late years, and has found a place in the margin of the Revised Version of 1881—a rendering which states no illustration from wind at all, and confines the language to a direct and exclusive description of the work of the Holy Ghost. "The Spirit breatheth where He willeth, and thou hearest His voice, but canst not tell whence He cometh, and whither He goeth : so is every one [born] who is born of the Spirit."

At each stage of these statements and explanations by the Saviour, Nicodemus has and expresses his own difficulties, wherein he strangely resembles the woman at the well of Jacob in her parallel conference. How like is his notion of the second bodily birth to her notion of Jacob's well and the living water! Both are instances of the natural man savouring not the things that be of God. And instead of blaming or pitying either, we may rather look around in our own day and see whether there are not some or even many who yet stumble as awkwardly in the early stages of spiritual experience.

Our Lord's answer, by insisting on the necessity of being born again, had a special adaptation to the present state and previous training of Nicodemus. As a Pharisee (and he is a specimen of such at their very best) he would be a conscientious observer of the law, diligently obedient in the firm persuasion that the multiplication of observances is the fulfilment of duty and the certainty of salvation. His defect lies in his seeing in Jesus rather a teacher than the Teacher, an honoured servant of Jehovah rather than His only Son. With this defective view of Christ's person, Nicodemus has a correspondingly defective view of Christ's work, of the blessing it brings, of the change it implies and produces, and of the new and far higher position into which it lifts up both the individual believer and the whole Church. What Jesus was, did, and spake, formed not so much an addition to an old series as rather the first of a new ; not a new prophet to be added after Malachi, but a new covenant to be added to the old ; the opening up of heavenly privilege to Jew and Gentile. And all this was to be realised through the unrestrained communication of the Holy Ghost, that Third Person of the glorious Godhead hitherto dimly revealed either to the knowledge or the experience of men. In truths that are now familiar to the Christian child, this master in Israel was a stranger and a stumbler. But such stumbling is neither inconsistent with reason nor sincerity at the time, nor with faith and salvation afterwards. It marks a man who is feeling his way, who has the principle of progress in him, and who is likely to come to more in the long-run than a disciple who believes just at once all that he is told at first. With a man of this sort Jesus takes pains of careful instruction, for the inquirer, though timid, is honest. Thus did that evening leave Nicodemus a master in Israel, while morning found him a humble disciple of Jesus. That we are entitled to reckon him as a believer from this date, born again in the very course of the conference with Jesus, the expression and contrast that introduce the narrative imply and prove—Jesus not committing Himself to some, but dealing differently with Nicodemus, to whom He made special revelation of His divine nature and office, and of the fundamental doctrine of His kingdom in the new birth needful for all its citizens.

Only twice else is Nicodemus alluded to in Scripture, and both times by reference to the characteristic feature of this first meeting—Nicodemus that came by night. On the next occasion, in vii. 50-52, we find Nicodemus in a friendly spirit calmly interposing for fairness of investigation and trial at a time when His enemies had begun to gather around clamouring for immediate death. "Doth our law judge any man before it hear him?" The reference is to such passages as "Hear the causes between your brethren, and judge righteously between every man and his brother." "At the mouth of two witnesses, or at the mouth of three witnesses, shall the matter be established." And most important of all was the principle of giving every accused person an opportunity of self-

defence, either personally or by agent, or both ways. Yet
this fundamental law of all civilised judicial procedure the
Sanhedrim in Jerusalem were for putting aside in their eagerness for the condemnation and death of Jesus. For restraining this headstrong haste by reminding them of the form of
process, Nicodemus was taunted with Galilean leanings. "They
answered and said unto him, Art thou also of Galilee ? Search,
and look: for out of Galilee ariseth no prophet." That might
be true as to Galilee, and yet Jesus might be Messiah after all ;
they were hastily, and, as we know, erroneously, taking for
granted that Jesus was born and bred in Galilee.

But the friendly interposition on this public occasion on
the part of Nicodemus is only one element; an element even
more important in its bearing on his character and disposition
lies in observing more closely the nature of the interposition :
it was only on a point of form, it bore no indication of personal
sympathy, although we may be sure, from our knowledge of the
first interview by night, and from anticipation of what came
later on, that the personal sympathy was there. Now the avoidance of any expression of personal sympathy reveals to us the
man on his weak side, that constitutional timidity which led him
to prefer the screen of night for his original interview. While
Nicodemus was untainted by any hypocrisy, he is very far off
from anything like Christian decision or heroism. Fear of man,
and perpetual remembrance of office and status, are too powerful with him ; there is hardly a germ of martyrdom in his soul.

When Nicodemus reappears the last time, xix. 39, it is after
the injustice above threatened by the Sanhedrim had been
accomplished ; and then do we find this ruler of the Jews advancing openly the length of a Christian profession, and tenderly performing for Jesus those last offices of love and reverence and worship which so few then cared or dared to do.
"And there came also Nicodemus, (which at the first came to
Jesus by night,) and brought a mixture of myrrh and aloes,
about an hundred pound weight. Then took they the body of
Jesus, and wound it in linen clothes with the spices, as the

manner of the Jews is to bury." Now at last has he succeeded in overcoming his fear of man, or constitutional timidity, or whatever it was, that for three years delayed a personal profession. Now we may regard him as clear in knowledge, strong in faith, and in possession of hope and love; for surely it needed these in no stinted measure thus to hold fast to Jesus even in death. And yet when we look more narrowly into the sacred narrative, we still find a very characteristic token of the original disposition surviving. Vastly better is his attitude towards Jesus in now providing myrrh and aloes and linen for the burial, and in helping to take down the body from the cross, than in the mere technical check imposed on the rashness of his colleagues; but in this great advance he only follows in the wake of Joseph of Arimathea, a man of his own station in life, and a member, like himself, of the Sanhedrim. It is not an independent or original act, and might never have been ventured on at all had not Joseph in a much bolder spirit cleared the way by going in person direct to Pilate and asking for the body to be granted to him for burial. Thus, from beginning to end of the history of Nicodemus, the three passages maintain a marvellous unity in the delineation of the man's character which could only have been drawn from life. It is like a tune all in a minor key, like a landscape painted in mist. The good man has a touch of mouse or hare nature all through his constitution; not a man to lead an enterprise, not a man to face rack or stake or gibbet in times of persecution, and yet a man quite honest and candid though unheroic.

In another line also, from our Lord's point of view, may we join the earlier and later Nicodemus. In the first conference-night the Lord won a heart that was yet to follow Him to the grave. Knowing what was in man, He foresaw the growth of Nicodemus in grace. In well-placed confidence He said to him, " As Moses lifted up the serpent in the wilderness, even so must the Son of man be lifted up." And the very man to whom this was spoken was afterwards one of two who helped down from the cross the Saviour's body, so that we may say

of Nicodemus's conversion as was said of the alabaster box of
ointment, "It was done for His burial." Wondrous are the
undercurrents that connect different parts of the sea of life;
one golden thread of Providence runs through and binds together the events of men's lives. And as for Nicodemus himself, how must he have recalled on occasion of that lifting
down, Christ's first word prophetic of the lifting up, and the
whole interview of that first blessed night! In Nicodemus it
is not a bare name we have, but a full character, a man of
whom we can conceive a definite image, as we can of Peter or
John or Paul. What most strikes us is the advance made in
spiritual insight between the first stumbling at the explanation
of the new birth in its nature and need, and his final triumph
over adverse outward circumstances, so that he recognised the
loftiness and purity of Jesus' character even amid the fresh
shame of the accursed tree, and contributed of his wealth to
bury Him with the honour due to a true Saint and the King
of saints, because their Redeemer.

In Joseph of Arimathea we meet a manlier and higher type
of disciple than Nicodemus. Arimathea seems the same as
Ramathaim - zophim, the birthplace of the prophet Samuel.
While we find Nicodemus in one gospel only, we meet Joseph
in all the four, and in the synoptical three he had a place for
thirty or forty years before Nicodemus attracted the attention
which S. John secured for him by the striking record of his
nocturnal interview, which is the real source of his fame
in Christendom. Not only had Joseph an earlier place in
the gospels than his colleague, but it is to Joseph that the
main, if not exclusive, reference is in Isaiah liii. : " And he
made his grave with the wicked, and with the rich in his
death." It was Joseph who boldly went in unto Pilate and
craved the body of Jesus. It was Joseph who provided
honourable burial for our Lord in his own new tomb in his
garden, which happened to be close by the place of crucifixion,
and the nearness of which suggested its use in the haste of
the "preparation" eve. The best single narrative of the

synoptists is that of S. Luke : "And, behold, there was a man named Joseph, a councillor ; and he was a good man, and a just : (the same had not consented to the counsel and deed of them :) he was of Arimathea, a city of the Jews : who also himself waited for the kingdom of God.   This man went unto Pilate, and begged the body of Jesus.   And he took it down, and wrapped it in linen, and laid it in a sepulchre that was hewn in stone, wherein never man before was laid.   And that day was the preparation, and the Sabbath drew on.   And the women also, which came with Him from Galilee, followed after, and beheld the sepulchre, and how His body was laid." How is every feature emphasised in the sacred fourfold narrative !   The tomb was new, wherein never man lay ; it was Joseph's "own," intended for himself ; it was situated in his garden, or surrounded with a garden as belonging to it ; it was a cave in nature and shape in the solid rock ; it was closed with a great boulder ; the first use of it was watched by some of the ministering women ; there the watch of four soldiers was posted ; there the priest's seal was put on the stone ; there the earthquake betokened the risen Redeemer ; there the grave-clothes were laid in folded order aside ; there the ministering women came to complete the embalming ; there the two angels were stationed at the head and foot of the resting-place ; there Peter and John came and saw.   Joseph by taking part in the burial of Jesus would render himself ceremonially unclean for a week, and would be unable to join in the Passover on that occasion : "He that toucheth the dead body of any man shall be unclean seven days."— Num. xix. 11.   Joseph's rock-hewn tomb was the scene of the greatest miracle of all that ever occurred on earth, and which forms the sure foundation of all Christian joy and hope. The Holy Sepulchre was the holiest of all Holy Places in the East, and its possession gave rise to the Crusades.   The name of S. Joseph of Arimathea is associated with Glastonbury Abbey in Somersetshire, said to be founded in 60 A.D. by the saint himself, whose pilgrim staff, according to legend (also told of others), when stuck into the ground grew into a thorn which blossomed on Christmas-day. Putting legend aside, there can be no doubt of Glastonbury being a very early Christian settlement, and that it had Joseph of Arimathea for its patron saint. His day in the Calendar is 17th March, the same day as S. Patrick.

The Good Centurion of Capernaum.

COLLECTS.—*O Christ our Lord, who art the Physician of salvation, grant unto the sick the aid of heavenly healing. Look upon all faithful people who are sick, and who love to call upon Thy name, and take their souls into Thy keeping, and vouchsafe to deliver them from all sickness and infirmity.*[1]

Visit Thy servant, O Lord, as Thou wast pleased to visit Peter's mother-in-law and the centurion's servant. Restore him, O Lord, to his former health, that he may be enabled to say in the courts of Thine House, The Lord hath chastened and corrected me, but He hath not given me over unto death, He who is the Saviour of the world. Grant this, O Lord, who with God the Father and the Holy Spirit livest and reignest, God, throughout all ages.[2]

> Thine arm, O Lord, in days of old,
>   Was strong to heal and save ;
> It triumphed o'er disease and death,
>   O'er darkness and the grave.
> To Thee they went, the blind, the dumb,
>   The palsied and the lame,
> The leper with his tainted life,
>   The sick with fevered frame.

---

[1] Mozarabic Liturgy, Bright's Collects, p. 111.
[2] Sarum Manual, Bright's Collects, p. 111.

And lo ! Thy touch brought life and health,
    Gave speech and strength and sight ;
And youth renewed and frenzy calmed
    Owned Thee, the Lord of light :
And now, O Lord, be near to bless,
    Almighty as of yore,
In crowded street, by restless couch,
    As by Gennesareth's shore.

Be Thou our great Deliverer still,
    Thou Lord of life and death ;
Restore and quicken, soothe and bless,
    With Thine Almighty breath :
To hands that work and eyes that see,
    Give wisdom's heavenly lore,
That whole and sick, and weak and strong,
    May praise Thee evermore.
                              —DEAN PLUMPTRE.

"And when Jesus was entered into Capernaum, there came
    unto Him a centurion, beseeching Him, and saying,
    Lord, my servant lieth at home sick of the palsy, and
    grievously tormented."—S. MATT. viii. 5-13.

AS this famous incident occurred at Capernaum in the territory under Herod Antipas, we may take for granted that
the centurion was an officer in that service and not directly in
the Roman army.   Herod's little army would be modelled on
that of Rome, but its officers would be Greek or Syrian rather
than Italian.

The time of the incident was very early in our Lord's public
ministry, for the record of it in S. Matt. viii. and S. Luke
vii. is placed in each just after the Sermon on the Mount and
before the ordination of the Twelve. The difference between
the two narratives is slight. In S. Matthew the centurion
directly speaks to Jesus, whereas in S. Luke it is a deputation
of the elders of the Jews who are sent by the centurion. They
alone could have introduced the building of a synagogue and
loving the nation of the Jews; for the centurion was not a
man to blow his own trumpet. When Jesus had agreed and

was on His way to the house, S. Luke states that "the centurion sent friends to Him, saying unto Him, Lord, trouble not Thyself; for I am not worthy that Thou shouldest enter under my roof: neither thought I myself worthy to come unto Thee: but say in a word, and my servant shall be healed." Immediately after this second deputation the centurion himself appears, because the last verse in S. Matthew's narrative reads as spoken face to face. "And Jesus said unto the centurion, Go thy way; and as thou hast believed, so be it done unto thee. And his servant was healed in the self-same hour." This brings the two narratives entirely parallel as regards the action. And the only remaining difference is the omission by S. Luke of what fills two verses in S. Matthew as to Gentiles sitting beside the Hebrew patriarchs sharing their blessings, while some of their descendants would be rejected as worse than heathen. Both evangelists record the Lord's admiration, "Verily I say unto you, I have not found so great faith, no, not in Israel;" but S. Matthew alone adds, "And I say unto you, That many shall come from the east and west, and shall sit down with Abraham, and Isaac, and Jacob, in the kingdom of heaven: but the children of the kingdom shall be cast out into outer darkness: there shall be weeping and gnashing of teeth." As an evangelist specially to the Jews, Matthew needed to lay this warning before them; but writing for Gentiles, it was enough to state the glad tidings apart from the fate of Israel.

These things cleared, we are now free to trace the working of the centurion's mind and heart, and why his conduct so favourably impressed our Lord. The proper starting-point is furnished by the elders, "He loveth our nation, and he hath built us a synagogue." This was antecedent to his servant's illness, perhaps by some years. This building and gift was the outcome of his love to the Jews. Whether technically a proselyte of the gate or not, the centurion's heart was with Israel, sharing knowledge of the God of their fathers, rejoicing in the hearing of the law and prophets weekly in public worship, and cherishing with Israel the hope of a coming Messiah, as so clearly announed by Isaiah in particular, whose book would be dear to him, as it was a little later in similar circumstances to the eunuch of Ethiopia, who read it aloud by himself in the desert. With these feelings, when he observed a deficiency in the ordinances of religion—no synagogue, or too small a one, or one that was naked and tasteless—at his own cost he provided a suitable house of God for Capernaum.

And the public liberality which thus indicated the genuineness and degree of his appreciation of religious ordinances, had itself a further evidence of sincerity in his concern when now his servant or slave was stricken with paralysis and "grievously tormented." Many a good giver and good church-goer fails to stand the home test of kindness and gentleness to wife, children, servants, and work-people; but here is a man whose whole place in the Gospel turns on his deep concern for his sick slave, and the peculiar method which he adopted to commend his slave's case to the gracious notice of the great Prophet. The domestic kindliness of the centurion may be interpreted as a fruit growing from his faith; or antecedently, as a rich natural soil wherein, by God's blessing and reward, faith sprang up with peculiar vigour of life.

A further element in the man, that goes still deeper into the revelation of his nature and character, is to trace his method and reasons for approaching the great Prophet with his slave's case in the indirect way adopted. It was from a feeling of lowliness and unworthiness as a Gentile stranger that he asked the mediation of the elders, "Neither thought I myself worthy." And the elders had asked more than he had directed or intended when they asked Jesus to come. It was healing without coming that was in the centurion's mind. Thus "when Jesus went with the elders, and was now not far from the house," this very promptness so disconcerted and overwhelmed the humble spirit of the kindly and devout man, that he hastily sent friends with a fresh message to explain that all he wanted was one word spoken, "Lord, trouble not Thyself; for I am not worthy that Thou shouldest enter under my roof : . . . but say in a word, and my servant shall be healed." Scarce was the message delivered when the centurion in person appeared to state the sum of his wishes. And when his own statement came, it came with a reason at once so lowly, mighty, and true, as to cause even the Son of God to marvel at the clearness and firmness of the faith that spoke from the lips and heart of the stranger and soldier. "Say in a word, and my servant shall be healed. For I also am a man set under authority, having under me soldiers ; and I say unto one, Go, and he goeth ; and to another, Come, and he cometh ; and to my servant, Do this, and he doeth it." Here the most hasty or least skilled reader cannot fail to observe the contrast between the elders' estimate of the centurion and his own. "They besought Jesus instantly, saying, That he was worthy for whom he should do this." On the other side, "Lord, trouble not Thyself; for I am not worthy that Thou shouldest enter under my roof: wherefore neither thought I myself worthy to come unto Thee." Usually in the world the difference is in the opposite way ; applicants put their own case at its highest, and leave the other side to find out any drawbacks. Good Bishop Hall of Norwich, in one of his Contemplations, puts the point quaintly thus : "Many a one, if he had been in the centurion's coat, would have thought well of it : a captain, a man of good ability and command, a founder of a synagogue, a patron of religion ; yet he overlooks all these, and when he casts his eye upon the divine worth of Christ and his own weakness, he says, 'I am not worthy.' True humility will teach us to find out the best of another and the worst piece of ourselves ; pride, contrarily, shows us nothing but matter of admiration in ourselves, in others of contempt."

Another striking feature of the incident is the very close companionship shown to exist between the grace of humility and the grace of faith. In ordinary popular Christianity we hear too often of faith and too seldom of humility as an aim and means of the soul's life and progress. Without humility there can be no true reverence, and without reverence no true worship. Humility is the climax of the three things named by the prophet Micah as constituting religion,—"What doth the Lord require of thee, but to do justly, and to love mercy, and to walk humbly with thy God?" And doubtless it was from the centurion's extraordinary humility that his correspondingly pre-eminent faith arose.

At this point can we best see the relation of the faith of our centurion to the other faith of the nobleman or courtier whose case is recorded only by S. John iv. 46—a case which belongs also to Capernaum, which happened only a few months before this, and would certainly be known to the centurion, and perhaps help to guide him. In the courtier's case it was his own son who was the sufferer, the disease was fever, and the anxious father pressed Jesus to come down from Cana to Capernaum, sixteen miles or so of distance. But Jesus refused, and simply said, "Go thy way; thy son liveth. And the man believed the word that Jesus had spoken unto him, and went his way." Thus, while the courtier in one part received a refusal, and in the main part received a lesson joined with the miracle, the centurion, on the other hand, received Christ's consent in the matter of going to the house, and it was only the greatness of his faith that interposed, so that the miracle, instead of ending with a lesson for increase of faith, ends with a strong commendation of faith already possessed. In the case where the ruler pleaded for his own son and said, "Come down," Christ stirred not, but only spoke the word. In the case where he was not asked to go, but only to speak the word, Jesus agrees to go, although it was only to heal a man's slave —the treatment being modified to suit more exactly the spiritual state of each suitor.

Now are we ready to glance at the beautiful Gentile and military parable by which the centurion supports and explains his confidence in Christ's healing power by word apart from presence. "For I am a man under authority, having soldiers under me: and I say to this man, Go, and he goeth; and to another, Come, and he cometh; and to my servant, Do this, and he doeth it." Although primarily the image rests on the small army and limited monarchy of Herod Antipas, in which the centurion held office, yet, considering how that army was modelled on and almost was part of the Roman military system, we may at once widen the idea to the whole empire.

The Imperator or Cæsar was commander-in-chief of all the legions, and the legions were scattered over all the provinces, —in Gaul and Britain in the west; in Pannonia and Thrace on the north; in Persia and Scythia in the east; in Libya and Egypt in the south. The emperor's command was the supreme law to every legion wherever posted, directing their movements and controlling their operations. The emperor had no need to visit provinces for the purpose of ruling; enough that his decree was issued. The centurion's parable bore that all this was true of the great Prophet, who was also a great King, ruling provinces more and wider than belonged to Rome, ruling hosts of angels marshalled under great leaders like Michael and Gabriel and Raphael. And in this spiritual empire communication from the centre to the extremities, from the great King to the humblest of the angel host, was no slow process of marching and sailing, but of instantaneous speed like that of lightning, which defies distance. Such was the centurion's creed, professional in form, touching the power and authority of our Lord. And with a creed so simple and strong, it was only natural for him to think and say that the Lord's word alone would suffice for the healing of his servant. "He felt that the Cause of causes is a Person.[1] Hence he could trust the living will out of sight. This is the highest form of faith, and he learned it through his own profession. The argument ran thus. I by the command of will obtain the obedience of my dependants. Thou by will the obedience of Thine: sickness and health are Thy servants. To him this world was a mighty camp of living forces in which authority was paramount. Trained in obedience to military law, accustomed to

<hr>

[1] Robertson of Brighton, Sermon ii. 132.

H

render prompt submission to those above him, and to exact it
from those below him, he read law everywhere, and law to him
meant the expression of a personal will." [1]

" When Jesus heard it, He marvelled, and said to them that
followed, Verily I say unto you, I have not found so great
faith, no, not in Israel.   And I say unto you, That many shall
come from the east and west, and shall sit down with Abraham,
and Isaac, and Jacob, in the kingdom of heaven : but the
children of the kingdom shall be cast out into outer darkness :
there shall be weeping and gnashing of teeth."   It surprises
us to think of Jesus thus made to marvel although He was the
reader of all hearts and ruler of all events.   We see herein a
glimpse of how real was the human nature which He possessed
in union with His divine Sonship.   Such marvelling is recorded
of Him only twice, and both occasions connected with men's
faith ; this time with faith's greatness, the other time with
faith's absence on the part of His own neighbours in Nazareth.
" And He could there do no mighty work, save that He laid
His hands upon a few sick folk, and healed them.   And He
marvelled because of their unbelief."—S. Mark vi. 5.   The
reasons for our Lord marvelling here were evidently two, to find
faith so strong in the heart and confession of a man who
laboured under the double disadvantage of Gentile race and
military profession.   " A soldier, and therefore exposed to a
recklessness and idleness and sensuality which are the temptations of that profession.   But he turned his loss to glorious

---

[1] The centurion of Capernaum is only one of four centurions all favourably mentioned in the New Testament.   Next after him is the one on
duty at Calvary : "Now when the centurion saw what was done, he
glorified God, saying, Certainly this was a righteous man."—Luke xxiii.
47.   The third is he of Cæsarea : "Cornelius, a centurion of the band
called the Italian band, a devout man, and one that feared God with all
his house, which gave much alms to the people, and prayed to God
alway."—Acts x. 1, 2.   The last is S. Paul's friend Julius, a centurion of
Augustus's band, who at Sidon courteously entreated Paul, and gave
him liberty to go unto his friends to refresh himself ; and who at the
end of the shipwreck saved Paul's life by keeping the soldiers from slay-
ing the prisoners.—Acts xxvii.

gain. The Saviour's comment therefore contained the advantage of disadvantages, and the disadvantage of advantages. The former, 'Many shall come,' &c. The latter, 'The children of the kingdom,' &c. There are spirits which are crushed by difficulties ; others gain strength from them. Moses, Elijah, Abraham, the Baptist, the giants of both Testaments, were not men nurtured in the hothouse of religious advantages. Many a man would have done good, if he had not had a superabundance of the means of doing it. Many a spiritual giant is buried under mountains of gold." [1]   On the same principle, one of the chief reasons of the low spiritual state of Scotland is its multiplication of sects and churches, which degrades all religion by perpetual competition.

But the most interesting point of all is our Lord's view of the centurion as the first-fruits of the calling of the Gentiles into Christendom, and the transfer of privilege from unfaithful Israel. Anticipations of this meet us all along the line of the Old Testament in Melchizedek of Salem, Hobab of Midian, Ruth of Moab, Naaman the Syrian ; as also in the temple-dedication prayer of Solomon. The star to the Magi from the East was its entrance into the Gospel ; while the crumbs of the children's bread given to the Canaanite mother form a parallel to this faith seen at Capernaum. After Pentecost it reached its blessed climax in Cornelius the centurion, to whom S. Peter was sent by heavenly vision. Here, in the very heart of our Lord's own ministry, is a distinct case clearer than any in the Old Testament, and containing an authoritative anticipation of all that characterised the apostleship of S. Paul as distinguished from the specially Jewish apostleship of S. Peter. Let us therefore glorify God for the centurion of Capernaum, in whom we see so early and clearly the blessedness in Christ of all Gentile men and nations.

Pleasant as is the prospect of many Western and Eastern Christians sitting down with the Hebrew patriarchs in the kingdom of heaven, very sad is the other half of our Lord's

---

[1] Robertson of Brighton, ii. 135.

saying as to the rejection of Israel to a large degree and for a long time. Yet this is not Christ's doing, but their own (as the parable of the wicked husbandmen tells us)—the righteous and unavoidable retribution on the men who refused the fruits of the vineyard, and killed the heir of the householder. Well warned of their danger were the Jews as far back as the picture of the vineyard wasted with fire and inroaded by wild beasts in Ps. lxxx.; and again in the parable in Isaiah v., of the degenerate vineyard that brought forth only wild grapes, and was given over to briers, thorns, and drought. All this was terribly fulfilled in 70 A.D., when Jerusalem was stormed by the Romans, 97,000 Jews made captives, and above a million killed by famine, fire, and sword; and every religious rite suppressed for generations on that Holy Hill where sacrifice had been daily offered for above 1000 years.

Many and varied are the lessons that connect themselves with the faith of the centurion at Capernaum, and with the healing of his servant, once grievously tormented. The whole man and his history declare, as by a special revelation, how true character grows from true religion. We have, moreover, a lesson of caution and charity as to the tracing and measuring of genuine faith: it may be found sometimes in the most unlikely persons and callings; and may fail in persons, places, and communities where externals and opportunities seem entirely favourable.

In this good and most worthy soldier we see the power of man to overcome moral and religious obstacles; we see the beauty and profitableness of the grace of humility toward God; we see the blessedness of brotherly sympathy with a man's own dependants, especially in seasons of sickness and pain; we see the blessedness of sympathy with and co-operation in God's kingdom in places of worship and ordinances therein; above all, we see the blessedness of that nobler form and degree of faith which is contented with the mere but sure word of God and of Christ, as all our hope and trust.

On a side higher still—that of Christ's own relation to this faithful centurion,—have we not a great insight into the true manhood of our Lord and Saviour in His marvelling over this man's degree and mode of faith ; an additional lesson on the Godhead of Christ in His healing of the servant without seeing him ; and in the world-wide graciousness of the great Prophet in admitting Gentiles to share the privileges of the Jews, and even of their most honoured patriarchs ? Finally, have we not here also a very solemn lesson touching the Judgeship of Christ in the rejection of the unbelieving Jews.

A good and faithful man is this centurion of Capernaum, worthy to be named in the company of apostles, evangelists, martyrs, and confessors of the best days of the early Church.

Lazarus, Mary, and Martha.

COLLECTS.—*Almighty and everlasting God, who dost en- kindle the flame of Thy love in the hearts of the saints, grant to our minds the same faith and power of love ; that as we rejoice in their triumphs, we may profit by their examples ; through Jesus Christ our Lord.*[1]

Almighty and everlasting God, be Thou present to our duties, and grant the protection of Thy presence to all that dwell in this house ; that Thou mayest be known to be the Defender of Thy family, and the Inhabitant of this dwelling ; through Jesus Christ our Lord.[2]

Flagrans amore, perditos Dum nos Redemptor quæreret, Defessus ad Martham Deus Sese recepit hospitam.	When, with love burning, the Saviour was seeking us who were lost, wearied and yet divine to Martha went He, for repose and food.

---

[1] Gothic Missal, Bright, Collects, p. 69.
[2] Gelasian Sacramentary Collects, p. 103.

Beata, quæ tantum suis
Amica tectis hospitem
Fovere gaudet, et Deo
Inferre convivæ dapes !

Happy was she beneath her roof
as friend, so great a guest
to entertain devoutly and God
　　Himself
to wait on at her table.　·

Dum Martha pascit, pascitur
Maria felix ; ac sedens,
Magnoque tuta Judice,
Partem potitur optimam.

The earthly table is Martha's care;
　　but happier　　　　　　[sitting
is Mary at the heavenly feast, where
at the feet of the great Judge
　　Himself
she gains the better part.

Nunc, Martha, nunc sedens Deo,
Et ipsa Verbo pasceris ;
Et juge se tuus tibi
Conviva dat convivium.

Now, Martha, now sitt'st thou down,
thou too feasting on the Word
　　divine ;
for thy Guest gives Himself to thee
a spiritual feast and for ever.

Da, Christe, sanctorum quies,
Sic nos ad unum tendere
Per multa, posthac optima
Ut parte possimus frui.
　　　—Cluniac Breviary, 1686.

Grant, O Christ, who art Thy saints'
　　repose,
that we one goal may reach,
although by many paths, so that
　　above
we may the better part enjoy.

Intrante Christo Bethanicam do-
　　mum,　　　　　　　[didam
Curramus omnes : hospite splen-
Simone cœnam præparante,
Tam celebrem penetremus aulam.

As Jesus enters the house at Beth-
　　any
haste we all, while Simon as host
makes ready his banquet rich,
and enter we the famous hall.

Hic dum ministrat Martha celer
　　gradu,
Fraterque lœtas assidet ad dapes ;
Maria, Christo tu fragranti
Vasa reples pretiosa nardo.

Here as Martha deftly serves [joy,
and her brother sits at the feast of
thou, O Mary, in honour of the
　　Christ　　　　　　　[sweet.
bearest the vase with its spikenard

Pedes inungens, tergere crinibus
Gaudes ; liquorem fundis et in
　　caput ;
Et, vase fracto mox inundans,
Tecta novo recreas odore.

Anointing His feet, with thy hair
　　thou driest them ; [perfume ;
over His head too pourest thou the
and the whole house with the fra-
　　grance is filled
when the vase has been broken to
　　free its treasure.

Sed cur iniquo dente lacesseris,
Dum gloriosis obsequiis vacas ?
Unguenta fundens, antevertis
Exequias morientis Agni.

But why art thou assailed by the carper ? [seest :
A great entombment thou fore-offering thine ointment, beforehand art thou [of God.
the death-feast keeping of the Lamb

Quantum per orbem Christiadum fides
Diffusa vastas subjiciet plagas,
Tantum Mariæ grande factum
Per populos resonabit omnes.
—*Cluniac Breviary*, 1686.

Whatever of the globe the Christ-ian faith [spread,
subduing wide realms shall over-there shall Mary's deed of devotion
find its fame through nations all.

"Jesus answered and said unto her, Martha, Martha, thou art careful and troubled about many things ; but one thing is needful : and Mary hath chosen that good part, which shall not be taken from her."—S. LUKE x. 41.

THE contrast that here marks the sisters of Lazarus has attracted attention in all ages of the Church. Exactly the same contrast is traceable in what is recorded of the sisters by S. John. Thus the harmony of representation by the evangelists and by Jesus Himself, whose estimate they record, carries a strong token of living truthfulness. Diversity of gifts and graces of Christian character is a matter of much practical importance, as showing different ways of acceptably serving God, and as teaching much-needed lessons of tolerance one with another, even in our unlikeness, provided our unlikenesses to each other keep within the wide circle of God's attributes and commandments.

Our information regarding the family of Bethany with its three saints, whose day is 2d September, is confined to three places of Scripture—viz., S. Luke x., containing Martha's complaint made to Jesus as to Mary's neglect of household duties ; S. John xi., with the account of the sickness, death, and resurrection of Lazarus ; and S. John xii., recording the anointing of Jesus by Mary with ointment of spikenard—the same incident being also recorded by S. Matthew xxvi. and S. Mark xiv.

Bethany was a village about two miles from Jersusalem, and situated on the northern road by which persons would travel to and from Galilee. On the first occasion when S. Luke mentions Martha and Mary, the village where they dwelt is not named: "Now it came to pass, as they went, that He entered into a certain village: and a certain woman named Martha received Him into her house." Besides omitting the name of the village, he makes no allusion to the existence of a brother as the head of the house. Nor is Lazarus named by Matthew or Mark in their record of the anointing. Even Mary herself is not named, but only referred to as "a woman"; and the scene of the incident is in Bethany, in the house of Simon the leper. It has been supposed that this omission of names was intentional on the part of the first three evangelists, so as not needlessly to point out for persecution this pre-eminently Christian household. Whereas S. John wrote so much later that all three were probably dead a good many years before, and full details might safely be furnished. That such danger was real is expressly stated by S. John: "But the chief priests consulted that they might put Lazarus also to death; because that by reason of him many of the Jews went away, and believed on Jesus."

This situation of Bethany made it convenient for Jesus to avail Himself of during His visits to Jerusalem at the great yearly festivals. It was remote enough from the capital to form a quiet retreat; and yet it was also near enough to allow of a daily walk to and from the Temple, throughout the octave of each festival. We are distinctly informed that Jesus did not sleep in Jerusalem on these occasions. "And in the day-time He was teaching in the Temple; and at night He went out, and abode in the mount that is called the Mount of Olives. And all the people came early in the morning to Him in the Temple, for to hear Him."—Luke xxi. 37. How long our Lord's use of the hospitality continued is unknown, but probably it extended over the three years of His public ministry. Possibly it went back over some of those years of obscurity from the age of twelve to thirty, during which Jesus would conform to the law and custom of statedly appearing in Jerusalem. Clearly something more than one or two eight-day visits would be required to justify the use of expressions so pointed as, "Our friend Lazarus;" "Lord, behold he whom Thou lovest;" "Behold how He loved him!" Our Lord's own homelessness, together with His frequent experience of suspicion, hostility, and persecution, would cause Him to prize the more the kindly shelter and sympathy of a family so peaceful and pure, and where every member vied with each other in different forms of devotedness to this wonderful guest whom the holy seasons attracted to the Temple and to their house. He was not priest, Levite, or scribe in the ordinary sense; yet these festivals were more to him, and He more to them, than in the case of any official person in the whole Jewish Church, for the place of common resort was His Father's house.

On this foundation of place and circumstance rest those traits of individuality on the part of the three inmates of the cottage in Bethany which form a sacred idyl. But while they are three in counting, there are really only two to discriminate, because Lazarus is passive all through, although he is the natural head of the house, and the great centre of affectionate interest to the whole of the little circle. The Gospel records no single word or act of Lazarus save his presence after his resurrection at the feast in Simon's house, where Martha served, and Mary anointed the feet of Jesus. It tells not where he stood in the family in order of years; it tells not whether the house was his or Martha's; it tells not how long he survived his resurrection. Only this is clear: he was intensely beloved by each of his sisters, so that his death was their supreme calamity, as his restoration from the grave was their best blessing and joy. Moreover, he drew the love of Jesus toward himself more than any other disciple save S. John. The one grand outstanding fact regarding Lazarus is, that

he was the subject of the greatest of all our Lord's miracles;
as markedly the greatest as that at Cana was the first.

The first mention of the sisters of Lazarus in S. Luke
x. is also the most distinctive. Martha appears receiving
Jesus as a guest in the house, and exerting herself to the
utmost to show Him honour by having all things at their best.
This was thoroughly right: her heart was in her household
duties, and she rejoiced in these as to be made tributary to
Jesus. But while she was thus absorbed in her own line,
her sister was equally absorbed in hers, which was different:
"She had a sister called Mary, which also sat at Jesus' feet,
and heard His word." There was thorough agreement between
the sisters in accepting Christ's presence under their roof as a
singular honour and privilege. The one showed her esteem
by promoting everything within the house that could tend to
honour the Guest; while the other gave her esteem a more
spiritual form by quiet observance of every word of doctrine
that flowed from the Guest's lips. The two forms of testimony
and homage might well have gone on side by side in the same
house: each was genuine, although one might be better than
the other. As it happened, the one was impatient and intolerant of the other; and the impatient and intolerant one was
the more outward and inferior. Martha carried her intolerance
so far as to embody it in a direct complaint to Jesus. "Lord,
dost Thou not care that my sister hath left me to serve alone?
bid her therefore that she help me."

How bold and tender was the reply! He might have declined to interfere, as being only a guest in the house; or he
might have yielded to the urgency of a bustling and commanding woman, who spared neither hands nor tongue. Instead of
either, he decided in favour of the weaker and quieter sister,
and administered to the domestic devotee of cookery, crockery,
and napery a rebuke as good-natured as it was real and just.
"Martha, Martha, thou art careful and troubled about many
things: but one thing is needful: and Mary hath chosen that
good part, which shall not be taken away from her." Here

was acknowledgment and appreciation of Martha's diligence in her own chosen sphere, but at the same time a restraining of her from forcing her ideas on her sister, whose heart led her in another and better direction in search of duty and happiness. The words of Jesus were of such a kind as to put Martha right without enraging her. Moreover, they not only shielded Mary, but greatly encouraged her. Her aim and zeal were toward what was highest and most enduring. Far beyond comfort, order, and domestic economy, her motto was, "Thou shalt guide me with Thy counsel, and afterward receive me to glory. Whom have I in heaven but Thee? and there is none upon earth that I desire besides Thee. My flesh and my heart faileth : but God is the strength of my heart, and my portion for ever." Here was Jesus in private life carrying out His public teaching, "Take no thought, saying, What shall we eat? or, What shall we drink? or, Wherewithal shall we be clothed? for your heavenly Father knoweth that ye have need of all these things. But seek ye first the kingdom of God, and His righteousness ; and all these things shall be added unto you."

The second scene of contrast between the sisters arises out of the somewhat long and very solemn record of the sickness, death, and resurrection of their brother Lazarus in S. John xi. Both are at one in desiring the presence of Jesus when their brother is dangerously ill, and they send a joint message. "His sisters sent unto Him, saying, Lord, behold, he whom Thou lovest is sick." They wish and expect Him to come, yet they do not directly ask Him : they simply describe their distress, and leave the rest to His well-known compassion and affection, for it is said, "Now Jesus loved Martha, and her sister, and Lazarus."

Their great trust receives a great trial, for Jesus did not at once quit Peræa and Bethabara (John x. 40, i. 28), but continued His present work for two days before starting westwards for Bethany. Martha, in accordance with her greater activity, is the first to hear of Christ's approach ; and, in accordance also with her independent and managing nature, she sets out alone to meet Jesus without informing her sister. At all events, while she went forth, " Mary sat still in the house." Having met and conversed with Jesus, she returns and conveys a secret message to her sister, the terms of which are interesting as marking their estimate of Jesus and their way of naming Him, " The Master is come, and calleth for thee." Deep as was Mary's grief, and calm as was her ordinary manner, it is twice mentioned in the holy page that the reception of this message quickened her to haste. " As soon as she heard that, she arose quickly, and came unto Him." " The Jews then which were with her in the house, and comforted her, when they saw Mary, that she rose up hastily and went out, followed her, saying, She goeth unto the grave to weep there." This haste, as being the contrary of her usual disposition, is a token of the inner ardour of soul the moment that the Master is near. The meeting with Jesus has also its own mark. While she uses the same words as Martha, " Lord, if Thou hadst been here, my brother had not died," she prefaces them with an action of intensity that made them expressive of a breaking and burning heart, for " when Mary was come where Jesus was, and saw Him, she fell down at His feet." This was the intensity of faith, love, and grief, that drew sympathetic tears to the eyes of the accompanying Jews and of Jesus Himself. Thus while both sisters were genuine in faith and sorrow, excellence in these pertained to her whose place for hearing and worship and anointing was at Jesus' feet.

Arrived at the grave, when Jesus directed the stone to be taken away from the opening, it was Martha who spake deprecatingly ; her construction of the whole scene being of a material sort, probably that Jesus was indiscreetly desirous once more to look on the features of His departed friend. For this she was gently reproved : " Said I not unto Thee, that, if thou wouldest believe, thou shouldest see the glory of God ?" No mention here of Mary. She was present, but looked on in silence, probably in hope and faith within the silence. In her view Jesus would be incapable of any rashness in word or deed. It was strange that He should seek to remove the stone from the grave's mouth where her brother lay; but she would give Jesus time, and trust Him to justify the strangeness.

There seems on the part of their neighbours a token of appreciation of the character of Mary as finer and deeper, in that case where her name occurs alone. " Then many of the Jews which came to Mary, and had seen the things which Jesus did, believed on Him." People would go more readily to condole with a woman of a quiet devout disposition, than with one full of activity in all household affairs. They would judge in the latter case that the activity would be partly an antidote to sorrow. Moreover, persons who were kindred enough in feeling to come and sympathise with a woman like Mary, would be specially likely to have kindred feelings toward Jesus, to be better specimens of Jews, and accordingly more open to conviction and conversion.

The third scene of contrast for the sisters of Bethany is that which occurs in three of the Evangelists, but in S. John xii. with precise insertion of the names concerned. The date was subsequent to the raising of Lazarus, and only six days before the Passover at which our Lord was crucified. The scene was Bethany, which furnished temporary home-quiet to Jesus from the crowds and plots and unbelief of Jerusalem. And the special house in Bethany was that of Simon the leper, probably one of those cured beforetime by Jesus. Here Martha appears in her former capacity, serving during the supper, and superintending all domestic arrangements. Let us not disparage such work. It was done heartily; it was that in which she was most at home; it is good and needful in every dwelling. Here it was done in reverence, love, and gratitude most special toward Jesus, and equivalent in spirit to any church service. This time we meet no word or hint of any forwardness or materialism on Martha's part that needed check or reproof. Probably the fresh remembrance of the restoration of her brother to life, and the sight of that brother at the table, would so solemnise her words and her work that all she did would secure the full approval and blessing of the Master.

Her severest reproof had been on the first occasion ; a gentler reproof was at the grave ; now no reproof at all appears. And we may perhaps fairly infer that, while still strongest in handiwork, her handiwork is doue in less bustle, and also with more reverence, humility, and sympathy with persons and ideas of a spiritual nature.

Meanwhile takes place at that supper one of the most impressive actions of combined devotion, humility, gratitude, and affection ever witnessed on earth. "Then took Mary a pound of ointment of spikenard, very costly, and anointed the feet of Jesus, and wiped His feet with her hair : and the house was filled with the odour of the ointment." What gift too precious for Him whose conversation and discourse are a revelation from heaven, of all wisdom and of all grace ! What gift too precious for Him who had recalled to life her dear and only brother ! Unbelief and strife are across the Kedron at Jerusalem, but here in Bethany are reverence, love, and gratitude.

It was needful here, too, for Jesus to defend Mary ; but now the defence is not again a misunderstanding of Martha, but again a perversion of Judas Iscariot. Once she had been charged with idleness or sloth ; now she is charged with waste and extravagance. How touching and complete was Christ's defence ! "Let her alone : against the day of my burying hath she kept this. For the poor always ye have with you ; but me ye have not always." To which S. Mark adds, "Verily I say unto you, Wheresoever this gospel shall be preached throughout the whole world, this also that she hath done shall be spoken of for a memorial of her."

> When Lazarus left his charnel-cave,
>   And home to Mary's house return'd,
>   Was this demanded—if he yearn'd
> To hear her weeping by his grave ?

"Where wert thou, brother, those four days?"
   There lives no record of reply,
   Which telling what it is to die
Had surely added praise to praise.

From every house the neighbours met,
   The streets were fill'd with joyful sound,
   A solemn gladness even crown'd
The purple brows of Olivet.

Behold a man raised up by Christ !
   The rest remaineth unreveal'd ;
   He told it not ; or something seal'd
The lips of that Evangelist.

Her eyes are homes of silent prayer,
   Nor other thought her mind admits
   But, he was dead, and there he sits,
And He that brought him back is there.

Then one deep love doth supersede
   All other, when her ardent gaze
   Roves from the living brother's face,
And rests upon the Life indeed.

All subtle thought, all curious fears,
   Borne down by gladness so complete,
   She bows, she bathes the Saviour's feet
With costly spikenard and with tears.

Thrice blest whose lives are faithful prayers,
   Whose loves in higher love endure ;
   What souls possess themselves so pure,
Or is there blessedness like theirs ?
          —TENNYSON, *In Mcm.*, xxxi., xxxii.

Seeking for lessons taught by these incidents, some of the lowliest but not least needful or valuable connect themselves with what should be the plan of education for girls. Probably no kind or amount of training in earlier life would have made these two sisters alike in disposition and taste. We should not only note the difference as a fact, but give room for the fact to work itself out in distinct lines. We deal wrongly with the narrative when, as is often done, we speak disparagingly of Martha, whose choice was quite lawful and praiseworthy in being greatly taken up with all household work and provisioning. She was thoroughly right while she tried to honour the Master by means of these. Her error lay in not agreeing to let her sister choose another way, which happened also to be a better way to the same end. By a strange turn, in our own generation we require to urge our women and girls to imitate Martha rather than Mary. At present there is a frightful neglect of home training as regards cookery and tidiness and doing things economically at home, to save paying people outside. The want of Martha's talent is what makes so many workmen's dwellings uncomfortable ; table-covers unknown save at christenings, marriages, and funerals ; the commonest food ill prepared ; nourishing food neglected, and men left to do a hard day's work on dry bread and cheese, or sickened by the perpetual teapot. One merit of the old Jewish life was its home and family character, full of skill and industry, and feelings of kinship and mutual helpfulness. Bible readings, cookery recipes, and other useful arts were not jostled aside by cheap novels, illustrated fashion-books, and sham "accomplishments."

We meet here also a great lesson as regards tolerance of variety of character and development. To seek for one uniform line of acquirements or accomplishments or cast of character is mere tyranny, and destined to issue in great loss to society. If we find, as here, such diversity in two sisters, both excellent Christian women, how much more may we expect diversity in different towns, kingdoms, and races ! As regards forms of worship and expression of religious feeling, it would be a pitiable ignorance alike of Scripture and our own nature to expect all men to conform to our own pattern here and now. Some people are more lively and superficial in their emotions, and may find the noisy shallowness of revivalists and the Salvation Army to suit them best. Some may be gloomy and severe in their religion, and can best express themselves by a bare and long service in church, and by three such diets of worship in one day, and by sitting the rest of the day in their houses speechless and with drawn blinds, and by puritanically naming the day Sabbath. Some again may prefer cheerfulness and taste, and seek to express these in a well-built church, in skilful music, in poetic hymns, in short and carefully expressed prayers, and in orderly arrangement of the whole church service. Were due allowance made for such diversity, there might be much more of peace among Christians of different communions. Why should we so readily unchurch one another altogether? Why not be content to grade churches as we do nations, into civilised, half civilised, and savage? A low type of Christianity does not absolutely make a man a heathen, any more than a low degree of culture takes away his claim to be human.

But the great lesson of the subject is more domestic than ecclesiastical. It points to the cultivation of simple Christian hospitality as distinguished from vain and wasteful parties. It points to useful arts in housekeeping as superior to idle pauper gentility. It points to household piety as the best of all home gifts, while a fair and reasonable proportion is to be assigned to a variety of gifts among members of the same family.

Zaccheus of Jericho.

COLLECTS. — *Almighty and everlasting God, who hatest nothing that Thou hast made, and dost forgive the sins of all them that are penitent; Create and make in us new and contrite hearts, that we worthily lamenting our sins and acknowledging our wretchedness, may obtain of Thee, the God of all mercy, perfect remission and forgiveness; through Jesus Christ our Lord. Amen.*[1]

Look upon us and hear us, O Lord our God; and assist those endeavours to please Thee which Thou Thyself hast granted to us; as Thou hast given the first act of will, so give the completion of the work; grant that we may be able to finish what Thou hast granted us to wish to begin.[2]

For the Epistle.—Rev. xxi. 1-5.

The Gospel—S. Luke xix. 1-10.

[*Appointed in Consecration of Churches.*]

"And Zaccheus stood, and said unto the Lord; Behold, Lord, the half of my goods I give to the poor; and if I have taken anything from any man by false accusation, I restore him four-fold."—S. LUKE xix. 8.

IN this verse, which tersely makes acknowledgment of the value and need of practical righteousness, lies the real kernel of the happy meeting at Jericho between Christ and Zaccheus. All else led up to this point, and without the principle here laid down, the expression "this day is salvation come to this house" could not have given its glorious close to the incident. Fully to appreciate the narrative, we must add to xix. 1-10, the passage xviii. 31-43, from which we learn the time and chief circumstances.

---

[1] Angl. Collect for Ash Wednesday.

[2] Mozarabic Brev., Bright's Collects, p. 93.

It was at the very end of our Lord's public ministry, the last stage of the journey, and within five or six hours' walk of Jerusalem. He and His disciples were going thither to celebrate the Passover for the last time; and before entering Jericho the Saviour plainly announced to the twelve the fate of betrayal, mockery, scourging, and death that lay immediately before him. But "they understood none of these things, and this saying was hid from them." Apparently their blindness arose from a preconception of their own in the contrary direction, that the approaching crisis was to be no disaster at all, but the opening up of a new career of victory and authority, when evil and evil men were to be subdued, and righteousness to be vindicated, the old world wound up and a new inaugurated. The parable of the pounds, which succeeds the narrative as to Zaccheus, was spoken to correct this error. "And as they heard these things, He added and spake a parable, because He was nigh to Jerusalem, and because they thought that the kingdom of God should immediately appear. . . . And when He had thus spoken [as in the parable], He went before, ascending up to Jerusalem." Within these limits—*i.e.*, before reaching and after leaving Jericho— there occurred two great incidents. The earlier, at the close of chapter xviii., was the miracle of healing on blind Bartimæus, which need not here be further alluded to. The other is the meeting with Zaccheus, the scene of which was, not after Jericho had been passed, but, according to the literal translation of xix. 1, when Jesus, having entered Jericho, was passing through it—*i.e.*, in the first suburb of Jericho, before entering the closer built town streets. And the very recent miracle on Bartimæus, probably not a mile back, would cause all the more eagerness in the townspeople, and among the fellow-travellers who, like Christ and His apostles, were journeying to the Passover.

The city which formed this resting-stage for a night to Jesus on His way to crucifixion was six miles from the Jordan, and fifteen miles from Jerusalem, the road to which was a long

slow ascent through a rocky glen infested by robbers.   This
road is the scene of the parable of the good Samaritan in S.
Luke x.   It was largely a priestly city, and also a centre of
revenue collection ; taxes being laid on balsam, which was a
great product of the district, and other taxes being exigible
on goods passing between Roman territory and the province
under Herod Antipas.   The Roman revenue at and around
Jericho would probably be farmed by some wealthy Roman
speculator, under whom Zaccheus would act as receiver-general
of the taxes ; and thus the head of the *publicani* would be a
man of prominence and power in the district.

But the more zealous among the Jews regarded the whole
Roman rule and finance in the land as an odious and impious
bondage, and for a native Israelite to help the foreigner, and
to earn his living in their service, and that by collecting
forcibly their hard taxes, was deemed the lowest sink of
degradation.   And in a city where priests and their families
formed a considerable proportion of the population, these
feelings of scorn would be much intensified.   All over Judea
the feeling was so violent that publican or taxgatherer had become synonymous with sinner, and even with harlot, as we
find again and again in the gospels, when the sentiments of
scribes and Pharisees are represented.

In these circumstances the wealth of Zaccheus would give
him little comfort in his own mind, and little respect in the
community.   Rather it would tend to embitter his neighbours
the more, for they would look on his prosperity as proportionate
to his rapacity, extortion, and fraud.   These self-called patriots
and self-righteous men would consign to hopeless reproach a
man like Zaccheus, who differed from them on the question
of the lawfulness of tribute, so absolutely sure were they of
their own infallibility of judgment.   It is marvellous to see
to what extent civil and religious life, even in Great Britain,
is still split and embittered by parallel prejudices and feuds.
In the matter of drink, some modern theorists challenge the
almost universal usage of mankind and the freedom of the

Word of God, and try to create a new standard of virtue, as if it were an unchallengeable axiom that total abstinence excels temperance. Other theorists deal with capital, property, rank, and culture as if each of these was in itself dangerous, whereas it is these that have the whole history of civilisation in their favour, and the theorists who write with such self-assurance have yet to prove their fundamental principles. There are men in Scotland and Wales who profess themselves Christians, yet are so blinded and degraded by Dissent that they cry and plot for the overthrow of larger, older, and more intelligent bodies of Christians, as if there were no way of getting to religious equality except by levelling down, and as if the principle itself were as sure as that $2 + 2 = 4$, whereas it is a delusive theory unattainable in practice, but useful as a stimulus to destruction, like the singing of revolutionary songs. There are also associations of Protestants whose delight and principle consist in slandering the adherents and ritual of Rome, as if these were the embodiment of all evil, whereas it is these so-called Protestants who form a blot upon the several Churches which they think they represent in greatest purity. So also on the other side, men of pedigree and fashion in many cases regard the people who constitute the bulk and strength of town and country as men of inferior clay, and not fit to be trusted with public business. Evangelicals in the Church, in like manner, inveigh against men of culture and taste who follow Scripture and history instead of accepting the narrow platitudes and repetitions of windbag revivalists.

In the midst of parallel feuds and prejudices the lot of Zaccheus was cast in these old days at Jericho, when the visit of Jesus took place. But the supposed wickedest man of that city is the man whom, under the teaching of our infallible Lord, we are now trying to analyse and honour as a pattern of righteousness to all Christians. It has been suggested that Zaccheus was awakened to repentance under the ministry of John the Baptist, when "came also publicans to be baptised, and said unto him, Master, what shall we do ? And he said unto them, Exact no more than that which is appointed you." —Luke iii. 12. Another has suggested (Dean Plumptre) that the publican in the parable in S. Luke xviii. 10, who "smote upon his breast, saying, God be merciful to me a sinner, and standing afar off, would not so much as lift up his eyes unto heaven," was no other than Zaccheus of Jericho—all the more as our Lord here addresses him by name at first meeting. While both of these suggestions are highly probable, we have no means of absolutely deciding upon them ; and for really solid material we must begin and end within the scope of the ten verses at the opening of S. Luke xix.

The first notable feature there—and it means a very great deal—is the eagerness and determination of Zaccheus " to see Jesus who He was ; and could not for the press, because he was little of stature." Considering what follows, we are safe to characterise this eagerness as religious in its nature, and not the mere product of curiosity. We may take for granted that he had never as yet spoken to Jesus ; and we may also take for granted that the eagerness was of older date than the very recent miracle on blind Bartimæus, for Christ's three years' ministry must in many a rumour have reached the ears of a man holding an important although despised office in Jericho. Particularly would Zaccheus be likely to have heard that the Prophet of Galilee was not unkindly to publicans, and that one of them had even been chosen an apostle. The knowledge of the Prophet's sympathy with publicans would be to Zaccheus like a ray of sunshine in his dark lot of life.

Whatever the exact source of the eagerness in circumstances or date, it is clear that the feeling was a strong one, as proven by the trouble he took and the ingenuity he exercised to over-come two obstacles—of the crowd and his own shortness—in order to gain his point of seeing the Prophet in the by-passing. He got over the one difficulty by running on in front, and he got over the other difficulty by climbing a tree. The kind of tree is very distinctly named, being a fig-mulberry or Egyptian fig—so called from having leaves like a mulberry, while the fruit is fig-like but harsh-tasted. Its low-growing and abundant branches would make it easily climbable. Much has been written allegorising this part of the narrative, but such spinning resembles ingenious play rather than useful doctrine. Enough if we see in the running and climbing on the part of Zaccheus a good evidence of the strength of his desire and determination to see Jesus; and also a good illustration of the saw that "where there's a will, there's a way."

From his coign of vantage Zaccheus not only sees but is seen, and, far beyond his intention or anticipation, attracts both the special observation and conversation of the great Prophet. "And when Jesus came to the place, He looked up, and saw him, and said unto him, Zaccheus, make haste, and come down; for to-day I must abide at thy house. And he made haste, and came down, and received Him joyfully." How it came that Jesus addressed him by name we cannot say. It might be by exercise of His supernatural power, whereby He knows every man in all the world, and even the most secret thoughts of each heart. Or it might be from some unrecorded word dropped at the moment by some one in our Lord's company; and who more handy for such a purpose than the apostle who had himself been called from the receipt of custom in Galilee, and was sure to know his brother in trade at Jericho? The construction that seems best to suit the whole case is this,— that Jesus did exercise His prophetic gift of reading the heart in this special instance; that He saw and read something in the eyes, in the face, in the attitude of the earnest and reverent little man in the tree, which He knew to be significant spiritually in a high degree, which drew forth His own sympathy, and led Him to the assurance that this would be returned in like spirit. As some on whom miracles were wrought showed by their wistful gaze and solemn demeanour that they had faith to be healed, so may we lawfully think that a corresponding sign shone from Zaccheus, and that sign, whatever it was, could not appeal in vain to Him whose office was "to seek and to save that which was lost." But, however it happened in exact way and order, it did come about most blessedly at the right spot and moment that the divine love and the human love recognised one another and exchanged their joy. It is quite as true, and in fact more true, that Jesus sought Zaccheus, than that Zaccheus sought Jesus. The record of the latter meets us in the middle of the narrative, while the record of the former meets us at its close, and there marks the principle which was really the deeper and earlier of the two, and which has a width which goes far beyond Jericho and Zaccheus, extending to the whole sinful world.

What passed so well as between the Saviour and the publican was very differently regarded by the multitude : "And when they saw it, they all murmured, saying, That he was gone to be guest with a man that is a sinner." As Bishop Hall in one of his "Contemplations" says, "Four vices met here at once—envy, scrupulousness, ignorance, pride ; their eye was evil because Christ's was good. I do not hear any of them invite Christ to his home, yet they snarl at the honour of this unworthy host: they thought it too much happiness for a sinner, which themselves willingly neglected to sue for." What happens with Zaccheus at Jericho is a repetition of what happened two or three years before at Capernaum on occasion of a parallel entertainment in the house of Matthew. "As Jesus sat at meat in the house, behold, many publicans and sinners came and sat down with Him and His disciples. And when the Pharisees saw it, they said unto His disciples, Why eateth your Master with publicans and sinners? But when Jesus heard that, He said unto them, They that be whole need not a physician, but they that are sick."—S. Matt. ix. 9.

The scene of what follows with Zaccheus, and which is the climax of the occasion, is not quite clear, whether it occurred on the road after he had come down from the tree, or whether it occurred (as seems more probable) immediately in front of Zaccheus's house, before Jesus and His disciples entered—when

the murmuring of the crowd would be at its height, and the
statement of Zaccheus would be timely both to vindicate himself and Jesus, and when also our Lord's allusion to the house
and salvation together would be no less apt. Or perhaps the
most appropriate and effective of all points whereat the words
could have been spoken would be at the leave-taking, when
the meal was over, when the spiritual discourse with which
it had been associated had produced its full effect on Zaccheus,
when the Saviour and His disciples were now on the road to
resume the journey to Jerusalem, and when the crowd had
afresh been stirred to interest by the appearance of Jesus.[1]

At this solemn moment, stepping forward in the hearing and
sight of all, Zaccheus might well give relief to his fulness of
heart towards the Master, now that he belonged to His kingdom,
and understood it in its charity and righteousness. "And
Zaccheus stood, and said unto the Lord; Behold, Lord, the
half of my goods I give to the poor; and if I have taken any
thing from any man by false accusation, I restore him four-
fold." To give half of his wealth to the poor was a very
liberal thing indeed to be done in a man's lifetime, which
makes all the difference. There are many who are apparently
liberal at death; but such profusion is often more deserving
of condemnation than praise. It may be done selfishly as a
personal monument; it may be done spitefully to show malice
and defraud relatives; it may be done lovelessly, because a
man does not see what else he can do, when his own turn
has been served. It is only living gifts that yield true certifi-
cates of character as in God's sight, for they alone imply self-
denial.

The other branch of his statement, of four-fold restitution
for all extortion, implied a consciousness of integrity in the
main in his past life, that his wealth had not been gained
unscrupulously, but by lawful charges and savings. We have
here a brave challenge proceeding from an honest man who is

---

[1] This is the view taken by Archbishop Trench, 'Studies in the
Gospels,' 273.

now a converted and pious man, and takes all his neighbours and even his enemies to witness what course he is to pursue, and how he is ready to make full and instant amends for any past offences, even beyond the measure prescribed by any laws of God or man as to restitution. The law in Numbers (v. 7) is the principal *plus* one-fifth. David in the case of the ewe lamb (2 Samuel xii. 6) names four-fold, but that was in a heat of indignation.

Here comes in a question of interpretation. "I give," and "I restore,"—do these refer to the past or the future—*i.e.*, do they express a habit or a vow? Robertson of Brighton takes the *habit* view; while Stier, Trench, and Farrar take the *vow* side, and rightly as it would seem. Had Zaccheus been in the habit of bestowing half of his income year by year on the poor, he could not have done so without its being known, and helping to break down popular prejudice. Had that been his habit, he would then in Scripture take rank with Cornelius the centurion; and in that case it would have been quite inappropriate for the Lord to have said, "This day is salvation come to this house," and to have made allusion to "saving that which was lost," when the man had been living for years a devout life, full of charity and righteousness.

The true theory of Zaccheus is to begin with regarding him as a member of a bitterly hated and despised profession; as a man who had all along felt socially crushed and ill-used; who had doggedly stuck to his trade; who had made considerable money in it; who had carried on his trade on fair principles, although unpopular; who, however, felt sore at heart because his money was doing him no good; who missed sorely the goodwill of his neighbours, and got small comfort from anything he believed, or from any synagogue or temple services. Yet, like other children of Abraham, he cherished the Hope of Israel; he had heard of mighty works done by this Galilean Prophet; most of all, he had marked the stories of the Prophet's kindliness, that He had a fellow-feeling for sick folks and poor folks and houses visited by death, and did not join. in the hue and cry against lawful taxation and its collectors. I should like to see the good man myself, was his thought.

When he not only saw the Prophet, but received a recognition and kindness, and was publicly honoured and made a personal friend of and recognised, more than any man or man's house in all Jericho, this touch of sympathy and divine love suddenly ennobled Zaccheus with a happiness and self-respect unknown before. Moreover, while he listened to the good man's conversation during the meal, and saw the reverence with which His disciples regarded Him, and saw the ex-publican Levi respected and respecting like the rest, there was in his house and heart a strange sunshine. He could wish with his whole soul that this gentle Prophet would agree to stay at Jericho and sweeten its society by his new kingdom, where men are brothers, and where God is so loving and fatherly, and where prayer is so simple and free ; where thereby heaven is so near, and Paradise and the patriarchs are brought back.

But now the meal is over, and the Prophet and His company are starting on the weary road, and afresh has the crowd collected around them. This solemn moment of adieu, after a service of hospitality more blessed than any service ever known by him in synagogue or temple, brings Zaccheus's heart to his mouth, and impels him to speak out a hot vow to the living Messiah as a farewell word of love and thanks and promise, forming a declaration of attachment to His person and cause, now and henceforth. "Behold, Lord, the half of my goods I give to the poor ; and if I have taken any thing from any man by false accusation, I restore him four-fold."

This is Christianity true and deep : love to the person of Christ is its essence, and determination to act charitably and uprightly is its proof. For a thousand years past or more the Church has shown its high appreciation of this history of Zaccheus by selecting it as the Gospel of the day on occasion of the Consecration of Churches, or services commemorative of Consecration. The corresponding Epistle for use on the same occasion is Rev. xxi. 1-5. "In the latter we have the consummation of salvation in the new world, the tabernacle of God, of which all houses of God typically prophesy; in the former, the gentle commencement of salvation in the individual, in the midst of the confusion of the old world, in the hastening of the Redeemer to His cross. There all is new and openly revealed; here we have the new heart with its first confession wrought by secret grace. There is the tabernacle of God; here our own house, whose best guest is the Son of God abiding in it."[1]

How much of the world's wealth needs specially to be purified like that of Zaccheus! How many a calling which brings to men their income needs to be braced up by Christian principle, and then it would be harmless, and cause no shame or scandal!

Nought remains but the beautiful parting comment of the Saviour, clenching the vow of Zaccheus: "This day is salvation come to this house, forsomuch as he also is a son of Abraham. For the Son of man is come to seek and to save that which was lost."

With a sentence of meditation and prayer from Bishop Hall we may leave the subject: "O Saviour, when Zaccheus was above, and Thou wert below, Thou didst look up at him; now Thou art above and we below, Thou lookest down upon us; Thy mercy turns Thine eyes every way towards our necessities. Look down upon us that are not worthy to look up unto Thee, and find us out, that we may seek Thee."

[1] Stier on S. Luke xix. 27; also Trench, Studies in the Gospels, 274.

S. Mary Magdalene,

AND THE HOLY WOMEN.

DAY, JULY 22.

COLLECT.—*Largire nobis, clementissime Pater, quod sicut beata Maria Magdalena Unigenitum tuum super omnia diligendo suorum obtinuit veniam peccatorum: ita apud misericordiam tuam sempiternam nobis impetret beatitudinem.   Per eundem.*

For the Epistle.—Prov. xxxi. 10-31.
The Gospel.—S. Luke vii. 36-50.

Procul maligni cedite spiritus ;
Nunc imperanti cedite Numini,
Fessamque duris Magdalenam
Parcite nunc agitare pœnis.

Begone and afar, ye spirits of evil,
yield ye now to the God, the great
King :
and her of Magdala long afflicted
cease ye to vex with your bondage
hard.

Christi jubentis numine territi
Fugere septem : mox sibi reddita,
Te, Christe, sectatur unum,
Et memori tibi mente servit.

Quaking at the word of the Christ
commanding
fled seven fiends.   To herself restored,   [forth,
Mary, O Christ, follows Thee hence-
minist'ring aye from a grateful
heart.

Quin et cruenta de tabe pendulo
Christo litabat mille doloribus :
Quam vellet insontis magistri
Sola graves tolerare pœnas.

And ah me ! with woes unutter-
able
waited she on Christ as He bled on
the Rood :   [as He
for a Master so holy and harmless
her own life there could she have
laid down.

Miscere fletus sanguinis æmulos
Non cessat, adstans victima victimæ,
Christus, silendo, nil rependit :
  Quam melius probat hinc amantem.
    —*Brev. of Paris*, NEWMAN, 135.

Waiting a victim, nigh the Victim
    divine,   [flowing blood :
her flowing tears respond to His
no answer makes the Christ, in
    death all silent ;
but the Magdalene's love has re-
    ward yet to come.

Maria sacro saucia vulnere, [doles ?
Non jam dolendum quid Dominum
Semper renascens hic amoris
Unde tibi violentus ardor ?

O Mary, stricken by a holy woe,
why mournest thou when cause of
    grief is gone ?   [still
why hour by hour renewest thou
thy heart's wild wail of grief ?

Quem quæris ipso funeris in sinu,
Victo triumphat funere clarior,
Vivit : retecto jam sepulcro,
Ecce jacent revoluta saxa.

He whom in the cold cave thou
    seek'st
is victor over death, and lives more
    glorious   [ulchre ;
even than before : void is the sep-
lo ! the great stones lie there rolled
    back.

Myrrham quid affers, vanaque bal-
    sama ?
Hæc luce functis debita munera :
Mox ille donandos Olympo
Non eget his redivivus artus.

              [and balsam ?
Why vainly bring'st thou myrrh
those gifts men render to the dear
    departed :   [mould,
now blest with body of celestial
He needs not such averters of de-
    cay.

Ingens amantem te dolor indicat ;
Amans vicissim se Deus obtulit :
Agnosce vocem tu Magistri
Nomine te proprio vocantis.

              [love ;
Thy mighty grief proclaims thy
God in His love responsive comes to
    thee :
mark thou the Master's voice
thee calling by thy name of Mary.

Tu prima testis, primaque nuntia,
Velox in urbem protinus advola ;
Christique nutantes ministros
  Plena Deo propiore firma.
    —*Brev. of Paris*, NEWMAN, 137.

First witness as first herald of the
    Risen One,   [tidings,
haste to the holy city with the
and there Christ's drooping ser-
    vants fill
with thine own firm assurance.

"Now when Jesus was risen early the first day of the week,
He appeared first to Mary Magdalene, out of whom He
had cast seven devils."—S. MARK xvi. 9.

FOUR women of distinguished piety are mentioned in the
gospels as bearing the name of Mary. Nor is there any
risk of confounding one with another. The most eminent of
all is Mary the Blessed Virgin, the mother of Jesus. The
next in prominence is Mary Magdalene, whose career and
character are now to be traced. The third is Mary of Bethany,
the sister of Martha and Lazarus. The last is Mary the wife
of Cleophas or Alphæus, probably a sister of Mary the Virgin.
She is that "other Mary" who with Mary Magdalene attended
the body of Christ to the sepulchre when taken down from
the cross. This last Mary, wife of Cleophas, was the mother
of James the less and of Joses. Three of these four Marys
were present at the crucifixion of Jesus, the absent one being
Mary of Bethany; at least there is no mention anywhere of
her presence.

Although no confusion is ever or almost ever made among
these four, there is a very common and ancient confusion made
of one of them—viz., Mary Magdalene—with another woman
mentioned but not named in the gospels. There were two
occasions when, at an entertainment, the feet of Jesus were
anointed with precious ointment, and wiped with women's
tresses. One of these was at Bethany, when Martha served
and Mary her sister did the anointing, and Judas Iscariot
demurred to the waste of the ointment. The other occasion
was in Jerusalem in the house of a Pharisee named Simon,
when Simon himself demurred, not to the waste or expense,
but to the character of the woman. "This man, if He were
a prophet, would have known who and what manner of woman
this is that toucheth Him; for she is a sinner"—where "sinner"
clearly means a woman of no virtue, a dissolute woman. Many
have confounded Mary Magdalene with this woman. It is on
the assumption that they are the same that the name of Mag-

dalene Hospital or Asylum has been applied to institutions that have for their aim the reclamation of fallen women; on the same assumption that the Gospel for 22d July, the Day commemorative of S. Mary Magdalene, is S. Luke vii. 36-50, which contains the history of the anointing of Jesus in Simon the Pharisee's house; and on the same assumption that the old Latin hymns for Magdalene's Day make particular allusion to many grievous sins and their gracious forgiveness, as in this case, by Jesus. The hymn, *Lauda, Mater Ecclesia*, in the Breviary of York, actually confounds the woman in Simon's house with Mary Magdalene, and then confounds her again with Mary the sister of Lazarus. Moreover, the error is scores of times embodied in Church statuary and sacred painting by giving to the Magdalene a vase of alabaster in her hand, as S. Peter has a key or S. Paul a sword.

But there is not a particle of Scripture evidence to support this ancient and so general assumption. Probably the chief source of the confusion is that while S. Luke viii. 2 mentions the real Magdalene in connection with the holy women who ministered to Jesus of their substance, vii. 36-50 immediately precedes with the narrative of the anointing done by the anonymous woman, " who is a sinner." The allusion to the Magdalene and the others has no trace of disorderly life, but only of mental disease and bodily infirmity, which Jesus had healed, and for which, being in good worldly circumstances, they showed their gratitude by meeting the expenses of His table. " He went throughout every city and village, preaching and showing the glad tidings of the kingdom of God: and the twelve were with Him, and certain women, which had been healed of evil spirits and infirmities, Mary called Magdalene, out of whom went seven devils, and Joanna the wife of Chuza Herod's steward, and Susanna, and many others, which ministered unto Him of their substance." There is only one hint as to the previous history of Mary Magdalene, which occurs in S. Luke viii. 2, and in S. Mark xvi. 9—" Out of whom he had cast seven devils." To have been at one time under

demoniacal possession, the thrall of a company even of seven
evil spirits, is quite a different thing from having been a
person of dissolute life.   Jesus healed many demoniacs during
His ministry; but not one of these cases points to any connection with immorality.   Some of them took the outward
form of *dumbness;* several seem to have had a *violent* aspect,
as tearing of clothes, bursting of bonds, moody dwelling
among tombs, and using language under compulsion.   These
manifestations are more akin to certain forms of mania or
insanity than anything else we know of.   If those possessed
in that manner still retained some consciousness of their
proper selves thus enslaved and victimised by evil spirits,
their state must have been inexpressibly bitter, as constantly
linked to, and at the mercy of, a veritable fiend, with all his
crookedness and vileness and profanity.   To be shut up in a
dark and filthy dungeon, merely the body confined, would not
be so bad.   To be shut up in the company of criminals and
coarse companions in the same room would not be so bad; for
demoniacal possession implied that the loathsome companion
had intimate and mysterious access within the heart, mind, or
soul itself of the unhappy victim.   The cure of one thus
afflicted implied deliverance from a living and present hell.
Exodus from this state by the healing word of Jesus brought
back self-possession, with reason clear, the heart at peace, God
near in His grace and love, together with the daily use of
religious exercises and holy fellowship in the household of
faith.   Is a greater change or a greater boon than this possible
on earth?   This seems to have been the boon conferred by
Jesus on Mary Magdalene.

Restored to her right self, she seems to have been a woman
specially noble and tender of feeling, capable of appreciating
more than ordinary so marvellous a deliverance.   There seems
to have arisen in her soul from the day of her restoration to
reason a strong sense of gratitude,—that there was no reverence too deep, no offering too precious, to be rendered to her
divine Benefactor.   To minister to His wants, to be near His

person, to hear His doctrine, to behold His gentleness, to have a share in His kingdom,—this absorption, sympathy, and devotion to the divine Man constituted for her all happiness and duty. Such seems to have been the foundation and animating principle of her discipleship.

We now proceed to consider the special acts of piety with which her name is associated in the later chapters of the gospels. The first time when the name of Mary Magdalene occurs is in that comparatively early passage in S. Luke viii. already quoted, where she is mentioned as the foremost of a holy and devoted company of women who followed the Lord and His apostles in their sacred journeys and labours, specially ministering unto Jesus of their substance. This waiting upon Jesus existed at least during the second half of our Lord's ministry. Like the apostles themselves, these women, by being constant witnesses of Christ's miracles of mercy, hearers of His teaching, and sharers of His private intercourse, could not fail better to understand and appreciate all that pertained to our Lord's work and character. Yet, for all their faithfulness and usefulness, we find no further trace of them till we come to the closing scenes. There, however, they shine clearly forth, conspicuous like a cluster of stars on a dark night. In connection with the crucifixion they are twice mentioned ; at one time as standing in a group close by the cross, and at another (whether later or earlier, is not said) standing afar off, sorrowfully watching the sufferings and death of the Holy One. "Now there stood by the cross of Jesus His mother, and His mother's sister, Mary the wife of Cleophas, and Mary Magdalene. When therefore Jesus saw His mother, and the disciple standing by whom He loved, He saith unto His mother, Woman, behold thy son !" This shows the nearness of conversation from the cross, recorded by S. John, who was present. S. Matthew, after recording the centurion's words, "Truly, this was the Son of God," adds, "And many women were there beholding afar off, which followed Jesus from Galilee, ministering unto Him : among which was Mary Magdalene, and

Mary the mother of James and Joses, and the mother of Zebedee's children."

The next scene is on the evening of the same day, when the body of Jesus was taken down from the cross by Joseph of Arimathea, assisted by Nicodemus, and laid in the new tomb in Joseph's garden. "And there was Mary Magdalene, and the other Mary, sitting over against the sepulchre." Besides recording this watching at the tomb, S. Luke (xxiii. 56) adds their return to the city to prepare what was necessary for more careful and honourable burial. "And the women also, which came with Him from Galilee, followed after, and beheld the sepulchre, and how His body was laid. And they returned, and prepared spices and ointments; and rested the Sabbath-day, according to the commandment." Then at the earliest lawful moment possible this faithful company of holy women, venturing through the lingering darkness of night and to the entrance of the vaulted sepulchre, sought their Lord's body to render the intended tokens of affection. "And when the Sabbath was past, Mary Magdalene, and Mary the mother of James, and Salome, had bought sweet spices, that they might come and anoint Him." They were the first to discover the stone rolled away from the sepulchre ; to behold the attendant angels ; and to receive from them intimation of Christ's resurrection. And as they had the first tidings, so had they the first vision of the risen Saviour. This was to Mary Magdalene by herself, as is minutely narrated in S. John xx. But besides the appearance to her who was forbidden to touch Jesus at that time, there was another appearance not much later to the other holy women after they had seen the empty tomb and been spoken to by the angels. "And as they went to tell His disciples, behold, Jesus met them, saying, All hail ! And they came and held Him by the feet, and worshipped Him. Then said Jesus unto them, Be not afraid : go tell my brethren that they go into Galilee, and there shall they see me."—S. Matt. xxviii. 9.

The only other passage needful to be quoted in this connection is Acts i. 14, which refers to the time immediately preceding the day of Pentecost, when the apostles had witnessed their Lord's ascension, and were waiting in Jerusalem for the fulfilment of the great promise touching the Holy Ghost. "And when they were come in, they went up into an upper room, where abode both Peter, and James, and John. . . . These all continued with one accord in prayer and supplication, with the women, and Mary the mother of Jesus, and with His brethren."

By this method of passing from point to point in the Gospel history wherever the name of Mary Magdalene occurs, and joining these notices together, we are enabled to gain a glimpse of a life of extraordinary devotion, gratitude, and love to Jesus. As an example of faithfulness and affection, perhaps it is the most perfect and beautiful on record. Surely we are warranted to interpret in this light the fact of her being privileged as the first to behold and converse with the risen Saviour. That the earliness implied privilege is apparent in the case of S. Peter, to whom Jesus appeared before He did so to the other apostles. Now here, where a privilege was given even in advance of Peter, how strong and pure must have been the preceding faith and devotion! As Peter's early confession of Christ drew forth the promise, "Thou art Peter, and on this rock will I build my Church;" as the Syrophenician's meekness was rewarded by her daughter's cure; as S. John had his gentleness recognised in the legacy of the mother of Jesus; as the loving hospitality of Martha and Mary was repaid by the restoration of Lazarus,—so are we to see in Mary Magdalene's first beholding of the risen Christ the divine prize of a pre-eminent piety. Under this feeling it seems to have been in medieval times that a goodly number of churches were dedicated to S. Mary Magdalene; just as others were dedicated to S. Luke, S. Mark, S. John Baptist, besides to the apostles one by one. It was in the Chapel of the Hospital or Maison Dieu of S. Mary Magdalene in the Cowgate of Edinburgh that the first General Assembly was held of the Reformed Church of Scotland. There was a Magdalene Chapel in Dundee, the name of which survived in "Maut's Close" and "Magdalene Green."

Hospitals or Maisons Dieu dedicated to S. Mary Magdalene existed also in Linlithgow, Legerwood, Old Roxburgh, and Rutherford in Maxton.

Looking now to Mary Magdalene as the chief of the holy women who ministered to the Lord of their substance, we may widen the lesson of piety and privilege, and consider the mutual relation of the Gospel toward women, and of women toward the Gospel. No other religion is so favourable as Christianity to the weaker and gentler half of mankind. Islam does not credit women with the possession of a proper soul; while every religion that sanctions polygamy thereby stamps inferiority on the whole sex. Islam not only sanctions polygamy here, but tries to transplant it to heaven by the promise of four wives in glory to every true Moslem—a sensual view of heaven very different from the Saviour's doctrine that there "they neither marry, nor are given in marriage, but are as the angels of God."

One special blessing for which women are indebted to the Gospel is its assertion of the indissoluble nature of the marriage tie. Wherever divorce is easy, woman's position is insecure and mean. Another and wider phase of the same blessing is traceable in the whole circle of domestic life. How pointed is the New Testament in setting forth the respective duties of all those whom nature guides to live together under one roof, and with one interest in common to bind them sacredly to one another —husband and wife; father and mother; son and daughter; also, master and servant! Nor is it mere matter of regulation, defining each member's position relative to the others; but each position has a high and holy sanction of God in Christ. In the case of parents and children the rule is, " Children, obey your parents in the Lord : for this is right. And, ye fathers, provoke not your children to wrath : but bring them up in the nurture and admonition of the Lord." In the case of wives and husbands the rule is, " Wives, submit yourselves unto your own husbands, as unto the Lord. Husbands, love your wives, even as Christ also loved the Church, and gave Himself for it."

To these corresponds the rule for servant and master, " Servants, be obedient to them that are your masters according to the flesh, with fear and trembling, in singleness of your heart, as unto Christ. And, ye masters, do the same things unto them, forbearing threatening : knowing that your Master also is in heaven ; neither is there respect of persons with Him." These are the influences that have lent to home its sweetness and sanctity, the charm of home being essentially feminine—in wife, daughter, sister, and mother. And the key-note of this Gospel benediction was not gathered from experience, but struck at creation, "And the Lord God said, It is not good that man should be alone ; I will make him an help meet for him."

Correspondent to the holy women in the gospels who ministered of their substance to Jesus, and were most of all faithful in the agony and gloom of death, were those good women whose names abound in the Old Testament—Sarah, Rebekah, Rachel, Miriam, Hannah, Ruth, and the Shunamite. Besides these living examples, we have in Prov. xxxi. 10-31, —given for the Epistle for S. Mary Magdalene's Day in the Sarum Breviary—an ideal picture of womanly virtue and grace.

Just as the sufferings and death of Jesus affected Mary Magdalene, and the other Mary, and Salome, and the women from Galilee, more powerfully, and caused them to cluster round the foot of the cross when all the apostles except John were scattered in fear—just as the same women watched Christ's burial, and devoutly prepared spices and ointments worthy of a king, when the apostles were idle and despondent in Jerusalem —so have the services and mysteries of the Christian Church ever appealed with special success to the hearts and minds of women. This patent fact is sometimes alluded to with scorn, as if the special relation of the Gospel to women and well-trained children were a mark of weakness on both sides. But the real interpretation of the fact is, that it denotes strength in both, the strength that comes from purity and gentleness. In the Gospel there are certain elements of tenderness, patience, compassion, sympathy, hope and longing, peace and purity, which, so long as human nature and society continue, cannot fail to gain special consideration and favour from those women who are the truest and best representatives of their sex. And similarly, the example and instructions of devout women are sure in the long-run to make the deepest impression on the members of their own family circle, and even on many beyond. And thus in this feature of female piety we have a sure pledge of continued honour to this great feature of our faith.

Like as to Mary of Magdala, the root of the believer's attachment to the Saviour is remembrance of a great change passed through, wherein Jesus was his physician and benefactor. Although this change is now purely spiritual, yet how great and real is the difference between the state of the soul before and after conversion! We may still use the experience of the ancient demoniacs as a lively representation of it. Satanic influence is now more limited; it takes no longer the shape of deafness, or dumbness, or subjection to fury. Yet how terrible is the same influence in the common form of an unbelieving heart that is a prey to evil passions and evil thoughts—a heart prejudiced against Jesus Christ, against public worship, and against heaven as revealed in Scripture!

Like Mary of Magdala, who waited and watched in faith although in sorrow over her crucified Lord, so should we make special exercise of our Christian grace in connection with the celebration from time to time of our Lord's death. We need more of the habit of meditation on Christ and the chief scenes in His work on earth, especially those associated with Gethsemane, the Prætorium, Calvary, and the Entombment. Devotional reading of the closing chapters of the four gospels, above all at Communion seasons, is the simplest and best form which such meditation can take.

Considering that the proper sequel to all Christian zeal is the Magdalene-like privilege of knowing the risen Lord, that also is twofoldly within our reach—in the great Christian doctrine of the high-priesthood of Jesus at the right hand of the Father, and in the great promise of the Lord's second coming.

S. Peter,

THE APOSTLE.

ORATIONES.—*Deus qui beato Petro apostolo tuo collatis clavibus regni cælestis animas ligandi atque solvendi pontificium tradidisti: concede propitius ut intercessionis ejus auxilio a peccatorum nostrorum nexibus liberemur.   Qui vivis et.* (In Cathedrn S. Petri apostoli, February 22.)
> The Epistle.—1 Peter i. 1, 2.
> The Gospel.—S. Matt. xvi. 13-19.

Deus qui beatum Petrum apostolum a vinculis absolutum, illæsum abire fecisti: nostrorum, quæsumus, absolve vincula peccatorum, et omnia mala a nobis propiciatus exclude.   Per Dominum.   (Petri ad vincula, August 1.)
> For the Epistle.—Acts xii. 5-11.
> The Gospel.—S. Matt. xvi. 13-19.

Deus qui hodiernam diem apostolorum tuorum Petri et Pauli martyrio consecrasti: da ecclesiæ tuæ eorum in omnibus sequi præceptum, per quos religionis sumpsit exordium.   Per Dominum.   (Petri et Pauli apostolorum, June 29.)
> For the Epistle.—Acts xii. 5-11.
> The Gospel.—S. Matt. xvi. 13-19.

COLLECT.—*O Almighty God, who by Thy Son Jesus Christ didst give to Thy Apostle Saint Peter many excellent gifts, and commandedst him earnestly to feed Thy flock; Make, we beseech Thee, all Bishops and Pastors diligently to preach Thy Holy Word, and the people obediently to follow the same, that they may receive the crown of everlasting glory; through Jesus Christ our Lord.   Amen.*   (S. Peter's Day, June 29.)
> For the Epistle.—Acts xii. 1-11.
> The Gospel.—S. Matt. xvi. 13-19.

Forsaken once, and thrice denied,
The risen Lord gave pardon free,
Stood once again at Peter's side,
    And asked him, "Lov'st thou me ?"

How many times with faithless word
Have we denied His holy Name,
How oft forsaken our dear Lord,
    And shrunk when trial came !

Saint Peter, when the cock crew clear,
Went out and wept his broken faith ;
Strong as a rock through strife and fear,
    He served his Lord till death.

How oft his cowardice of heart
We have without his love sincere,
The sin without the sorrow's smart,
    The shame without the tear !

Oh oft forsaken, oft denied,
Forgive our shame, wash out our sin ;
Look on us from Thy father's side
    And let that sweet look win.

Hear when we call Thee from the deep,
Still walk beside us on the shore,
Give hands to work, and eyes to weep,
    And hearts to love Thee more.
        —Mrs C. F. ALEXANDER.

"Thou art the Christ, O Lord,
The Son of God most high."
For ever be adored
That Name in earth and sky,
In which, though mortal strength may fail,
The Saints of God at last prevail.

O surely he was blest
With blessedness unpriced,
Who, taught of God, confessed
The Godhead in the Christ !
For of Thy Church, Lord, Thou didst own
Thy Saint a true foundation-stone.

Thrice was he put to shame,
Thrice did the dauntless fall ;
But, oh, that look that came
From out the judgment-hall !
It pierced and broke the spell-bound heart,
And foiled the tempter's sifting art.

Thrice fallen, thrice restored !
The bitter lesson learnt,
That heart for Thee, O Lord,
With triple ardour burnt.
The cross he took he laid not down
Until he grasped the martyr's crown.

Oh bright triumphant faith !
Oh courage void of fears !
Oh love most stroug in death !
Oh penitential tears !
By these, Lord, keep us lest we fall,
And make us go where Thou shalt call.

—Bishop How.

"Thou art Peter, and upon this rock I will build my Church ;. and the gates of hell shall not prevail against it."—S. Matt. xvi. 18.

THE original name of S. Peter was Simeon or Simon, a name of common occurrence in Jewish families. His father was Jonas = John ; and this is applied to the apostle in two forms, "Simon, son of Jonas" and "Simon Bar-jona." His birthplace was Bethsaida, a town of Galilee, on the west side of the lake. His worldly calling was that of a fisherman. Both in this and in his Gospel calling he was closely joined with his brother Andrew. When their names first occur in S. John i. 40, Andrew has the precedence, and brings his brother to Jesus, telling beforehand, "we have found the Messias." Even at that first meeting Jesus performed the striking and decisive act of giving to Simon a new name—a deed in the highest spirit of prophecy. "And when Jesus beheld him, He said, Thou art Simon the son of Jona: thou

shalt be called Cephas, which is, by interpretation, Peter."—
(R. V. of 1881.)   Of this in S. John i. 42 we find the development on another occasion in S. Matt. xvi. 18 : "Thou
art Peter [*Petros*], and upon this rock [*petra*] I will build
my Church."

There is a feature in the record of the first call of the two
brothers that gives us a glimpse into their earlier religious
history.   "The next day after, John [Baptist] stood, and two
of his disciples ; and looking upon Jesus as He walked, he saith,
Behold the Lamb of God !   And the two disciples heard him
speak, and followed Jesus.   One of the two which heard John
speak, and followed Him, was Andrew, Simon Peter's brother."
It is not said that Peter himself was also one of the Baptist's
disciples, but the likelihood is that he was, when we consider
the thorough sympathy between the brothers, and when we
further take into account that Andrew's companion when the
Lamb of God was pointed out was S. John the Evangelist,
who all through the New Testament appears as the dear
friend of S. Peter.   Moreover, Andrew seems to have been
more to the Baptist than a common disciple ; he appears like
a personal friend in privileged converse.   This relation to the
preparatory ministry of John, certain in the case of Andrew,
and highly probable in the case of Peter, indicates to us the
bent of mind in the family, and opportunity of training.   At
this point Peter was probably a man in middle life, for we
afterwards find him as one of the oldest of the apostles, a circumstance which causes him to speak sometimes representa-
tively for the rest.

An interval of perhaps two or three months intervenes ; once
more the two brothers are by the side of the lake, and Jesus
has now begun His more active ministry.   The people in considerable numbers are following, anxious to hear the new
Prophet's words, and to witness His mighty works.   To gain
a better position from which to address the crowd, Jesus enters
into the fishing - boat of the sons of Jonas.   When the discourse was finished, Simon having been doubtless an attentive

listener, Jesus directed the owners to push the boat farther out and drop their nets. This was done, although the whole of the previous night had been unsuccessful. The result was an immense and evidently miraculous draught—a kind of sign peculiarly appreciable by Simon, and which impressed him so strongly that he exclaimed, "Depart from me; for I am a sinful man, O Lord." On this Jesus called him to follow Him as an apostle, and turned the sign just witnessed into a prophetic figure of Simon's new calling and of its success. "Fear not; from henceforth thou shalt catch men." Here already we perceive much of what later events confirm as characteristic of the man. He is earnest almost to vehemency; he has a lively simple faith, to which he entirely yields himself, and by which he is suddenly carried too far; he is a man of sudden and generous impulse, true-hearted and outspoken.

To these two scenes there are seven to be added within the compass of the gospels which mark the training through which the apostle passed. Besides these, in order to show the peculiarly close relation of Peter to Jesus, we must include a series of three solemn occasions when Peter, in connection with James and John, was privileged beyond the rest of the twelve. These occasions were—the raising of Jairus's daughter, the scene of the Transfiguration, and the scene in the garden of Gethsemane,—all fitted to inspire and confirm faith in Jesus as a Prophet with a wonderful commission, which at one time led Him to scenes of heavenly glory, and at another to a bitterness of experience that stood in some dark relation to the sinner's deepest anguish and God's fiercest judgment.

We may review in rapid succession a series of four incidents, the first instalment of the above seven, wherein Peter is the prominent figure—viz., his walking on the sea, his avowal of Jesus as the Christ, his rash rejection of Christ's intimation of His death, and the washing of his feet (S. Matt. xiv. 22, xvi. 13, xvi. 21; S. John xiii. 4).

It was night and stormy, and in the storm were caught the disciples of the Lord, and tossed about for several hours in

great peril. In the fourth watch came help, but in a form
which at first only increased the disciples' alarm. What
seemed a storm-spirit resolved itself into their living prophetic
Master, who had come on an errand of comfort and aid. Peter
first and most strongly seized both—so much so that he asked
leave, received it, and used it to go to Jesus on the water.
But the step was too bold to be continuously sustained, and
the heroic attempt very soon declined to fear and a greater
danger than had been before Jesus appeared. On Peter's side
was a cry, "Lord, save me." And on Christ's side was a
reproof, "O thou of little faith, wherefore didst thou
doubt?"

The Saviour's ministry was at the next point well advanced,
and it was becoming the great question of the day, What
think ye of Christ? Who is this man of Nazareth? Jesus
Himself questioned His disciples, "Whom do men say that I
the Son of man am?" Some told what they had heard, but
Peter took the bolder course of telling his own mind, and that
without reserve, "Thou art the Christ, the Son of the living
God." This was wonderfully true, full, frank, and early. It
resembled a gleam of youthful genius, worthy of admiration
and encouragement. Such did it receive from Jesus on the
instant, and in words that would carry back Peter's thoughts
to his first interview with this Master, with whom a quick,
intimate, and mutual bond had been even then formed.
"Blessed art thou, Simon Bar-jona: for flesh and blood hath
not revealed it unto thee, but my Father which is in heaven.
And I say also unto thee, That thou art Peter, and upon this
rock I will build my Church; and the gates of hell shall not
prevail against it. And I will give unto thee the keys of the
kingdom of heaven: and whatsoever thou shalt bind on earth
shall be bound in heaven; and whatsoever thou shalt loose
on earth shall be loosed in heaven." Let us take these words
to mark Christ's great favour to S. Peter without reference to
the painful and endless controversy between Catholics and
Protestants as to their exact and full meaning; only this being

noted, that, in a general way, the Catholic interpretation has a more natural as a more hearty aspect.

But, just as Peter's boldness of faith in venturing on the water had its check in his partial sinking, so had this grand and early appreciation of the claims of Jesus its counterpoise too; for in the same chapter we find a further incident wherein, after Jesus had foretold His sufferings and death, this was demurred to by Peter, and deprecated in the words, "Lord, this be far from Thee." Such an idea was a flat contradiction to the real aim of Jesus in this world, and reduced to nullity the view already expressed by Peter. How severe was the rebuke administered by Jesus! "Peter, Get thee behind me, Satan: thou art an offence unto me; for thou savourest not the things that be of God, but those that be of men." This again is singularly characteristic of Peter: he had spoken in the eagerness of his love to his Lord, but that love was defectively enlightened regarding Christ's plan, and pointed in such a direction as would have done Jesus more injury than even the treason of Judas—hence in the rebuke the strong allusion to Satan.

Parallel to that error of hastiness in regard to Christ's words touching His death, was another impulsive speech at a later period when Jesus girded Himself with a towel to wash the feet of His disciples, in a great act of symbolism setting forth love, devotion, humility, and purity. Peter at first refused to receive the Lord's ministry of condescension, while misapprehending its purpose and importance. But no sooner had he gained a glimpse of what was being done, than he turns from the position of resistance to that of asking more than Jesus would yield or than the disciples required. "Lord, dost thou wash my feet?" "Thou shalt never wash my feet." "Lord, not my feet only, but also my hands and my head." Such were the wonderful changes of this honest, earnest, impulsive man.

There remains now, so far as the four gospels are concerned, only a closely connected series of three incidents, the second instalment of the above seven—viz., the vaunt of superior allegiance ; the denial thereafter and penitence ; his restoration (S. John xiii. 36 ; S. Matt. xxvi. 75 ; S. John xxi. 15). The washing of the disciples' feet by their Lord and Master im-, mediately preceded the Passover at which the Holy Supper was instituted ; the sad scene of the rash boast immediately followed the same event. The Saviour, when preparing to go forth to die, to be betrayed by a disciple, and when speaking of this final journey and doom, said that Peter could not follow Him now. Hereon Peter protested not only his willingness to follow, but also his readiness to lay down his life for Jesus' sake. This was as usual spoken warmly, and truthfully meant at the time ; but it was spoken in ignorance of his own weakness, and of the sudden temptation to which he was soon to be subjected. The great Judge of men, the reader of hearts and foreseer of events, revealed in startling words the coming truth or falsehood (either word is applicable) in all its sadness and shame. "Jesus answered him, Wilt thou lay down thy life for my sake ? Verily, verily, I say unto thee, The cock shall not crow, till thou hast denied me thrice."

No need to describe in detail the awful and complete fulfilment of this prediction. Only let us recall, on Peter's third denial, the things that happened,—viz., the look of Jesus on the poor perjured apostle ; his outgoing ; his bitter weeping. To an earnest soul like that of Peter, this was a fearful experience, and heavy must his heart have been day by day, day and night, with the remembrance of this transcendent sin and shame. And how would this bitterness of soul be intensified by what happened to Jesus Himself meanwhile ! There was first of all the crucifixion, then there was the dreary interval of entombment. Even when the resurrection came, and even though Peter himself was the first apostle to whom the risen Saviour appeared, there was still this burden on his heart : no explanation had taken place ; no direct forgiveness had been vouchsafed ; the forfeited place had not been distinctly restored.

The exceeding value of the third of the incidents above specified is, that it restores S. Peter to his Lord's heart and cause as before, and removes the burden from the apostle's soul.   Corresponding to the three times that Peter had denied his Master, are the three times that Jesus asks of him, "Lovest thou me?"   And correspondent to the three times that Peter in denying his Master had forfeited his apostolic commission, are the times when Jesus anew appoints him to apostolic labours, "Feed my lambs;" "Feed my sheep;" "Feed my sheep."   Thus in this threefoldness there was fulness of forgiveness and of restoration.   The dark blot was washed out.   The apostle began a new course.   The Saviour anew said to him, "Follow me," recalling the original summons three years or so previously given.

In this review we have gone over a greater series of nine events in the gospels wherein S. Peter is the prominent figure, and have instanced a smaller series of three events which mark the close relation in which he stood to his Master.   The gospels contain not a few other references to S. Peter, but the above embrace the great turning-points of his career, and show the lineaments of the man.   We must, however, also take into account the length of time over which these incidents extended; and the usual course and manner of life during that period when Peter with the other apostles enjoyed the company and converse of Jesus, hearing almost all His teaching, and witnessing almost all His works of power and mercy as He passed from village to village and from city to city.   It was this three years' familiarity and privilege which gave such darkness to the sin of Peter's fall; and it is the same circumstance which so exceedingly magnifies the loving grace of Jesus in forgiving, uplifting, and restoring one who had fallen so far.

In the further part of S. Peter's history given in the Acts we find the apostle's character greatly altered and improved: he is no longer rash and impulsive, but manifests a dignity and firmness more consistent with the new name given to him

by the Lord at their first meeting. The change, while decided
and permanent, did not destroy the former lineaments of his
character. These still remain and mark the natural and moral
identity of the man, but they are henceforth influenced by a
faith and love not so liable to fluctuation as before. We see
the same thing happening continually. Conversion does not,
as the sillier class of evangelicals suppose, mould all believers
into one monotonous pattern of creed, practice, or spiritual
taste. There is as much and healthy variety among true
Christians as there is among the most worldly and wicked of
mankind. Every man has certain peculiarities of heart, temper,
disposition, and thought about him; and it is the work of
God's grace through the Holy Ghost to consecrate these by
cleansing them and giving them right direction. So with
S. Peter; his old rashness becomes now a holy and well-
ordered zeal. He could never under any circumstances have
become a timid, bashful, backward man, like good, honest
Nicodemus : that was not the direction in which grace would
work here. The direction was this, to retain his forwardness,
but guide it and proportion it, so that it would not appear
when not wanted, and would not go beyond the point at which
it was wanted.

Two influences seem to have led to this blessed result in
S. Peter's later character and conduct. The one of these is
the abiding impression made by his Lord's death and resurrection; the other is the direct grace of God fulfilling the
Saviour's special personal promise and prayer, "Simon, Simon,
behold, Satan hath desired to have you, that he may sift you
as wheat : but I have prayed for thee, that thy faith fail not :
and when thou art converted, strengthen thy brethren."—S.
Luke xxii. 31.

In the book of the Acts S. Peter's name is the predominant
one in twelve out of the twenty-eight chapters, just as S. Paul's
name is in the other sixteen chapters. Where so much is to
be dealt with as twelve consecutive chapters, it will be enough
to mark the emphatic points in the narrative.

I. 15. At the election by lot of Matthias in preference to Joseph Barsabas Justus to fill the vacant place in the apostolic college, at a meeting of 120 disciples, "Peter stood up in the midst and spoke."

II. 14. At Pentecost, fifty days after the Passover, Peter delivered the first Christian sermon expository of the gift of the Holy Spirit as fulfilling the prophecy of Joel, and when 3000 were converted to the faith of Christ. "But Peter, standing up with the eleven, lifted up his voice, and said unto them, Ye men of Judea."

III. Peter and John at the ninth hour heal a lame man above forty years of age, whose begging-station was the Beautiful gate of the Temple ; whereafter Peter preaches a second time salvation through Jesus Christ.

IV. 8. The disciples now numbered 5000 : Peter and John were apprehended and imprisoned for a night ; and next day Peter boldly declared to the Council concerning Jesus, "This is the stone which was set at naught of you builders." "And being let go, they went to their own company, and reported all that the chief priests and elders had said unto them." Then in a thanksgiving service application was made of Psalm ii. to the occasion.

V. In the discipline and judgment on Ananias and Sapphira it is Peter who presides. Sick persons are healed by Peter's shadow. He is imprisoned, but an angel opens the prison-door : is again brought before the Sanhedrim, but, on the advice of Gamaliel, let go free after warning.

VIII. 20. Peter resists Simon Magus in Samaria, saying, "Thy money perish with thee."

IX. 32. At Lydda Peter heals Æneas of palsy after he had been bedridden eight years. At Joppa he raises from death the charitable disciple Tabitha Dorcas.

X. 5. At Joppa Peter has one vision, while at Cæsarea, Cornelius, centurion of the Italian band or cohort, has another. The Holy Ghost fell on them that heard the word ; and they were baptised ; whereafter the whole matter of the admission of Gentiles to the Christian Church was reported by Peter to the apostles at Jerusalem.

XII. 5. Peter was imprisoned by Herod Antipas, who had just beheaded James the brother of John, and intended Peter as a second victim. The day before his intended death, the apostle was liberated by an angel. This great deliverance was made the subject of a special commemoration on 1st August in the early Church.

XV. 6. At the first Church Council in Jerusalem, when the question of the continuance of circumcision and Jewish ordinances was discussed, Peter spoke in strong terms for freedom, and supported his view by referring to the case of Cornelius, where the Holy Ghost was given as to others. And yet at Antioch Peter was rebuked by Paul for dissembling on this point in the presence of Bishop James of Jerusalem (Gal. ii. 11).

After the Council at Jerusalem, there is little more in Scripture of S. Peter's personal history beyond a very few hints in his own epistles, and yet he survived for fourteen or fifteen years. One hint touches his very friendly relation to Mark the evangelist, from whom he sends a salutation, "Marcus my son" (saluteth you) (1. v. 13); so that at this point Mark was with the apostle. Now the tradition as to the second gospel is, that it was written at Rome, and for Romans specially, and under S. Peter's guidance. This hint seems contradicted by another in the same verse. "The church that is at Babylon, elected together with you, saluteth you." Here, however, church is untenable, being a mere guess of a suitable noun. An easier way is to supply nothing, but take the feminine adjective as denoting a female disciple sending a salutation along with that of S. Mark. And what simpler than to take the apostle's wife as the disciple, especially when the very next clause conjoins a salutation from the apostle's son (in the faith)? Babylon, according to early and almost universal tradition, is not the city on the Euphrates, but a name for Rome, just as in Rev. xvii. Thus all may accord with Rome as the apostle's place of writing his epistle to the Diaspora on the north and west shores of the Black Sea. In these dispersed Jews S. Peter had a two-fold interest—as the apostle of the circumcision, according to the arrangement with S. Paul in Gal. ii. 9—because he had visited them at a certain point in his travels, probably 49-59 A.D., and because he wished to warn and guide them as to certain trials and dangers. There are a few more personal hints in the second epistle. As to the date of writing, it was very near the apostle's end (i. 14). New troubles for the Church are indicated in ii. 1, 10, iii. 3. The reference to S. Paul in iii. 15 is specially interesting in view of the early meeting and fare-well of the two great apostles on the day of their martyrdom. A doctrinal feature of the two epistles is seen in four passages relative to Noah, the judgment, and the intermediate state (1. iii. 20, 1. iv. 6, 2. ii. 5, 2. iii. 6), and yet these mysterious passages have a real basis in the gospels (S. Matt. xxiv. 37, 38, xxv. 46 ; S. Luke xiii. 23, xvii. 26-30).

Far more than in any other apostle, tradition has been busy in gathering incidents to attach to the history of S. Peter. Partly this is natural, because no other man save S. Paul occupied so large a space in the early Church. Partly it is questionable, because the apostle's greatness is mixed up with the claims of one particular bishopric to an inheritance of his greatness. On the other hand, the sources of the Petrine tradi-tions have been subjected to keen research and criticism of en-venomed enemies who have had a *cacoethes dubitandi et negandi*, as others have had a scribbling or speechifying disease. Tradi-tion as to S. Peter has not only continued his history beyond the point of its being dropped in Scripture, but has also (which is less common) inserted parentheses here and there between the Scripture incidents. Nearly all of these ecclesiastical traditions contain genuine historical facts or statements with a very high degree of probability, notwithstanding the rage of ultra-Protestant controversialists, who are blinded by prejudice and often write with unchristian malice. The following is an outline of these traditions.

Four years after our Lord's death—*i.e.*, 33 A.D. (the real date of birth being 4 B.C.)—Peter left Jerusalem for Antioch, where he laboured seven years and was succeeded by Euodius. But during this period neither his home nor work was continuous there, for in 37 A.D. Paul met him at Jerusalem and stayed with him fifteen days (Gal. i. 18). It was during this Antioch period that Peter visited the Jews of the Diaspora in Pontus, Galatia, Cappadocia, Asia, and Bithynia, to whom afterwards he wrote his epistle.

In 40 A.D., after the murder of James the brother of John by Herod, and after the death of the mother of Jesus, the apostles separated to labour in different parts, and Peter's choice as his sphere was Rome. After he had begun there he travelled to Jerusalem and shared in the persecution by Herod, and on being delivered from prison by the angel, returned to Rome, which is the " other place " in Acts xii. 17. In 49 A.D. a decree of Claudius against the Jews drove Peter with them from Rome, so that he was in Jerusalem in 51 A.D. at the Council of Jerusalem. On leaving Jerusalem he revisited Antioch, and it was now that he received the rebuke from Paul as stated in Gal. ii. 11.

On his return to Rome this time the apostle changed his abode from the Transtevere quarter, where hitherto he had lived among his countrymen, to the house of the Senator Pudens (named in 2 Tim. iv. 21) on the Viminal Hill, where he baptised Pudens and his two daughters, Praxedis and Pudentiana, the church of S. Pudentiana standing on the site of the house of Pudens. The Roman Christians who met S. Paul at Tres Tabernæ (Acts xxviii. 15) were sent by Peter. While at Rome S. Peter encountered his old enemy of Acts viii. 20, Simon Magus of Samaria, whose sorcery was in favour with people and emperor; but he experienced an exposure and judgment on descending ignominiously and breaking his limbs as the issue of an attempt at flying, the judgment following on prayer by the two apostles. Persecution of Christians arose, 64 A.D., partly from Nero's blaming them with his own crime of setting the city on fire, and partly in revenge for the defeat of Simon Magus.   In the persecution Peter was urged to flee, and taking the Via Appia, when he had got beyond the Porta Capena, he met the Saviour, to whom he said, " *Domine, quo vadis ?* " (" Lord, whither goest Thou ?"), and got for answer, " *Iterum crucifigi* " (" To be crucified again "). Under this rebuke the apostle returned to the city to meet his fate, and was imprisoned in the Tullianum or Mamertine.

Paul had become involved in the same persecution ; and the same day, but at different parts of Rome, was fixed for their deaths.   The two apostles met and embraced, and parted on the Via Ostia at a spot marked by a small oratory.   S. Paul suffered by beheading at the Three Fountains, which sprang up where his head fell and rebounded.   S. Peter suffered by crucifixion, head downwards, on Janiculum, beyond the Tiber, the place of his first residence among the Jews.   The death of S. Peter was in the thirteenth year of Nero, and after he had been twenty-five years Bishop of Rome.   It is this double martyrdom of the two greatest men among the apostles that is commemorated on 29th June.   The following hymn for the day, as given in the Sarum Breviary, is traceable to the sixth century, and was used in the Anglo - Saxon Church :—

<table>
<tr><td>

Aurea luce et decore roseo
Lux lucis omne perfudisti seculum
Decorans cœlos inclyto martyrio
Hac sacra die quæ dat reis veniam.

</td><td>

It is no earthly summer's ray
   That sheds this golden brightness round,
Crowning with heavenly light the day
   The Princes of the Church were crowned.

</td></tr>
<tr><td>

Janitor cœli, doctor orbis pariter
Judices secli, vera mundi lumina
Per crucem alter, alter ense triumphans
Vitæ senatum laureati possident.

</td><td>

The blessed Seer, to whom were given   [school;
   The hearts of men to teach and
And he that keeps the keys of heaven
   For those on earth that own his rule.

</td></tr>
</table>

Jam bone pastor Petre clemens
accipe   [cula
Vota precantum : et peccati viu-
Resolve tibi potestate tradita
Qua cunctis cœlum verbo claudis,
aperis.

Doctor egregie Paule, mores in-
strue   [satage :
Et mente polum nos transferre
Donec perfectum largiatur plenius,
Evacuato quod ex parte gerimus.

Olivæ binæ pietatis unicæ,   [mæ
Fide devotos, spe robustos maxi-
Fonte repletos caritatis geminæ,
Post mortem carnis impetrate
vivere.

Fathers of mighty Rome ! whose
word   [death,
Shall pass the doom of life or
By humble cross and bleeding sword
Well have they won their laurel
wreath.

O happy Rome ! made holy now
By these two martyrs' glorious
blood,
Earth's best and fairest cities bow,
By thy superior claims subdued.

For thou alone art worth them all,
City of martyrs ! thou alone
Canst cheer our pilgrim hearts, and
call   [throne.
The Saviour's sheep to Peter's
—F. W. Faber.[1]

The weak points in the traditionary accounts of S. Peter are
chiefly two. First, the alleged seven years' episcopate, 33-40
A.D., at Antioch, does not fit well into Acts xi. 19-30, which
associates Barnabas and Paul with the Church there. But as
Antioch was a Christian stronghold, and not remote from
Jerusalem, Peter appears to have been repeatedly there, and
more so as he travelled considerably, and along with his wife.
Even at Corinth there were disciples who used his name for
party purposes (1 Cor. ix. 5). Secondly, there is no real
evidence for the alleged twenty-five years' episcopal rule of the
apostle at Rome. It should be observed that the claim is
made only with qualification, because it is admittedly mixed
up with long absences, and journeys voluntary and involuntary.
The closing residence and martyrdom at Rome ought frankly

[1] This translation, used in the modern Roman service, is not made
from the older hymn *Aurea luce* direct, but from a new version of it,
Decora lux æternitatis, given in Newman's ' Hymni Eccl.,' p. 284. There
is also a very fine hymn on the same subject on exactly the same lines,
Felix per omnes festum mundi cardines, given in Newman, p. 356, from
the Breviary of York, and in the Anglo-Saxon Hymns printed by the
Surtees Soc., p. 160.

to be admitted, and also some amount of work for several months, or even a year. But any official rule for a whole quarter of a century is silently but significantly opposed by the absence of any greeting to S. Peter when, in 58 A.D., S. Paul wrote his Epistle to the Romans ; by a similar absence of allusion to Peter touching Paul's two whole years' stay in Rome in 61-63 A.D., as stated at the end of the Acts ; and by a third absence of allusion to Peter in the two Epistles to Timothy in S. Paul's latest writing very shortly before his own martyrdom.

But although the twenty-five years' primacy at Rome be rejected, there is still the original promise of the Lord in S. Matthew as to the rock and the keys, which Protestants, like the priest and Levite in the parable, persist in passing by on the other side, and taking no notice of, if they can help it. Now, this is simply not honest ; for it is a promise of no common order, and beyond all question it has received a rich historical fulfilment, and that in Rome above all places in the world. There has been an unbroken line of bishops in Rome from the first to the nineteenth century ; and these bishops have all honoured S. Peter as their founder. Moreover, whatever bigots may say, the Roman Church has been the mightiest branch, if not stem, of Christendom, and is so at this moment. It is silly nonsense of wilful ignorance or self-deception for a host of sects, constantly at war with one another, to try to combine against Rome, and call it corrupt, and the enemy of light and liberty, and on its way to extinction. In spite of the lavish abuse heaped on it for three centuries past, the Roman bishopric at this moment is as energetic and lifelike as any branch of the Church whatever, and much more lifelike than the majority of branches. It has its faults, and among its faults are exaggerated claims ; but it has done, and is still doing, more good work than any single Church that can be named in the past or the present. And therein lies the fulfilment of our Lord's great promise of the rock and the keys ; and the reason of the festival of Peter's Chair on 22d February.

One of the most important of all points connected with S. Peter is his very precious contribution to Christian doctrine and life. He has of course contributed nothing new or original, for Christ and the Spirit are the only lawful sources of faith; but in co-operation with Paul, John, and James, he has the credit of developing a special aspect of Christianity on the side of authority and practicalness. His first epistle (wisely selected by our own Leighton for exposition) is entitled to a higher place in Christian meditation and preaching than it has yet received among biassed Protestants, who are far too argumentative and controversial, but slender in devotion and virtue and efficient church government.

S. John,

EVANGELIST AND APOSTLE.

DAY, DECEMBER 27.

ORATIO.—*Ecclesiam tuam, quæsumus, Domine, benignus illustra: ut beati Johannis Apostoli tui et Evangelistæ illuminata doctrinis ad dona perveniat sempiterna. Per Dominum.*

The Epistle.—Ecclesiasticus xv. 1-6.
The Gospel.—S. John xxi. 19-24.

COLLECT.—*Merciful Lord, we beseech Thee to cast Thy bright beams of light upon Thy Church, that it being enlightened by the doctrine of Thy blessed Apostle and Evangelist Saint John, may so walk in the light of Thy truth that it may at length attain to the light of everlasting life; through Jesus Christ our Lord. Amen.*

The Epistle.—1 S. John i. 1-10.
The Gospel.—S. John xxi. 19-25.

The life which God's Incarnate Word
  Lived here below with men,
Three blest Evangelists record
  With heaven-inspirèd pen :

John soars on high with eagle wing,
  To God the Father's throne ;
And shows the mystery wherein
  The Word with God is One.

Best loved one, on his Saviour's breast
  Invited to recline,
'Twas thence he drew in moments blest
  Rich stores of truth divine.

There too with that angelic love
  Did he his bosom fill,
Which, once enkindled from above,
  Breathes in his pages still.

                   —E. CASWALL.

    An exile for the faith
    Of his Incarnate Lord,
Beyond the stars, beyond all space,
    The loved disciple soared ;

    There saw in glory Him
    Who liveth and was dead ;
There Judah's Lion and the Lamb
    That for our ransom bled ;

    There of the kingdom learnt
    The mysteries sublime ;
How sown in martyr's blood, the faith
    Should spread from clime to clime :

    There new Jerusalem
    Bathed in her Spouse's light,
Pure seat of bliss, his spirit saw,
    The land that hath no night :

    There heard through highest heaven
    The Alleluia sound,
The loud Amen that ever rolls
    The eternal throne around.

> He now calls all to drink
> Of streams of life their fill,
> From out the Lamb's clear fount : O Lord,
> In us this thirst instil ;
>
> And grant us now with him
> On those blest courts to gaze,
> To see the rainbow round the throne,
> And join those songs of praise.
>
> —E. Caswall.

"Again, the next day after, John stood, and two of his disciples; and looking upon Jesus as He walked, he saith, Behold the Lamb of God! And the two disciples heard him speak, and they followed Jesus."—S. John i. 35.

S. JOHN the Evangelist was one of the sons, probably the younger son, of Zebedee and Salome. Salome being a sister of the Blessed Virgin Mary, her son was first cousin to our Lord. The manner in which the two brothers James and John are designated as Zebedee's children indicates that the father was a well-known man, holding a respectable social position. This idea is confirmed by his having hired servants in his employment; and still more by the fact that Salome was one of the holy women who ministered to Jesus of their substance, and at His death prepared costly spices for His embalming. In the same connection it has been customary to recall that at our Saviour's trial John shows acquaintance of a personal kind with the High Priest. And yet further confirmation appears in the house of John being chosen by Jesus on the cross for the future home of Mary His mother ; for no one would think of adding in that way another inmate to any poor struggling household.

The real commencement of the spiritual history of S. John lies in our text, where he informs us that Andrew (Peter's brother) and himself were disciples of the Baptist; and that when their first master pointed out Jesus as the Lamb of God, they at once followed and accepted Jesus as their Master henceforth. It was at the same date that Peter himself, through the instrumentality of Andrew, was brought into contact and discipleship with Jesus. So that here also we have the root of the spiritual friendship that afterwards so notably·existed between Peter and John—meeting us in their joint visit to the empty sepulchre, and in their joint entry into the Temple when the lame man was healed at the Beautiful gate.

It is worthy of observation how readily John followed Jesus on His being clearly and authoritatively pointed out by the Baptist as the promised Messiah. The token of great confidence thereby shown in the Baptist's teaching was a happy augury of a like confidence and impressibleness for the still more potent teaching of Jesus. And this was just what was realised as months and years passed on of Christian discipleship; for John became one of a group of three attached to Jesus by special ties of personal affection and devotion. Peter, James, and John were chosen from the twelve to witness the raising of Jairus's daughter; the glory on the Mount; and the agony in the garden. And even of the three John was unquestionably the first; as is proven by his usual seat next to Jesus and leaning on His bosom; and still more decisively by the legacy on the cross, as also in express words in his attribute twice occurring of "the disciple whom Jesus loved," an epithet recalling the distinction of David as "the man after God's own heart."

> " Much he asked in loving wonder,
>   On Thy bosom leaning, Lord !
> In that secret place of thunder,
>   Answer kind didst Thou accord,
> Wisdom for Thy Church to ponder
>   Till the day of dread award."
> —KEBLE, on *S. John's Day*.

But this attribute of the beloved disciple suggests to us that John, in company with his brother, had been early called by Jesus, Boanerges—a name which points in another and almost opposite direction from affection, for it means "sons of thunder," and refers more immediately to their intolerant and cruel zeal when they were for calling down fire from heaven on an unbelieving and inhospitable village—a false zeal which Jesus rebuked by the word, "Ye know not what manner of spirit ye are of." This incongruity of sweet water and bitter from the same fountain is a characteristic still of those who as "evangelicals" claim greatest nearness to Jesus, for they above all men sharing the Christian name are inclined to curse and persecute those who differ even a little from them. The disposition of the super-evangelical is one which Jesus has tenderly presented yet clearly exposed in the servants in the parable of the tares among the wheat, "Wilt thou then that we go and gather them up? But he said, Nay; lest, while ye gather up the tares, ye root up also the wheat with them."

Kindred to this fault of facile ecclesiastical banning is another early flaw in the beloved disciple, wherein he is the precursor of much ecclesiastical ambition and place-hunting. But here John stands in company with mother and brother. "Then came to Jesus the mother of Zebedee's children with her sons, worshipping Him, and desiring a certain thing of Him. And He said unto her, What wilt thou? She saith unto Him, Grant that these my two sons may sit, the one on Thy right hand, and the other on the left, in Thy kingdom." It was natural that the ten should be moved with indignation when they heard of this petition, which, though based on a high and lively view of Christ's destiny, proposed to utilise the estimate for the promotion of private greed. Yet another instance is recorded in which John manifests an exclusive and over-zealous spirit requiring correction. "John answered Him, saying, Master, we saw one casting out devils in Thy name, and he followeth not us: and we forbade him, because he followeth not us. But Jesus said, Forbid him not: for there is no man which shall do a miracle in my name, that can lightly speak evil of me. For he that is not against us is on our part." —Mark ix. 38.

These four incidents—the name Boanerges from Jesus, the desire of immediate judgment on the Samaritan village, the ambition of the two archbishoprics, and the prohibition of the unenrolled worker—are the only unfavourable traits known of the beloved disciple.   They all point in one direction, and mark a spirit aiming high, but needing both curb and guidance before it can be in unison with the character of Jesus and the sober principles of His kingdom.   Such chastening and toning down, John seems to have received with comparative ease and earliness under the teaching of the great Master.

We hear of and can trace no continuance of these blemishes in the later part of the apostle's history, even when we confine ourselves to the first division of his career as contained in the gospels.   The only thing at all similar is the strong passage in his second epistle against entertaining those who abide not in the doctrine of Christ.   "If there come any unto you, and bring not this doctrine, receive him not into your house, neither bid him God speed : for he that biddeth him God speed is partaker of his evil deeds."   A kindred vehemence is traceable in a saying in the first epistle, "If we say that we have fellowship with Him, and walk in darkness, we lie, and do not the truth."   Similarly, on the authority of Polycarp, who was a disciple of John, Eusebius relates that once in Ephesus, when the apostle entered a public bath and saw the heretic Cerinthus, he turned back saying, "Let us flee, lest the building should fall that contains Cerinthus, the enemy of the truth."   This legend, if accepted, reveals a glimpse of his old intolerance and excess of zeal.

In the Gospel history few special incidents are recorded of S. John ; but from the fulness with which he himself preserves the Saviour's discourses, it is evident that he must have been one of the most attentive and receptive of all the apostles. And this is increased when we consider the long period generally admitted to have elapsed before the fourth gospel with its rich treasure of the Lord's words was written, probably in 96 A.D.—*i.e.*, more than sixty years after the crucifixion. Laying full stress on John's quiet earnest watchfulness of Christ's conversation, and on his deep personal sympathy with Jesus all through the three precious years of apostolic training, we come to that point whereat he shines forth for fidelity and boldness far beyond any of the chosen twelve. When, at the crisis of the betrayal, trial, and crucifixion, all fled or held back, and Peter was guilty of denial, John, on the contrary, never deserted Jesus, but lingered near as a sorrowful helpless witness, animated by intense compassion and love. At the awful scene of Calvary he was the only believing disciple within speaking and hearing of the dying Redeemer, except the small company of the holy ministering women; love to Jesus proving in each case superior to all fear, whether of soldiers, rulers, or multitude. Partly in reward of this pre-eminent faithfulness did S. John receive from Jesus then and there the great legacy of love and confidence in the charge of the Blessed Mary.

How long the mother of Jesus survived with her meekness, piety, holy sorrow, and unparalleled reminiscences, to beautify and enrich the house of S. John, we know not. But that it was some considerable number of years we may infer from John's apparently continuing at Jerusalem until he left it to succeed S. Paul in the care of the churches in Asia. He was in Jerusalem, and (with James and Peter) is spoken of as a "pillar" of the Church when S. Paul made his second visit after his missionary journeys. Mary is traditionally said to have died in the forty-eighth year of the Christian era. If she thus survived the crucifixion of Jesus for fifteen years, and during all that period dwelt with S. John, what marvellous opportunity was here for John to learn from his aunt more than any living man ever could of the history, mind, and character of the Holy Child of Bethlehem and Nazareth! And yet it is not S. John, but S. Luke who is communicative as to the Saviour's early and more domestic history. John in his gospel entirely omits the Incarnation of the Son of God, so far as concerns the circumstances of the Nativity; and presents only that other and more mysterious side which reaches back through all eternity in the coexistence and unity of the several Persons of the Godhead. S. John in his gospel also omits the direct history of Christ's Baptism, the Last Supper, and the Ascension.

The last reference to S. John in his own gospel is that which corrects a current misrepresentation of certain words of Jesus touching John's end, as if Christ had predicted for him to survive till the second advent. "Jesus said not unto him, He shall not die ; but, If I will that he tarry till I come, what is that to thee?" The hint as to tarrying was indeed fulfilled ; for we have good authority, though not express Scripture, for believing that the beloved disciple survived every one of the apostles, dying at an advanced age, near or even above one hundred years.

In the Acts of the Apostles the allusions to S. John direct and indirect are the following :—He was present with the eleven on their return to Jerusalem from Olivet after the Ascension, and his name is third on the list in i. 13 : " Peter and James and John." His presence at Pentecost is implied, although not expressly mentioned. In the third chapter he is thrice named (1, 3, 11) as in close connection with Peter on occasion of the miraculous healing of the lame man at the Beautiful gate of the Temple. In chap. iv. 13, 19, he is twice named, again in connection with Peter as suffering a night's imprisonment, and then brought before the Council. The continuation of the narrative (v. 23) tells of their being let go, and their going "to their own company" to report the treatment which they had received in the Council. John's name is not expressed but is implied.'

The only further appearance, in Acts xv., is at the Council of Jerusalem in 50 A.D., where the speaking is done by Peter, and James the Lord's brother, now Bishop of Jerusalem. John is not named in the minutes of Council furnished by S. Luke, but his presence is certified by S. Paul (Gal. ii. 9); and his presence has this peculiarity, that it is the last trace of S. John in Jerusalem, that its record is associated with recognition of his high standing as one of the three " pillars of the Church," and that it is the only record we have of a meeting between S. John and S. Paul, fourteen years after the conversion of the latter. It was an entirely friendly meeting, because, although no public word of John's is mentioned, his special friends Peter and James were distinctly on the side of Paul and Barnabas on the occasion of the decree, which was valuable as giving to the two apostles to the Gentiles the full sanction of apostolic authority in the mother Church at Jerusalem for the admission of believers of the Gentiles without their submitting to the Jewish rite of circumcision and keeping the other points of Jewish observance.

In later life S. John's home and work were at Ephesus, and he had special charge of the seven churches in Asia, whose separate epistles form chapters ii. and iii. of the Apocalypse. The commendations and warnings that fill these epistles show in the midst of what ecclesiastical things good and bad the apostle was called to live and labour and die. At what date the transference to Ephesus took place, or at whose instance, we know not; nor do we know the date of the exile or retreat to Patmos, which was a small rocky isle in the Ægean, reachable from Ephesus in a day. Much has been written on the question, Was the apostle's exile to Patmos under Nero, who reigned 54-68 A.D., or was it under Domitian, 81-96 A.D.? If the former, then Revelation would be written about 68 A.D.; if the latter, then c. 95. The earlier date accords best with the inferior character of the Greek of Revelation, as indicating a point when the apostle had not long before left a Hebrew community to reside where Greek was spoken. It accords best with a period of special violence and change, when Paul and Peter were martyred, when Nero was at the height of his fury, when Jerusalem was nearing its fall, when the old order of things was ending. It accords best also with the Gospel and Epistle of John, that were to come about twenty years further on, when Greek had become familiar to the apostle, when his mind had recovered its peace after the fall of Jerusalem and cessation of the Temple service, and when the new world of Christian truth had come to be fully realised as the second advent (in a sense) of the Son of man. The Apocalypse in no small degree is an expansion of the twenty-fourth chapter of S. Matthew, and it is full of the old figures familiar to Ezekiel and Daniel. The book has been the favourite study of fanatics and dreamers, and too much neglected by quiet practical Christians. In recent days great advance has been made by scholarly and more sane interpreters, so that now a very large part of the book is rescued from controversy, and is no longer spitefully interpreted by one branch of the Church against another, nor madly mixed up with contemporary politics or guesses as to the world's end or millennial dreams. Whereas the English Lectionary of 1662 made use of only three chapters out of the twenty-two—viz., i., xix., xxii.—the new Lectionary of 1871 uses all except three,—viz., ix., where is the Apollyon difficulty; xiii., where is the too famous number of the beast; and xvii., where is the scarlet woman.

Apart from its difficult figures and shifting visions, the Apocalypse is remarkable for the way in which it opens heaven to us, and shows the kingly and priestly place there occupied by that Lamb of God which the Baptist had first pointed out to his namesake apostle. To a contemplative, affectionate, and earth-weaned spirit like that of S. John, what an appropriate reward and consummation was this privilege at Patmos! Specially dear to him must heaven have been, where Jesus and the Blessed Mary had gone before, and where Peter and James had also gone, and Paul too, the first great Ephesian church-planter. Yet of all the loved ones that heaven contained, practically the only one mentioned by name is Jesus Himself—He, however, how often, and with what circumstances of grandeur and glory! As for the Blessed Virgin, she is never once named, nor is she even alluded to; for in chapter xii. the woman clothed with the sun, and having the moon under her feet, and on her head a crown of twelve stars, is a figure for the Church of God.   Similarly there are no references to the apostles regarded as intercessors, but simply to them as servants of Christ in high honour in His kingdom.   While they are honoured as foundations in the wall of the city of New Jerusalem, and joining in celestial praise, they never appear as helping the prayers of Christians on earth.

Tradition assigns the origin of the Gospel of S. John to a solemn request and pressure by the Presbyters of Ephesus and neighbourhood that the venerable apostle, the last survivor of the twelve who had seen the Lord and were His commissioned witnesses, should confer one more boon on the Church before his departure, by doing what no other man living could, and giving a fresh and final account of the Lord's life as they had been used to hear it from him in precious particulars beyond what were familiar in the Church service in the writings of Matthew, Mark, and Luke.   It is said that the apostle withdrew voluntarily to Patmos as a retreat suitable for the composition of such a work; but enough for us to associate it with Ephesus, and to regard it as the ripest work of S. John, embodying twenty years of added experience of Asiatic Christendom, and recalling with the freshness of yesterday the old scenes and words of sixty years ago, especially those in and around Jerusalem.   The fourth gospel is that which will commend itself more and more to believers as they ripen in grace glorywards, being that which is pitched on the highest key.   The first three deal faithfully and well with the events of our Lord's life on earth, especially with his northern ministry in Galilee, the native province of the most of the twelve.   But the fourth gospel deals mainly with Christ's discourses, which show His mind and heart, and with the southern ministry, which, as regards the destiny of the nation and their official representatives, was the more decisive field of action, being the scene alike of atoning Death and vindication by Resurrection.   The other gospels are of the nature of memoirs, while this is akin to a great epic, an ideal work whose hero is the Son of God.   Notwithstanding the important things that John has left unnoticed—viz., Incarnation, Baptism, Last Supper, Ascension—his gospel has a wonderful plan of its own in four parts. First comes the sublime preface, containing the noblest and clearest of all statements of Christ's eternal and essential Godhead. Then in chapters i.-xii. follows a section of the book describing the public functions of Christ, how He taught in and about Jerusalem and met ever-growing hostility from the priests and rulers. Then in the second section of the book, in chapters xiii.-xx., comes the history of our Lord's Passion and Resurrection. And last of all, in a chapter of appendix, is a formal conclusion. Bishop Westcott has named as peculiarities of S. John's Gospel these four points—viz., exhibition of the mystical relation of the Son to the Father, the relation of the Redeemer to believers, the Spirit as the Comforter, and the importance of Love. Comparing the first three gospels with the last, Canon Farrar says:[1] "They had reported some of the public sermons of Jesus, but they had not preserved any memorial of such private discourses as that to Nicodemus and the woman of Samaria, or as those divine farewells delivered at the Last Supper. Nor, again, had they spoken of Christ's pre-existence; nor had they used that title of 'the Word,' which was now so frequently on the lips of S. John, and to which he gave such pregnant significance; nor did they furnish a final insight into the two natures in the one Person of the Son of man." The aim of the fourth gospel as a whole is stated by the evangelist himself at the close: "Many other signs truly did Jesus in the presence of His disciples, which are not written in this book: but these are written, that ye might believe that Jesus is the Christ, the Son of God; and that believing ye might have life through His name."

S. John's remaining book, his epistle (taking the first alone), is the latest part of the New Testament writings, and follows his gospel as a fresh presentation of leading principles of Christian life apart from narrative, and apart also from argu-

---

[1] Early Days of Christianity, ch. xxxi.

ment, so effectively and systematically used by S. Paul. There is no more authoritative or simple statement of Gospel truth than this final book in five short chapters, the ripest fruit of the earthly experience of the beloved disciple and the last survivor of the Apostolic College. All is clear, firm, peaceful here compared with the change and violence and mystery in the early Apocalypse. Yet the Church has dangers as great, though less noisy and violent. In the Apocalypse time, twenty years earlier or more, there was one coarse antichrist at Rome; now there are more numerous antichrists of a subtler type claiming the Christian name and fellowship. Against these in Gnostic and kindred heresies is S. John's final warning.

Two touching stories are told of the apostle's later days. One is of a young man intrusted to a certain presbyter to be trained as a Christian. Returning to the city, S. John inquired for the youth, and was distressed to hear that he had fallen into evil courses and become head of a band of robbers. The apostle at once mounted horse, and got a guide to show him the way to the robbers' hold. When they were made prisoners, he said this was what he wanted, as he desired to speak with their captain. When the youth saw the venerable John he began to tremble, and attempted to escape; but the apostle insisted on a conversation, which ended in the robber abandoning his crimes, and returning to enjoy all the privileges of the Church and lead an honourable life.

The other story is, that when the apostle was too frail to preach, he was carried to the church and placed in the midst of his flock, repeating often as he sat, " Little children, love one another." The people wondered at the monotony, but S. John replied, " It is the commandment of the Lord; and if this is done, enough is done."

The most reliable account of his end places his death in the hundredth year of the Christian era, at the age of ninety-four, making him twenty-five years old at the Crucifixion. His grave was regarded with superstitious reverence, and legends arose in mistaken honour to his name. His best and only monument is the inestimable treasure of his three books— Apocalypse, Gospel, and Epistle—so full of highest truth, charity, Christ, and heaven.

S. Andrew,

THE APOSTLE.

DAY, NOVEMBER 30.

ORATIO.—*Quæsumus, omnipotens Deus, ut beatus Andreas apostolus tuum pro nobis imploret auxilium: ut a cunctis reatibus absoluti a cunctis etiam periculis eruamur. Per Dominum.*

The Epistle.—Rom. x. 9-18.
The Gospel.—S. Matt. iv. 18-22.

COLLECT.—*Almighty God, who didst give such grace unto Thy holy apostle Saint Andrew, that he readily obeyed the calling of Thy Son Jesus Christ, and followed Him without delay; Grant unto us all that we, being called by Thy Holy Word, may forthwith give up ourselves obediently to fulfil Thy holy commandments; through the same Jesus Christ our Lord.* Amen.

The Epistle.—Rom. x. 9-21.
The Gospel.—S. Matt. iv. 18-22.

Jesus calls us ; o'er the tumult
Of our life's wild restless sea
Day by day His sweet voice soundeth,
Saying, "Christian, follow me : "

As of old Saint Andrew heard it
  By the Galilean lake,
Turned from home and toil and kindred,
  Leaving all for His dear sake.

Jesus calls us from the worship
  Of the vain world's golden store,
From each idol that would keep us,
  Saying, "Christian, love me more."

In our joys and in our sorrows,
  Days of toil and hours of ease,
Still He calls, in cares and pleasures,
  That we love Him more than these.

Jesus calls us : by Thy mercies,
  Saviour, make us hear Thy call,
Give our hearts to Thine obedience,
  Serve and love Thee best of all.
                    —Mrs C. F. ALEXANDER.

When brothers part for manhood's race,
  What gift may most endearing prove
To keep fond memory in her place,
  And certify a brother's love ?

Who art thou, that wouldst grave thy name
  Thus deeply in a brother's heart ?
Look on this saint, and learn to frame
  Thy love-charm with true Christian art.

First seek thy Saviour out, and dwell
  Beneath the shadow of His roof,
Till thou have scanned His features well,
  And known Him for the Christ by proof ;

Such proof as they are sure to find
  Who spend with Him their happy days,
Clean hands, and a self-ruling mind
  Ever in tune for love and praise.

Then, potent with the spell of Heaven,
  Go, and thine erring brother gain,
Entice him home to be forgiven,
  Till he, too, see his Saviour plain.
                    —KEBLE, *on S. Andrew's Day.*

"One of the two which heard John speak, and followed Him,
   was Andrew, Simon Peter's brother."—S. JOHN i. 40.

IN the case of the patron saint of Scotland, the apostle S.
   Andrew, while we cannot claim for him so large a place
in Scripture as for some others of the twelve, especially Peter
and John, yet have we regarding him more frequent notices
than in the majority of the twelve. In one particular he
occupies a very honourable position as the earliest of all "the
glorious company" in the date of his call, which, in the Greek
Church, gained him the epithet of Protoclet = first called ;
parallel to S. Stephen's attribute of Protomartyr.

It is noticeable that our chief information touching Andrew
is given in the Gospel of S. John, and proceeds not only from
companionship in office, but from partnership in business, and
from a warm family friendship which united the sons of Zebedee to the sons of Jonas ; all four being fishers and joint
owners of boats and nets, but by Jesus turned into fishers of
men. We can note three stages in the call and appointment
of Andrew. The first is recorded in S. John i. 35-42, and
marks the transition from discipleship with the Baptist to
discipleship with Jesus. The second is in Mark i. 14-20, also
in Matt. iv. 12-22, at the point when the Baptist was cast into
prison by Herod. The third is in Matt. x. 1-42, when the
full appointment to apostleship took place. As there are three
stages in the call, so are there further on three stages again in
the conveyance of the full commission : the first in S. John
xx. 21-23, when the Saviour, after His resurrection, breathed
on them, and gave authority to remit and retain sins ; the
second at the end of "the Great Forty Days," in Matt. xxviii.
16-20, when they were commissioned to teach and baptise ;
the third in Acts ii. 1, "when the day of Pentecost was
fully come."

At the earliest call of Andrew what happened was this :
The Saviour had been baptised, and the forty days in the wilderness had passed, and Jesus had returned to where the Bap-

tist still laboured surrounded by crowds of people, and by
some closer followers called disciples. On the very day of the
Lord's return from the wilderness had the Baptist pointed to
Him, saying, " Behold the Lamb of God, which taketh away
the sin of the world ! " Next day this testimony was repeated
by the Baptist, not for the crowd at large, but for the special
benefit of two of his disciples, one of whom was Andrew and
the other the evangelist John, who modestly refrains from
naming himself. " The two disciples heard him speak, and
followed Jesus." Their following was noted by Jesus, who
turned and addressed to them the question, " What seek ye ? "
Their reply was in Scots fashion by a question, " Rabbi, where
dwellest Thou ? " To which the Lord's answer was the extremely simple and direct one, " Come and see." The issue
was, " They came and saw where He dwelt, and abode with
Him that day : for it was about the tenth hour." The tenth
hour was four o'clock in the afternoon, so that they spent
several hours, the remainder of the day, and probably stayed
overnight with Jesus in whatever sort of temporary lodging
the Lord then occupied. The house where this occurred we
may pass over ; but we may well ponder the precious hours of
that first Christian conference between Jesus, Andrew, and
John. We may judge of the impression it made on John
when we find him so many years afterwards, in distant Ephesus, giving every detail of day and place and persons with such
wonderful reminiscence at the opening of his gospel. " Before
they lay down to sleep they knew and felt in their inmost
hearts that the kingdom of heaven had come, that the hopes
of long centuries were fulfilled, that they had been in the presence of Him who was the desire of all nations, the Priest
greater than Aaron, the Prophet greater than Moses, the King
greater than David, the true star of Jacob and sceptre of
Israel." [1]

Part of this first call of Andrew is beautifully associated
with his instrumentality in promoting the call of his brother

---

[1] Farrar, Life of Christ, ch. x.

Peter, who so soon attained to the first place among the twelve.
" He first findeth his own brother Simon, and saith unto him,
We have found the Messias.　And he brought him to Jesus.
And when Jesus beheld him, He said, Thou art Simon the son
of Jona : thou shalt be called Cephas, which is, by interpretation, Peter."　Under the expression " he first " lurks a curious
and precious meaning almost wholly concealed by John's
modesty—viz., that he did the same brotherly and Christian
service to James that Andrew did to Peter ; Andrew doing it
first, and John following the good example.　These, then, were
our Lord's first four disciples, and afterwards apostles ; in the
order of call, Andrew, John, Peter, James—a noble beginning
truly.

It is in the second stage of our Lord's ministry, when its
sphere is in Galilee and in Capernaum in particular, that the call
of these four disciples receives repetition and a fresh development ; as recorded in S. Matthew and S. Mark at a point when
the ministry of the Baptist was now closed by his imprisonment, but previous to his beheading.　In this interval between
the two calls there had taken place the following great Gospel
events—the further calls of Philip and Nathanael Bartholomew ;
the marriage at Cana with the first miracle ; Jesus' first visit to
Jerusalem, with the cleansing of the Temple and the conference
with Nicodemus ; the latter part of the Baptist's ministry and
testimony ; the return of Jesus from Jerusalem to Galilee
through Samaria, when at Jacob's well the discourse with the
woman took place, and His revelation of His office ; and, most
recently, at Cana the cure of the nobleman's son at Capernaum.
All these things, belonging to the Judean and early ministry of
Jesus, are consecutively recorded by S. John in his first four
chapters.　And it is specially the Judean ministry that S. John
records ; while it is mainly the northern Galilean ministry
that is recorded by the other three evangelists.

When we next meet the name of Andrew in the list of the
twelve as given in the three synoptic gospels, his place is
second in S. Matthew, next after Peter ; fourth in S. Mark,

after Peter, James, and John ; second in S. Luke, after Peter ;
but fourth in S. Luke's second list in Acts, after Peter, James,
and John.   This order is evidently guided by three facts—his
being brother to Peter, the earliness of his own call, and the
future distinction of Peter and John over Andrew in point of
work.   This to Andrew and the rest was far more than a call ;
it was a most solemn and final selection and ordination, preceded by a night of prayer on the part of the divine Head of the
Church, and followed by a most solemn charge to the twelve,
and by a full and careful outline of the new kingdom in its
great principles addressed both to the apostles and to the multitude who had gathered to hear and see the great Prophet,
without knowing that the Sermon on the Mount was in store
for them on the occasion.   In such circumstances, how would
the charge by the Lord, and a public sermon thereafter, in the
case of Andrew have a place in his memory and heart beside
the conversation of that first evening which he and John spent
by invitation in the Lord's lodging on the day after His return from the wilderness to the old scene of the Baptist's
ministry !

From this point onward through the course of our Lord's
ministry we come upon the apostle Andrew only three times
by name.   The first of the allusions is in S. John vi. 8, on
occasion of the miracle in Galilee of the feeding of the five
thousand.   "One of His disciples, Andrew, Simon Peter's
brother, saith unto Him, There is a lad here, which hath five
barley loaves, and two small fishes : but what are they among
so many ?"   Jesus had previously to this passed over Philip's
reply to the question, "Whence shall we buy bread, that these
may eat ?   Philip answered Him, two hundred pennyworth of
bread is not sufficient for them, that every one of them may
take a little."   It was on the fact supplied by Andrew that
the miracle proceeded ; and at the close they "filled twelve
baskets with the fragments of the five barley loaves, which
remained over and above unto them that had eaten.   Then
those men, when they had seen the miracle that Jesus did,

said, This is of a truth that prophet that should come into the world."

The next occasion of the three is in the same gospel (xii. 22), just after Palm Sunday, when Jesus made His entry into Jerusalem as the King of Zion, sitting on an ass's colt. Certain Greeks who came up to worship at the feast desired to see Jesus, and made this known to Philip. He hesitated to act alone, and consulted Andrew ; indicating by the choice that the two were friends, and that Andrew was recognised as a man of judgment and influence. "Philip cometh and telleth Andrew : and again Andrew and Philip tell Jesus." It is remarkable as a point of contact with these Greeks that both Philip and Andrew bore distinctly Greek names—and in these days names were given for definite reasons, and not founded on fancy or sound ; so that the having of genuine Greek names probably arose from family relationship to men of Greek extraction. But the main element of the incident was its close relation to the revelation then made by Jesus as to His immediately approaching end and its manner. "I, if I be lifted up from the earth, will draw all men unto me,"—a saying which followed on the miraculous voice which came from heaven, bearing thus for the third time the Father's testimony to the Son. To these Greeks, as to Philip and Andrew who introduced them, how precious in after-years would be this experience of the great and final Passover week of the Crucifixion ! what an aid to the faith of every one then privileged to see and hear !

To the same Passover week belongs the third occasion of the mention of Andrew's name in S. Mark xiii. 3. Our Lord in visiting the Temple had predicted its coming overthrow, when not one stone would be left upon another. "And as He sat upon the Mount of Olives, over against the Temple, Peter and James and John and Andrew asked Him privately, Tell us, when shall these things be ? and what shall be the sign when all these things shall be fulfilled ?" How lifelike and striking thus to find a confidential group at the end, consisting of the very same four whom we met at the beginning in S. John i. as the earliest called of the twelve! Only once more in the New Testament do we meet Andrew's name, in a formal list of the eleven in Acts i. 13, after their return to Jerusalem from witnessing our Lord's ascension, and before they proceeded to fill the place vacated by the betrayer of Jesus. And there the first four of the eleven names occur in exactly the same order as in the verse just quoted from S. Mark, thus furnishing an indication of Andrew's place and standing in the Apostolic College.

In leaving Scripture, as we now must needs do, further to trace our apostle, one of the things that meets us is that he is credited with the writing of two books called Acts of Andrew and Gospel of Andrew. These are mentioned by Eusebius, Epiphanius, and others: but their spurious character may be inferred from the fact that they are used by early heretics to prop up their irregular tenets; that they are deliberately shut out of the Canon of Scripture; and that so early as 500 A.D. they are expressly declared apocryphal by Pope Gelasius, one of the three great Pontiffs (Leo and Gregory being the other two) who did so much to regulate the ancient Church service.

As to the sphere of Andrew's labour when the apostles quitted Jerusalem to fulfil the great commission recorded at the end of S. Matthew, Scythia, Greece, and Thrace are variously named, and would agree well with the Grecian element already referred to in his career. On the ground of his Scythian mission Andrew has been selected as the patron saint of Russia. Thirty years after the crucifixion of Christ he met his death by crucifixion at Patræ in Achaia, on a special form of cross like the letter X, technically known as *crux decussata*. Patræ, now Patras, is a town on the northern end of Peloponnesus, near the entrance to the Gulf of Corinth. In classic times it was one of the four cities of the Achæan league, and gives its name to the Bay of Patras. It is said that the relics of Andrew were brought in 357 from Patræ to Constantinople (in company with the relics of Luke and Timothy),

to confer prestige on a splendid new church of the apostles there
erected by the Emperor Constantine the Great.   One thing
that corroborates these traditions by carrying us back a very
long way is, that Venerable Bede of Jarrow (b. 672, d. 735), a
most careful historian, wrote a hymn usually entitled *S. Andreas
alloquitur crucem*, versifying a passage quoted in Alban Butler's
'Lives of the Saints,' 30th November, of which the original
is in Lectio VI. for S. Andrew's Day in the Sarum Breviary.
In the nine Lections in the Sarum Breviary for S. Andrew's
Day, I.-V. are occupied with dialogue between the Proconsul
Egeas and the apostle, which we cannot suppose to be authentic,
but which yet has extraordinary verisimilitude and vigour.   It
is strange that the nine Lections of Salisbury are reduced to
three in the Aberdeen Breviary of Bishop Elphinstone.   Can
this arise from Aberdeen jealousy of St Andrews as the Scots
Metropolitan See ?

Salve, tropæum gloriæ,
Salve, sacrum victoriæ
Signum, Deus quo perditum
Mundum redemit mortuus.

Quondam genus mortalium
Metu premebas pallido,
At nunc reples fidelium
Amore læto pectora.

En ! ludus est credentium
Tuis frui complexibus,
Quæ tanta gignis gaudia,
Pandis polique januas.

Sic tu libens me suscipe,
Illius, alma, servulum,
Qui me redemit per tuam
Magister altus gloriam.

Sic fatur Andreas, crucis
Erecta cernens cornua,
Tradensque vestem militi,
Levatur in vitæ arborem.
—VENERABLE BEDE.

Cross whereon my Saviour bled,
  Dying to redeem our loss,
Now with living trophies spread,
  Welcome, welcome, happy cross !

Sickening once with hope delayed,
  Paling all our hearts with gloom,
Then a tree of life displayed,
  Budding with eternal bloom.

Cross ! thy loving arms embrace,
  Clasps my Saviour to my soul,
Heaven, to bring us face to face,
  Rending wide from pole to pole.

Where to buy me Jesus died,
  How shall I, poor serf, recline ;
To Thy gauging standard tied,
  Measure all his love with mine ?

Thus his cross beholding nigh,
  With its horns athwart the sky,
Andrew spake, then doffed his vest,
  Ere they lift him to his rest.
—H. KYNASTON.

Then as to the connection of Andrew with Scotland, whereby he became our national patron saint, whose day on 30th November is the first saints' day in the old Church Calendar, in deference to his being first called of the apostles, it happened thus: The original form of the story is, that S. Regulus or Rule, who in 360 flourished at Patras, and was custodier of the relics of S. Andrew, sailed with them towards Scotland, and was wrecked at Muckross = Boar's-point or Kilrymont, now St Andrews, where in 369 he erected a cross, and afterwards got from the Pictish king, Hungus, a great grant of land there. But this story confounds two or three distinct pieces of old local history. St Andrews was the site of an old Celtic church and monastery as far back as the time of S. Columba. Regulus or Rule, whose name to this day attaches to the tall square Tower, was an Irish monk, S. Riagail of Muic-inis = Boar-isle in Loch Derg, who visited Scotland in 573. About the same period, within ten or twenty years, another famous Irish saint, Cainnech or Kenneth, (b. 517, d. 598), lived in the monastery at St Andrews, then called Cill-righmonadh or Kilrymont. In this monastery, fully 100 years later—*i.e.*, in 731—during troubles and persecution in the north of England, a certain Bishop Acca of Hagustald or Hexham, on the Tyne between Newcastle and Carlisle, took refuge in the country of the Picts. Hexham was famous for its devotion to S. Andrew, and the exiled bishop seems to have carried certain relics of the apostle. And from this date the place bore its present name; and the city being the ecclesiastical capital of Scotland, its new patron saint became the patron saint of our nation. Moreover, the Pictish king, Hungus or Angus, gave large additional endowment to the place, in fulfilment of a vow at Athelstaneford in Lothian, to dedicate one-tenth of his inheritance to S. Andrew. Such is the historical clearing of the confused legend, as wrought out by Dr Skene in his 'Celtic Scotland,' vol. ii. pp. 271-277. Thus the relics of the apostle did not come direct from Greece, but had been venerated for some centuries in a monastery in Northumberland, which was then part of the Lothians.

Now there are many in our age who are utterly incredulous as to the existence of genuine relics, and who jeer at the whole system as a piece of debasing superstition. That short way, however, will not do. In these early days relics of the old servants of God, especially of those who had suffered martyrdom or done great mission work in converting whole provinces or kingdoms to the Gospel, were carefully treasured, apart from worship rendered to them. And surely such men deserved honour.

If any one is inclined to mock at religious relics, let him ponder the amazing fact that the present scientific and enlightened age is extremely busy collecting and preserving all sorts of secular relics, and yearly celebrating all sorts of secular birthdays, not to speak of jubilees and centenaries. In the case of Shakespeare there are museums where every scrap connected with him is carefully arranged, annotated, and venerated. The same holds good of our own national poet. A Burns snuff-box, shoe-buckle, old chair, scrap of MS., or first Kilmarnock edition makes a house famous. The average and annual proceedings which occur at a Burns Club festival on 25th January, were this the place realistically to describe the food, liquor, and sentiments, would form a curious *per contra* to even a crude medieval *feria* like a Breton *Pardon* or a German *Kirch-weih*. Let the two fashions, ancient and modern, saint and hero, be fairly weighed in the balance of reason, and surely it is ten times better sense to respect a silver-shrined arm-bone of S. Andrew in a Church festival, than to glorify over a Burns snuff-box or a Kilmarnock edition. And why should the one group be called idolaters, and not the other also?

It is a noble thing every S. Andrew's Day when the thriving colony of Scotsmen in London meet in connection with the Scottish Hospital, as it is called, founded in 1665 for the relief of indigent Scots in the metropolis, and organise a fresh year's work of patriotic charity, and encourage one another in the glorious history of their fatherland, which, though the smallest of the three kingdoms, is the most energetic and independent, both in Kirk and State.

We have a Scottish order of knighthood, called the Order of S. Andrew or of the Thistle, with the threatening motto befitting a brave land, *Nemo me impune lacesset.* This order goes back to the legend already referred to, that a St Andrew's Cross appeared in the sky to Achaius, King of Scots, and Hungus MacFergus, King of the Picts, as a sign of the victory which they should gain the following day over Athelstane, the general of Eadbert, king of Northumbria, and their vow on fulfilment of the prophecy to bear that cross on their ensigns and banners. The place where this cross appeared bears the name of Markle = Miracle, in the parish of Prestonkirk.[1] Thus is the very name of our ancient ecclesiastical metropolis, new named in 731, commemorative of an earlier Bannockburn, wherein a king of Scots and a king of Picts defeated and drove back an English invader. It is a Scottish version of the cross in the sky that appeared to Constantine with the motto, *Hoc signo vinces.*

While some parts of the Church legend regarding the apostle S. Andrew are open to question, it is certain history that since 731 A.D. he has counted as the patron saint of Scotland; that a vow associated with his cross and relics was made by King Angus at the battle of Athelstaneford; that thereafter relics, believed for centuries earlier to be his, were brought to the old monastery in the East Neuk of Fife; that the old name of Kilrymont was then changed to St Andrews; and that the church there was then enriched with fresh endowments. Farther back still we may rest assured of the truth of the apostle's death by crucifixion, c. 62 A.D., at Patræ; and we may safely believe that for thirty years he industriously served Christ in Greece and Scythia.

But for the main purpose of edification our preponderating

---

[1] Ritchie, Churches of S. Baldred, p. 123.

N

attention is due to the series of incidents contained in the gospels, particularly in that of S. John, his own and his brother's personal friend. There we learn of Andrew's first call at the Jordan; the renewal of the call in Galilee; the completion of it on the day of the Sermon on the Mount. There we meet the three incidents thereafter,—at the miracle of the feeding of the five thousand; the introducing of the Greeks at the last Passover; and the inquiry as to the date of the overthrow of the Temple. Thereafter comes the crowning fact of his presence at the meeting in Jerusalem between the Ascension and Pentecost. Although not in the foremost line of the twelve, Andrew is yet an honoured and active member of the Apostolic College.

S. Thomas,

THE APOSTLE.

DAY, DECEMBER 21.

ORATIO.—*Da nobis, quæsumus, Domine, beati apostoli tui Thomæ ita solennitatibus gloriari : ut ejus semper et patrociniis sublevemur, et fidem congrua devotione sectemur. Per Dominum.*

> The Epistle.—Eph. ii. 19-22.
> The Gospel.—S. John xx. 24-29.

COLLECT.—*Almighty and ever-living God, who for the more confirmation of the faith didst suffer thy holy apostle Thomas to be doubtful in Thy Son's resurrection ; Grant us so perfectly and without all doubt, to believe in Thy Son Jesus Christ, that our faith in Thy sight may never be reproved. Hear us, O Lord, through the same Jesus Christ, to whom, with Thee and*

the Holy Ghost, be all honour and glory, now and for evermore.
Amen.

The Epistle.—Eph. ii. 19-22.
The Gospel.—S. John xx. 24-31.

How oft, O Lord, Thy face hath shone
On doubting souls whose wills were true !
Thou Christ of Cephas and of John,
Thou art the Christ of Thomas too.

He loved Thee well, and calmly said,
" Come let us go and die with Him : "
Yet when Thine Easter-news was spread,
'Mid all its light his eyes were dim.

His brethren's word he would not take,
But craved to touch those hands of Thine :
The bruisèd reed Thou didst not break ;
He saw and hailed his LORD divine.

He saw Thee risen ; at once he rose
To full belief's unclouded height ;
And still through his confession flows
To Christian souls Thy life and light.

O Saviour, make Thy presence known
To all who doubt Thy Word and Thee ;
And teach them in that Word alone
To find the truth that sets them free.

And we who know how true Thou art,
And Thee as GOD and LORD adore,
Give us, we pray, a loyal heart,
To trust and love Thee more and more.
—Canon W. BRIGHT.

. . . One indeed I knew
In many a subtle question versed,
Who touched a jarring lyre at first,
But ever strove to make it true :

Perplext in faith, but pure in deeds,
At last he beat his music out.
There lives more faith in honest doubt,
Believe me, than in half the creeds.

> He fought his doubts and gathered strength,
>   He would not make his judgment blind,
>   He faced the spectres of the mind
> And laid them : thus he came at length
>
> To find a stronger faith his own ;
>   And Power was with him in the night,
>   Which makes the darkness and the light,
> And dwells not in the light alone.
>   —TENNYSON, *In Memoriam*, xcv.

" And Thomas answered and said unto Him, My Lord and
my God."—S. JOHN xx. 28.

ALTHOUGH the point of absorbing interest in this apostle's
history is his attitude towards the resurrection of our
Lord, there are a few things which require attention first.
Thrice in the Gospel of S. John, xi. 16, xx. 24, xxi. 2, and
there only, is given the Greek equivalent of the Hebrew name
Thomas, " who is called Didymus " = twin.   From the fact
that in the three Gospel lists of the twelve, which are mostly
arranged in pairs, the name of Thomas is linked with Matthew,
it has been supposed that these two were brothers and twins.
But the mere collocation of the names without other evidence
or hint is not a sufficient basis for the guess.   Another theory
of the Didymus name, is that it means the twin or double-
minded man, combining unbelief and faith as in S. James i. 8,
iv. 8, or like Esau and Jacob in Gen. xxv. 22.   It is further
supposed that the name was prophetically given by Jesus
Himself, as Peter to Simon, and Boanerges to the sons of
Zebedee ; but this also is a naked guess.

Besides the supreme incident in S. John xx. 24-29, there
are three other incidents all in the same gospel touching S.
Thomas—viz., a proposal on Christ's going to Lazarus, xi. 16 ;
a question put to Christ, xiv. 5 ; and Thomas's presence at
the Sea of Galilee after the resurrection, xxi. 2.   On S. John's
part this is the same peculiarity toward Thomas as already

seen in the case of Nicodemus, and afterwards to be seen again in the cases of Philip and Nathanael.

The first of these three incidents is the most important for the light it throws on the apostle's temperament. After hearing the message as to the sickness of Lazarus, Jesus remained two days in Peræa, and then intimated to His disciples His intention to go to Bethany. The disciples tried to dissuade Him on the ground of personal danger, "Master, the Jews of late sought to stone Thee ; and goest Thou thither again ? " But when others dissuaded, Thomas made proposal to go, even should it be at the cost of life to them as well as to Jesus. "Then said Thomas, which is called Didymus, unto his fellow-disciples, Let us also go, that we may die with Him." Here is love and boldness, and no reason to suspect the genuineness of either.

A little later, when our Saviour was speaking that part of his post-Communion address which mentions the many mansions in His Father's house and His going to prepare a place for His disciples, "And whither I go ye know, and the way ye know. Thomas saith unto Him, Lord, we know not whither Thou goest ; and how can we know the way ? " This is the interruption of a man who has more zeal than knowledge, a man whose mind was running materialistically. But however objectionable the interruption in form or source, we may be glad it happened, for it was the means of calling forth from the Lord that mighty name of Himself which has ever since been a chief Gospel motto, especially in the Latin alliteration, *Via, Veritas, Vita ;* "Jesus saith unto him, I am the way, the truth, and the life : no man cometh unto the Father, but by me."

The third incident wherein we meet Thomas, at the Sea of Galilee in company of six other apostles, who there saw and conversed with the risen Saviour, is mainly valuable as showing the close and blessed adhesion of Thomas to the apostolic company now when his temporary doubt was entirely overcome ; otherwise, it reveals no trait of character, as the two incidents preceding did.

Coming to the supreme incident in xx. 24-29, it is connected with two of the eleven appearances made by our Lord between resurrection and ascension. The two were fifth and sixth in order, and it will promote clearness to state the series up to this point. The first appearance of all was to Mary Magdalene, early in the morning of the first Lord's Day, and at the sepulchre. The next was still early the same morning, to the other Mary and Salome as they were returning from the tomb to Jerusalem. The third was on the afternoon of the same day, to Cleopas and the other disciple on the way from Jerusalem to Emmaus. The fourth was about the same time as the third, possibly before it, to Peter, by himself. The fifth was still the same day, but in the evening, and to ten of the apostles—*i.e.*, to all except Thomas. The sixth was on that day week (now called Low Sunday, and first after Easter), to the same ten as before, but now with the addition of Thomas.

The account of Thomas's thoughts and feelings regarding our Lord's death and resurrection naturally commences with noting the fact of his absence from the company of the apostles on the first occasion when Jesus reappeared among them : " But Thomas, one of the twelve, called Didymus, was not with them when Jesus came." For this absence there may possibly have been a sufficient cause ; but probably it arose from negligence, or, more probably still, from a feeling of melancholy and despondence that supervened in the peculiar temperament of the apostle after what he had seen in the crucifixion of his Master. The apostles seem, when Christ reappeared among them, to have been convened by appointment or for special prayer. Considering the date, so early after the crucifixion, and considering Christ's own pre-intimation of return, and looking to Thomas's subsequent unbelief, it can hardly be counted rash to suppose some degree of blame in our apostle, whereby he lost this first opportunity of acquaintance with the comforting doctrine of the rising of the Son of God from the dead.

"The other disciples therefore said unto him, We have seen the Lord. But he said unto them, Except I shall see in His hands the print of the nails, and put my finger into the print of the nails, and thrust my hand into His side, I will not believe." What a strange result is this on one apostle from an account solemnly accredited by the other ten ! Here they appear at the very start a house divided against itself : one faces ten with a boldly defiant contradiction, the subject of which is one of the most recent and essential matters of fact connected with the very Person of the Founder of Christianity. If one of their own number believes them not, how can they expect belief from enemies, or even from common disciples ?

There is something peculiarly stirring in observing the mental and moral movements of a man who, having fallen unawares into the wrong side of a question, opposes the truth earnestly and honestly, perhaps even stubbornly, until such time as greater light and deeper conviction reach him. Such a man, however, after having fought his way to the truth by the pathway of error and opposition, values it all the more afterwards, and is likely to become all the better a herald and defender of it. And that this doubt and conflict on the part of one of the eleven is put on record on the sacred page, is itself a token of the overwhelming testimony for Gospel facts. Scripture draws no veil over the faults of its greatest men : when truth demands it, the weakness and sin of Noah, Abraham, Moses, Aaron, David, Peter, Thomas are faithfully and circumstantially narrated. Of the Bible saints may be used, in a higher sense, the words of Joseph's brethren, " We are true men "—men truly with light and shadow according to life.

Thomas's failing seems to have had its origin in a disposition to hem in God's movements in providence and grace by a self-confident view of what was proper to a given end. Or if not wholly in presumption, partly in a kindred despondency because things have not followed our expectations, that we are unduly disappointed, and lose all hope of a good issue. When reflecting on Jesus' mission and death, Thomas quite omitted the idea of any further reappearance, deeming such useless or impossible. Rather than give up his preconceived idea of the requirements of the case, he violently sets aside the testimony of the whole body of the apostles. How unreasonable was this!—proud on his part, and insulting or disparaging to his brethren. Were not the slighted ten his own personal friends, and known to him as men of integrity, sense, and piety? Had not all the ten of them been familiar for several years with that Lord whom they affirmed they had seen again alive? They were therefore little likely to err in identification, and least of all to be unanimously mistaken. But all this is nothing to Thomas. "Except I shall see . . . I will not believe."

There is more in his attitude than mistrusting brethren for sense or integrity; there is a sort of dictation also to God. And great was the danger that God might leave so arrogant a man to himself to make shipwreck of his soul, and never vouchsafe to meet conditions thus high-handedly prescribed. Partly this was done; but mercifully only in part, and for a brief period. For an entire week this dark distressing doubt continued in the apostle's mind; by its bare existence working out the punishment of its cause. How different was that first week of the Gospel to the cold doubter as compared with the ten believing and rejoicing apostles, who knew the Saviour risen, and had already experienced the peace which He had brought from beyond the grave! "Then were the disciples glad when they saw the Lord."

Let us remember that the Gospel history was then only opening out. No life of Christ had yet been penned; and the full nature of our Lord's mission on earth was as yet very indistinct. The incompleteness was at a stage the most trying it ever was or could be—just on the very day of resurrection, previous to the certifying of the grand fact to the apostles by Christ's bodily presence and converse. For us who have never passed through these days of death and suspense as to Jesus,

it is difficult to conceive what a tide of thought and feeling
must have surged in the apostles' hearts in the first moments
of their Master's reappearance. Their experience had been for
three years to traverse Judea, Samaria, and Galilee in close
and sacred fellowship with this Teacher whom they believed
sent from God, yet who had met an end alike untimely and
unmerited on the cross. From their Master's lips day by day
and year by year had they been hearing words of wisdom and
goodness in similitudes and discourses, unparalleled even in
the history of the chosen people. By Him had such miracles
been performed on a vast variety of occasions as the Old
Testament prophets (though gathered all into one testimony)
had never equalled either in number or grandeur. In His
more private life they had witnessed such union of elevation
and simplicity, such devotion toward God and earnestness for
human welfare, as accorded even with His high claim to be
God's own Son, the predicted and long-expected Messiah.
Before His decease He had again and again discoursed to them
on themes that required and betokened the furthest reaches of
prophecy. His own death and many of its circumstances He
had foretold; a reappearance He had also spoken of, and a
divine Comforter to be sent. A heavenly kingdom He had
boldly predicted as to be set up on earth, which after many
and hard conflicts with the powers of darkness would finally
gain the ascendancy.

This prospect, vast as it was, under One so powerful over
the resources of nature, wise in doctrine, pure in life, and
divinely disinterested, might possibly be realised. But, de-
prived of the presence and aid of their Master, how could they,
ten or eleven poor feeble disciples, hope to accomplish what He
had planned? Their own experience in these years, and the
whole of sacred history from Malachi back to Genesis, contained nothing parallel. Now that their Master was removed,
and His doctrine and followers under the ban of all power,
civil and ecclesiastical, it seemed as if nothing remained but
to garner up in their hearts this beautiful vision, which might

at least cheer them man by man, and help them to follow, quietly and unobserved by the world, the footsteps of the great Prophet fallen in Israel three days ago.

When suspense and high hope might thus be subsiding—not into unbelief of the heavenly mission of Jesus, but into a much subdued estimate of its aim—then would this reappearance from the dead, and the exalted charge which Christ delivered to them, restore them to more than all their former anticipations. The charge is far higher and more real than poor sects that exaggerate preaching and glorify finance can ever appreciate—for the salutation of peace was followed by the breathing of the Holy Ghost into their souls, and by their endowment with the mysterious power of absolution. By these gifts, betokening a commission from above and a holy ministry on earth, they would be sustained against every taunt that unbelievers could throw at the death of their Master. Enough for them that Jesus still lives, that their Friend is God's Friend and Son, that the Father in heaven has set His seal of truth on the resurrection of Jesus on earth, that the offering made for sin has been divinely accepted, that human redemption has been achieved, and that a new age begins of higher privilege and closer communion.

But in all this uplifting of the soul from despondency, and nerving of it against taunts or persecution by new-born faith in the risen Christ, Thomas at first had no share. He was too much a disciple of sight and the other bodily senses : he must even add touch to sight, and touch most rigorously exercised, for he was not to be so easily gained as the credulous ten. "Except I shall see in His hands the print of the nails, and put my finger into the print of the nails, and thrust my hand into His side, I will not believe." He thought mainly of cross and grave ; of a dead, if not deceitful or victimised friend. He thought of a body, if not decaying in the grave, surreptitiously removed and made the basis of false doctrine. What a state of mind was this to be in for a whole week long, day by day and night by night; harassed by doubt, suspicions, suspense as to both earthly friendship and heavenly hope! In his reflective thoughts he would toilsomely climb upwards and truthwards for the hour; but the next hour would see him cast down, Sisyphus-like, from almost ascertained verity and peace to disorder, mistrust, and fresh bitterness of a struggling soul.

As regards temper and result, the harsh words of Thomas are to this day re-employed against the leading doctrines of the Gospel,—against the mysterious doctrine of the Trinity; against the union of the human and divine nature in Christ; against the agency of the Holy Spirit in conversion and sanctification. And, just as Thomas conceitedly took to himself over the ten credit for a higher development of reason, so ever since has party after party arisen among Christians, pretending to superior sense and caution, but in reality only waging war against everything in religion that transcends our limited understanding. Failing to obtain an answer reduced to the level of their own preconceptions, they drive certain doctrines from their creed; but only to their own loss.

Nor should we omit to note the closeness of connection between the unbelief of Thomas and his absence from the meeting on Easter Sunday. Had the apostle been then with the others, his unbelief could not have occurred; for the Saviour then and there spontaneously supplied those very proofs of reality which Thomas afterwards wrongly demanded. His after demand was unreasonable, for in making it he was guilty of despising the use of the eyes and other senses and integrity of ten honest and well-known men. The law of Moses stipulated for the testimony of two or three witnesses for establishing facts; but here were ten, each one specially trustworthy, and yet Thomas repudiates the whole. In refusing to believe at that stage, unless allowed to see and judge for himself, Thomas acted as unreasonably as we would do were we now to repeat his words. To meet demands for unlimited repetition is at variance with both the nature and use of a miracle; if it becomes common and ordinary, it loses its power of authenticating what is extraordinary.

More specially as to the absence itself; how many professing Christians are absent from public worship when they have no excuse valid before God or even their own conscience! Without supposing any special presence of Christ or outpouring of the Holy Ghost on a given Sunday, may we not justly believe that joining in the ordinary Church service in a right spirit would help us every day of the week in duty and trial? Though the difference arising from occasional absence may not produce a crisis in spiritual life, it is sure to tell in some not inconsiderable degree. And a few such degrees, added month by month and year by year, may ultimately weaken or destroy our faith, unless, as in the case of Thomas, God should compassionately interpose.

"And after eight days, again His disciples were within, and Thomas with them. Then came Jesus, the doors being shut, and stood in the midst, and said, Peace be unto you. Then saith He to Thomas, Reach hither thy finger, and behold my hands; and reach hither thy hand, and thrust it into my side: and be not faithless, but believing." How gracious is this condescension of the Lord of glory in stooping to meet even the excessive demand for evidence made by the wilful and wayward disciple whose words had done violence to both reason and reverence! How often has like compassion been extended to ourselves to meet doubts, prejudices, and errors, even in cases where, had we been duly diligent or humble beforehand, these difficulties would not have arisen. But, along with the loving-kindness that granted a reply to the scruples, there is conveyed a reproof all the more effectual by reason of its gentleness. The force of the reproof consists in the repetition by the Lord of the same strong form of words used by Thomas. As much as to say: It was no common evidence you asked—it is no common evidence I furnish. Be it sight —be it touch—and both keenly exercised; for I am He who who was dead and is alive. "Reach hither thy finger, and behold my hands; and reach hither thy hand, and thrust it into my side." Another element of the reproof, more direct but gentle still, lies in the added exhortation, "Be not faithless, but believing."

The arrow of conviction thus aimed stuck fast, and took effect. The demands of unbelief had been fulfilled to the letter, and the intractable apostle can hold out no longer. This divine and compassionate reproof has exorcised the evil spirit. Restored to his right mind, the apostle is overpowered by the clearness, greatness, and consolation of the present miracle. Before the eyes of the apostle stands the crucified Lord returned from the world of spirits, victorious over death, having recrossed, not as fugitive or favourite, but triumphantly, that bourn whence no human traveller ever returns. To Thomas the present miracle flashes backward and lights up the long train of Christ's miracles and teaching and holy life, giving them all a sudden and full interpretation. It gleams with a supernatural brightness across the field of Messianic prophecy, and discloses in this glorified presence the Redeemer of mankind, who must indeed be what He claimed and what the heavenly voice had declared, "The well-beloved Son of God." Under such impulse did Thomas answer to Christ's words in new fervour of faith and love, "My Lord and my God." So spake he not from surprise, inadvertence, or profanity, according to the brutal interpretation of Unitarians; but in deliberate confession and adoration of his Master's Messiahship and Godhead.

The apostle's confession in all its warmth is not only accepted by Jesus, but in the acceptance is included a couched censure for the error that prevented its earlier expression. Moreover, this confession of S. Thomas continued through life the joy of his soul and rule of his conduct; for he, like each of the ten, devoted himself to teaching and spreading the outstanding doctrine of which the apostles were made special witnesses—"Jesus and the resurrection." Nor was it merely by appearing alive with the marks of the five wounds that

Jesus corrected the error of His disciple, for He also employed words that have attained a proverbial character by throwing a precious light on the whole relation between seeing and believing. "Jesus saith unto him, Thomas, because thou hast seen me, thou hast believed: blessed are they that have not seen, and yet have believed." Here is the principle of faith in its noblest form, honouring to God and profitable to man. The honour to God by such faith lies in its readier perception of God's love in Christ's death, and of God's power in Christ's resurrection. The profit to man lies in the special blessing attached to such faith. Like a boat gently carried on a river's current, this noble blessing has floated for eighteen centuries with the stream of time. How many a believer's eye has it met and how many a heart has it gladdened along the ages? We cannot now see our Lord in the flesh; yet we are none the less blessed in our seeing by faith: "Whom having not seen, ye love; in whom, though now ye see Him not, yet believing, ye rejoice with joy unspeakable."

When afterwards the apostles quitted Jerusalem in order to carry the Gospel to all nations, Parthia, or Persia, seems to have been the sphere of Thomas. He is said to have suffered martyrdom at Meliapor, afterwards known as S. Thomas's, on the Coromandel coast. His body was carried to Edessa. In the sixteenth century the Portuguese found 15,000 S. Thomas Christians along the coast of Malabar. Two festivals were observed in his honour—one on Low Sunday (which is the first after Easter), when He confessed Christ, and the other, the principal feast, on 1st of July. The new town of S. Thomas was built around a church erected in the apostle's honour, when, in 1523, John III., King of Portugal, had dug under the ruins of a very ancient chapel outside the walls of Meliapor, and discovered a vault with remains supposed to be those of Thomas, and beside the body the spear that had caused his death-wound.

S. James

THE APOSTLE, THE SON OF ZEBEDEE.

DAY, JULY 25.

ORATIO.—*Esto, Domine, plebi tuæ sanctificator et custos :
ut apostoli tui Jacobi munita præsidiis, et conversatione tibi
placeat, et secura deserviat.   Per Dominum nostrum.*

The Epistle.—1 Cor. iv. 9-15.
The Gospel.—S. Matt. xx. 20-28.

COLLECT.—*Grant, O merciful God, that as Thine holy
apostle Saint James, leaving his father and all that he had,
without delay was obedient unto the calling of Thy Son Jesus
Christ, and followed Him ; so we, forsaking all worldly and
carnal affections, may be evermore ready to follow Thy holy
commandments ; through Jesus Christ our Lord.   Amen.*

The Epistle.—Acts xi. 27-xii. 3.
The Gospel.—S. Matt. xx. 20-28.

For all Thy saints, a noble throng,
  Who fell by fire and sword,
Who soon were called or waited long,
  We praise Thy name, O Lord.

For him who left his father's side,
  Nor lingered by the shore,
When, softer than the weltering tide,
  Thy summons glided o'er ;

Who stood beside the maiden dead,
  Who climbed the mount with Thee,
And saw the glory round Thy head,
  One of Thy chosen three ;

Who knelt beneath the olive shade,
  Who drank Thy cup of pain,
And passed from Herod's flashing blade
  To see Thy face again.

Lord, give us grace, and give us love,
  Like him to leave behind
Earth's cares and joys, and look above
  With true and earnest mind.

So shall we learn to drink Thy cup,
  So meek and firm be found,
When Thou shalt come to take us up
  Where Thine elect are crowned.
                    —Mrs C. F. ALEXANDER.

O great apostle ! rightly now
  Thou readest all Thy Saviour meant,
What time His grave yet gentle brow
  In sweet reproof on thee was bent.
Seek ye to sit enthroned by Me ?
  Alas ! ye know not what ye ask,
The first in shame and agony,
  The lowest in the meanest task.

Then be it so—my cup receive,
  And of My woes baptismal taste :
But for the crown, that angels weave
  For those next Me in glory placed,
I give it not by partial love ;
  But in My Father's book are writ
What names on earth shall lowliest prove,
  That they in heaven may highest sit.

If ever on the mount with Thee
  I seem to soar in vision bright,
With thoughts of coming agony,
  Stay Thou the too presumptuous flight :
Gently along the vale of tears
  Lead me from Tabor's sunbright steep,
Let me not grudge a few short years
  With Thee tow'rd heaven to walk and weep.
                    —KEBLE, S. James's Day.

"And going on from thence, he saw other two brethren,
James the son of Zebedee, and John his brother, in a
ship with Zebedee their father, mending their nets ; and
He called them. And they immediately left the ship
and their father, and followed Him."—S. MATT. iv. 21.

THIS apostle is usually known as S. James the Great, to
distinguish him from the other S. James, also an apostle,
the son of Alphæus, usually called S. James the Less; and
both are to be distinguished from another S. James who is
known as the Lord's brother, and is the author of the Epistle
of James, and the subject of a separate chapter here at the
close of the apostles.

Beginning with the call of S. James the Great as above
recorded in S. Matt., we learn that he was third in order of the
twelve in the date of his call; the two preceding him being
the brothers Andrew and Simon of Bethsaida (S. John i. 44).
James was not called alone, but at the same time and place
joined with his much more famous brother. It is noticeable
that as the seventy disciples were sent out two and two, so the
apostles both in their call and in the formal list of their names
are similarly grouped, in most cases as brothers or companions.
James, from the precedence of his name in the call, was probably the elder of the sons of Zebedee. The call of James and
John is also recorded in S. Mark i. 19, where the only additional feature is the hint of the father's circumstances enabling
him to have "hired servants" with him in the ship. In
S. Luke's narrative (v. 10) of the same call, James and John
are referred to as business partners with Simon in the lake
fishery. And a singularly significant fact there associated
with the call is the Saviour's discourse to the people from
Simon's boat, and, after discourse, the parable-miracle of the
great draught of fishes which brake the net and caused Simon
to prostrate himself before Jesus and say, "Depart from me ;
for I am a sinful man, O Lord;" whereat Jesus replied, "Fear
not ; from henceforth thou shalt catch men."

While this, as related by the Synoptists, was the effective or effectual call of the two pair of brothers to one of which James belonged, there was an earlier call, and at a different place, which is described in the fourth gospeL Its scene was at the Jordan near Bethabara, two days after the baptism of Jesus. The subjects of this earliest call were five—viz., Andrew, John, Simon, Philip, and Nathanael; the first three of whom reappear at the effective call renewed at Bethsaida. But there is no hint of James's presence on the Bethabara occasion; and from this absence it has been inferred, not at all conclusively, that he was not previously, like John, one of the Baptist's disciples.

It forms an element in any separate estimate of James as an apostle to notice how he stood in the favour of our Lord in company with Peter and John on three great occasions,—as witnesses together of the Transfiguration, Matt. xvii. 1; of the raising from death of Jairus's daughter, Mark v. 42; and of the Agony in the Garden, Mark xiv. 33. These conjunctions were determined by the choice of Jesus. Another conjunction of the same three, which proceeded from themselves, was when they asked, in company and privately, at Jesus, as to the destruction of Jerusalem, Mark xiii. 3. The incident in Luke ix. 54, when the sons of Zebedee desired to call down fire from heaven on the Samaritan village that refused to receive Jesus, shows the eagerness of their temper, which seems to have been already well known to Jesus when we find S. Mark (iii. 17) mentioning their surname of Boanerges, = Sons of Thunder, even in the dry list of the apostles' names. But with their fuller Christian training they outgrew the Elias spirit of Carmel, and gradually attained to the spirit of patience and forgiveness.

It is still as one imperfectly disciplined that James next appears in company with his brother and their mother Salome in Matt. xx. 22, as petitioning for the two best places in the Lord's kingdom, at His right hand and His left—a request that stirred the anger of the other apostles, as it met also refusal from Christ. And yet the request was so far granted as that in another sense it was promised to them by the prophetic Saviour anticipating His own sufferings and theirs. "Ye shall indeed drink of my cup, and be baptised with the baptism that I am baptised with." It is a striking thing that the name of James only occurs once, and that in a formal list of the twelve in Acts i. 13, where he is mentioned second in order, next after Peter, until the fulfilment of the Lord's prediction occurs in Acts xii.: "Now about that time Herod the king stretched forth his hands to vex certain of the Church. And he killed James the brother of John with the sword." Moreover, it is no less striking that the close of the same chapter which opens with this deed of persecution and murder, records the descent of the divine vengeance on the royal criminal: "And immediately the angel of the Lord smote him, because he gave not God the glory: and he was eaten of worms, and gave up the ghost." The Herod of this crime, committed in 42 A.D., was Herod Agrippa I., son of Aristobulus, and grandson of Herod the Great, the murderer of the Holy Innocents of Bethlehem forty years preceding.

Thus was S. James the first martyr among the apostles, which, with his eminent place beside Peter and John, has caused him to be distinguished as S. James the Great or the Elder, probably alluded to by Keble in the line, "O great apostle!" If under a ruler like Agrippa I. the martyr-apostle had any form of legal trial, probably the technical accusation would be the same as was urged against Stephen—a charge of speaking against the Temple and the Law. Early Church history contains a hint of the procedure at the martyrdom of the apostle James. Eusebius, ii. 9, following Clemens Alexandrinus, as embodied in Lectiones V. VI. for 25th July in the Sarum Breviary (Cambridge, 1886, iii. 536), tells how the high priest Abiathar, enraged at the success of S. James's ministry, raised a tumult, and got the apostle apprehended, accused, and condemned by Herod. On the way to execution he healed a paralytic, which so impressed the man who had charge of the apostle that he at once became Christian, was thereupon baptised by James, and after giving and receiving the kiss of peace, suffered the same death as the apostle himself.

Suffering martyrdom eleven years after the crucifixion of our Lord, the question suggests itself, How and where was James occupied as an apostle during that considerable period? He was evidently a man of zealous disposition, and he held a place in the first group of the twelve. And the tyrant's singling him out to begin upon, and trying to get Peter next, proves that he was a man of special work and worth, and a representative man in the youthful Christian community of the first decade. Wonderful is the silence of S. Luke, who has no hint of work, and only a single verse to note the death of one so prominent.

A very ancient tradition affirms that part of these eleven years between the crucifixion and the apostle's martyrdom was spent by S. James in Spain. This tradition goes back to S. Isodore, the Breviary of Toledo, and the Arabic Books of Anastasius of Antioch. And when we consider the early and firm hold of Christianity in Spain, there need be no difficulty in accepting such evidence, which some are too ready to scoff at in their violent prejudices against all that is Roman.

After James had been buried at Jerusalem, it is said that disciples carried his remains to Spain, to Iria Flavia, now El Padron in Galicia, whence in 829 A.D. they were translated by Alphonsus the Chaste, King of Leon, to a place four miles distant, called Ad S. Jacobum Apostolum, which became first Giacomo Postolo, then Compostella. Another derivation of the name of the famous shrine is Campus Stellæ, from a legendary star. The present cathedral of Santiago, or Sant Iago of Compostella, was founded in 1082. Santiago is the patron saint of Spain, and more than parallel to Andrew in Scotland or Mark in Venice. Besides Santiago de Compostella, there is a Santiago de Chili and a Santiago de Cuba in Spanish America. A military Order of S. James of Compostella was founded in 1175, and attained vast wealth in its three great, with nearly two hundred minor, Commanderies, which in 1522 were for safety subjected to the Spanish Crown.

S. Bartholomew,

THE APOSTLE.

DAY, AUGUST 24.

ORATIO. — *Omnipotens sempiterne Deus, qui hujus diei venerandam sanctamque lætitiam in beati Bartholomei apostoli tui festivitate tribuisti; da ecclesiæ tuæ, quæsumus, et amare quod credidit, et prædicare quod docuit.   Per Dominum.*
The Epistle.—1 Cor. xii. 27-31.
The Gospel.—S. Luke vi. 12-19.

COLLECT.—*O Almighty and everlasting God, who didst give to thine Apostle Bartholomew grace truly to believe and preach Thy Word; Grant, we beseech Thee, unto Thy Church, to love that Word which he believed, and both to preach and receive the same; through Jesus Christ our Lord.   Amen.*
The Epistle.—Acts v. 12-16.
The Gospel.—S. Luke xxii. 24-30.

"What word is this?   Whence know'st thou me?"
All wondering cries the humbled heart,
To hear Thee that deep mystery,
The knowledge of itself, impart.

The veil is raised; who runs may read,
By its own light the truth is seen,
And soon the Israelite indeed
Bows down t' adore the Nazarene.

So did Nathanael, guileless man,
 At once, not shamefaced or afraid,
Owning Him God, who so could scan
 His musings in the lonely shade ;

In his own pleasant fig-tree's shade,
 Which by his household fountain grew,
Where at noonday his prayer he made
 To know God better than he knew.

Oh happy hours of heavenward thought !
 How richly crowned ! how well improved !
In musing o'er the Law he taught,
 In waiting for the Lord he loved.

We must not mar with earthly praise
 What God's approving word hath sealed ;
Enough, if right our feeble lays
 Take up the promise He revealed ;

" The childlike faith, that asks not sight,
 Waits not for wonder or for sign,
Believes, because it loves, aright—
 Shall see things greater, things divine."

" Heaven to that gaze shall open wide,
 And brightest angels to and fro
On messages of love shall glide
 'Twixt God above and Christ below."

So still the guileless man is blest,
 To him all crooked ways are straight,
Him on his way to endless rest
 Fresh ever-growing strengths await.

God's witnesses, a glorious host,
 Compass him daily like a cloud ;
Martyrs and seers, the saved and lost,
 Mercies and judgments cry aloud.

Yet shall to him the still small voice,
 That first into his bosom found
A way, and fixed his wavering choice,
 Nearest and dearest ever sound.
    —KEBLE, *S. Bartholomew's Day.*

"Jesus saw Nathanael coming to Him, and saith of him, Behold an Israelite indeed, in whom is no guile!"—S. JOHN i. 47.

WITH this apostle the first thing to be done is the adjustment of his name. In the four places of Scripture which furnish a list of the apostles—Matt. x., Mark iii., Luke vi., and Acts i.—we find the name of Bartholomew immediately succeeding and also coupled with that of Philip, "Philip and Bartholomew;" in the last case with this slight variation, "Philip and Thomas and Bartholomew." In all four cases it is the bare name that meets us.

On the other hand, in two places of S. John, i. 45, xxi. 2, we find a man evidently an apostle under the name of Nathanael, a name which occurs in none of the four lists of the twelve. In the former passage the connection with Philip is exemplified, and is put so distinctly as to form an explanation of the conjunction above noted. "Philip findeth Nathanael, and saith unto him, We have found Him of whom Moses in the Law, and the Prophets, did write, Jesus of Nazareth the son of Joseph." The other passage, in xxi. 2, describes our Lord's appearing after His resurrection to seven apostles or disciples at the Sea of Tiberias. "There were together Simon Peter, and Thomas called Didymus, and Nathanael of Cana in Galilee, and the sons of Zebedee, and two other of His disciples." Put thus in the midst of apostles on a great occasion, the inference is plain that Nathanael was one of the eleven, of whom seven were there present. If so, he can be no other than Bartholomew. It helps this conclusion, if further help were needed, that Bartholomew is not an independent personal name, but a patronymic meaning Son of Tolmai; as Barjona = Son of Jonas. The apostle's full and proper name accordingly is Nathanael Bartholomew, or Nathanael the son of Tolmai. It is curious that in a case of identification where the evidence almost amounts to arithmetical demonstration, there should still have been hesitation of ancient date and among influential churchmen,—as we can infer from the fact that in selecting a Gospel lesson for S. Bartholomew's Day on 25th August, by far the most appropriate passage, in S. John i. 43-51, should have been passed over in favour of a general passage like S. Luke xxii. 24 by the Church of England; and in favour of a mere list of the twelve in S. Luke vi. 12, in the Church of Rome—simply because of the little explanation needed to vindicate the name Nathanael as also Bartholomew's.[1]

Having completed the adjustment of the name of our apostle, we have at the same time exhausted all that we know of him from Scripture, with one important exception in S. John i. 43-51, which ought to have been the Gospel lesson for S. Bartholomew's Day, and which we are now free and entitled to go back on, to see what light we there have on the character and disposition of Nathanael son of Tolmai.

Philip of Bethsaida was he who, in the gracious providence of God, was the means of communicating to Nathanael of Cana of Galilee the most precious tidings and discovery then possible, and which all were more or less on the outlook for— " We have found Him of whom Moses in the Law, and the Prophets, did write, Jesus of Nazareth the son of Joseph." Although himself a Galilean, Nathanael seems unwilling to accept the chance of a spiritual honour for his own district, " Can there any good thing come out of Nazareth ? " Probably the true explanation of Nathanael's words is not a slighting of Nazareth or Galilee as unworthy or incapable of good, but a latent reference to sacred prophecy, that there was no passage therein which could lead men to look in that direction for the appearance of the expected Messiah. Philip gives a short and practical answer—Don't let us enter on the difficult matter of searching the various things and places joined in Scripture

---

[1] Even Archbishop Trench, 'Studies in the Gospels,' p. 81, is not decided as to identity. Mr Ellerton, author of " King of Saints to whom the Number," in ' Hymns Ancient and Modern,' mars his fine hymn by hesitation. Keble, on the other hand, strikes a clear note.

with the Messiah, but just "come and see" the man I am speaking of, and judge for yourself whether He is not the Hope of Israel.

Here, however, comes in a sudden change and turn in the narrative. It is no longer a friendly comparison between Philip and Nathanael; but Jesus Himself anticipates and interposes, instead of passively waiting to be tested and made matter of consideration. The basis of our Lord's anticipation is His divine power of knowing men's hearts and histories, as anciently described in Ps. cxxxix., and as experienced at the well of Jacob by the woman of Samaria, and which forms one of His qualifications for the office of Judge at the end of the world. Exercising this heart-searching power, "Jesus saw Nathanael coming to Him, and saith of him, Behold an Israelite indeed, in whom is no guile! Nathanael saith unto Him, Whence knowest thou me? Jesus answered and said unto him, Before that Philip called thee, when thou wast under the fig-tree, I saw thee. Nathanael answered and saith unto Him, Rabbi, Thou art the Son of God; Thou art the King of Israel." Thus without any further intervention of Philip, and without any search of prophecy as to cities, families, or other tokens, Nathanael arrives at Philip's own conclusion and discovery by the shortest and surest of all roads. It was communication between spirit and spirit, as belongs to heaven itself, or to inspiration, or to the work of the great day of the Lord, when books and consciences are opened, and all concealment and doubt are ended. He was a good and guileless man before; but now in an instant of time, with a flash of spiritual recognition he is a believer in Jesus. And it was no flattery that Jesus spoke, but a true measure that He made of this beautiful and noble character free from all crooked ways. In the terms used there is a glance back at the character of the patriarch Jacob, who was originally cunning, subtle, and greedy, so that he supplanted his brother Esau, taking away his blessing, and deceived by an artifice and falsehood even his father Isaac. But here was no duplicity or craftiness, but a through

and through man of honest truth, artless as a child and trusty
as a friend. Such a man was representative of the very best
side and development of Hebrew life under the influence of
the grace of God, as when Jacob had outgrown his earlier
" pawky " character, and became a better man, deserving a new
name, the name Israel—a name which fitted this good man
without any waiting or change at all, for he had never been
anything else but honest, sincere, straightforward, "an Israelite indeed, in whom is no guile." Nathanael had none of the
old Jacob Jew and Yankee who cheated Isaac and Esau, and
Laban too, with his tricks for breeding beasts of colours to suit
his own bargain, while Laban intended only the ordinary natural proportion of speckled oddities. A man of the Nathanael
type, like Spenser's Una, "makes a sunshine in the shady
place." His complete honesty and " aefaldness " leave to conviction and conversion a short work, so that he reaches *instanter*
the grand conclusion which afterwards Martha reached through
a loving heart anticipating the miracle-power of resurrection in
the same Jesus. "Yea, Lord: I believe that Thou art the
Christ, the Son of God, which should come into the world."
As kindred-spirited to Martha, so was he to Peter in his great
confession, " Thou art the Christ, the Son of the living God ; "
and to Thomas in his abrupt but appropriate, " My Lord and
my God."

The remainder of the dialogue contains further praise of
Nathanael by Jesus, and the addition of a special promise.
The praise of his ready but just faith reminds us of parallel
words of Jesus to Thomas, where the faith was just but tardy ;
and the promise also associated with the Thomas interview, not
for Thomas himself, but for others more prompt of faith.
" Jesus answered and said unto Nathanael, Because I said
unto thee, I saw thee under the fig-tree, believest thou ? thou
shalt see greater things than these. And He saith unto him,
Verily, verily, I say unto you, Hereafter ye shall see heaven
open, and the angels of God ascending and descending upon
the Son of man." Here is a fresh allusion on our Lord's part

to Jacob. The reference before was to the slippery side of the patriarch's original disposition; now the reference is to Jacob's experience of light and comfort from the merciful vision divinely granted of the ladder that joined earth to heaven and heaven to earth through a ministry of angels constantly coming and going. Why Jacob should thus twice have been referred to does not appear, unless it may have been that this passage of Genesis was the Scripture lesson of the day or of last Sabbath, as we find Jesus on one occasion taking up the lesson of the day from Isaiah—Luke iv. 17.

Again, whether any special fulfilment of this promise was made to Nathanael, we know not. It was fulfilled in part, and literally, in the wilderness, in Gethsemane, and at the ascension. But the real fulfilment is probably to be found not thus, but in the graces, blessings, and gifts bestowed on believers in answer to their daily prayers, and through Jesus Christ as Mediator between heaven and earth. And surely a man in the early Church in the high office of the apostolate would find the joy and privilege of his life to consist in the verification day by day of this better Jacob's ladder in the new and full doctrine of the Mediatorship.

Here practically we part from Nathanael, although it is only the day of his call. For the next three years he would share the training of the twelve in the society of Jesus; but we have no special incidents on record as to his share. We have only, by S. John xxi. 2, the fact of Nathanael's presence with six others as a witness of the risen Saviour at the Sea of Tiberias; and in Acts i. 13 the mere mention of his name among the eleven who, after witnessing our Lord's ascension, returned to Jerusalem, and abode in an upper room waiting for the day and gift of Pentecost. Scripturally that is the very end.

Tradition says that Bartholomew travelled to India with the Gospel. Eusebius relates that S. Pantænus, c. 300 A.D., going to India to confute the Brahmins, found some Christians who still preserved a Hebrew copy of S. Matt. which Bartholomew had left. Afterwards, Bartholomew met his old friend S. Philip at Hierapolis in Phrygia, and thereafter he laboured in Lycaonia, finally suffering martyrdom in Armenia. His body is said to rest in a porphyry monument in the church of S. Bartholomew in an isle in the Tiber at Rome.

The saint's memory and day have grievously suffered from being associated with one of the most wicked events in modern history, when on 24th August 1572 the massacre of S. Bartholomew's Day took place under the instigation of Catharine de Medici, whereby above 2000 Huguenots were slain in Paris, and at least 20,000 all over France, at a time when, by the Peace of St Germain-en-Lay in 1570, full exercise of their religion was given to the French Reformed. It was surely by a strange perversity that the commemoration day of an apostle, who was an Israelite indeed, and a guileless man, should be fixed on for the perpetration of one of the most treacherous and cruel acts of all history.

In Tarves, in Aberdeenshire, is a Barthol (= Bartholomew) chapel, with an old fair on the saint's day.

S. Philip and S. James.

APOSTLES.

DAY, MAY 1.

ORATIO. — *Deus qui nos annua apostolorum tuorum Philippi et Jacobi solennitate lætificas ; præsta, quæsumus, ut quorum gaudemus meritis, instruamur exemplis. Per Dominum.*

The Epistle.—Wisdom of Sol. v. 1-5.
The Gospel.—S. John xiv. 1-13.

COLLECT.—*O Almighty God, whom truly to know is everlasting life ; Grant us perfectly to know Thy Son Jesus Christ
to be the way, the truth, and the life ; that following the steps
of Thy holy apostles Saint Philip and Saint James, we may
steadfastly walk in the way that leadeth to eternal life ; through
the same Thy Son Jesus Christ our Lord.   Amen.*

The Epistle.—S. James i. 1-12.[1]
The Gospel.—S. John xiv. 1-14.

Æterna Christi munera
Apostolorum gloria,
Laudes ferentes debitas
Lætis canamus mentibus.

The Lord's eternal gifts,
Th' apostles' mighty praise,
Their victories, and high reward,
Sing we in joyful lays.

Ecclesiarum Principes
Belli triumphales Duces
Cœlestis aulæ milites,
Et vera mundi lumina.

Lords of the Churches they ;
Triumphant chiefs of war ;
Brave soldiers of the heavenly
camp ;
True lights for evermore.

Devota sanctorum fides,
Invicta spes credentium,
Perfecta Christi caritas
Mundi triumphat principem.

Theirs was the saints' high faith ;
And quenchless Hope's pure
glow ;
And perfect charity which laid
The world's fell tyrant low.

In his Paterna gloria,
In his voluntas Spiritus,
Exultat in his Filius,
Cœlum repletur gaudiis.

In them the Father shone ;
In them the Son o'ercame ;
In them the Holy Spirit wrought,
And filled their hearts with flame.

Te nunc, Redemptor, quæsumus,
Ut ipsorum consortio
Jungas precantes servulos
In sempiterna sæcula.
   —AMBROSIAN, *in Anglo-Saxon
     Hymnary.*

[In love, Redeemer, grant
That we Thy servants here
Be joinèd with the Twelve on high
In glory's endless sphere.]
   —E. CASWALL.

---

[1] This lesson is evidently chosen on the theory that James the son of
Alphæus was the author of the Epistle of James. The same view is
distinctly expressed in Lectio II. in the Sarum Breviary. See chapter
here on S. James, the Lord's brother.

> "Philip saith unto Him, Lord, show us the Father, and it
> sufficeth us."—S. JOHN xiv. 8.

SUCH is the chief and best saying recorded of this apostle.
It is far from being perfect, as our Lord at once showed
on hearing it; but yet it contains, not only what was characteristic of the speaker, but what also is to his credit, and which,
with our Lord's correction of it, may form a most edifying
subject of meditation.

The material available for knowledge of the apostle Philip
is in a manner confined to the fourth gospel, in short passages
in chapters i., vi., xii., xiv., which fall to be considered in
order.

In the more strict and full call of the apostles, as recorded
in the first three gospels, the name of Philip stands fifth in
each list, as it does also in the list in Acts i. But in the
earlier call recorded in S. John i., preceding the official
appointment and solemn charge to the whole twelve, Philip
is fourth in order, immediately following on Andrew, John,
and Peter. And just as Andrew was instrumental in bringing forward his brother Peter, so was Philip in bringing
his friend Nathanael Bartholomew into the first early group
of special disciples soon to be promoted to the apostolate.
Philip's call was the day after that of Andrew and Peter and
John, and the event took place at or near the Jordan, where
John was baptising. It would seem that all of this first group
were already John's disciples; and by so early and frankly
joining the Saviour, they formed living tokens of how well the
Baptist was doing his work as Christ's herald. The action of
Philip on Nathanael, besides its blessing to the latter, throws
a very favourable light on Philip himself, as showing his great
confidence in Jesus, with whom Philip had been so impressed
and satisfied that he thought his friend Nathanael had only
to see Christ to be also similarly convinced. Moreover, the
method which Philip uses with his friend in the invitation
to "come and see," is exactly that which Jesus Himself had

already used so successfully with Andrew and John (John i.
39); so that Philip seems an apt scholar already. Nor is it
amiss to interject here, although it is an anticipation, that the
same method of learning and getting satisfied by "seeing"
meets us twice again in connection with Philip—when the
Greeks asked to see Jesus, and when Philip himself asked to
see the Father. Although not named, we may be sure that
Philip and the others who shared in the preliminary call would
be present to see the beginning of miracles in Nathanael's own
town of Cana, which was on the third day from the calling of
Philip, as appears from S. John i. 43, ii. 1. The formal call
to the apostolate occurred nearly a year later.

Philip's place in chapter vi. is on the occasion of the miraculous feeding of the five thousand with five loaves and two
fishes. The scene was on a mountain near the Sea of Galilee,
and the Passover was nigh, probably the Passover following
the death of the Baptist. "When Jesus then lifted up His
eyes, and saw a great company come unto Him, He saith unto
Philip, Whence shall we buy bread, that these may eat? (And
this He said to prove him, for He Himself knew what He
would do.)" To prove him, clearly means to test Philip's faith,
what solution he would propose for the difficulty—whether it
would occur to him to trust and call in the same power and
glory that had been manifested at Cana. But very lowly
and materialistic is his idea towards the solution: "Philip
answered him, Two hundred pennyworth of bread is not
sufficient for them, that every one of them may take a little."
He does not face a full meal, but thinks only of what children
call "a piece" between meals. And in judging of this he
estimates it as from the front of a baker's counter. On these
lines no action is taken, so that we must consider Philip as
failing to satisfy the proof which Jesus sought. What failed
in Philip was found in Andrew, whose allusion to the lad
with five barley loaves and two small fishes was made the
basis of the miracle. The conjunction of Andrew and Philip
here is noticeable as a hint of their being special friends.

In chapter xii., where Philip next appears, the time is about five days preceding the Passover of the Crucifixion, as appears from xii. 1 and xii. 12. "And there were certain Greeks among them that came up to worship at the feast : the same came therefore to Philip, which was of Bethsaida of Galilee, and desired him, saying, Sir, we would see Jesus." These *Hellenes*, born Gentiles, had probably become proselytes of the gate, and thus observers of Jewish feasts, and also evidently favourable towards Jesus. Their application to Philip seems to have arisen from some acquaintance connected with Beth-saida; and his Greek name might also furnish a point of contact, for his having it would probably imply Greek speaking or Greek business in his family Although the introduction requested seems a simple matter, Philip does not decide upon it without the help of his friend Andrew. "Philip cometh and telleth Andrew : and again Andrew and Philip tell Jesus."

On this slight beginning turned a very great Gospel incident —one of the three occasions when a voice from heaven bore testimony to the divine Sonship of Jesus. "And Jesus answered them, saying, The hour is come, that the Son of man should be glorified. . . . Now is my soul troubled. . . . Father, glorify Thy name. . . . I have both glorified it, and will glorify it again. . . . This voice came not because of me, but for your sakes. . . . I, if I be lifted up from the earth, will draw all men unto me. . . . These things spake Jesus, and departed, and did hide Himself from them." Thus was the seeing of Jesus on the part of these Greeks by the aid of Philip and Andrew, not only a great thing to the beholders, but a notable step in our Lord's career, now rapidly closing —only five days before the end.

In chapter xiv., which presents Philip for the last time within the compass of the gospels, he appears in a still more solemn scene. The traitor had received the sop, had gone out into the night self-excommunicated, xiii. 30, and with more freedom Jesus addresses the faithful eleven. "Therefore when he was gone out, Jesus said, Now is the Son of man glorified." This discourse had three interruptions: the first from Peter, "Lord, whither goest Thou?" which ended terribly for him in evoking the prophecy of his denial of his Master; the second by Thomas, "Lord, we know not whither Thou goest; and how can we know the way?" which evoked the inexhaustible answer, "I am the way, the truth, and the life," and the allusion thereon to the Father; the third by Philip, while Jesus was yet answering Thomas, "No man cometh unto the Father, but by me. If ye had known me, ye should have known my Father also: and from henceforth ye know Him, and have seen Him. Philip saith unto Him, Lord, show us the Father, and it sufficeth us. Jesus saith unto him, Have I been so long time with you, and yet hast Thou not known me, Philip? He that hath seen me hath seen the Father; and how sayest thou then, Show us the Father? Believest thou not that I am in the Father, and the Father in me? . . . If ye love me, keep my commandments. And I will pray the Father, and He shall give you another Comforter, that He may abide with you for ever."

The spiritual position of Philip here is this: as an honest practical man, seeing best the outside of things, and not grasping principles very firmly or readily, he recalls apparently that a little ago he had heard the Father's voice from heaven, when Jesus was speaking to the Greeks, while, just a moment ago, before Thomas interposed, Jesus had spoken of His Father's house with its many mansions, and had since added, "If ye had known me, ye should have known my Father also: and from henceforth ye know Him, and have seen Him." Philip's request, while it sprang from reverence, desire, and faith, was spoken too much from the outside of things, was deficient in love and spirituality, and indicated a slow mind for one who had been among the earliest called of the twelve. Philip, like the rest, understood but a little part of the life which they were privileged to see and hear so familiarly in Jesus. And so he and they remained dull and half blind till

Pentecost. Our Lord's question as to his non-intelligence is not so much reproachful as simply sorrowful, compassionate, and even tender, in the use of the apostle's name when addressing him. If Philip craved for a favour of sight in regard of the Father, like what was vouchsafed to Moses in the cleft of the rock, and if he did this remembering that Jesus was the Prophet like unto Moses, and yet greater, he was craving in a direction not consistent with the new economy. And it is this which the great Prophet tells to Philip, and to the rest of the eleven; and through him and them to us, in the lesson as to the Father and the Son which fills the wonderful passage xiv. 10-14. Thus the very slowness of Philip's mind has eventuated in a most precious lesson to us in the Saviour's answer and revelation. After such an instruction every Christian can now from day to day, with increase of light and firmness, repeat the venerable form of sound words: "I believe in God the Father Almighty, Maker of heaven and earth; and in Jesus Christ His only Son our Lord."

The last of all Scripture references to Philip is the mere mention of his name in Acts i. 13, as one of those present at Jerusalem in the meeting held after our Lord's ascension.

On the authority of Theodoret and Eusebius we learn that he preached the Gospel in Phrygia, and died there in the city of Hierapolis. He must have lived to a good old age, because Polycarp, the martyr-bishop of Smyrna, and disciple of S. John, whose conversion took place in 80 A.D., testifies that he had enjoyed the conversation of the apostle Philip. The Church of S. Philip and S. James at Rome, which was dedicated as early as 560 A.D., whatever was the cause of the joint dedication, may partly account for, or be a token of, the union of the two apostles in one commemorative day; for, so far as concerns personal intercourse, there appears no special reason for the conjunction in the lives of either.

S. JAMES THE APOSTLE, SON OF ALPHÆUS.

In the Roman Breviary and in the Anglican Prayer-book the commemoration of this apostle is on 1st May, and his name is joined with S. Philip, having the same Epistle and Gospel for both. At the sound of this saint's day one can hardly help wandering in reminiscence from Church ideas to the fields and gardens and hedges, with their fresh grass and lilies and hawthorn blossom, and larks' song, and children's excursion. Or rather, the visit to the fresh hill and woodland, with their Maydew of natural baptism, may well give new zest to both Church and Heaven, as in the sprightly ballad of Baring-Gould :—

> " Daily, daily sing the praises
>   Of the city God hath made ;
> In the beauteous fields of Eden
>   Its foundation-stones are laid.
>
> There the meadows green and dewy
>   Shine with lilies wondrous fair ;
> Thousand, thousand are the colours
>   Of the waving flowers there.
>
> There the forests ever blossom,
>   Like our orchards here in May ;
> There the gardens never wither,
>   But eternally are gay."

In the list of apostles in S. Matt. x., James the son of Alphæus is ninth in order. There is no Gospel incident associated with his name, as we find with Thomas, Philip, Bartholomew, Andrew, Peter, John, and Matthew ; so that practically our knowledge of him is limited very much to the four lists of the apostles.

Some have supposed him to be a brother of the apostle Matthew, who in Mark ii. 14 is called " Levi the son of Alphæus." But this depends on the Alphæus of Mark ii. 14 being the same as the Alphæus of Matt. x. 3. And when we consider the frequent repetition of the same name among the Jews, as seen in Simon, James, Judas, John, Moses, and Joseph, it would be very rash to assume this identity. Had Matthew and James been really brothers, surely some direct allusion would have been made to the fact, as in the cases of Andrew and Peter and the two sons of Zebedee. Another supposition is that James the son of Alphæus is a brother of the apostle Jude; but the reason against this may be reserved till we reach S. Jude.

Having put aside these brother connections, we come to a relationship that is as nearly as may be certain and reliable. It rests on S. Mark xv. 40-47, and xvi. 1, in his narrative of the Crucifixion. "There were also women looking on afar off: among whom was Mary Magdalene, and Mary the mother of James the less and of Joses, and Salome; (who also, when he was in Galilee, followed Him, and ministered unto Him;) and many other women which came up with Him unto Jerusalem. . . . And Mary Magdalene and Mary the mother of Joses beheld where He was laid. And when the Sabbath was past, Mary Magdalene and Mary the mother of James, and Salome, had bought sweet spices, that they might come and anoint Him." Describing the same scene, S. John xix. 25 says: "Now there stood by the cross of Jesus His mother, and His mother's sister, Mary the wife of Cleophas, and Mary Magdalene." Here arises the question, Are there four or three women alluded to?—i.e., does His mother's sister mean Mary the wife of Cleophas, or does it mean another person—viz., Salome mentioned above by S. Mark, and who was the mother of S. John himself, being the wife of Zebedee?—Matt. xx. 20. From the above it comes out that James the less (referring probably to stature) is the distinctive epithet of this apostle. Moreover, Alphæus and Cleophas are the same name as regards consonants, which are the determining force in Hebrew.

If this identification is correct, as it has every appearance of being, then it throws a very valuable light on the apostle himself. With a woman as his mother so devout, liberal, and full of personal regard for the Saviour, may we not picture a good portion of the same spirit as animating the son, especially as both of them are evidently related by close family ties to the Blessed Virgin Mary? There is no sweeter picture in the gospels than this of the little group of holy women who ministered to the Lord of their substance—who followed Him in His journeys, reverently treasuring His teaching—who watched His dying moments in loving sympathy—who watched the disposal of the body in burial—who returned with the earliest dawn to embalm the Prophet's body with precious spices worthy of a king's son. The disciple trained at home from boyhood under such a mother could not fail of a deep and hereditary attachment to Jesus, and was sure to be a faithful worker in His kingdom from the day of his call to the day of his death. No holier or mightier influence can work in a good man's soul than that of a saintly mother like the wife of Alphæus.

S. Simon and S. Jude,

APOSTLES.

DAY, OCTOBER 28.

ORATIO.—*Deus, qui nos per beatos apostolos tuos Symonem et Judam ad agnitionem tui nominis venire tribuisti: da nobis eorum gloriam sempiternam et proficiendo celebrare, et celebrando proficere. Per Dominum.*

The Epistle.—Eph. iv. 7-13.
The Gospel.—S. John xv. 17-25.

COLLECT.—*O Almighty God, who hast built Thy Church upon the foundation of the apostles and prophets, Jesus Christ Himself being the head corner-stone ; Grant us so to be joined together in unity of spirit by their doctrine, that we may be made a holy temple acceptable unto Thee ; through Jesus Christ our Lord.   Amen.*

The Epistle.—S. Jude 1-8.[1]
The Gospel.—S. John xv. 17-27.

Cœlestis aulœ Principes,
Sacri duces exercitus,
Bissena mundi lumina,
Olim futuri judices !

Captains of the saintly band,
Lights who lighten every land,
Princes who with Jesus dwell,
Judges of His Israel :

Mersis gravi caligine
Per vos dies renascitur ;
Quos vanus error luserat
Illustrat alma veritas.

On the nations sunk in night
Ye have shed the Gospel light ;
Sin and error flee away,
Truth reveals the promised day.

Non vi, nec armis militum,
Fandi nec ullis artibus,
Verbo sed irrisæ crucis,
Christo rebelles subditis.

Not by warrior's spear and sword,
Not by art of human word,
Preaching but the cross of shame,
Rebel hearts for CHRIST ye tame.

Quibus gemebat subditus,
Rumpuntur orbis vincula ;
Jam gaudet excusso jugo
Liber Dei sub legibus.

Earth, that long in sin and pain
Groaned in Satan's deadly chain,
Now to serve its God is free
In the law of liberty.

Vulgata terris omnibus
Per vos Dei mysteria ;
Sic vestra terris omnibus
Præclara facta personant.

Distant lands with one acclaim
Tell the honour of your name,
Who, wherever man has trod,
Teach the mysteries of God.

Uni sit et Trino Deo
Suprema laus, summum decus,
De nocte qui nos ad Suæ
Lumen vocavit gloriæ.
    —*Paris Breviary.*   NEWMAN,
    Hy. Eccl.

Glory to the THREE in ONE
While eternal ages run,
Who from deepest shades of night
Called us to His glorious light.
        —Sir H. BAKER.

---

[1] This selection for the epistle implies an opinion that Jude the apostle was the author of this epistle—an opinion, as will appear, very open to challenge.

> "And when it was day, He called unto Him His disciples:
> and of them He chose twelve, whom also He named
> apostles; Simon, (whom He also named Peter,) and
> Andrew his brother, James and John, Philip and
> Bartholomew, Matthew and Thomas, James the son of
> Alphæus, and Simon called Zelotes, and Judas the son
> [R. V. of 1881] of James, and Judas Iscariot, which also
> was the traitor."—S. Luke vi. 13-16.

AS no Scripture incident is recorded of the apostle Simon,
it is well to acknowledge frankly and at once that there
is really nothing to be stated about him beyond the fourfold
mention of his name in the lists of the twelve. In the two
lists given by S. Luke he is marked by a Greek surname
Zelotes, S. Luke being more classic in his style. In the other
two lists, by writers more strongly Hebraic, he is named as
"Simon the Canaanite," which does not refer to Canaan or
Cana geographically, but to an Aramaic word *kana*, meaning
zeal, and thus equivalent to Zelotes. The association of this
surname on each occasion when Simon is named serves two
purposes,—to distinguish him from others of the same name,
which was one of the commonest among the Jews; and also
to indicate the apostle's antecedents previous to his call by
our Lord. If he is thus carefully surnamed for distinctiveness,
it is simply a defiance of that caution to attempt to identify
him with the Simon, almost certainly a different person, named
in Matt. xiii. 55, and Mark vi. 3, as belonging to the household of the Blessed Virgin.

Nor need the other reasons for Simon's surname be long
dwelt on. The Zealot party, according to Josephus, was one
of four philosophic sects of the Jews, whose distinctive principle was a denial of the right of Gentiles to rule over the
people of God. They were Pharisees, but on a *political* basis;
whereas the Essenes, who were also Pharisees, were *doctrinal*.
The Zealots were extremists in the maintenance of the Mosaic
law, and apt to run or be led into armed resistance to Roman

rule and taxation. That Simon belonged to this rather danger-ous faction before his call, enables us to see the natural and original bent of his mind. But we have absolutely no means of knowing to what extent he retained any sympathy with his old views or associates when the new career of the apos-tolate opened before him ; or whether he might not even renounce and denounce his earlier self, as did S. Paul after his conversion.

The only observation of a practical nature that may be made on S. Simon is founded on noting the difference of date when his name occurs in Acts i. 13, as compared with the three occurrences in the Synoptic Gospels. These denote the original call as one of the twelve; and that call was followed by the solemn charge which after the Roll of the twelve fills S. Matt. x., and should ever form a special study when we consider the Apostolic College as a body of divinely commissioned men invested with the highest of sacred offices, and in the *Te Deum* fairly named " the glorious company of the apostles." This call and charge were followed by a deliberate course of instruc-tion and training by our Lord, parallel with the years of his public ministry. And when all had been completed on earth —the Crucifixion, the Resurrection, the great Forty Days, the Ascension—then, preceding the Pentecostal gift, which amounted to a fresh and full commission, it was fitting that the names of the eleven should again be put on record as the starting-point of the remainder of the New Testament, and also the starting - point of Church authority and Church history.

More directly the practical lesson of S. Simon's career is to demonstrate, from the case of a man occupying the highest of sacred offices, the compatibility of personal and historical obscurity with good Christian work. Probably not so much as one per cent of all men who for 1850 years past have faith-fully served Christ in the holy ministry, whether as deacons, presbyters, or bishops, are to be found at this moment trace-able even on tombstones any more in detail than this high servant of Christ in the apostolate. They have no record here, but their witness and record are on high. All such await "the manifestation of the sons of God." How much more is this true of the great body of the membership of the Christian Church, faithful men and women who have endured many a trial and exemplified many a virtue and grace in utter obscurity, yet for whom the happy greeting is in store, "Come, ye blessed of my Father, inherit the kingdom prepared for you from the foundation of the world"!

S. JUDE, THE APOSTLE.

For this apostle, the last of the eleven, the Oratio, Collect, Epistle, and Gospel are the same as for S. Simon Zelotes; and the same text in S. Luke vi. 13-16 may also serve; because here again it is a bare name that meets us, although the office is so high, above bishops and archbishops and even patriarchs.

Except one passage in S. John xiv. 22, which records a question put to Jesus by this apostle, no Scripture incident of word or deed of the man casts a single ray of light on his distinctive character or sphere. In the apostolic list of S. Matt. Jude is the tenth in order of the twelve. He comes between James the son of Alphæus and Simon the Canaanite thus: "and Lebbeus, whose surname was Thaddeus." In the list of S. Mark he is also tenth in order of the twelve, and with the same immediately preceding and following; but his own name occurs simply, "and Thaddeus." In the other two lists, both by S. Luke, his name is eleventh in order, standing after that of Simon; and in each case in a new form which literally is, "and Judas of James." In the Revised Version of 1881 this is correctly translated, "Judas the son of James;" a translation which had already been adopted by Tyndale and Cranmer, "Judas James' sone;" as also by Luther, "Judas, Jakobi Sohn." The origin of the twist in the Authorised Version of 1611, "Judas the brother of James," was a desire to make the two lists of S. Luke agree with the first verse of the Epistle of

Jude, " Jude, the servant of Jesus Christ, the brother of James."
A further aim of this forced harmony was to vindicate for that
epistle an apostolic authorship and authority. But it is not
necessary for a place in the New Testament Canon that a
writer should be an apostle : witness the Gospels of Mark and
Luke as sure cases, and the Epistle of James as next to
certainty. Inspiration and not apostleship is the test for canonicity. The author of the Epistle of Jude is to be found in
another man of the same name, which was very common among
the Jews. He has been already indicated as a son of S. Joseph
by his first marriage, and his position as " brother of James "
will appear under S. James, the Lord's brother. As to the
apostle " Judas the son of James," we must accept the simple
silence of Scripture, and interpret it as has been done in the
like case of S. Simon Zelotes. The solitary exception to the
silence is in a question put by Jude to our Lord in the course
of an address that had already been twice interrupted,—by
Thomas as to whither the Saviour was going ; and by Philip
as to seeing the Father. With like superficialness and rashness
Jude caught up the word *manifest*, and hung upon it a question
which sprang from his misconception of Christ's work in the
world, which was not external power and deliverance of Palestine from imperial Rome, but a kingdom of righteousness and
peace and prayer. " I will love him, and will manifest myself
to him. Judas saith unto Him, (not Iscariot,) Lord, how is it
that Thou wilt manifest Thyself unto us and not unto the
world ? " In this unspiritual conception of Christ's great aim
Jude was no worse than the rest of the apostles, with the exception perhaps of S. John. It was only after Pentecost that
this popular Messianic theory was laid aside. Then the Holy
Ghost became their teacher, according to the great promise
which immediately follows this rash question of Jude ; and
then also, in the practical work of preaching the Gospel according to the command of Christ, they learned the higher
nature of doctrine as compared with government. All along
the three years' ministry of Christ both the disciples and the

multitude wistfully looked on the succession of miracles as what might more profitably have been utilised against Cæsar than against the kingdom of Satan. Thus does even this incident throw hardly any light on the special disposition or work of S. Jude the son of James as one of the twelve.

S. Matthias,

THE APOSTLE.

DAY, FEBRUARY 24.

ORATIO.—*Deus qui beatum Mathiam apostolorum tuorum collegio sociasti: tribue, quæsumus, ut ejus interventione tuæ circa nos pietatis semper viscera sentiamus. Per Dominum.*
For the Epistle.—Acts i. 15-26.
The Gospel.—S. Matt. xi. 25-30.

COLLECT.—*O Almighty God, who into the place of the traitor Judas didst choose Thy faithful servant Matthias to be of the number of the twelve apostles; Grant that Thy Church, being alway preserved from false apostles, may be ordered and guided by faithful and true pastors; through Jesus Christ our Lord. Amen.*
For the Epistle.—Acts i. 15-26.
The Gospel.—S. Matt. xi. 25-30.

Who is God's chosen priest ?
He who on Christ stands waiting day and night,
Who traced His holy steps, nor ever ceased,
   From Jordan banks to Bethphage height :

Who hath learned lowliness
From his Lord's cradle, patience from His Cross ;
Whom poor men's eyes and hearts consent to bless ;
   To whom, for Christ, the world is loss ;

Who both in agony
Hath seen Him and in glory ; and in both
Owned Him divine, and yielded, nothing loth,
  Body and soul, to live and die,

In witness of his Lord,
In humble following of his Saviour dear :
This is the man to wield th' unearthly sword,
  Warring unharmed with sin and fear.

Dread Searcher of the hearts,
Thou who didst seal by Thy descending Dove
Thy servant's choice, O help us in our parts,
  Else helpless found, to learn and teach Thy love.
                    —KEBLE, *S. Matthias' Day.*

Annue, Christe, seculorum Do-
    mine,
Nobis per hujus tibi cara merita :
Ut quæ te coram graviter deliqui-
    mus
Hujus solvantur gloriosis precibus.

O Christ, Thou Lord of all,
  Thine ear to hear us bow,
On this the festival
  Of Thine apostle now ;
That all the weary load
  Of many a foul offence
May, as we sing His praise,
  Be lost in penitence.

Salva Redemptor plasma tuum
    nobile
Signatum sancto vultus tui lumine.
Ne lacerari sinas fraude dæmonum
Propter quos mortis exsolvisti pre-
    tium.

Redeemer, save Thy work,
  Thy noble work of grace ;
And shed on us the light
  That beameth from Thy face ;
Nor suffer us to fall
  To Satan's wiles a prey,
For whom Thou didst on earth
  Death's costly ransom pay.

Dole captivos esse tuos servulos,
Absolve reos, compeditos erige :
Et quos cruore redemisti proprio,
Rex bone, tecum fac gaudere per-
    petim.
        —*Anglo-Saxon Breviary.*[1]

Release Thy flock enthralled
  By sin's captivity :
Forgive each guilty soul,
  And set the bondmen free :
And those Thou hast redeemed
  With Thine own precious blood,
Grant to rejoice with Thee,
  Thou Saviour kind and good.
              —J. M. NEALE.

---

[1] This very ancient and simple hymn consisted of five verses as used
on the feast-day of each apostle. The last verse (here omitted) was a

"And the lot fell upon Matthias; and he was numbered with the eleven apostles."—ACTS i. 26.

CAREFUL though S. Luke's account be of the election of an apostle to fill the place vacated by Judas Iscariot, it is remarkable that neither before nor after this narrative of election have we one word anywhere in the New Testament touching the man so solemnly appointed. We know even less about him than about Simon Zelotes or Jude the son of James.

The method employed in filling the vacancy is therefore the main if not sole matter of interest. It is S. Peter who presides, showing how thorough was his restoration to his old place with the goodwill of the whole one hundred and twenty believers present. He begins by explaining the vacancy in connection with the fulfilment of two passages in the Psalter —lxix. 25, "Let their habitation be desolate, and let none dwell in their tents;" cix. 8, "Let his days be few, and let another take his office." He then lays down the limit of choice as regards qualification, that it must be of one conversant with the whole ministry of Jesus from His baptism to His ascension. Next he describes the particular work to which an apostle is called, "To be a witness with us of the Lord's resurrection." Then, having found and nominated two who were thus qualified, a special appeal was made in prayer for the divine guidance; and the final choice was left, by the use of the sacred lot, to God the Head of the Church. The lot was never appealed to after Pentecost; although it has often been superstitiously used in the form of accepting random passages of Scripture that happen first to catch the eye. The two chief points observable herein are,—acquaintance required with the whole course of Christ's public minis-

doxology. There were ten forms of the first verse, varied according to the commemoration, eight being for apostles, and two for S. Barnabas and Pope Gregory the Great. All the verses are given in the Anglo-Saxon Hymnarium, and also in the Sarum Breviary.

try ; and the special duty of testifying to the risen Redeemer. The defining of these points on this occasion throws a valuable light on the apostolic office, and it was only by miraculous vision and special training from heaven that S. Paul was enabled to become an apostle, notwithstanding the lateness of his conversion, and his inexperience of Christ's three years' ministry.

The principles here involved have been stated with singular clearness and force by Bishop Westcott in the following passage : [1]—

"The primary Gospel was proved, so to speak, in life before it was fixed in writing. Out of the countless multitude of Christ's acts, those were gathered, in the ministry of twenty years, which were seen to have the fullest representative significance for the exhibition of His divine life. The oral collection thus formed became in every sense coincident with the Gospel; and our gospels are the permanent compendium of its contents.

"This then was the first great stage in the apostles' work—the first step in the composition of the gospels—to adapt the lessons which they learned with Christ to the requirements of the growing Church. Every detail of their conduct tends to indicate the clearness with which they apprehended the requirements of their office, and fulfilled them by the guidance of the promised Spirit. They remained together at Jerusalem in close communion for a period long enough to shape a common narrative, and to fix it with requisite consistency. They recognised that their message was popular and historic. The place of instruction was the synagogue and the market-place, and not the student's chamber. The qualification for the apostolate was personal acquaintance with Christ ; and S. Paul admitted the condition, and affirmed that he had fulfilled it. Of the great majority of the apostles, all that we know certainly is, that they were engaged in this first charge of instructing orally

---

[1] Study of the Gospels, chap. iii.

the multitudes who were waiting to welcome their tidings. The common work of "the twelve" was *prayer and the ministry of the Word*, though the labours of all are summed up in the acts of two or three. The rest of the apostles were engaged with S. Peter on the day of Pentecost, and guided by their teaching the new converts. Signs were wrought by their hands to arrest the attention of their hearers and symbolise the purport of their message—*the testimony of the resurrection*. The apostles, in a body, were brought before the Council, and beaten and forbidden *to speak in the name of Jesus*. And when all others were scattered, they remained steadfastly at Jerusalem, watching the progress of the Church, supplying its wants and regulating its discipline. *The twelve foundations of the wall of the city of God bore the names of the twelve apostles.*"

This view of the relation of the apostles to the evangelists is at once historical and striking. The apostles are the true founders and teachers, the men of origination under the Church's divine Head; whereas, with all their dignity and usefulness and permanence of record, the evangelists are only secondary both in date and function. The evangelists, however, are much more to us now than they were to the first generation of believers who were still in living contact with the twelve; and for this reason their writing finds an opening place in the New Testament. To us and succeeding generations they do a large part of the work originally and so well done by the apostles. They are the four infallible teachers as to Christ from His birth to His ascension.

S. Stephen,

THE PROTOMARTYR.

DAY, DECEMBER 26.

ORATIO.—*Da nobis, quæsumus, Domine, imitari quod colimus, ut discamus et inimicos diligere: quia ejus natalitia celebramus, qui novit etiam pro persecutoribus exorare Dominum nostrum Jesum Christum Filium tuum.   Qui tecum vivit.*

For the Epistle.—Acts vi. 8-10, vii. 54-60.
The Gospel.—S. Matt. xxiii. 34-39.

COLLECT.—*Grant, O Lord, that, in all our sufferings here upon earth for the testimony of Thy truth, we may steadfastly look up to heaven, and by faith behold the glory that shall be revealed; and, being filled with the Holy Ghost, may learn to love and bless our persecutors by the example of Thy first martyr Saint Stephen, who prayed for his murderers to Thee, O blessed Jesus, who standest at the right hand of God to succour all those that suffer for Thee, our only Mediator and Advocate.   Amen.*

For the Epistle.—Acts vii. 55-60.
The Gospel.—S. Matt. xxiii. 34-39.

Heri mundus exultavit,
Et exultans celebravit
Christi natalitia
Heri chorus angelorum
Prosecutus est cœlorum
Regem cum lætitia.

Yesterday with exultation,
Joined the world in celebration
 Of her promised Saviour's birth;
Yesterday the angel-nation
Poured the strains of jubilation
 O'er the Monarch born on earth;

Protomartyr et Levita,
Clarus fide, clarus vita,
Clarus et miraculis,
Sub hac luce triumphavit
Et triumphans insultavit
Stephanus incredulis.

But to-day o'er death victorious,
By his faith and actions glorious,
 By his miracles renowned,
See the deacon triumph gaining,
'Midst the faithless faith sustaining,
 First of holy martyrs found.

Agonista, nulli cede ;
Certa certus de mercede,
Persevera, Stephane :
Justa falsis testibus,
Confuta sermonibus
Synagoga Satanæ.

Testis tuus est in cœlis,
Testis verax et fidelis,
Testis innocentiæ.
Nomen habes Coronati,
Te tormenta decet pati
Pro corona gloriæ.

Pro corona non marcenti
Perfer brevis vim tormenti,
Te manet victoria.
Tibi fiet mors, natalis,
Tibi pœna terminalis
Dat vitæ primordia.

Plenus Sancto Spiritu
Penetrat intuitu
Stephanus cœlestia.
Videns Dei gloriam
Crescit ad victoriam
Suspirat ad præmia.

En a dextris Dei stantem
Jesum, pro te dimicantem
Stephane, considera.
Tibi cœlos reserari,
Tibi Christum revelari
Clama voce libera.

Ne peccatum statuatur
His, a quibus lapidatur,
Genu ponit et precatur,
Condolens insaniæ :
In Christo sic obdormivit,
Qui Christo sic obedivit,
Et cum Christo semper vivit,
Martyrum primitiæ.
—Adam *of S. Victor :*
Trench, *Lat. Poetry*, p. 212.

Onward, champion, falter never,
Sure of sure reward for ever,
  Holy Stephen, persevere ;
Perjured witnesses confounding,
Satan's synagogue astounding
  By thy doctrine true and clear.

Thine own Witness is in heaven,
True and faithful, to thee given,
  Witness of thy blamelessness :
By thy name a crown implying,
Meet it is thou shouldst be dying
  For the crown of righteousness.

For the crown that fadeth never
Bear the torturers' brief endeavour ;
  Victory waits to end the strife :
Death shall be thy life's beginning,
And life's losing be the winning
  Of the true and better life.

Filled with God's most Holy Spirit,
See the heaven thou shalt inherit,
  Stephen, gaze into the skies :
There God's glory steadfast viewing,
Thence thy victor - strength renew-
  Pant for thy eternal prize.   [ing,

See as Jewish foes invade thee,
See how Jesus stands to aid thee,
  Stands at God's right hand on
      high :   [thee,
Tell how opened heaven is shown
Tell how Jesus waits to own thee,
  Tell it with thy latest cry.

As the dying martyr kneeleth,
For his murderers he appealeth,
  For their madness grieving sore ;
Then in Christ he sleepeth sweetly,
And with Christ he reigneth meetly,
  Martyr first-fruits evermore.
            —J. M. Neale.

"And they stoned Stephen, calling upon God, and saying,
Lord Jesus, receive my spirit. And he kneeled down,
and cried with a loud voice, Lord, lay not this sin to
their charge. And when he had said this, he fell
asleep."—ACTS vii. 59.

SPECIAL interest attaches to the name of Stephen as the
first Christian martyr, the first of believers in Jesus who
sealed his testimony with his blood. So many have followed
in different ages and countries, and by different forms of
death, and their deaths have contributed so much to commend to others the Gospel for which they suffered, that the
history of this class of witnesses, while one of the most sad, is
also one of the most splendid chapters of the general history
of Christianity. It so happens that in the first we have also
a typical example; for here martyrdom meets us at its noblest
as at its freshest. The commemoration of S. Stephen has
always been very hearty, even though it immediately follows
Christmas Day, and calls men from joy to sorrow, as emphasised in the opening verses of the grand hymn of Adam of
S. Victor at Paris.

Any proper appreciation of Stephen's faithfulness unto
death, and of the value of his testimony to the cross of Christ,
must rest on a careful consideration of what is stated as to
his office, conduct, and defence in Acts vi. and vii. These
chapters, with viii. 1-2, contain all that Scripture says directly
regarding him.

First comes his position as one of the seven deacons. While
in subsequent ages, and in none more than the present, men
have dogmatised about Church government and clerical orders,
it is remarkable how open on these points the New Testament
itself is. We have the name of one office here and of another
there, but they are never presented in the rigid method adopted
in most modern books on the subject. When deacons appear
in Acts vi. it is the first mention of any office distinct from the
apostolate; yet this mention comes in, not for the sake of the

office itself, but in connection with the appeasing of a certain discontent among the early disciples. And the allusion is so made as to imply that other deacons existed earlier than these seven. Each of the seven names in vi. 5 is "Grecian" or Hellenist, and it was in respect of the murmuring of Hellenists against native Hebrews for the neglect of their widows in the daily ministration that the seven were appointed. The previous Hebrew or native deacons are alleged to have been one-sided toward Hebrew widows. The daily ministration is in the original *deaconry;* thus implying that the same work already existed, and had it been in charge of the apostles, then the murmuring would have been against them; whereas it appears only to have been addressed to them for redress. Their position was : We will not leave our more spiritual work to put or keep right those of whose partiality you complain; but we will provide an additional staff and branch specially to attend to the interests alleged to be neglected. As regards modern sticklers for " orders," it is rather hard on their mathematically exact theories that the appointment of deacons here is not made by the apostles at all, but by popular election. " The saying pleased the whole multitude, and *they* chose." " Whom they set before the apostles : and when they had prayed, they laid their hands on them." The apostles only ratified the popular choice and ordained the men.

Three qualifications were named by the apostles to be attended to by the disciples in selecting and nominating. "Wherefore, brethren, look ye out among you seven men (first) of honest report, (second) full of the Holy Ghost and (third) wisdom, whom we may appoint over this business." In public office, secular or sacred, from the highest to the lowest, it is of great value that a man start with a fairly good name, which is what is meant by honest, honourable, or respectable report. As concerns the deacon, this has probably a main reference to report within the Christian community. In the case of the higher office of bishop, named before the deacon in 1 Tim. iii., it is specially said that the good report should exist even beyond the Christian circle. "Moreover he must have a good report of them which are without; lest he fall into reproach and the snare of the devil." As to the second qualification, being full of the Holy Ghost, that could be more definitely ascertained then than now, because there were spiritual gifts as well as graces in the early Church, and in these Stephen was specially distinguished. "And Stephen, full of faith and power, did great miracles and wonders among the people." Doubtless Stephen's eminence in gifts was accompanied by a corresponding richness in graces, which would, in fact, be the source of his remarkable zeal and success. But just as a good report is the foundation of fitness for office generally, so for a sacred office like the diaconate it was necessary that there should be that character regenerate and sanctified which proceeds from the operation of the Holy Spirit in the heart. The third qualification of wisdom or prudence has respect to the special duties of a deacon in the administration of temporal concerns in the case of the more necessitous. Without wisdom the fund of charity might have been misapplied. A quite different sort of knowledge and insight is required judiciously to assist the poor, as compared with the work of expounding Scripture or taking part in the deliberations of a Church court. And this special gift of discreetness and prudence was sought and found in all the deacons, and best of all in Stephen. Moreover, it is a common and probable supposition that Stephen was already a tried and well-known man in the Christian community; the idea being that he was one of the seventy disciples sent forth two and two to heal and teach in the cities and villages.

Having noted the method of appointment to office, another important matter touching Stephen is to observe from what source the opposition proceeded that had so sad a conclusion. Five synagogues, or rather one synagogue of fivefold composition of Grecian or Hellene Jews, were the instigators. "Then there arose certain of the synagogue, which is called the synagogue of the Libertines, and Cyrenians, and Alexandrians, and of them of Cilicia and of Asia, disputing with Stephen." Whatever the chapel arrangements among these five were, the general position of all, both toward Law and Gospel, was the same : for the Law they were zealous, and against the Gospel they were bitter. The zeal in the one case, and the bitterness in the other, were actually greater than in the case of native Hebrews.

Mixture of foreign training and experience doubtless tended in this direction. Some natures are affected thereby in the way of tightening bonds and increasing narrowness ; whereas others, in a better spirit, are led to liberality and higher culture. We see this in connection with distinctively Scottish literature in the case of our colonies as compared with those at home. Many of the greatest enthusiasts for Scott, Burns, and Ramsay, are men who never saw Scotland at all, but have good Scottish blood, and cherish fondly all Scottish associations in America or Australia or India. Others, again, so situated, have their intellectual horizon expanded, and escape from many prejudices which we at home must put up with, or perhaps fail even to discover the singularity of.

Both of these influences seem to be at work in the history before us. Stephen, as a representative Hellenist, is an example of a liberalised Jew who, by genial Grecian influences, had laid firm hold of the Christian system, so as early to find out for himself that it contained what was destined to have a far wider and freer course than the law of Moses ever had or could have. Stephen, in fact, was an anticipation of Paul— the most liberal-minded of the apostles, because of his connection with Tarsus, and his Grecian as well as Jewish culture. On the contrary, Stephen's Hellenistic opponents from the colonial synagogue were specimens of fossilised Jews, Pharisees of the Pharisees, and out-Heroders of Herod, prepared to go any length against any who hinted at a different view of the kingdom of God from their own. Thus the struggle here is really between two tendencies both characteristic of colonial Judaism —the centripetal and centrifugal.

It is a melancholy task to trace the conduct of this narrow
and intolerant party, whose zeal leads them on to fury and unscrupulousness.   Stephen's success in word and deed they cannot cope with on their side.   They cannot meet miracle with
miracle ; they cannot even meet argument with argument, or
Scripture with Scripture.   Doubly foiled, they resort to sub-
orning of false witnesses, prepared by gift or promise to bring
forward exaggerated or perverted versions of Stephen's sayings.
And they also prejudge the case by stirring up all the opposition they can among the people, elders, and scribes.   Then
they bring him to the Council of seventy-two members, the
supreme ecclesiastical court of the nation.   All the calm and
fairness that befit a legal trial are thus deliberately set at
nought : it is no real trial at all, but a persecution, like a
modern heresy-hunt, a scene of rage and violence.

A third prominent matter for consideration is Stephen's defence before the Council, as given in Acts vii. at length.   The
speech of Stephen is to be judged as an answer to the charges
that had been made against him.   Two versions of these
charges are given,—one, that he had spoken " blasphemous
words against Moses and against God ; " another, that he had
spoken " blasphemous words against this holy place and the
law."   The two versions of the charge easily coalesce,—Moses
and the law being one ; and God and the holy place the other.
Stephen's way of meeting the charge is peculiar ; not so direct
as we would have expected.   A large part of his speech goes
over an outline of Jewish history.   He mentions Abraham,
Joseph, Moses, Aaron, David, and Solomon, in such way as
to show that he and his hearers were at one in honouring all
these, and in believing that God held communication with
them all.   Now this contains in it a refutation of both of the
charges.   But he was interrupted and stopped before concluding his speech.   They refused to listen longer at a point where
he begins to *interpret* the history as to the outline of the facts
of which they were agreed.   His interpretation makes out
Israel in past ages to have been disobedient ; a point which

they violently deny. If he intended, as was likely, to close by an application of this to the history of Jesus and to his own present position, he was not allowed to do more than point that way. The last thought in his speech, as it stands, is this. "Ye stiff-necked and uncircumcised in heart and ears, ye do always resist the Holy Ghost : as your fathers did, so do ye. Which of the prophets have not your fathers persecuted? and they have slain them which showed before of the coming of the Just One ; of whom ye have been now the betrayers and murderers."

There is but faint trace in the speech of what we would have expected declarative of the great principle that the whole Jewish system was to prepare the way for a wider Church, wherein all men would be equal in the sight of God, and all lands equal in privilege and nearness. The allusion to Solomon's words at the Temple-dedication is of this kind ; but they are a mere germ compared with our Lord's saying to the woman of Samaria as to spiritual worship, or compared even with a few Isaiah passages (ii., ix., lx.) as to the spread of Messiah's kingdom. What we should have expected from Stephen was a short version of what is so fully done in Hebrews, which explains the relation of priest, altar, and offering to the wider and more spiritual system of the New Testament, showing that there is consistency between Old and New, and that the New confers fresh honour on the Old, instead of disrespectfully pushing it aside. Something like this was actually done by our Lord Himself in the Sermon on the Mount, when He was charged with preaching doctrine at variance with the law. He took up a series of specific points, and gave them wide and stringent application to practical righteousness and true piety. "One jot or one tittle shall not pass from the law till all be fulfilled."

It was at a conviction for blasphemy that alike the accusers and judges of Stephen were aiming. Probably they would have arrived at that conclusion had the case come to a regular end. As it was, the foregone conclusion was reached, not from materials in the case proper that was before the court, but from a special incident which happened when Stephen spoke describing what he saw, whether in external reality, or in an inner vision of prophecy, is disputed. "Behold, I see the heavens opened, and the Son of man standing on the right hand of God. Then they cried out with a loud voice, and stopped their ears, and ran upon him with one accord, and cast him out of the city, and stoned him." Thus was the knot cut instead of being untied. There was no sentence, no authority, only tumult. Not only was there no sentence; but, as we know from the death of Jesus, even had there been sentence of death by this court, they could not have carried out capital punishment without sanction of the Roman governor.

The noblest of all as concerns Stephen yet remains—his conduct in the presence of death, wherein was neither fear nor anger. Hasty and cruel as was the closing scene, his piety and charity are undisturbed. For his fidelity to the Crucified One he incurred danger and death. He was faithful to the last unto Jesus, to whom specially it was that his dying prayer was addressed; and that prayer accordingly forms one of the strongest Scriptural evidences of our blessed Lord's divinity. "Lord Jesus, receive my spirit." Could such a prayer be addressed to one less than divine? more especially when the very occasion of his dying was the question of what was due to God and what constituted blasphemy. Here is Stephen at one with Thomas in his no less significant words, "My Lord and my God." As to charity, Stephen is of the same spirit with his divine Master on a like occasion, but where to martyrdom was added an infinite sacrifice. Jesus said, "Father, forgive them: they know not what they do." Similarly did Stephen, "He kneeled down, and cried with a loud voice, Lord, lay not this sin to their charge. And when he had said this, he fell asleep."

The whole narrative implies that Stephen was a comparatively young man. His activity and zeal, and partly the very office of deacon, point this way. As we look admiringly on the many excellent things in his career and character, we are led keenly to regret his early removal from the scene of his labours and success and further promise. We cannot help counting up the elements of his fame,—his high place at first in the confidence of his fellow-Christians—his large faculty in spiritual and miraculous gifts—his skill in arguing and pleading for the Christian cause—his precocious enlightenment as to the Gospel superseding legal ordinances, and the Temple giving place to sanctuaries in all lands—his boldness in speaking before the Council—his acquaintance with the Old Testament and with commentaries and traditions—his bold statement of his prophetic vision—his pious commendation of his soul—and his charitable intercession for his murderers. Seeing these manifold and noble features in a comparatively young Christian, we are apt to think, had he been spared to a ripe old age thus firmly and judiciously working, what a gain it would have been to early Christendom! This is natural and right; but his actual fate, very untimely from a human point of view, has perhaps profited the Church really more than prolonged work and a natural death would have done. Here very strikingly has God made the wrath of His enemies to praise Him. Stephen's early death is not a wasted life. Who can tell to what degree we are indebted to Stephen's end for Paul's beginning? The two men and their careers, the one taking up the other's work after a marvellous interval of struggle between the persecutor Saul and Paul the apostle, seem almost like a transmigration of souls. Moreover, who can tell how many a persecuted Christian has both lived and died the calmer for Stephen's example? Nobler beginning could not have been to "the noble army of martyrs." And apart from the extreme case of martyrdom altogether, who can tell how many now glorified or now converted souls have been led to think seriously and favourably of the Gospel by reading of Stephen's boldness, calmness, and charity? Just as our Lord Himself, by being lifted up, draws all men to Him, so does a death like Stephen's work towards attraction of men by begetting a marvellous sympathy. This is what has been expressed so well in the famous axiom or proverb of Tertullian — *Sanguis martyrum, semen Christianorum;* martyr blood, Christian seed.

In connection with Christian martyrs a very striking thing is to note at whose hands or instigation they suffer. There were hundreds and thousands in early times who were put to death for Christ's sake at the hands of heathen persecutors, such as Roman emperors and governors of provinces, while yet the old worship of the gods of Olympus was the religion of the State. Similarly in modern times, in connection with Christian missions, we see sometimes the best of men made victims of savage fury. So happened it to many converted natives of Madagascar in their first conflict with the heathenism of their native island. So happened it to Bishop Patteson, perhaps the noblest of our modern missionaries, when he was betrayed and massacred by enraged Polynesians. Such martyrdoms are comparatively natural in the course of the mighty struggle between light and darkness.

But as many or more martyrs come from the struggles of one branch of the Christian Church against another. These are inexpressibly sad and shameful. There is not a branch almost of the Church but has had martyrs made by fratricidal hands under the influence of bigotry and ambition and revenge. Scotland itself has seen martyrs to four creeds at least, Celtic, Roman, Episcopal, and Presbyterian. And not much better than the wickedness of Christians fratricidally making martyrs is the historic dishonesty of each Church denying the existence of martyrs outside of itself, or evading to tell of them, or saying that they deserved what they suffered. In Stephen's case it is a specimen of this sadder kind of martyrdom that we witness. His death was compassed, not by heathen Romans, Greeks, or outer barbarians, but by the members of a colonial synagogue in Jerusalem—*i.e.,* by men who worshipped the same Jehovah, sang the same Psalms, and read the same Law and Prophets. The worst wounds of the Christian Church have ever been those received in the house of its friends. By its mutual martyrdoms, and by those hatreds and strifes of which martyrdom has so often been the index and climax, the Christian Church has hindered and scandalised itself more perhaps than the world and Satan have done.

It is usual to point to martyrs like Stephen as our examples; and this is certainly the highest and best use to which their deaths can be put by those who read their histories or keep their commemoration days. Happily there is no need in our quiet time to prepare men for these earlier hardships. We sit peacefully under the shade of our vine and fig-tree, no man making us afraid. What we now need is to remember gratefully the sore sufferers of former ages, and to imitate the spirit that sustained them in their last hour. Some portion of Stephen's spirit is still a necessity of the true and earnest Christian. We may copy his faithfulness and constancy even in the plainer path of modern life Let us learn to fortify ourselves against seductions, jeers, and intimidation. When we see the line of duty clear before us, let us manfully tread the straight and narrow way, turning neither to the right nor to the left. The Christian of our day who is firm in principle, ready to meet profit or loss indifferently, ready to win or lose a friend indifferently, ready to face popularity or unpopularity with the same pure heart and unbending purpose, is a man who has in him the germ of martyrdom. And that is a type greatly needed in our easy, and luxurious, and fashionable, and popular age, to give some pith and backbone to society and the Church.

It may almost seem like a descent, after tracing a martyr's career and crown, to allude to Stephen in his simple official capacity as one of the seven deacons; and yet this is the most useful of all lights in which he can be viewed. The diaconate is a grossly misunderstood office in the Presbyterian Churches. But taking it in the Scriptural and historical sense, as has been well preserved in the Roman and Anglican Churches, there is a great deal of material for encouragement and guidance in the narrative of the election and ordination of the first seven, among whom Stephen was of such outstanding fame and glory.

More pointed allusion will be made to clerical orders under the names of Philip and Timothy; but meanwhile it may be appropriate to quote a very ancient prayer on behalf of deacons on the solemn occasion of their being ordained to office.

COLLECT.—*O Lord our God, who by Thine own presence dost shed the abundance of the Holy Spirit on those who are set apart, by Thine inscrutable power, to become ministers and to serve Thy spotless mysteries; Keep Thy servant whom Thou hast willed to be promoted to the ministry of a deacon, that he may hold the mystery of the faith in a pure conscience with all virtue; vouchsafe him the grace given to Thy first martyr Stephen, who was first called by Thee to the work of this ministry; and enable him to administer according to Thy good pleasure the degree assigned to him by Thy goodness, for they that minister rightly purchase to themselves a good degree; and fill him by the presence of Thy holy and life-giving Spirit, with all faith and love and sanctification. For Thou art our God, and to Thee we render glory. Father, Son, and Holy Spirit, now and ever and unto ages of ages.*[1]

S. Philip,

THE DEACON.

COLLECTS.—*Grant, O Lord, we beseech Thee, that the course of this world may be so peaceably ordered by Thy governance, that Thy Church may joyfully serve Thee in all godly quietness; through Jesus Christ our Lord. Amen.*[2]

[1] Ordinal of the Eastern Church, Bright, Collects, p. 176.
[2] Fifth Sunday after Trinity.

Almighty God, who by Thy Divine Providence hast appointed divers orders of ministers in Thy Church, and didst inspire Thine apostles to choose into the order of deacons the first martyr, Saint Stephen, with others; Mercifully behold these Thy servants now called to the like office and administration; replenish them so with the truth of Thy doctrine, and adorn them with innocency of life, that, both by word and good example, they may faithfully serve Thee in this office, to the glory of Thy name and the edification of Thy Church; through the merits of our Saviour Jesus Christ, who liveth and reigneth with Thee and the Holy Ghost now and for ever. Amen.

Almighty God, giver of all good things, who of Thy great goodness hast vouchsafed to accept and take these Thy servants unto the office of deacons in Thy Church; Make them, we beseech Thee, O Lord, to be modest, humble, and constant in their ministration, to have a ready will to observe all spiritual discipline; that they, having always the testimony of a good conscience, and continuing ever stable and strong in Thy Son Christ, may so behave themselves in this inferior office, that they may be found worthy to be called unto the higher ministries in Thy Church; through the same Thy Son our Saviour Jesus Christ, to whom be glory and honour, world without end. Amen.[1]

The Epistle.—1 Tim. iii. 8-13.
The Gospel.—S. Luke x. 1-9.

"Then Philip went down to the city of Samaria, and preached Christ unto them. . . . But when they believed Philip preaching the things concerning the kingdom of God, and the name of Jesus Christ, they were baptised, both men and women."—ACTS viii. 5-12.

FEW Scripture biographies are so clear as that of Philip the Deacon, which is all contained in one book, filling Acts viii.; his bare name and office being given in advance in vi. 5,

---

[1] Common Prayer, Ordering of Deacons.

and his abode and family mentioned xxi. 8. And the history is no less interesting than simple.

The name of Philip stands second in the list of the seven; and he is the only one of the deacons besides Stephen of whom we have any personal record. Although his appointment took place at Jerusalem, he seems to have belonged by birth and abode to Cæsarea. There was his home with his daughters, when twenty-three years later he entertained Paul and his company for several days in 58 A.D. at the close of the apostle's third great missionary journey. His work in Samaria, and especially in the coast towns from Gaza to Cæsarea, points in the same direction. And there is the express testimony of S. Isodore of Pelusium at the mouth of the Nile, and thus near to part of Philip's sphere of work.[1]

The origin of this mission in Samaria, which is associated with the name of Philip, was "the great persecution against the Church which was at Jerusalem: and they were all scattered abroad throughout the regions of Judea and Samaria, except the apostles. . . . Then Philip went down to the city of Samaria, and preached Christ unto them." Thus it was Philip's own choice of sphere, not a command by the apostles; and the choice seems determined by his own early familiarity with the district. The nature of his work and method is exactly defined. His preaching of Christ was earnest and telling—the more so as it was accompanied by miraculous signs which benefited the people and drew their attention to his doctrine, while the fame of the miracles drew others to see and hear for themselves. Three classes of miracles are named—viz., cures of demoniacal possession, palsy, and lameness. These works were confined to Philip's own action in the first instance; for it was only after the arrival of Peter and John from Jerusalem that power to work miracles through the gift of the Holy Ghost was conferred on any of the new and ordinary disciples. "And the people with one accord

---

[1] Alban Butler, Lives of the Saints—under 6th June, the day of Philip the Deacon in the Calendar.

gave heed unto those things which Philip spake, hearing and seeing the miracles which he did. For unclean spirits, crying with loud voice, came out of many that were possessed with them : and many taken with palsies, and that were lame, were healed. And there was great joy in that city. . . . Now when the apostles which were at Jerusalem heard that Samaria had received the word of God, they sent unto them Peter and John : who, when they were come down, prayed for them, that they might receive the Holy Ghost. (For as yet He was fallen upon none of them : only they were baptised in the name of the Lord Jesus.) Then laid they their hands on them, and they received the Holy Ghost."

One of those baptised by Philip was Simon Magus, born at Gitton in Samaria, and who had already gained a great name and influence among his countrymen. This consummate scoundrel requires careful attention here on his first appearance, because very soon afterwards he was more sharply and properly dealt with by Peter than by Philip ; and a quarter of a century later the arch-impostor reappears in Rome under the patronage of Nero, and has a certain share in the persecution associated with the joint martyrdom of Peter and Paul. Before Philip's ministry he had carried the people with him to assent to his wild claims to not only a heavenly commission, but to being himself a demiurgos, or manifestation of the divine, parallel to the Word or the Paraclete in Christianity. Thus he "bewitched [= amazed] the people of Samaria, giving out that himself was some great one." Philip's practical and merciful healings of demoniacs, palsied, and lame persons, as compared with Simon's barren marvels, based on a few chemical secrets or sleight of hand, drew away the people from the impostor : and the cunning fellow, instead of making an outcry and opposition, pretended to fall in with Philip, and got himself baptised, evidently in hope of learning Philip's secrets (for he regarded him only as a more powerful cheat). "He continued with Philip," marks an observer, hanging on for mischief and his own ends ultimately. On the coming of Peter and John, the superior craft (as it appeared to Simon) was so plain in not only themselves doing wonders but conferring like power on others, that Simon was carried away to a hasty proposal to buy a power so suitable to his own line of business, that even a large price could soon be recouped by selling it over the country. Great must have been the surprise of the artful merchant at S. Peter's vehement denunciation of the proposed bargain; for the two men belonged to absolutely different worlds of principle and aim. This living specimen of a Gnostic and his system embodied in a few verses in Acts viii. explains to us sufficiently not only the fire and indignation of Peter at the moment, but also the angry energy of his denunciation in the second chapter of his second Epistle when the system had become wider spread; and explains also the still greater vehemence of S. Jude in his Epistle, dealing with the same arch-deceivers and corrupters.

The close of this short and special mission of the two apostles is noticeable for this, that after their work in the city of Samaria, on their return journey to Jerusalem they "preached the Gospel in many villages of the Samaritans"—which is the very same course as was followed a little later by Philip with the line of coast towns between Azotus and Cæsarea, where he sowed the seed of the kingdom literally by the wayside, after accomplishing what falls now to be stated.

Very striking and picturesque is the narrative in the second half of Acts viii. An angelic order directed Philip to leave his Samaritan work and go to the Jerusalem and Gaza road. A second communication of a supernatural kind directed him to join himself to a chariot in which a traveller sat reading a book aloud, according to an Eastern custom that has some advantages for impressiveness and understanding and memory, although more laborious and slow. Philip's question, "Understandest thou what thou readest?" brought the two men into spiritual contact; and Philip being invited to explain Isaiah liii., which was the passage read aloud, gave the best possible opportunity of presenting the fulfilment in Jesus of Nazareth.

The happy issue was an additional baptism on their coming
to a stream crossing or alongside their path.   The baptismal
question and answer in verse 37 is probably no part of S.
Luke's narrative, only the later gloss of some doctrinarian; but
the simple extempore baptism is all the more beautiful for its
rustic air.   The convert so marvellously won was the treasurer
of Queen Candace of Ethiopia, the modern Nubia and Abys-
sinia, of which the northern part called Meroë was Candace's.
This laid the foundation of a Christian mission through the
treasurer and the members of his suite, who would see and
hear all that passed between Philip and their master.   The
close of the narrative in the rapture of Philip when his work
was done, reminds us of Obadiah, in 1 Kings xviii. 12, speaking of Elijah.   No details are given of Philip's preaching in
the coast-line of towns between Ashdod and Cæsarea, but the
conclusion at Cæsarea is indicative of home, when we consider
that on his reappearance, twenty-three years later, in xxi. 8, we
find him settled there with his four unmarried daughters, and
entertaining S. Paul and his company.   Here a fresh name
is applied officially—"we entered into the house of Philip the
evangelist, which was one of the seven;" and the additional
name throws some light on early church life.   While Philip's
original appointment was to the diaconate, and expressly associated with the daily ministration and the serving of tables,
vi. 1, 4, as distinguished from prayer and the ministry of the
Word, the fact of his preaching faculty seems to have drawn
him aside and upward from the humbler service, so that actually
we have no record whatever of his deacon work, and everything
told of him, with the exception of his first appointment to office,
belongs to missionary and evangelistic work in the strict and
higher sense.   Whether formally or not appointed as such, he
must have virtually held the status of a presbyter; but as his
work was largely itinerant or missionary, the name of evangelist
would be excellently descriptive.   In recent days the honest
old name has been grievously vulgarised by being applied to and
usurped by a coarse class of religious tramps hawking about

town and country making a muddle of Christianity, and occupying a sort of intermediate position between Simon Magus and Philip. Philip's four prophesying daughters form an ecclesiastical puzzle in point of classification. Their prophesying undoubtedly means some kind of preaching, such as could not be very Pauline according to 1 Tim. ii. 12; but they might be deaconesses like Phebe, Rom. xvi. 1, without being nuns under a vow as some suppose, seeking for a foundation for subsequent usages. The best interpretation is to take them as earnest Christian women, worthy daughters of a noble father, like-minded, and working as his assistants, apart from all theories as to orders; and forming lawful models to as many modern women as choose thus to serve the Divine Master.

As regards the office to which alike Stephen and Philip were ordained by the laying on of hands, it is rather remarkable that in neither case does the biography throw one particle of light on deacon duties properly so called. Each of the two, in fact, was so good, that he may be said to have at once risen above his office into a higher sphere. It was the preaching and argumentative power of Stephen, and not his administrative prudence in economics or his kindness to the poor of the Church, that drew down upon him the rage of the colonial synagogue that ended in his glorious martyrdom. So is it by his preaching in Samaria, Ashdod, and Cæsarea that we know Philip as we do, and not for diaconal work in the sense of Acts vi. 1, 4, or of 1 Tim. iii. 8-13, where the duties are not directly named at all, but only the qualities that are required in the man.

The duties anciently associated with the diaconate are three: to assist the presbyter in the celebration of the sacrament of the Supper; to baptise in absence of the presbyter; and to preach the Word. A fuller list is sometimes given[1]—to take care of the holy table, its ornaments and vessels; to receive the people's offerings; to read the Scripture lessons in church; to assist in the Eucharist by distributing the elements, especially

---

[1] Bingham, Antiq. of the Christian Church, Bk. ii. ch. xx.

the cup; to baptise; to bid prayer to the congregation (*i.e.*, to act as sacred crier announcing the parts of the service); to preach, with the bishop's sanction; to correct irregular behaviour in church. The relation of the deacon to the presbyter corresponded to that of the Levite to the priest in Judaism. In both of these views of the deacon's functions there is practically a total omission of the original duty of caring for widows and tables. And it is also to be noted that while S. Paul carefully separates presbyters and deacons in 1 Tim. iii., he entirely omits deacons in his directions to Titus for Crete. Probably the reason of the omission is that, as Crete consisted of a long line of shore with many villages of no great size, it was considered enough of a beginning to plant a presbyter in each who could take charge of everything, at least for a time, without any assistant.

Thus, while the deacon's office is of apostolic institution, and requires ordination by the laying on of hands, and is inferior to the office of presbyter, there is evidently considerable latitude left as to the range of duties, the independent celebration of the Holy Supper being perhaps the only act that is clearly reserved as a function peculiar to the presbyter. In these circumstances the great question for the present day and for the future is a calm consideration, in the light of Scripture, reason, and usage, of the comparative merits of the two systems, adopted respectively by Rome on the one side, and by Presbyterian Churches on the other. In the Roman Church (and the same holds good of the Anglican) the diaconate is practically an initial stage of the priesthood or presbyterate, and the deacon is in no sense a layman or the representative of the laity. Given respectable literature and conduct, he passes on, almost as a matter of course, to the position of presbyter, often within a single year, so that the partition between the two offices is extremely thin. The special basis of this arrangement is 1 Tim. iii. 8-13.

The deacon of the Presbyterian Churches is a considerably different man, whose special basis is Acts vi. 1, 4. He is a sacred official, with ordination by laying on of hands, but not in one case in five hundred is there any intention or likelihood of his ever passing on from deacon to presbyter. His primary duty is the care of the poor and of Church alms; but he helps at communion and in maintenance of discipline, and is a member of all Church courts, with vote equal to and at same time as the presbyters; he visits the sick or the careless, or any members of the Church, at his discretion, usually having an assigned district; he is not expected to pray or preach at canonical hours, but yet on occasion, especially if an educated man, as many are, he may do both with great advantage; he is distinctly restrained, no matter what his education, from celebrating baptism, communion, or marriage; he is expected to keep to his business or trade, without his ordination making any difference. Thus in every way he is of the people and for the people, and is not a professional man like a presbyter; because no qualification is exacted in point of literature, though he is often well educated as a business man. Surely both types of deacon are alike Scriptural; but the Presbyterian type has greatly the advantage in point of flexibleness, and as a bond of union between the professional class of the presbyterate and the common membership of the Church; yet he cannot be called more Scriptural.

It is a grievous calamity that the Presbyterian type of deacon, so well founded in Scripture and utility and usage, has been marred by putting alongside of him the Puritan mongrel of a Mosaic "elder," as again pointed out here under S. Timothy, where the presbyter is further discussed. Yet this "elder," in spite of his blundering name, is substantially a good honest deacon, and the so-called deacon is really a non-entity. It is a melancholy muddle of names; two are used (elder and deacon) where only one (deacon) should have been. And, through a curious timidity and blindness, hardly a single Presbyterian writer ventures a critical whisper touching a gross blunder, which is both demonstrable and ridiculous in the face of Scripture and Church history.

S. James,

THE LORD'S BROTHER.

COLLECTS.—*Almighty and everlasting God, who adornest the sacred body of Thy Church by the confessions of holy martyrs; Grant us, we pray Thee, that both by their doctrines and their pious example, we may follow after what is pleasing in Thy sight; through Jesus Christ our Lord.*[1]

Lord God of powers, do Thou sanctify the pastors and prelates of Thy sheep; that our adversary the devil, overcome by their faith and holiness, may not dare to touch or violate the flock of the Lord; through the same our Lord Jesus Christ.[2]

O God, of unchangeable power and eternal light, look favourably on Thy whole Church, that wonderful and sacred mystery; and, by the tranquil operation of Thy perpetual providence, carry out the work of man's salvation, and let the whole world feel and see that things which were cast down are being raised up, and things which had grown old are being made new, and all things are returning to perfection through Him from whom they took their origin, even through our Lord Jesus Christ.[3]

The Epistle.—S. James i. 1-12.
The Gospel.—S. Matt. vii. 7-14.

"And the day following Paul went in with us unto James; and all the elders were present."—ACTS xxi. 18.

SUCH is the last mention of this S. James in the Acts; and, beginning here, his office and personality, and how

[1] Sacramentary of Leo the Great, Bright, p. 68.
[2] Gothic Missal, Bright, p. 102.
[3] Gelasian Sacramentary, Bright, p. 98.

he grew into his office, may be traced most conveniently backwards.

As already said under S. James the son of Zebedee, there are three saints of this name in the New Testament, of whom two were apostles—viz., James the son of Zebedee and James the son of Alphæus. The James of Acts xxi. 18 is distinctively "James the Lord's brother." All three, however, were relatives of Jesus. James the son of Zebedee was a cousin, his mother being Salome, a sister of the Blessed Virgin Mary. James the son of Alphæus was the son of a Mary who was the wife of Clôpas = Alphæus, and another sister of the mother of Jesus. While both of these were thus first cousins of Jesus, James the Lord's brother was a son of S. Joseph, the Blessed Virgin's husband; but a son by a former marriage.

Usually the second and third of these three saints are regarded as one; and the result of this has been, that S. James the Lord's brother is left without Day of Commemoration, without Hymn for his Day, without special Collect, and without special Epistle and Gospel Lessons; unless we give up his separate existence or repeat the Day, Hymn, Collect, and Lessons which were partly intended for him under S. James the son of Alphæus.

In Acts xxi. 18 the date is 58 A.D., fully two years before Paul was taken to Rome; the bulk of these years being spent in his imprisonment at Cæsarea—xxiv. 27. S. Paul had just completed one of his great missionary journeys—the third of the series, the record of which fills xviii. 22–xxi. 17; the time occupied being about four years; the places visited being —Phrygia, Galatia, Ephesus, Macedonia, Philippi, Achaia (Greece), Macedonia again, Troas, Philippi, Miletus; landing at Tyre, and proceeding by Ptolemais and Cæsarea to Jerusalem. The companions of Paul, besides Luke, as named in xx. 4, were, "Sopater of Berea; and of the Thessalonians, Aristarchus and Secundus; and Gaius of Derbe, and Timotheus; and of Asia, Tychicus and Trophimus." From his four years' journey the apostle of the Gentiles brought to

Jerusalem collections from Macedonia, Achaia, and Galatia. " Now after many years I came to bring alms to my nation, and offerings."—Acts xxiv. 17, with 1 Cor. xvi. 1, Rom. xv. 26.

Arriving thus in Jerusalem, which is clearly recognised as the headquarters of the Christian Church, by whom is it that Paul and his seven companions are publicly received, and to whom do they make their formal and official report and hand over the funds intrusted to them? First, there is a hearty welcome on the day of arrival by " the brethren "—*i.e.*, all and sundry of believers, in more or less of a promiscuous gathering. But, next day was held a solemn business meeting, when the leaders of the Christian community met in official capacity evidently as a Church court. . And after Paul's detailed account had been given of his work, a speech is made in reply by James in his capacity of president or bishop. And the speech is the more evidently from James that it proceeds exactly on the lines of a previously recorded speech of his, dealing with the adherence of Jews to their old customs, and defining what of these were needful to be laid upon believers of the Gentiles.

Thus James's official speech in xxi. 20-25 carries us back to the speech in xv. 13-21, even more distinctively official, in which Peter is honourably referred to, but in which the speaker uses a more authoritative voice than Peter himself, beginning, " Hearken unto me," and ending, " Wherefore my sentence is." And it was that motion, clearly and firmly put from the chair of the moderator-bishop, that was unanimously adopted. " Then pleased it the apostles and elders, with the whole Church, to send. . . . And they wrote letters by them after this manner; The apostles and elders and brethren send greeting unto the brethren which are of the Gentiles in Antioch and Syria and Cilicia. . . . For it seemed good to the Holy Ghost, and to us, to lay upon you no greater burden than these necessary things; That ye abstain from meats offered to idols, and from blood, and from things strangled, and from fornication : from which if ye keep yourselves, ye shall do well. Fare ye well." According to all fair interpretation of Scripture, this first decree of the first ecclesiastical Council at Jerusalem in 51 A.D. is still binding as a rule of duty on all Christendom, and permanently lays down the line of demarcation ceremonially as between Judaism and Christianity.

There is only one other distinct reference to the same James in xii. 17, where we have the testimony of S. Peter to his prominence or pre-eminence. Peter, on his miraculous escape from Herod's prison, sends a message from the house of Mary the mother of John Mark, " Go show these things unto James, and to the brethren."

These three proofs of the position of James as the recognised president or bishop of the mother-Church of Jerusalem, and which carry us back to the year 44 A.D., are strengthened by two autobiographical passages of S. Paul in Gal. i. 19, ii. 9. "Neither went I up to Jerusalem [after the vision on the road to Damascus] to them which were apostles before me ; but I went into Arabia, and returned again unto Damascus. Then after three years I went up to Jerusalem to see Peter, and abode with him fifteen days. But other of the apostles saw I none, save James the Lord's brother." Here is a hint of the distinctive name which we ought to apply to this saint. Here, too, at the date of 37 A.D., we find Peter prominent and James secondary. In the other reference in Gal. ii. 9, of date 52 A.D., we find the name of James in front of that of Peter, indicating that in the interval that change had taken place which we are engaged in tracing. "Then fourteen years after I went up again to Jerusalem with Barnabas, and took Titus with me also. . . . And when James, Cephas, and John, who seemed to be pillars, perceived the grace that was given unto me, they gave to me and Barnabas the right hands of fellowship ; that we should go unto the heathen, and they unto the circumcision." Three verses further down is a continuance of the reference, which shows James to be a man of

more firmness and consistency than Peter even yet, and gives
a hint of higher status in the mother-Church at Jerusalem.
"But when Peter was come to Antioch, I withstood him to
the face, because he was to be blamed. For before that
certain came from James, he did eat with the Gentiles: but
when they were come, he withdrew and separated himself,
fearing them which were of the circumcision."

This exhausts the information given in Acts, with one important exception in i. 13, where James is not named, but
where the brethren of Jesus are alluded to in a clause *apart*
from the apostles, to whose number they did not belong; but
indicating that *now* they were in sympathy with the apostles as
believers. Having just witnessed our Lord's ascension, "then
returned they unto Jerusalem from the mount called Olivet.
And when they were come in, they went up into an upper room,
where abode both Peter, and James, and John, and Andrew,
Philip, and Thomas, Bartholomew, and Matthew, James the son
of Alphæus, and Simon Zelotes, and Judas the brother of James.
These all continued with one accord in prayer and supplication,
with the women, and Mary the mother of Jesus, and with his
brethren." Although he is not here named, this is the place
where the James who became Bishop of Jerusalem first appears
in Scripture as a *believer*. And his being "the Lord's brother,"
taken along with his own firmness and ability, explains to us
why he rose so rapidly in the confidence of the early Church,
as we have traced in three chapters of the Acts, confirmed by
three passages in S. Paul's autobiography in Galatians.

This is the man who alone could write officially, and did
write the epistle which bears his name. He was no apostle,
and does not call himself so; but "James, a servant of God
and of the Lord Jesus Christ, to the twelve tribes which are
scattered abroad, greeting." As Bishop of Jerusalem he was
entitled to write authoritatively to the Jews of the dispersion.
As Bishop of Jerusalem and also "the Lord's brother," his
Epistle, in arranging the books of the canon of Scripture, is
granted precedence even of the two Epistles of S. Peter and

the three Epistles of S. John; following thus the arrangement of names in S. Paul's autobiography, "James, Cephas, and John, who seemed to be pillars."

But to enable us better to understand both the man and his epistle, it is needful to make a second backward journey over the Gospels, as over the Acts. "The Lord's brother" means that James was a son of S. Joseph, the husband of the Blessed Virgin Mary, by a *former* marriage; more strictly, it is half-brother of the Lord, as in the eye of Jewish law. But with perfect exactness, in view of the miraculous conception of Jesus by the Holy Ghost, James bore no blood-relationship to Jesus at all; but only they were brought up together as brethren, living under the same roof, the one governed by his own father, the other governed by his own mother. And, as father and mother were wedded husband and wife, each of the two young men would be dutiful and obedient to both; for both were true saints of God, as they have always been of His Church, when not blinded and degraded by Puritanic or *quasi*-Puritanic controversy. And here I declare my reverential adherence to the most ancient and reasonable tradition of the Christian Church regarding the perpetual virginity of Mary after the miraculous birth of her Divine Son, her and our Lord. With the high secret which Mary knew and which Joseph knew—each on the authority of an angel from heaven—this consecration would best agree, although it is never expressly declared in Scripture.

The Holy Family being thus constituted, we can think of the elder brothers, four in number, James, Joses, Simon, and Judas, watching the growth of Him who "increased in wisdom and in stature, and in favour with God and man."[1] Their training had been after the pattern which prevailed in all devout Jewish houses. They heard the Holy Scriptures daily at home and on Sabbath in the synagogue. At length Joseph their father dies; some of them leave the old home

---

[1] Several paragraphs here are abridged from Dean Plumptre's Introduction to S. James, pp. 18-24, in the Cambridge Bible for Schools.

and marry (1 Cor. ix. 5); and perhaps leave their step-mother,
the Blessed Virgin, to be partly or mainly supported by her
own Divine Son, who had learned carpentry with Joseph.
So the years pass on till the preaching of the Baptist breaks
through the orderly routine with the energy of a new force.
The brothers go from Nazareth as others go from Capernaum
to hear the Voice in the wilderness; and James learns the
lessons which he afterwards reproduces in his epistle, and
adopts the Nazarite rule (perhaps adopted even earlier) against
wine and flesh, for rigorous observance of which he was afterwards conspicuous. Then comes what to him and others in
Nazareth was a stumbling-block, that the younger Brother proclaims in the synagogue (Luke iv. 17), on the great day of
Atonement, that the lesson of the day containing the greatest
promise in the book of Isaiah was fulfilled in Himself. James
would fear lest this should rouse the scribes and Pharisees,
and even Herod Antipas, and bring harm on the whole family.
So would he hold back from joining his foster-brother's disciples, and cause Jesus to complain of a prophet's lack of
honour in his own country. Some months later James would
hear that Pharisees were come from Jerusalem to watch the
new Teacher (Luke v. 17), and in league with Herodians
are plotting against His life—Mark iii. 6. In their anxiety
for Jesus, Mary and James and other of her step-sons and
daughters come from Nazareth and appear on the outskirts of
the crowd at Capernaum, just when danger is at the greatest—
Matt. xii. 46. Their wish is to warn and restrain; but Jesus
has higher cares, and says in their hearing, " Behold my mother
and my brethren ! For whosoever shall do the will of my
Father which is in heaven, the same is my brother, and sister,
and mother." A little further on Jesus appears afresh in the
synagogue of Nazareth, when James and the rest of the family
listen, but without faith, to their own relative. Neither do
the villagers yet believe, but are more boldly unbelieving than
before; and even appeal or refer by name to the members of
the family over whom the Blessed Virgin presided as step-

mother. " Is not this the carpenter's son, Himself a carpenter?
Is not His mother called Mary? Are not His brethren, James,
and Joses, and Simon, and Judas, with us?"—Matt. xiii. 55;
Mark vi. 3. At an earlier period, just after the calling of the
twelve, His brethren, seeing the crowds and His zeal in teaching
them, had said, "He is beside Himself."—Mark iii. 21. At the
last feast of Tabernacles preceding the crucifixion His brethren
had said, not in a kindly spirit, "Depart hence, and go into
Judea, that Thy disciples also may see the works that Thou
doest." And S. John, vii. 5, explains the harshness by inter-
jecting, "For neither did His brethren believe in Him." On
that occasion Jesus did not go with them, but went later and
privately, and appeared in the Temple in the midst of the feast;
and managed to escape yet for a little from His enemies.
When the last Passover came, and the brethren as well as the
mother of the Lord would be in Jerusalem, it is remarkable
that He did not eat the Paschal lamb with His own family
according to the flesh, but with the new family of twelve of
which He was the Divine Head. At the crucifixion we hear
nothing of any of the four brethren, although they were doubtless not only in Jerusalem but in the Calvary crowd. They
did not yet believe; and it is only the believing part that is
noticed in the sacred record. The Blessed Virgin is there in
faith, love, and anguish; and none of her step-sons, although
there were four of them, bear her company, for at this point
not one of them was a believer in Jesus as the Christ. The
only companion and guardian of the holy mother of sorrow
was her nephew S. John, and son of her sister Salome, and the
beloved disciple of the suffering Messiah.

Thus, up to the crucifixion, the relation and attitude of our
Lord's brethren to the Divine Son of their step-mother Mary
was—unbelief, doubt, hesitation, some measure of alienation,
fear for the sanity of Jesus, and fear for the good name of the
family as respectable Galilean citizens. But to them as to
many more, the resurrection of Christ made a marvellous
change. Their unbelief was suddenly thawed; their fears of

a family blot scattered ; and, being honest although prejudiced men, faith came at last to their minds and hearts when they saw the Son of Mary alive again after all that had happened at Calvary. It is a clear evidence of this mighty change in the brethren of our Lord that we have already seen in Acts i. 14, when, after the ascension of Christ, the apostles returned to Jerusalem, the eleven names being all mentioned one by one expressly ; and then it is added, quietly but significantly, "These all continued with one accord in prayer and supplication, with the women, and Mary the mother of Jesus, and with His brethren."

Of these four brethren the eldest was James, who as eldest was the chief representative of the family, especially of his father S. Joseph, deceased a number of years before. But this James was already a man of strong and distinctive character, known as James the Just, with reference to his Nazarite vow. That vow debarred him from eating flesh and drinking wine, and it imposed on him the wearing of long hair—Numbers vi. He seems to have gone beyond even this vow in restricting himself in clothing to the exclusive use of white linen ; in this particular more rigid than the priests, who wore woollen undergarments when not on duty in the Temple.

But the most notable thing of all connected with James remains to be stated—that, on the authority of S. Paul, 1 Cor. xv. 7, a special vision and conference with the risen Saviour were granted to James by himself alone. "After that, He was seen of James ; then of all the apostles. And last of all He was seen of me also, as of one born out of due time." This vision and conference of the risen Saviour for the personal conviction and conversion of James, amounts to a special call and appointment, parallel somewhat to that of Paul himself, received on the Damascus road. And such a call, given to a man already of a strongly devout heart, could not but add strength to his devotion, and point him out as specially fitted to be the leader of Jewish believers in Palestine. Accordingly, ere long the matter ended in the formal recognition and appointment of James as

Bishop of Jerusalem, and also attaching to him the distinctive title of " the Lord's brother "—which would serve to mark him off from the two Jameses who were apostles among the original twelve, whereas this James the son of S. Joseph could not have been an original apostle, because he did not then believe in Jesus Christ at all.

These things biographical to James, and carefully traced from Scripture, help very greatly towards simplifying and commending to all Christians his epistle, primarily addressed to the twelve tribes of the Dispersion. The type of Christian doctrine there found is seen to harmonise at once with the character and antecedents of the man. In pleading for a religion which finds scope in holy and useful work among the poor and afflicted, feeding the hungry and clothing the naked, instead of a merely orthodox creed, he is not making thrusts at S. Paul's preaching or writing; but, apart from controversy, is expressing his own earlier view of Gospel duty, joined to a little of the Nazarite asceticism which he had before his conversion to the full and free Gospel of the risen Redeemer. Probably his epistle was written even before the Council at Jerusalem in 51 A.D. If so, it would be the first written of all the epistles, and even the earliest book of the New Testament, except the first Hebrew edition of S. Matthew's Gospel. Nay, it was probably this very man, the Bishop of Jerusalem and the earthly head of the family of which the Blessed Virgin Mary was a member by marriage, who supplied to S. Matthew for his gospel the copy of the genealogy which forms its first chapter; for the family papers would belong to James by legal inheritance as Joseph's eldest son.

The epistle is very happy in its division into five chapters, which correspond to its contents. Chapter i. gives a deeper and higher view of temptation or trial; interpreting it hopefully from a disciplinary stand-point, that evil is associated neither with men's circumstances nor with God's providence, but comes from man's own lusting heart, wilfulness, and lawlessness. Chapter ii. exposes and corrects one of the most clamant wrongs both in world and Church—the mean and unjust deference paid to the rich and great, while any scrap of place or notice is counted good enough for the poor. One great aim of the Church is to be the defence and refuge of the poor and the oppressed and the stranger; to maintain their cause in the struggle of class against class, of man against man, of labour against capital, or of plebeian against patrician; with a view to brotherhood, justice, and peace. Chapter iii. grapples with another of the great sources of mischief in life—the abuse of the gift of speech, writing and (now) printing to the injury of charity and consistency and edification. The glory of the chapter is its last two verses, which worthily led his contemporaries to characterise Bishop James as "the Wise" besides "the Just." "The wisdom that is from above is first pure, then peaceable, gentle, and easy to be entreated, full of mercy and good fruits, without partiality, and without hypocrisy. And the fruit of righteousness is sown in peace of them that make peace." How different this practical sense from the blatant and sentimental rubbish associated in modern times with popular and evangelical preaching! Chapter iv., in tracing war to lust and pride, gives a true pedigree. And no better counteractive to these evils can be found than in that spirit of humility and of trusting the future to God, that are inculcated as our best way of life on earth. The last chapter is practical intensely, like all the rest of the noble epistle—warning the rich afresh, earnestly inculcating patience, self-restraint, avoidance of rash appeals to heaven, and the quiet confident use of prayer as a mighty spiritual instrument.

It took a little time for the strikingly characteristic epistle of Bishop James of Jerusalem to find its full place in the Canon of the New Testament; but it was acknowledged in 363 by the Council of Laodicea, and in 397 by that of Carthage, while all along from the first it met general if not universal recognition.

Scripture says nothing of the end of Bishop James the Lord's brother—by far the greatest of the three S. Jameses—

but Eusebius, History, ii. 23,[1] quoting an earlier writer, Hegesippus, *c.* 170 A.D., says he was killed by a fuller's club about 62 A.D., at the instigation of the scribes and Pharisees; and that, Stephen-like and Christ-like, in his dying moments he prayed to God for the forgiveness of his murderers.

The one great lesson of his life and epistle is a clear testimony in favour of practical Christian duty and usefulness as a higher type of religion than dogma or ecclesiasticism. And herein he occupies a sure place alongside of the teaching of our Lord Himself in His Sermon on the Mount, and in His picture of the day of judgment in S. Matt. xxv., where the supreme test is no mere creed, but the practice of the seven works of mercy—in relief of hunger, thirst, stranger, naked, sick, prison, and burial. These had an honoured place in our older Christian systems; but they are searched for in vain among more modern system spinners and weavers.

S. Paul,

THE APOSTLE.

DAY, JANUARY 25.

ORATIONES.—*Deus qui universum mundum beati Pauli apostoli tui prædicatione docuisti: da nobis, quæsumus, ut qui ejus hodie, conversionem colimus, per ejus ad te exempla gradiamur. Per Dominum nostrum.*

The Epistle.—Gal. i. 11-20.
The Gospel.—S. Matt. x. 16-22.

[1] Dean Plumptre, Introduction to S. James.

Deus qui hodiernam diem apostolorum tuorum Petri et Pauli martyrio consecrasti : da ecclesiæ tuæ eorum in omnibus sequi præceptum, per quos religionis sumpsit exordium. Per Dominum.   (June 29.)

> For the Epistle.—Acts xiii. 5-11.
> The Gospel.—S. Matt. xvi. 13-19.

Deus qui multitudinem gentium beati Pauli apostoli tui prædicatione docuisti : da nobis, quæsumus, ut cujus natalicia colimus ejus apud te patrocinia sentiamus.   Per Dominum. (June 30.)

> The Epistles.—Gal. i. 11, 12 ; 2 Tim. iv. 7, 8.
> The Gospel.—S. Matt. xix. 27-29.

COLLECT.—*O God, who through the preaching of the blessed apostle Saint Paul, hast caused the light of the Gospel to shine throughout the world; Grant, we beseech Thee, that we, having his wonderful conversion in remembrance, may show forth our thankfulness unto Thee for the same by following the holy doctrine which he taught ; through Jesus Christ our Lord.* Amen.

> For the Epistle.—Acts ix. 1-22.
> The Gospel.—S. Matt. xix. 27-30.

Pastore percusso minas	The Shepherd now was smitten ;
Spirabat et cædes lupus ;	The wolf was ravening near ;
Sparsumque vastabat gregem,	The scattered flock he threatened,
Te, Christe, Saulus nesciens.	But knew not whose they were.
Et jam catenas stringere,	In zealous fury seeking
Ferox parabat, jam cruces ;	To bind and crucify,
Sed O ! repente sternitur,	A sudden voice withheld him,
Verboque perculsus ruit.	A loud and startling cry :
Quid, Saule, Saule, quid struis ?	"Saul ! Saul ! why blindly daring
Agnosce victricem manum :	To persecute thy Lord ?
Cœlo reluctari nefas ;	'Tis Jesus whom thou hatest ;
Absiste Jesum persequi.	Rebel not at my word."

Jam tendit imbelles manus ;
Jam colla submittit jugo :
Stupens jacet, clamat tremens :
Quid, Christe, quid victor jubes ?

Ex hoste miles, ex lupo
Agnus, gregi se devovet ;
Et raptor ipse nobili
Raptus triumpho ducitur.

O celsa cedrorum, Deus,
Qui voce vertis culmina !
O qui potenti subjicis
Mentes superbas gratiæ !

Tu, Pastor, infensas tuo
Vires ovili contere ;
Et nostra, si quid devium,
Ad te reflecte pectora.
—GUILLAUME DE LA BRUNETIÈRE.
   Cluniac Breviary, 1686 ; NEW-
MAN, p. 106.

Then forth in prayer he stretcheth
  Those hands prepared to slay ;
"What wouldst Thou with Thy
    servant ?
  My Lord and Master, say."

Christ's foe becomes His soldier,
  The wolf destroys no more,
A gentle lamb he enters
  The sheepfold by the door.

O voice of God Almighty,
  What wonders hath it wrought !
It rends the lofty cedars,
  It bends the haughty thought.

Jesu, our Shepherd, cease not
  Thy flock from harm to free ;
And, when Thy sheep are wandering,
  O lead them back to Thee !
          —F. POTT.

COMMEMORATION, JUNE 30.

Sat, Paule, sat terris datum
Post multa te certamina,
Cursu peracto, debita
Corona jam cœlo manet.

Quot tu mari periculis,
Terraque jactatus malis !
Quot saxa, virgæ, compedes !
Quot damna, curæ, funera !

Nunc ille confixum suæ
Qui te cruci dudum tenet,
Te Christus ad vitam vocat ;
Tibique lucrum jam mori.

Enough, O Paul, enough on earth
    is done :
after full many struggles
thine earthly goal is reached, and
    crown
thee waits in heaven well earned.

How many perils of the stormy
    deep !   [thine !
what hardships of long marches
what pains of stoning, beating,
    chaining !   [capes !
what losses, cares, hairbreadth es-

Now Christ, who long has held thee
bound like Himself unto the cross,
calls thee to life above ;
and sure 'tis gain to die.

Sed caritatis viscera
Strictis coarctant nexibus ;
Christoque quos tu parturis
Patrem reposcunt filii.

Verum paratur jam tibi
Finis laboris ardui,
Mercesque : bissenos thronus
Te poscit inter judices.
  —DE LA BRUNETIÈRE.—*Sens
  Breviary, 1726 ; NEW-
  MAN, p. 131.

Yet love's sweet bonds
constrain thee with strong tie,
and many a convert son [God.
would fain detain his aged father in

It may not be ; for ready now
the great reward of many a weary
 day :
a throne awaits thee, yonder,
'mong Israel's judges twelve !

"Saul, Saul, why persecutest thou me ?"—ACTS ix. 4.
"I am now ready to be offered, and the time of my departure
 is at hand. I have fought a good fight, I have finished
 my course, I have kept the faith : henceforth there is
 laid up for me a crown of righteousness, which the Lord,
 the righteous Judge, shall give me at that day."—2 TIM.
 iv. 6.

IN the case of the apostle of the Gentiles, materials are so
 abundant that it is not easy to compress even an outline of
them into our limits here. It will be observed that anciently
the Church honoured S. Paul by three festivals,—of his conversion on 25th January ; of his martyrdom along with S.
Peter on 29th June ; and a separate commemoration on 30th
June. Although Paul did so much in the original planting of
the standard of the Cross throughout the world—far more than
any other single apostle—and though by his writings he has
done more than the rest combined to fix the Church's doctrine,
yet he was not one of the original twelve, nor had he any
share in their personal training during Christ's public ministry.
This is the reason of the festival of his conversion, because in
his being won to the Gospel so much was won. His conversion is united to a clear, bold prophecy by Jesus touching the
career that lay before him—a prophecy parallel to that which
accompanied the call of S. Peter and the change of his name.

"He is a chosen vessel unto me, to bear my name before the Gentiles, and kings, and the children of Israel." In his first appearance at the stoning of S. Stephen, he is named Saul; and the first use of the name Paul is in Acts xiii. 9, when he came in contact with Sergius Paulus in Cyprus. The apostle was born at Tarsus, the capital of the province of Cilicia, his father being a Jew of the tribe of Benjamin, a strict Pharisee, and also a Roman citizen. How his Roman citizenship was gained does not appear from Scripture; but neither birth nor residence at Tarsus would carry with it the privilege which again and again served the apostle in good stead. Neither father's nor mother's name are anywhere stated, but there is allusion to their piety in 2 Tim. i. 3, "I thank God, whom I serve from my forefathers with pure conscience." Paul's only relatives referred to are a sister and her son, specially useful in the crisis in Acts xxiii. 16. Andronicus and Junia (or Junias) are named as "kinsmen"; but this may mean only as Benjamites. The apostle's age is not stated at any point, but two circumstances help us near it: his being called "a young man" at Stephen's death, and his having then or soon after a formal commission from the priests against the Christians (Acts xxvi. 9-12). No man much under thirty years would be likely to have so responsible a commission, especially as it was joined with a seat and vote in the Council—"When they were put to death, I gave my voice against them"—a promotion probably in reward of his zeal against Stephen.

Paul's birthplace was extremely favourable for a good education, as it ranked with Athens and Alexandria in possessing a great school or academy of learning and philosophy. The aim of his training was to qualify for a doctor of the law at Jerusalem, to which he would probably proceed about the age of fourteen, after preparatory schooling at Tarsus, where also he would learn his trade of tent-making; otherwise translated carpet, mat, leather, and tent cloth. The trade was added to the book-lore on the proverb, "He who does not teach his son a trade teaches him to steal;" or on the sounder principle of joining bodily exercise to the sedentary work of study. At Jerusalem the lad from Tarsus was enrolled under Gamaliel, Acts v. 34, one of seven famous teachers known by the higher style of Rabban ; so that both ways, at Tarsus and Jerusalem, Saul had the best academic training of his age, as the dialectic, literary, theological, and legal quality of his speeches and letters amply prove. Although in Jerusalem at the date of Stephen's death, Saul must have been quite away from Palestine during all the years of our Lord's ministry, for there is no hint of his seeing or hearing Jesus until the vision on the Damascus road.

Saul's position at the time of his conversion to the Gospel of Christ was that of a red-hot inquisitor against the Gospel, holding an official appointment from the Council at Jerusalem, and himself a member of that Council. His determination and theirs was to root out the Gospel as a pestilent heresy. He was acting from conviction ; and so soon as he was made to see his error in all its perverseness by the Lord's miraculous appearance to him and the Lord's words pointedly addressed to him by name, at once the fierce inquisitor became a humble believer and disciple of the Lord Jesus. One effect of the vision was that Saul was struck blind, and continued so for three days until miraculously restored by Ananias in Damascus, who was divinely sent to Saul's lodging in the house of Judas in "Straight street." Thus cured, the future apostle at once began his new work : "Straightway he preached Christ in the synagogues, that he is the Son of God, . . . and confounded the Jews which dwelt at Damascus, proving that this is very Christ." The disappointment and rage of the Jews at the conversion of the inquisitor, his loss to them and gain to the other side, led them, "after that many days were fulfilled, to take counsel to kill him." Although they watched the gates day and night, they were baffled by his being let down by the wall in a basket by night and escaping to Jerusalem. But his conversion was so recent, and his previous repute so evil, that the disciples there hesitated to receive him, until, by the intervention, explanation, and assurances of Barnabas, their fears and suspicions were at last removed.   At Jerusalem Paul resumed his preaching of Christ, specially arguing with "the Grecians," who had been Stephen's opponents already, and were now quickly enraged against Paul to murder-heat, to escape which the brethren helped him away, first to Cæsarea, and then to Tarsus. The impulse to this withdrawal, however, came neither from the brethren nor from Paul himself, but, as mentioned later in the speech on the stairs, Acts xxii. 17-21, came directly from revelation and command given by Jesus to His new servant in the Temple. "It came to pass, that, when I was come again to Jerusalem, even while I prayed in the temple, I was in a trance; and saw Him saying unto me, Make haste, and get thee quickly out of Jerusalem: for they will not receive thy testimony concerning me. And I said, Lord, they know that I imprisoned and beat in every synagogue them that believed on Thee: and when the blood of Thy martyr Stephen was shed, I also was standing by, and consenting unto his death, and kept the raiment of them that slew him. And He said unto me, Depart: for I will send thee far hence unto the Gentiles."

But into S. Luke's narrative in Acts ix., covering the period from conversion till the first return to Jerusalem, and the escape to Cæsarea Philippi and Tarsus, we require to insert details given by Paul himself in Gal. i., which furnish clearer ideas as to the time occupied at the several points mentioned. "When it pleased God . . . to reveal His Son in me, . . . immediately I conferred not with flesh and blood: neither went I up to Jerusalem to them which were apostles before me; but I went into Arabia, and returned again unto Damascus. Then after three years I went up to Jerusalem to see Peter, and abode with him fifteen days. But other of the apostles saw I none, save James the Lord's brother." This temporary retreat in the solitude of Arabia, which seems to have taken place very soon after the restoration of his sight and his baptism by Ananias, may have been of weeks' or months' duration, and its purpose apparently was for the

apostle to adjust his thoughts to his new position, and perhaps
to receive special and direct instruction by heavenly vision,
such as he alludes to in 1 Cor. xi. 23, when, speaking of the
Holy Supper, he says, "For I have received of the Lord that
which also I delivered unto you." The "many days" of Acts
ix. 23 are defined in Gal. i. 18 as nearly three years. When
he reached the safety of Tarsus, Paul spent several years there,
we may be sure not idle, but preaching the Gospel in his
native town, and probably over the province of Cilicia; but as
to this there is no express Scripture. In fact, Paul was out of
sight for several years, and such a stranger to the disciples,
that at length Barnabas went to Tarsus from Antioch to "seek
Saul: and when he had found him, he brought him unto Antioch. And it came to pass, that a whole year they assembled
themselves with the Church, and taught much people."—Acts
xi. 25. During this Antioch ministry Barnabas and Saul were
deputed by the disciples at Antioch to carry to Jerusalem a fund
raised for the relief of disciples suffering there in a time of
dearth and famine. This errand accomplished, Paul and Barnabas returned to Antioch, which counted as *their* headquarters,
taking with them from Jerusalem Barnabas's nephew John
Mark, afterwards the evangelist. This brings us to the close
of one distinct epoch in Saul's career—viz., from his conversion till the date of leaving Antioch again on his first great
missionary journey under full and direct sanction of the Church
and command of the Holy Ghost. It is estimated that a period
of no fewer than ten years elapsed between Saul's conversion
and his ordination at Antioch—*i.e.*, 36-46 A.D. (taking 29 A.D.
as the date of the Crucifixion).[1]

Within this period we have come on two visits of Saul to
Jerusalem. As the Jerusalem visits of the apostle are important landmarks in his career, it may be well here to arrange
them all in order, even though part of them are anticipatory
of what follows. *First visit*, Acts ix. 26, Gal. i. 18, three
years after conversion, when a fortnight's stay was made with

---

[1] See Canon Norris on the Acts, App. V., on the Chronology.

Peter. *Second*, Acts xi. 30, xii. 25, when with Barnabas as a deputation from Antioch with relief fund. *Third*, Gal. ii. 1-10, accompanied by Barnabas and Titus; a private visit to confer with James, Cephas, and John, who gave the right hand of fellowship, and arranged with Saul that he should work among the heathen and remember the poor disciples in Judea.[1] *Fourth*, Acts xv. 2, when Paul and Barnabas were sent from Antioch to consult the apostles and elders on the question of the relation of the Gentiles to the law of Moses. *Fifth*, Acts xviii. 22, a very short visit at the close of the apostle's second great missionary journey. *Sixth*, Acts xxi. 17, at the close of his third great journey, when he made a report to James and the elders. After this arose the tumult in the Temple, and Paul's apprehension and trial, and voyage to Rome as a prisoner; and Jerusalem was seen by him no more.

I. Paul's first apostolic journey had for its starting-point and conclusion Antioch, the capital of Syria, and mother-Church of the Gentiles, and one of the original four bishop-rics and patriarchates—viz., Jerusalem, Antioch, Rome, and Alexandria. This journey took place about 43-45 A.D., and is notably clear in its outline, being comprised in exactly two chapters, Acts xiii., xiv.

The origin of the Church at Antioch is traced in Acts xi. 19 to the effect of the persecution at Jerusalem in which Stephen perished. The places of refuge were Phenice, Cyprus, and Antioch. "And a great number believed, and turned unto the Lord." Hearing this at Jerusalem, the Church there sent Barnabas to Antioch. After labouring a while, he went to Tarsus in search of Saul, and returned with him to Antioch, where the two and others laboured a whole year. Prophets and teachers at Antioch were Barnabas, Simeon Niger, Lucius of Cyrene in North Africa, Manaen = Menahem, foster-brother

---

[1] On the order and reason of this visit, see Wheeler's 'Analysis and Summary of New Test. History,' Part II. § 93. §§ 52-353 contain one of the best outlines of S. Paul's life anywhere to be found, especially clear in geographical explanations.

of Herod Antipas the tetrarch, and Saul. "As they ministered to the Lord, and fasted, the Holy Ghost said, Separate
me Barnabas and Saul for the work whereunto I have called
them. And when they had fasted and prayed, and laid their
hands on them, they sent them away." The ordination or
dedication service here, by laying on of hands, is very noticeable. In Paul's case it connects him for the first time with
the controversial subject of Orders, although, antecedent to
this, he had a direct commission first from Christ at conversion
and baptism and in the Arabian retreat; and here from the
Holy Ghost by revelation in addition.

Antioch on the Orontes was 300 miles north of Jerusalem
and 30 miles from the sea. Their start was from Seleucia,
the seaport of Antioch, whence they crossed to Cyprus,
Barnabas's birthplace. Landing at Salamis on the east side,
they crossed to Paphos on the west. Here they met Sergius
Paulus the proconsul, and a Jewish sorcerer, Bar-jesus Elymas, who was struck blind. At Antioch and on to Paphos
the narrative gives Barnabas precedence over Saul, but from
Paphos onward Saul has precedence and is marked as Paul.
The handling of Elymas as a bold and mighty act seems to be
the turning-point—xiii. 9-13. "Then Saul, (who also is called
Paul,) filled with the Holy Ghost, set his eyes on him. . . . .
Now when Paul and his company loosed from Paphos, they
came to Perga in Pamphylia: and John departing from them
returned to Jerusalem." It was 80 miles north from Perga,
the capital of Pamphylia, to Antioch in Pisidia, and through
a wild country which seems to have scared Barnabas's nephew.
The discourse of Paul at this Antioch, xiii. 16-41, is singularly interesting as a specimen of the first shape of the oral
Gospel for practical mission-work. They next proceeded to
Iconium, the capital of Lycaonia, 75 miles farther, and 120
from the sea; then to Lystra in the same province, where a
cripple was healed, and Paul was taken for the god Mercury,
but soon after stoned nearly dead. Retiring from Lystra to
Derbe, they then retraced their steps to Lystra Iconium and

Pisidian Antioch, confirming the first settlements and ordain-
ing presbyters in every Church, and after prayer and fasting,
commending them to the Lord, and leaving them to minister to the believers and make more. They sailed from the
port of Attalia in Pamphylia, back to Seleucia and Antioch,
their starting-point. "And when they were come, and had
gathered the Church together, they rehearsed all that God
had done with them, and how he had opened the door of
faith unto the Gentiles. And there they abode long time
with the disciples."

II. S. Paul's second and greater apostolic journey had again
Antioch for its start and conclusion. The chronicle of it is
Acts xv. 36–xviii. 22, and the period of it was 49-52 A.D.

In the four years' interval between the first and second
journey, occurred the private visit of Paul, Barnabas, and
Titus to Jerusalem concerning the preaching to the Gentiles,
as told in Gal. ii. 1-10. Later came the public visit of Paul
and Barnabas to Jerusalem concerning circumcision, as told
in Acts xv. 1-35 ; a question which was determined in the
first Council of the Church, and embodied in a letter sent to
Antioch by Paul and Barnabas accompanied by Judas Barsabas and Silas.

Paul's companion on this second journey was Silas, after an
opening disagreement with Barnabas as to the assistantship
of his nephew Mark. At starting they were recommended in
prayer by the brethren to the grace of God. Their course was
by land through Syria to Cilicia, Paul's native province, where
he strengthened churches probably founded by himself shortly
after his conversion, before being taken by Barnabas to Antioch.
Then he visited Lystra and Derbe again, meeting Timothy at
Lystra, and starting his long and profitable connection with him
by circumcision. Paul, Silas, and Timothy next turn south
through Phrygia and Galatia ; then west through Mysia and
to Troas, a port on the west coast of Asia Minor on the Ægean
Sea. Here the three were joined by Luke, and were called by
a vision to cross the sea into Europe. "Come over into Mace-

donia, and help us." The crossing was from Troas to Neapolis, taking the small island of Samothracia on the way. Landing at Neapolis, they proceeded inland and northward to Philippi, the capital, where they had among their hearers and converts Lydia of Thyatira. The healing of a damsel possessed by a spirit of divination brought trouble, whereby Paul and Silas were apprehended, brought before the Duumviri, beaten and imprisoned. After the miraculous opening of the prison, the conversion and baptism of the jailer, and leaving Luke behind, they proceeded south-westward through Amphipolis and Apollonia to Thessalonica, twenty miles from Philippi, where they were lodged with Jason, whose house was assaulted and Jason himself summoned before the magistrate. Driven thus by Jewish venom from Thessalonica, their next stage was Berea, where the reception was kindly, until the envenomed Jews overtook them afresh, whereon Paul was withdrawn to Athens, while Silas and Timothy stayed at Berea. Here the apostle made his famous defence on Mars' Hill; but only a few believers were gained, including Dionysius and Damaris. From Athens Paul proceeded to Corinth, where he found and dwelt with Aquila and Priscilla. Corinth was a large seaport, and capital of the Roman province of Achaia, where Gallio was proconsul, and by a certain contempt for Jewish peculiarities, xviii. 12-17, was the means unintentionally of defending the apostle from Jewish persecution. Here Paul stayed a year and six months, both firmly founding a church, and by his letters greatly helping some of those already founded elsewhere. To this year and a half belong three of Paul's epistles, afterwards so precious to all churches—viz., Galatians, and 1 and 2 Thessalonians. For more definite and thoughtful use of Scripture, and to escape the degrading lucky-bag system of the baser sort of Christians who merely deal out texts, it is of vast importance to note the real order of the inspired books, and in what particular circumstances and with what aim each was written. In Corinth, Paul was rejoined by Silas, who prolonged his stay at Berea, and also by Timothy, who had been told off for Thessalonica. This strengthening of the apostle's hands gave him fresh heart, so that he turned his attention specially to the Gentiles in Corinth, and marked the change of charge by a change of abode, now taking up his quarters in the house of Justua. Moreover, he had another source of courage and success in a special revelation in a vision of the Lord, " Be not afraid, but speak, and hold not thy peace : for I am with thee, and no man shall set on thee to hurt thee : for I have much people in this city." While thus busy and cheery, the apostle received some pecuniary help from his converts in Philippi. At the close of this happy period Paul embarked at Cenchrea, the eastern port of Corinth, where he shaved his head in terms of a vow. His companions in the voyage to Syria, which was broken at Ephesus, were Aquila and Priscilla, Silas, Timothy, Erastus, Gaius, and Aristarchus. Landing at Cæsarea Stratonis, thirty-five miles north of Joppa, he went to Jerusalem, saluted the Church there, and then proceeded for rest at the close of his circuit to Antioch, the headquarters of the Church of the Gentiles and cradle of the Christian name.

III. In his third great missionary journey, begun in the same year, 52 A.D., in which he returned from the second, again he started from Antioch ; but his return was to Jerusalem to make his official report, and particularly to Bishop James the Lord's brother, at this date the supreme Bishop of Christendom. The record of this tour fills Acts xviii. 23-xxi. 19. The journey is long and successful, and there is no controversial element in it; and a meagre list of the places visited may suffice, because the great point of interest lies in noting its close at Jerusalem, which led to the apostle's two years' imprisonment at Cæsarea, and his being sent to Rome as a prisoner for other two years. He began by visiting the churches of Galatia and Phrygia ; and in this was accompanied, xix. 22, by Timothy and Erastus. The Galatian Church, like that at Corinth, Gal. ii. 10, 1 Cor. xvi. 1-2, gave the apostle hearty help for the poor Christians at Jerusalem. He now made a second visit to Ephesus, where he met Apollos of Alexandria, an earnest and learned man, who did a great work at Corinth ; watering what Paul had planted. Here twelve disciples of the Baptist received Christian baptism. Two years of steady work were devoted to Corinth, and the work was commended by special miracles done by Paul, as well as by the exposure of false miracles of the sons of Sceva. From Ephesus he sends Timothy and Erastus to Macedonia (= Northern Greece), and Achaia (= Southern Greece), especially Corinth, to fulfil what at first he intended to have done himself, but now, instead, prosecutes his work in Lydian Asia. At this point he wrote 1 Corinthians, and sent it by Titus. A hint of a previous letter now lost is given in 1 Cor. v. 9. The occasion of 1 Corinthians was the arrival at Ephesus of three deputies, Stephanas, Fortunatus, and Achaicus, with fresh information and a letter asking guidance on certain special questions. Paul's stay in Ephesus had to be closed hastily owing to a tumult excited by Demetrius. He left for Macedonia, going by Troas, where he was disappointed at not finding Titus, but on going further, probably at Philippi, found both Timothy and Titus, and on their fresh news from Corinth, sends Titus and two brethren to collect alms and deliver the second Epistle to the Corinthians.

After visiting the Churches in Macedonia he proceeded north-west to Illyricum, Rom. xv. 19, then to Corinth, for the second time, where he stayed three months. This residence is notable, because then was written the Epistle to the Romans, dictated to Tertius and sent by the deaconess Phebe of Cenchrea. This ends the apostle's literary work on the Scriptures up to his imprisonment at Cæsarea, and the total is six epistles —viz., Galatians, 1 and 2 Thessalonians, 1 and 2 Corinthians, Romans.

It had been Paul's intention to sail from Corinth direct to Syria, but hearing that Jews were on the watch to assassinate him, he changed his route and went northward to Philippi, for the third time, accompanied by these seven brethren—viz., Sopater, Aristarchus, Secundus, Gaius, Timothy, Tychicus, and Trophimus. These proceeded to Troas and waited for

Paul (and Luke, who had joined at Philippi), who got to Troas in five days and stayed a week. Luke and others took ship from Troas to Assos, nine miles, to which Paul walked. Then all sailed to Mitylene in Lesbos, thirty miles; then to Chios; thence to Trogyllium in Samos; and on the fourth day reached Miletus, twenty-eight miles south of Ephesus, to which Paul sent a message to the presbyters to come and see him. After conference the voyage was continued round the south corner of Asia Minor, past Coos, Cnidus, and Rhodes to Patara; then direct from Patara to Tyre, where was stay of seven days, whereafter luggage was repacked, and they got to Jerusalem, lodging in the house of Mnason, an old convert from Cyprus. " And when we were come to Jerusalem, the brethren received us gladly. And the day following Paul went in with us unto James; and all the presbyters were present. And when he had saluted them, he declared particularly what things God had wrought among the Gentiles by his ministry."

The interval between S. Paul's third and fourth journey now calls for brief notice. Although it was the advice of Bishop James and the Jerusalem presbyters that Paul should associate himself in his own vow with four other vow-men of poor degree, the advice seems to have been injudicious, in the light of what followed: first, because it was partly a make-believe to half-cheat the Jews; and second, because it did not lessen one whit their hatred, but furnished cause of tumult which led to the apostle's apprehension. The speech on the stairs of the castle of Antonia was a daring but unsuccessful venture of Paul to quiet an angry mob. Inside the castle he only escaped scourging by pleading his Roman citizenship. Next day he was presented by Lysias, the Roman tribune, to the chief priests and Sanhedrim, when he declared himself a Pharisee, and escaped by dividing the Council against itself; whereupon Lysias carried him off into the castle. Next day more than forty Jews conspired to kill Paul. The plot was checkmated by Lysias sending Paul strongly guarded to Felix the Procurator at Cæsarea Stratonis. After five days Paul was tried

before Felix ; Ananias the high priest, and some of the Sanhedrim, being accusers, and Tertullus their law-agent. Judgment was deferred till Lysias should come to Cæsarea. Mean-
time the apostle was called to speak before Drusilla, the Jewish
wife of Felix, and they "heard him concerning the faith in
Christ." Under Felix Paul remained two years at Cæsarea,
and, with the measure of freedom which he had, was able to
do a good deal of Church work, especially as Philip the evangelist was here, xxi. 8, and Luke also. At the end of the two
years, when Felix was deposed from office, he did a mean trick
on the apostle in making his imprisonment more severe—xxiv.
27. Porcius Festus, who succeeded Felix, was asked by the
high priest to bring Paul to Jerusalem for trial—this in collu-
sion with assassins to act by the way ; but Festus refused. Ten
days later he returned to Cæsarea, and next day Paul was
brought on for trial, his accusers from Jerusalem making
charges which they could not prove. Festus asked Paul to
consent to change the venue to Jerusalem ; but he, seeing the
double risk of assassination on the road or condemnation at the
trial, refused, and appealed to Cæsar. Shortly after this, on a
ceremony visit of Agrippa II. and Bernice to Festus, Paul was
brought into the Prætorium to state his case before the visitors,
when Agrippa was candid enough to say that the prisoner
might have been set at liberty had he not already appealed.

After this comes the voyage by Cæsarea to Sidon, round
Cyprus to Myra in Lycia ; then to Cnidus and the Fair-
Havens in Crete. Leaving this to get to Phenice or Phœnix,
a better Cretan harbour forty miles to the west, the ship was
caught in a wind called Euroclydon (in R.V. Euraquilo) = a
Levanter or typhoon, and was driven to Clauda = Gozzo. On the
fourteenth night from Fair-Havens they sounded for land, and
cast anchor, and at daybreak found themselves in Malta. Their
next stage was to Puteoli ; thence by land Romewarda. They
were welcomed by two deputations of believers at Appii Forum,
forty miles, and at Tres-Tabernæ, thirty miles from the capital.
The apostle was handed over to Burrhus, the Prefect of the Præ-

torian guard, and, after two interviews with the Jews, was left with the soldier that guarded him. "And Paul dwelt two whole years in his own hired house, and received all that came in unto him, preaching the kingdom of God, and teaching those things which concern the Lord Jesus Christ, with all confidence, no man forbidding him." The leisure of this imprisonment was partly occupied in the writing of a fresh group of Epistles—viz., Ephesians, Colossians, Philemon, and Philippians.

IV. S. Paul's second imprisonment at Rome is matter of controversy as to the fact of it, but involves nothing of doctrine. The Roman Church holds by one imprisonment; but the arguments for a second seem quite conclusive. They are well stated by Dr Macknight.[1] The imprisonment in Acts xxviii. 30 was easy compared with the severity in 2 Tim. ii. 9. "Wherein I suffer trouble, as an evil-doer, even unto bonds." At the first he had freedom and others had boldness, Phil. i. 14; the others including companions like Timothy, Luke, Tychicus, Aristarchus, and those named in Col. iv. But now in the second imprisonment he had none with him, either as assistants or brethren, save Luke, 2 Tim. iv. 11-16. So close was the confinement the second time that Onesiphorus had to search the different prisons of the city to find Paul. "The Lord give mercy unto the house of Onesiphorus; for he oft refreshed me, and was not ashamed of my chain: but, when he was in Rome, he sought me out very diligently, and found me."—2 Tim. i. 16. After his first defence in his second imprisonment his judges were enraged, and he looked for immediate condemnation. "I am now ready to be offered, and the time of my departure is at hand." The first imprisonment was only for heresy, whereas at the period of the second Rome had been set on fire by Nero, 10th July 64 A.D., and the blame cast on the Christians, the result being the first general persecution, in which the apostle was caught and severely dealt with as a Church leader.

Thus, making two imprisonments at Rome, we have between

[1] Trans. of the Apostolical Epistles, Pref. to 2 Tim.

them the apostle's fourth great missionary journey.   Rome
itself may be regarded as the starting-point this last time ; and
Paul's companions were Timothy and Titus, and the faithful
Luke.   Titus had previously been sent from Philippi to
Corinth (2 Cor. viii. 16), but seems to have rejoined Paul at
Rome.   The first visit paid on leaving Rome was probably to
Crete, where Titus was left in charge.   The next visit seems
to have been to Colossæ and Ephesus.   At the former, Paul
would occupy the lodging bespoken in Philemon 24 ; and at
the latter, Timothy was left in charge, the station being very
important and the state of the Church critical.   " Unto
Timothy, my own son in the faith. . . . As I besought thee
to abide still at Ephesus, when I went into Macedonia, that
thou mightest charge some that they teach no other doctrine."
—1 Tim. i. 2, 3.   Leaving Ephesus, Paul is traceable next in
Macedonia, apparently fulfilling the promise in Phil. ii. 24,
"But I trust in the Lord that I also myself shall come
shortly."   In going from Ephesus to Philippi he seems to
have taken Troas on the way, and when lodging with Carpus
to have left the cloak and parchments mentioned in 2 Tim.
iv. 13.   From Philippi he proceeded to Nicopolis, on the coast
of Macedonia facing the south of Italy ; and it was at this
stage that the First Epistle to Timothy and the Epistle to
Titus were written and sent.   "When I shall send Artemas
unto thee, or Tychicus [who had probably joined at Colossæ],
be diligent to come unto me to Nicopolis : for I have determined there to winter."—Titus iii. 12.   In spring he intended to pass to Ephesus.   "These things write I unto thee,
hoping to come unto thee shortly : but if I tarry long, that
thou mayest know."—1 Tim. iii. 14.   But having ordered Titus
from Crete to Nicopolis, as above, Titus gave such an account
of Crete as led Paul to return with him and give Crete a second
visit.   And it was now, on hearing of the sore persecution of
the Christians in Rome by Nero, that Paul sailed then with
Titus from Crete to Italy, in the end of autumn 65 A.D., to
assist the afflicted Church of the metropolis.   On arrival,

Paul's activity and ability would make him obnoxious to the
heathen priests, angry at the desertion of their temples, and
also to the unbelieving Jews ; so that he soon came to be discovered to the magistrates, and closely imprisoned, as above
said, in the end of 65 or early in 66 A.D. We do not know
how long he was in prison before his first answer, nor what
space intervened between his first and second ; but his writing
to Timothy a second epistle, the latest of all his epistles, and
expecting the arrival of Timothy before his death, implies
some considerable time, with which his and S. Peter's Day in
the Calendar (29th June) would very well accord as regards
the season of the year for his martyrdom. And the thirteenth
year of Nero, = 67 A.D., may represent the year ; although
both a year earlier and a year later are assigned by careful
chronologists.

As already stated under S. Peter, he and Paul, the two
greatest pillars ever the Church had, met, embraced, and
parted on the Via Ostia, each on the way to martyrdom on
the same day. S. Paul suffered by the sword, which is his
emblem in Christian art, being beheaded at the Three Fountains,
said to have sprung up where his head thrice rebounded on
the ground. Let us remember S. Paul's share of the grand
old Latin hymn already given under S. Peter, especially the
verse beginning *Doctor egregie Paule.*

The following may be set down as the chief features of this
great saint : 1. His early education of the best sort. 2. One
wonderful change from persecutor to believer in Christ.
3. His training and action directly under Jesus, and largely
independent of the twelve. 4. His bitter opposition met
from unbelieving Jews. 5. The amount of his travels and
adventures. 6. His method of working through a large staff
of trained assistants. 7. His being the chief doctrinal ex-
pounder of Christianity. 8. His being the first master of
Christian oratory. 9. His calm preparedness for death. By
these he verified the Lord's prophetic word to Ananias at
Damascus, "He is a chosen vessel unto me."

S. Barnabas.

ORATIO. — *Ecclesiam tuam, quæsumus, Domine, beati Barnabæ apostoli tui commendet oratio: et pro ea interventor existat, quam doctrina et passione illustrat.   Per Dominum.*

For the Epistle.—Acts xi. 21-26 ; xiii. 1-3.
The Gospel.—S. Matt. x. 16-22.

COLLECT.—*O Lord God Almighty, who didst endue Thy holy apostle Barnabas with singular gifts of the Holy Ghost ; Leave us not, we beseech Thee, destitute of Thy manifold gifts, nor yet of grace to use them alway to Thy honour and glory ; through Jesus Christ our Lord.   Amen.*

For the Epistle.—Acts xi. 22-30.
The Gospel.—S. John xv. 12-16.

O Son of God, our Captain of Salvation,
  Thyself by suffering schooled to human grief,
We bless Thee for Thy sons of consolation,
  Who follow in the steps of Thee their chief ;

Those whom Thy Spirit's dread vocation severs
  To lead the vanguard of Thy conquering host ;
Whose toilsome years are spent in brave endeavours
  To bear Thy saving name from coast to coast ;

Those whose bright faith makes feeble hearts grow stronger,
  And sends fresh warriors to the great campaign,
Bids the lone convert feel estranged no longer,
  And wins the sundered to be one again ;

And all true helpers, patient, kind, and skilful,
  Who shed Thy light across our darkened earth,
Counsel the doubting, and restrain the wilful,
  Soothe the sickbed, and share the children's mirth.

Such was Thy Levite, strong in self-oblation
  To cast his all at Thine apostles' feet;
He whose new name, through every Christian nation,
  From age to age our thankful strains repeat.

Thus, Lord, Thy Barnabas in memory keeping,
  Still be Thy Church's watchword, " Comfort ye ;"
Till in our Father's house shall end our weeping,
  And all our wants be satisfied in Thee.
                                    —J. ELLERTON.

" He was a good man, and full of the Holy Ghost and of faith."
—ACTS xi. 24.

THE first mention of Barnabas is at the end of Acts iv.,
where several important points of information are grouped
together. "And Joses, who by the apostles was surnamed
Barnabas, (which is, being interpreted, The son of consolation,)
a Levite, and of the country of Cyprus, having land, sold it,
and brought the money, and laid it at the apostles' feet." This
shows that he was an early convert, because it happened just
after Pentecost ; in fact, he is supposed to have been one of
the seventy disciples in Luke x. The interpretation of his
name as son of consolation, while not inaccurate, does not present the first and more usual meaning of the word, which is
son of prophecy. If we include prophecy, the allusion will be
to his eminence as a Christian teacher ; and in Acts xiii. 1, he
is named and described as one of four " prophets and teachers
in the church that was at Antioch." The alliance of the two
functions of consolation and prophecy is seen from the account
of the decree of the first Council, " which when they had read,
they rejoiced for the consolation. And Judas and Silas, being
prophets also themselves, exhorted the brethren with many
words, and confirmed them."—Acts xv. 31. At an earlier stage
in their respective careers Barnabas occupied a more important
position in the Church than Paul. " And when Saul was come
to Jerusalem, he assayed to join himself to the disciples : but
they were all afraid of him, and believed not that he was a

disciple. But Barnabas took him, and brought him to the apostles, and declared unto them how he had seen the Lord in the way, and that he had spoken to him, and how he had preached boldly at Damascus in the name of Jesus."—Acts ix. 26. There is an old tradition that Barnabas had been a fellow-student with Saul under Gamaliel, and that meeting in Jerusalem on the above occasion, he had once more asked Saul to become Christian, whereupon he told of his conversion by the heavenly vision. In Acts xi. 19-30 we have quite a series of allusions to Barnabas: that his birthplace, Cyprus, had its first Gospel mission in the persecution that arose about Stephen—that men of Cyprus at once became preachers of the Gospel to the Hellenes of Antioch—that when news of this reached Jerusalem, Barnabas was sent by the Church there to labour in Antioch—that after labouring a while with success, he went to Tarsus to seek Saul—that on the return of the two to Antioch they wrought together for a year—that it was out of their success there that the name of "Christians" was originated to discriminate the new communion—that alms collected to help Judea in a dearth were sent from Antioch to the Jerusalem presbyters "by the hands of Barnabas and Saul." But perhaps the chief feature of the narrative is S. Luke's personal reference to Barnabas, "For he was a good man, and full of the Holy Ghost and of faith: and much people was added unto the Lord."

When this ministry of the alms had been accomplished, Barnabas and Saul returned to Antioch, taking with them John Mark, the nephew of Barnabas, whose mother, the sister of Barnabas, was a prominent member of the Jerusalem Church, and a special friend of S. Peter. It was very soon after this return that the two were selected from the leaders of the Church at Antioch by supernatural direction of the Holy Ghost, and set apart by fasting, prayer, and laying on of hands, for a special mission, already described as the first of four with which S. Paul was associated. It was in the early part of this mission, in Cyprus, that Barnabas fell back into the second place and

S. Paul came to the front, as stated in Acts xiii. 9. When
they began the Asia Minor part of the work, John Mark left
them and returned to Jerusalem. No heat arose over this at
the time, but subsequently at the beginning of a second missionary journey it was the ground of a separation of the two
great missioners. When Paul went up on a private visit to
Jerusalem to confer with the leading men of the Church fourteen years after his conversion, Gal. ii. 1, Barnabas was with
him in the capacity of one of the leaders of the Church of
the Gentiles. And the same two were sent from Antioch to
Jerusalem in a representative capacity on occasion of the first
Council—Acts xv. Previous to this, in Acts xiv. 8-12 we gain
a curious glimpse of the contrast in the *physique* of the two
missioners at Lystra, when Barnabas by his stature and dignity
was taken for Father Zeus, while the lesser and voluble Paul
was taken for the god Mercury. After Paul's unfortunate dispute with Barnabas over his nephew, Barnabas and Mark made
a missionary tour of their own in their own isle of Cyprus—
Acts xv. 36-39 ; and at this point Barnabas disappears from
S. Luke's narrative.

There are a few additional references in the epistles, but
they contain limited information compared with the preceding.
From 1 Cor. ix. 5, 6, we can infer that Barnabas was unmarried,
and partly supported himself by a trade, like Paul himself.
From Gal. ii. 11 we learn that he was temporarily carried away
by Peter's dissimulation in the matter of eating with Gentiles.
In 2 Cor. viii. 18, 19, is the question as to the " brother whose
praise is in the Gospel throughout all the churches "—whether it
is Luke or Barnabas that is meant ; but the balance of evidence
rather points to the former. And finally, the three entirely
favourable references to Mark by Paul—Col. iv. 10, Philem.
24, 2 Tim. iv. 11—show that the old dispute regarding him
was wholly overcome, and no bitterness remained either toward
nephew or uncle. Moreover, the absence there and elsewhere
of any reference to Barnabas almost certainly implies that
Barnabas had already passed away; the more as Alexander, a

Cyprus monk of the sixth or seventh century, records a tradition of his death as happening 53-57 A.D.

A book called *Actio et Passio Barnabæ in Cypro*, forged in the name of S. Mark, says that he was killed by being stoned at Salamis in Cyprus, by Jews from Syria under Bar-jesus—a not unlikely fate when we consider the persecutions of S. Paul. There is a legend that in the second half of the fifth century Barnabas appeared three times by night to tell the Bishop of Salamis where his body lay, and that beside it was a copy of S. Matthew's Gospel, which would help in a dispute then raging against Peter Fullo, a Monophysite Patriarch of Constantinople, who was claiming superiority over the Church in Cyprus.

Another book which occupies a much better position is the Epistle of Barnabas. This is given in full in Hefele's *Patres Apostolici*, as in other similar collections. The epistle is in twenty-one short chapters, treating of the abrogation of the Mosaic dispensation, and of types and prophecies of Christ, ending with practical directions and exhortations. The book is of a genuine nature, but seems the work of a somewhat *later* Barnabas of Alexandria. It is referred to in the ninth century in lists of sacred books, but was discovered only in the sixteenth century by Jacob Sirmond, a scholar of the Society of Jesus. It holds an honourable place among apocryphal books suitable to be read for edification, although not part of the rule of faith.

Before leaving Barnabas, allusion may be made to the question of his proper designation: is he to be called an *apostle*, using the word in its stricter sense? The title of apostle is given ecclesiastically both in the Latin and English collect for S. Barnabas's Day prefixed to this article. And the Scripture basis of the designation thus adopted is traceable in Acts xiv. 4, 14. " Which when the apostles, Barnabas and Paul, heard of," &c. " But the multitude of the city was divided : and part held with the Jews, and part with the apostles." Here is the word undoubtedly applied to Barnabas, and twice; but this is not decisive as to its full import—as used of " the twelve" or of "the eleven" in the Gospels. Barnabas and Paul, all through Acts xiii. xiv., are linked by a special tie as the *messengers* of the Holy Ghost and of the Church at Antioch. The meaning of the word by derivation, = one who is sent, appears in S. John xiii. 16, and also in the messengers (lit., *apostles*) of the churches sent to carry alms or special messages in writing, 2 Cor. viii. 23 : used of Epaphroditus, Phil. ii. 25 ; and of Apollos, 1 Cor. iv. 6-9. Paul himself was an apostle in the full sense, as he claims repeatedly, 1 Cor. ix. 1, 2 Cor. xii. 12, Acts xxvi. 16-17, 1 Tim. ii. 7, 2 Tim. i. 11. But no such specialty can be claimed for Barnabas. And to widen the name to include him introduces confusion into that Scripture representation of apostles which traces their call and commission directly to the Lord Jesus, as stated in S. Matt. x., confirmed in S. John xx. 21-23, S. Matt. xxviii. 18-20, implied in Acts i. in the appointment of Matthias to fill the one vacant place in the college ; and again implied in Rev. xxi. 14, although in a figure—" The wall of the city had twelve foundations, and in them the names of the twelve apostles of the Lamb."

But while firmly resisting the application of the style of apostle in its proper sense to Barnabas, it is needful to recognise most heartily how, partly through seniority in years, and partly through earlier connection with the Church, he really occupied for a time—*i.e.*, up to the end of Acts xiv.—an ecclesiastical position that gave him precedence even of Paul. And it may be added that, in all probability, or rather, certainly, Barnabas would have occupied a Scripture place even above the high place he now holds, had he not been carried away by an early death, which prematurely closed his career by martyrdom in his native island ; so that in one respect we may compare him to S. James the son of Zebedee, and say that he was a greater man in promise and potency than the years of his brief life could give development to. And part of his work and spirit passed over into his beloved nephew, S. Mark, an equal favourite with S. Paul and S. Peter.

S. Silas.

COLLECTS.—*Graciously cast Thy light, O Lord, upon Thy Church; that Thy flock may everywhere go on and prosper, and its pastors, by Thy governance, may become acceptable to Thy name; through Jesus Christ our Lord.*[1]

O God, who hast promised that Thou wilt never be absent from Thy Church unto the end of the world, and that the gates of hell shall never prevail against the apostolic confession; Graciously make Thy strength perfect in our weakness, and show the efficacy of Thy divine promise, while Thou deignest even to be present in Thy feeble ones. For then do we beyond doubt feel Thy presence when Thou dispensest to each one at all times, in fitting manner, things desirable, and by perpetual protection guardest us from the attack of all our adversaries.[2]

For the Epistle.—Acts xvi. 25-34.
The Gospel.—S. Luke x. 1-9.

"Then pleased it the apostles and elders, with the whole Church, to send chosen men of their own company to Antioch with Paul and Barnabas; namely, Judas surnamed Barsabas, and Silas, chief men among the brethren. . . . And Paul chose Silas, and departed, being recommended by the brethren unto the grace of God."—ACTS xv. 22, 40.

FROM the first mention of Silas in the above circumstances, it appears that he was then resident in Jerusalem, and one of the foremost among the believers in Jesus Christ. It further appears in the same chapter that Silas was a preacher besides being a believer, and that being in Antioch he pro-

---

[1] Leonine Sacramentary, Bright's Collects, p. 180.　　　[2] Ibid., p. 97.

longed his stay on his own and the Gospel's account. "And Judas and Silas, being prophets also themselves, exhorted the brethren with many words, and confirmed them. And after they had tarried there a space, they were let go in peace from the brethren unto the apostles. Notwithstanding it pleased Silas to abide there still." Then when the dispute arose between Paul and Barnabas over Mark, "Paul chose Silas, and departed, being recommended by the brethren unto the grace of God. And he went through Syria and Cilicia, confirming the churches." All the other allusions to Silas in the Acts belong to this second of the missionary journeys of S. Paul. In xvi. 25, Silas shares Paul's imprisonment at Philippi. In xvii. 4, 10, 14, 15, after trouble at Thessalonica, Paul and Silas were sent off by night to Berea, where Silas with Timotheus remained after Paul had to withdraw again before the Jews. In xviii. 5, Silas and Timotheus rejoin Paul at Corinth, and there all three laboured with vigour and success. "For the Son of God, Jesus Christ, who was preached among you by us, even by me and Silvanus and Timotheus, was not yea and nay, but in Him was yea."—2 Cor. i. 19.

The other allusions to Silas are all in the epistles, where his name uniformly occurs as Silvanus, and where thrice in the same conjunction, "Paul and Silvanus and Timotheus" (2 Cor. i. 19 ; 1 Thess. i. 1 ; 2 Thess. i. 1). The reason for the conjunction of the three names in salutations to the Churches of Macedonia and Corinth lies in the narrative in the Acts above quoted. It is not certain, but in a high degree probable, that it is the same Silvanus who appears in 1 Peter v. 12 as the bearer of that epistle. "By Silvanus, a faithful brother unto you, as I suppose, I have written briefly, exhorting, and testifying that this is the true grace of God wherein ye stand."

"The circumstances of the life of Silas [1] obviously gave him special qualifications for maintaining or restoring unity of teaching and feeling between the Jewish and Gentile sections

[1] Dean Plumptre on 1 Peter v. 12, in Camb. Bible for Schools.

of the Church. Trained in the Church of Jerusalem, and known as possessing prophetic gifts (Acts xv. 32), he had been chosen with Barsabas to be the bearer of the encyclical letter from the Council of apostles and presbyters, and to enforce its purport orally. Throwing himself so heartily into the work of preaching to the Gentiles that he was chosen by S. Paul as his companion on his second missionary journey, travelling with him and Timotheus through Galatia, Troas, Philippi, Thessalonica, and Corinth, he was conspicuously fitted to carry on the work which Paul had begun. The scattered notices above referred to do not carry us further than his work at Corinth, and we are left to conjecture how he had filled up the interval that had elapsed since that date [52-66 A.D.] What we now read suggests (1) that he had been working among the churches of the provinces of Asia Minor named in chapter i. 1, and had gained their confidence; (2) that after S. Paul's final departure from those regions he had turned to S. Peter as still within reach, and had brought under his notice the sufferings of the Christians there; and (3) that he was sent back with the epistle that was to guide and comfort them. It is a probable conjecture that S. Peter may have received from him copies of the epistles of S. Paul to which he refers in 2 Peter iii. 15-16. The Greek verb for "I have written," as being in the epistolary aorist, is rightly taken as referring to this epistle, and not, as some commentators have thought, to a lost earlier one. The words "by Silvanus" may imply that he was either the amanuensis or the bearer of the letter, or possibly that he united the two characters."

Apollos.

COLLECTS.—*Blessed Lord, who hast caused all Holy Scriptures to be written for our learning; Grant that we may in such wise hear them, read, mark, learn, and inwardly digest them, that by patience and comfort of Thy Holy Word, we may embrace, and ever hold fast the blessed hope of everlasting life, which Thou hast given us in our Saviour Jesus Christ. Amen.*[1]

Almighty and everlasting God, who alone workest great marvels; send down upon our bishops and curates, and all congregations committed to their charge, the healthful Spirit of Thy grace; and that they may truly please Thee, pour upon them the continual dew of Thy blessing. Grant this, O Lord, for the honour of our Advocate and Mediator, Jesus Christ. Amen.[2]

For the Epistle.—Acts xviii. 24-28.
The Gospel.—S. Luke xxiv. 44-53.

"I have planted, Apollos watered ; but God gave the increase."
—1 Cor. iii. 6.

APOLLOS, = Apollonius, appears first and suddenly in Acts xviii., where five closely compacted verses are devoted to him. "And a certain Jew named Apollos, born at Alexandria, an eloquent man, and mighty in the Scriptures, came to Ephesus. This man was instructed in the way of the Lord ; and being fervent in the spirit, he spake and taught diligently the things of the Lord, knowing only the baptism of John. And he began to speak boldly in the synagogue : whom when Aquila and Priscilla had heard, they took him unto them, and expounded unto him the way of God more perfectly. And when

---

[1] The Second Sunday in Advent.
[2] Morning Prayer, For Clergy and People.

he was disposed to pass into Achaia, the brethren wrote, exhorting the disciples to receive him: who, when he was come, helped them much which had believed through grace: for he mightily convinced the Jews, and that publicly, showing by the Scriptures that Jesus was Christ." In the Revised Version of 1881 "eloquent" is replaced to great advantage by *learned*, which is a more literal translation of *logios*, and is explained or confirmed by "mighty in the Scriptures," as by his Alexandrian education. The abundance of Jews at Alexandria appears from Acts vi. 9, and it was for the use of these at an earlier period that the Septuagint version of the Old Testament was made. Moreover, it was the seat of a school of philosophy famous at this very period for the teaching of Philo, under whom in all probability Apollos had studied. Thus would Apollos in his line of training greatly resemble S. Paul himself, whose work he so much helped, first at Ephesus, mainly at Corinth, and later at Crete, as we may judge from Titus iii. 13. Very interesting is it to note the exact doctrinal and ecclesiastical position occupied by Apollos before he was taken in hand by Priscilla and Aquila (for here the wife comes first, probably as a Jewess married to a Gentile). They appreciated the solid learning, devout zeal, and honest reasonableness of the Alexandrian, and privately communicated to him that distinctively evangelical element which was lacking owing to the circumstances of his education. In trying to enumerate the points in which this distinctively Christian element consisted, High Churchmen seize the opportunity for laying the usual emphasis on sacramental doctrine; but the clear and simple thing required was to state to Apollos all that had happened to and through the Lord Jesus since the imprisonment and beheading of the Baptist, of which the two sacraments were part, but only a part, and in the written Gospels not the most prominent part. Soon after he had been instructed in the completed Gospel by Priscilla and Aquila, Apollos removed from Ephesus to Corinth, and with letters of introduction from the one Church to the other, his intention being to see and join in the

work of the great apostle of the Gentiles. It seems somewhat
of an exaggeration to regard Apollos as the representative of a
party in the Corinthian Church, although his name is used
by Paul himself in that aspect. The use is not absolute, but
only for convenience to expose the wrongness of the Corinthians in clustering round certain objectionable teachers whom
Paul did not wish to name, but illustrated the evil of parties
in the Church by taking the good and quite friendly name of
Apollos simply as one familiar. And he used his own name
in the same way, although he had done nothing partisan.
" These things, brethren, I have in a figure transferred to
myself and to Apollos for your sakes; that ye might learn in
us not to think of men above that which is written, that no
one of you be puffed up for one against another."—1 Cor. iv. 6.
At the same time, while the two men were so friendly and
alike in their training and method, Apollos seems to have been
the smoother of the two in his Old Testament arguments with
the Jews, laying more stress on the evanishing law than Paul
did, and less stress on the full openness of the door of entry to
the Gentiles.

After Apollos had laboured with great success at Corinth,
for some time he paid a visit to Paul at Ephesus, and gave
an account of the Corinthian Church, supplementary to the
accounts from the house of Chloe and the deputation consisting of Stephanas, Fortunatus, and Achaicus, as to strife and
immorality—which led the apostle who founded it to write a
long and severe letter, now forming sixteen chapters. It was
probably in view of these divisions that Apollos declined to
return for the present, even though urged by Paul himself.
" As touching our brother Apollos, I greatly desired him to
come unto you with the brethren : but his will was not at all
to come at this time; but he will come when he shall have convenient time."—xvi. 12.

It was about 56 A.D. that Apollos first appeared at Ephesus—
about 59 that 1 Corinthians was written, after which probably
Apollos would return to Corinth after the first epistle had done

the good work alluded to in 2 Cor. vii. At a later point again, in Titus iii. 12, written about 64 A.D., we hear of Apollos in connection with a journey to Crete. Jerome says that it was only now, when S. Paul's letters had served to quieten and discipline the Corinthian Church, that Apollos went back and became the bishop of the place. Beyond this we have no record of the man.

His name has been associated with the extremely discussed question of the authorship of the Epistle to the Hebrews, especially in two recent books of Canon Farrar. No historic evidence points toward Apollos. Luther made a cleverish guess, which has been adopted by, among others, De Wette, Bleek, and Farrar. It is quite true that the training and ability of Apollos, as above traced, mark him as competent for the authorship; but the good old-fashioned ascription to Paul had really the same reason, *plus* the very important addition of historical evidence back to the second century. Even if Apollos had some special training that shows traces in the Hebrews, he might during his not brief and very cordial intercourse with S. Paul have communicated these to the apostle; and the apostle was a man capable enough of appreciating and utilising such intercourse, which would form a part of his wider lifelong education. And all this might with special advantage fill part of his two years' first and easier Roman imprisonment.

Timothy.

COLLECTS.—*O God, who providest for Thy people with tenderness, and rulest over them in love; Give the spirit of wisdom to those to whom Thou hast given the authority of government; that from the wellbeing of the holy sheep may proceed the eternal joy of the pastors; through Jesus Christ our Lord.*[1]

It is meet for us to beseech Thy majesty, that we may be found at our Lord's coming ministering to our fellow-servants their portion of meat in due season; that in our dealings with Thy servants we may be careful to join affection with rebuke and needful censure with love; and that wisely discharging the service committed to us, we may not incur the guilt of neglecting to increase our Lord's deposit, but may receive profit from having multiplied God's talents, whereof we have been the stewards.[2]

The Epistle.—2 Tim. iv. 1-5.
The Gospel.—S. John xx. 19-23.

Lord, pour Thy Spirit from on high,
  And Thine ordainèd servants bless;
Graces and gifts to each supply,
  And clothe Thy priests with righteousness.

Within Thy temple, when they stand
  To teach the truth, as taught by Thee,
Saviour, like stars in Thy right hand
  Let all Thy Church's pastors be.

Wisdom, and zeal, and love impart,
  Firmness with meekness from above,
To bear Thy people in their heart,
  And love the souls whom Thou dost love;

----

[1] Gregorian Sacramentary, Bright, p. 182.
[2] Leonine Sacramentary, Bright, p. 178.

To love, and pray, and never faint,
  By day and night their guard to keep,
To warn the sinner, form the saint,
  To feed Thy lambs, and tend Thy sheep.

So when their work is finished here,
  They may in hope their charge resign !
So when their Master shall appear,
  They may with crowns of glory shine !
—J. MONTGOMERY.

"Paul, an apostle of Jesus Christ by the commandment of God our Saviour, and Lord Jesus Christ, which is our hope; unto Timothy, my own son in the faith : Grace, mercy, and peace, from God our Father and Jesus Christ our Lord."—1 TIM. i. 1.

TIMOTHY belonged to Lystra in Lycaonia, his mother Eunice being a Jewess, and his father a Greek. He first appears in Acts xvi. in connection with S. Paul's second apostolic journey. "Then came Paul to Derbe and Lystra : and, behold, a certain disciple was there, named Timotheus (the son of a certain woman, which was a Jewess, and believed; but his father was a Greek:) which was well reported of by the brethren that were at Lystra and Iconium. Him would Paul have to go forth with him; and took and circumcised him because of the Jews which were in those quarters : for they knew all that his father was a Greek." Two passages in 2 Tim. i. 3 tell with great beauty and tenderness Paul's affection for his young friend, and the manner of his early training. "Without ceasing I have remembrance of thee in my prayers night and day; greatly desiring to see thee, being mindful of thy tears, that I may be filled with joy; when I call to remembrance the unfeigned faith that is in thee, which dwelt first in thy grandmother Lois, and thy mother Eunice; and I am persuaded that in thee also. Wherefore I put thee in remembrance that thou stir up the gift of God, which is in thee by the putting on of my hands." "Neglect not the gift that is in thee, which was given thee by prophecy, with the laying on of the hands of the presbytery."   "Continue thou in the things which thou hast learned and hast been assured of, knowing of whom thou hast learned them; and that from a child thou hast known the Holy Scriptures, which are able to make thee wise unto salvation through faith which is in Christ Jesus."   No two men working together in the Gospel as senior and junior are united by the tie of personal sympathy and affection so strongly and tenderly as are Paul and Timothy. "Unto Timothy, my own son in the faith."   "This charge I commit unto thee, son Timothy, according to the prophecies [1] which went before on thee, that thou by them mightest war a good warfare."—1 Tim. i. 2, 18.   "For this cause have I sent unto you Timotheus, who is my beloved son, and faithful in the Lord, who shall bring you into remembrance of my ways which be in Christ, as I teach everywhere in every church." —1 Cor. iv. 17.   "Timotheus my work-fellow."—Rom. xvi. 21. "Paul, an apostle of Jesus Christ by the will of God, and Timotheus our brother, unto the Church of God which is at Corinth, with all the saints which are in all Achaia."—2 Cor. i. 1.   "Wherefore, when we could no longer forbear, we thought it good to be left at Athens alone, and sent Timotheus, our brother, and minister of God, and our fellow-labourer in the Gospel of Christ, to establish you, and to comfort you concerning your faith."—1 Thess. iii. 1.

Found by S. Paul at Lystra, highly recommended by the brethren there, already from infancy carefully educated in religion, Timothy was taken in hand by the apostle as a valuable acquisition to the Gospel, and in view of his acting as an assistant, was at once circumcised, so as not to offend the stricter Jews among the disciples.   We are not told when or where the laying on of hands took place.   Perhaps it was done at once at Lystra; but more likely it was after some prelimi- nary testing of the young man's actual behaviour and capacity

---

[1] "Prophecies" here and "prophecy" above in 1 Tim. iv. 14, evidently contain an allusion to the ordination sermon on occasion of Timothy's consecration, probably preached by Paul himself.

for ministerial work, and in some larger place like Philippi, Corinth, or Ephesus, where believers were more numerous, and where several presbyters already existed. Apart from the where and when, the consecration service for Timothy was the occasion of anticipations or actual predictions made in the sermon (as twice above alluded to) that no ordinary man was being set apart to the holy ministry. And the man himself, after ordination and in the course of his performance of special duties at Ephesus, whereto he was appointed by his senior, has for eighteen centuries had this distinction attached to his name, that S. Paul's letters of charge for his guidance contain more clear and pointed instruction touching the Christian ministry than all the rest of the New Testament put together. The similar Epistle to Titus is a useful compend of the two Epistles to Timothy, but it is the latter that are emphatically "the pastoral epistles," in so far as Holy Scripture furnishes an ordinal to the Church, not in the technical and ecclesiastical sense, but in a readable outline of sound general principles combined with certain specific details.

Thus adopted on S. Paul's staff of personal assistants, Timothy labours stage by stage to the end of the apostle's second great journey, in the midst of which he was assumed. No less is he associated with the third and fourth journeys. But his particular value lay in his suitableness to be told off at any crisis to act as the apostle's deputy or representative. This most responsible and honourable class of work he did in three different places in succession. His missions to Thessalonica and Corinth, 1 Thess. iii. 1-3, 1 Cor. iv. 17, were each of a more temporary and occasional nature; whereas his connection with Ephesus, 1 Tim. i. 3, was that of a settled charge, and for the surrounding province as well as the city proper; so that herein he followed S. Paul the founder, and preceded S. John his great successor, in this chief centre of Christian work and rule in Asia.

From Heb. xiii. 23, probably written by S. Paul towards the end of his first Roman imprisonment about 62 A.D., we learn incidentally that Timothy had also for a time been in prison at Rome. "Know ye that our brother Timothy is set at liberty; with whom, if he come shortly, I will see you." Who the *you* are depends on what Hebrews received the original epistle; those of Judea being commonly understood. After this come the whole of the references in 2 Timothy, the latest of S. Paul's writings, and of peculiar solemnity and pathos for allusions to the apostle's coming martyrdom, its earnest renewal of points in the original ordination sermon to Timothy, and repeated entreaty to Timothy to start from Ephesus (for the work at which Tychicus had already been despatched by Paul), and hasten to Rome himself and bring Mark also, both for fresh work and final farewell. All this and much more is in the last chapter of the apostle's tearful, pleading, yet brave and peaceful letter. "I have fought a good fight, I have finished my course. . . . Do thy diligence to come shortly unto me. . . . Only Luke is with me. Take Mark, and bring him with thee: for he is profitable to me for the ministry. And Tychicus have I sent to Ephesus. . . . Do thy diligence to come before winter." We may safely believe that this urgent summons to the death - scene of Timothy's heroic "father in God" would be as fervently responded to as it was sent; and that thus the youthful Bishop of the Ephesians, in the course of his absence from his people, would have the mournful satisfaction of adding to the peace and comfort of the last days, not only of Paul, but of Peter too, on that 29th June, which bereft the Church of the two chiefs of the apostolic college.

Hi sunt olivæ duæ coram Domino,	These be the two olive-trees before the Lord, [ent,
Et candelabra luce radiantia,	the candlesticks brightly resplend-
Præclara cœli duo luminaria,	the two great luminaries of heaven :
Fortia solvunt peccatorum vincula,	these unloose the strong bonds of sin,
Portas Olympi reserunt fidelibus.	these unlock heaven's gates to the faithful.

O Roma felix, quæ tuorum princi- pum	O happy Rome, with the precious blood
Es purpurata pretioso sanguine,	of thy chiefs empurpled ! [est,
Excellis omnem mundi pulchritu- dinem, [meritis,	all the world's beauty thou excell- not by thy fame, but by the merits
Non laude tua sed sanctorum	of saints [swords.
Quos cruentatis jugulasti gladiis.[1]	slain of thee by blood-stained

After his sad duties and experience at Rome, Timothy seems to have returned to Ephesus, and laboured on faithfully in his diocese till 97 A.D., when tradition says he was beaten to death by stones and clubs on a heathen festival on 22d January. His day in the Calendar being 24th January, he would seem to have survived this assault for two days. His full and proper designation is S. Timothy, Bishop and Martyr.

Touching the great question of Orders, the *locus classicus* of which is 1 Tim. iii., I may here, as a presbyter of the Church of Scotland, writing mainly for Scottish Churchmen, criticise the relation of the Reformed Church of Scotland, as represented by Knox, Melville, and Henderson, to the two orders of presbyter and deacon authoritatively prescribed and described for Timothy's guidance. Other New Testament names—*e.g.*, apostle, prophet, evangelist, teacher, worker of miracles, healer, interpreter, exhorter, as in 1 Cor. xii. 8-10, 28-30, and Rom. xii. 6-8—are practically irrelevant for the present purpose; because belonging to offices that had no succession, or that represented passing phases of ministry associated with extraordinary gifts of the Holy Ghost. Any real view of the practical question of orders turns on the Scripture use and interpretation of the three words bishop, presbyter, and deacon. In the Scripture itself it is now generally admitted that bishop and presbyter are synonymous terms, used interchangeably, the proof passages being Titus i. 5, 7, and Acts xx. 17, 28, which it is simply impossible to

---

[1] Part of hymn beginning *Felix per omnes*, which is an ancient version in another metre of the still older hymn *Aurea luce et decore roseo*, quoted under S. Peter the Apostle.

interpret honestly in any other sense.   To these may be
added, as adminicles of proof, Phil. i. 1 and 1 Tim. iii. 1, 8,
where two offices and no more are named, the list being
evidently complete, and one of the two being a different office
altogether from bishop or presbyter—viz., deacon, which is not
matter of controversy in the same sense at all.   Separate
choice and ordination for presbyters and deacons, as also
distinct duties, are clear from 1 Tim. iii. and Acts vi. 5, 6.
But no separate or additional appointment or consecration can
be proven from Scripture for bishops as distinct from presbyters.   It is simply the same office and status; but when the
office was held by a man of superior energy or ability, or when
the sphere of office was a more prominent place, then came in
a difference, which quickly grew to be marked by one of the
two words rather than the other, and a distinct form of
ordination was invented.   Thus bishop, = overseer or superintendent, acquired a technical meaning; and it is very foolish
and unhistorical for Presbyterians not to acknowledge heartily the naturalness and usefulness of this development, even
though it has no Scripture proof, and no basis in any higher
ordination or consecration.   Why may there not be presbyters
and presbyters; just as there are squires and squires?   So
long as overseers, superintendents, or bishops are ordained by
a body of presbyters, there is no interference with the real
principle of presbytery.   And without some such recognition
of superior attainments, ability, and experience, there can be
no efficient rule or supervision among a body of clergy where
every man thinks himself as good as his neighbour, and every
man has his turn of the top like the spokes of a wheel.

The Church of Scotland, which in modern times is the
original and normal pattern of Presbytery for all English-
speaking people, has had three successive presentations of
ecclesiastical offices, not one of which accords with 1 Tim. iii.;
and of which the first is by far the best, because of its greater
approximation to Scripture and common-sense.

The First Book of Discipline in 1560 lays down five offices,

—viz., minister, reader, superintendent, elder, and deacon. Three of these five are distinctly Scriptural—viz., minister and deacon as corresponding to presbyter, and deacon. Superintendent is as good as Scriptural, because it represents bishop when it began to be partly discriminated from presbyter. Reader was an extremely useful office when presbyters were few, or when congregations were small or remote; but it need not have been formally inserted in the list of offices at all. The great objection lies to elder, and on two grounds; because really drawn from the Old Testament (Num. xi. 17), and in so far as it has New Testament root it makes inextricable confusion with presbyter on the one hand and deacon on the other. Presbyter is robbed of his name by translation, and deacon is ousted from his duties by a nondescript intruder. Some attempt to justify the intruder by calling him a *ruling* as distinguished from a *preaching* elder, and appeal to 1 Tim. v. 17, " Let the elders that rule well be counted worthy of double honour, especially they who labour in the word and doctrine." This is a violent absurdity, because it is presbyters alone that are there spoken of, and among presbyters certain more efficient in ruling gain more honour than ordinary presbyters; so that the whole text, instead of pointing downward to an intermediate class or office between presbyter and deacon, points *upward* to a superior grade of presbyters, already provided for in the superintendent. To use plain language, the introduction of elder in the First Book of Discipline in 1560 is a monstrous hash. Nor need one scruple to use a strong term of condemnation, because two other gross blunders were made in the same book touching offices. Ordination itself was actually discontinued for a short period; and both elders and deacons were at first appointed to office only for a year's tenure ! !

The Second Book of Discipline in 1578, and for which Andrew Melville was mainly responsible, made matters worse instead of better by a restatement of offices as four—viz., minister, doctor, elder, and deacon. Here the nondescript blundering elder is retained ; the Scriptural superintendent and useful reader are both dropped ; and a new office of doctor or teacher, partly referring to universities, is introduced for the first time.

In 1645 the Westminster "Form of Presbyterian Church Government " retains the same four as were laid down in 1578, but changes the names of two of them, thus : pastors, teachers, elders, deacons.   Here pastors mean presbyters, which the whining Puritans seem to wish disguised ; teachers, as already said, are a nonsensical branch of presbyters, quite out of place in such a list ; elders are first put as "other church governors " in the heading, and then explained from the Jewish Church as parallel to the elders joined with the priests and Levites, an illustration which betrays gross ignorance of the first principles of Christian order. Thus all through the three systems of 1560, 1578, and 1645, this bogus "elder," sometimes called "lay" and sometimes "ruling," comes into collision with the real and Scripture deacon, who is made a mere *nominis umbra*.   In practice the Presbyterian system honestly consists of two orders, presbyter and deacon, in conformity with 1 Tim. iii., but a frightful confusion is made in the nomenclature by calling the deacon Judaically an elder. Moreover, a great loss has been suffered by dropping the superintendent recognised by Knox, which makes government almost necessarily in-efficient, and puts a premium on the degrading and unnatural principle of parity and rotation, whereby courts are constructed on the cart-wheel principle of each spoke having its turn of the top.

Titus.

COLLECTS.—*O Lord, we beseech Thee to keep Thy Church and household continually in Thy true religion ; that they who do lean only upon the hope of Thy heavenly grace may evermore be defended by Thy mighty power ; through Jesus Christ our Lord. Amen.*[1]

Almighty God, the Giver of all good gifts, who of Thy divine providence hast appointed divers Orders in Thy Church ; Give Thy grace, we humbly beseech Thee, to all those who are to be called to any office and administration in the same ; and so replenish them with the truth of Thy doctrine, and endue them with innocency of life, that they may faithfully serve before Thee, to the glory of Thy great name, and the benefit of Thy holy Church ; through Jesus Christ our Lord. Amen.[2]

The Epistle.—Titus iii. 1-8.
The Gospel.—S. Matt. vii. 21-27.

" Paul, a servant of God, and an apostle of Jesus Christ, . . . to Titus, mine own son after the common faith : Grace, mercy, and peace, from God the Father and the Lord Jesus Christ our Saviour."—Titus i. 1.

ALTHOUGH part of his work comes within the period embraced by S. Luke in the Acts, the name of Titus is not once mentioned there ; so that all our knowledge comes from S. Paul's own allusions in his epistles, and particularly in that addressed to him by name, for guidance in his duties in Crete. The first mention of Titus is in Gal. ii. 1, 3 : " Then fourteen years after I went up again to Jerusalem with Bar-

---

[1] Fifth Sunday after Epiphany.
[2] Anglican Prayer-Book, Occasional Prayers.

nabas, and took Titus with me also. . . . But neither Titus, who was with me, being a Greek, was compelled to be circumcised." We are not told where Titus belonged to by birth, how or when he was converted, or at what point he joined S. Paul. But we may reasonably associate all these particulars with Antioch, where both he and Paul were previous to the above journey to Jerusalem. It is clear that the connection of Titus with the great apostle continued from that point in 50 A.D. to 67 A.D., S. Paul's martyrdom.

There is trace of the presence and work of Titus in Corinth at an early stage of the history of the Church there. "Whether any do inquire of Titus, he is my partner and fellow-helper concerning you."—2 Cor. viii. 23. He seems twice to have visited Corinth; to begin the collection for the poor saints, and, after a year or more, to complete it. "Insomuch that we desired Titus, that as he had begun, so he would also finish in you the same grace also. . . . But thanks be to God, which put the same earnest care into the heart of Titus for you. For indeed he accepted the exhortation; but being more forward, of his own accord he went unto you. And we have sent with him the brother, whose praise is in the Gospel throughout all the churches."—2 Cor. viii. 6, 16, as again referred to in xii. 18: "I desired Titus, and with him I sent a brother. Did Titus make a gain of you?" We see from the above that in the matter of the collection Titus was the apostle's chief agent, and that "the brother whose praise is in the Gospel" (probably S. Luke) was only subsidiary.

After the tumult at Ephesus, Acts xix., Paul went to Troas expecting to meet Titus, probably on his way back from delivering the First Epistle to the Corinthians, and was greatly disappointed at not meeting him. "Furthermore, when I came to Troas to preach Christ's Gospel, and a door was opened unto me of the Lord, I had no rest in my spirit, because I found not Titus my brother: but taking my leave of them, I went from thence into Macedonia."—2 Cor. ii. 12. This anxiety soon after came to an end, for in Macedonia, to which Paul had gone, Titus joined him with good news of Corinth. "When we were come into Macedonia, our flesh had no rest, but we were troubled on every side; without were fightings, within were fears. Nevertheless God, that comforteth those that are cast down, comforted us by the coming of Titus; and not by his coming only, but by the consolation wherewith he was comforted in you, when he told us your earnest desire, your mourning, your fervent mind toward me; so that I rejoiced the more. . . . Therefore we were comforted in your comfort; yea, and exceedingly the more joyed we for the joy of Titus, because his spirit was refreshed by you all. . . . Even so our boasting, which I made before Titus, is found a truth. And his inward affection is more abundant toward you, whilst he remembereth the obedience of you all, how with fear and trembling ye received him."—2 Cor. vii. 5-15. These circumstances associated with Titus were largely the occasion of the writing of S. Paul's second letter to the Corinthian Church, which seems to have been sent by the hands of Titus and Luke, and to have been written at Philippi or Thessalonica about 57 A.D.

From the date of the delivery by Titus of the Second Epistle to the Corinthians we have no further account of him till 62 A.D., when he was left by the apostle in Crete "to set in order the things that were wanting, and to ordain presbyters in every city."—Titus i. 5. Crete, now Candia, is the largest of the isles of Greece, lying across the opening of the Ægean Sea, about 160 miles in length and from 5 to 35 in breadth, once so thickly peopled that Homer calls it hecatompolis, from its 100 cities: it contained Mount Ida, and was associated with legends of Jupiter, Europa, Pasiphaë, Ariadne, Dædalus, and the Corybantes. It was brought under Roman rule by Metellus Creticus, and with Cyrenaica formed a province for a proconsul. The date of its first receiving the Gospel is unknown. Some think of the record of Pentecost, where the people of both halves of the proconsular province are named,—"the parts of Libya about Cyrene, . . . Cretes.

and Arabians."—Acts ii. 10. Others think of a visit of Paul himself at the close of his first Roman imprisonment ; but that is clearly too late a date, and too brief and recent a stay, to have produced so many converts that now presbyters were needed to be ordained by Titus for every city. The true origin must go back to the Pentecost disciples who came from Jerusalem, or some intermediate preachers of whose labours we have no definite record. The field was a comparatively large one for Titus, forming the better half of a proconsular province, and would give full scope for the youthful bishop's zeal and prudence for a series of years in organising congregations and settling presbyters in terms of his apostolic commission.

After three years more or less of this good work in the diocese of Crete, Bishop Titus was hastily and earnestly summoned to Nicopolis in Macedonia by S. Paul, who also provided a substitute in Artemas or Tychicus to carry on the superintendent's duties in absence—Tit. iii. 12. This being done by Titus, it appears from 2 Tim. iv. 20, that Paul visited Crete and left Trophimus sick there in Miletus,[1] the visit being of course in company with Titus. After this visit to Crete, Titus seems to have accompanied Paul to Rome to help the Christians there in the persecution. Before or during the apostle's second Roman imprisonment, Titus was sent, about 65 A.D., on some mission to Dalmatia, on the north-eastern coast of the Adriatic—2 Tim. iv. 10—which is the latest Scripture notice of Titus. From notices in early Church history, he seems to have returned from Dalmatia to Crete, where he laboured on till his death in his ninety-fourth year. He was regarded as the first archbishop of Gortyna, the capital of Crete, which was destroyed by the Saracens in 823 A.D., whereafter Candia became the capital; and the cathedral there is dedicated to S. Titus. According to Malte Brun

---

[1] Both Homer and Strabo certify a Miletus in Crete. Had it been the Miletus of Ephesus at which Trophimus had been left, who was an Ephesian, it would have been useless to tell Timothy, who was himself there.

and Balbi, the population of Crete in 1839 was 158,000 ; and
Alban Butler, under S. Titus, whose day is 4th January, says
that the metropolitan of the island has eleven suffragan bishops
of the Greek communion.

S. Jude,

THE BROTHER OF JAMES.

COLLECTS.—*O Lord Jesus Christ, who at Thy first coming didst send Thy messenger to prepare Thy way before Thee ;
Grant that the ministers and stewards of Thy mysteries may
likewise so prepare and make ready Thy way, by turning the
hearts of the disobedient to the wisdom of the just, that at Thy
second coming to judge the world we may be found an acceptable people in Thy sight, who livest and reignest with the
Father and the Holy Spirit, ever one God, world without end.
Amen.*[1]

*O Lord, raise up (we pray Thee) Thy power, and come
among us, and with great might succour us ; that whereas,
through our sins and wickedness, we are sore let and hindered
in running the race that is set before us, Thy bountiful grace
and mercy may speedily help and deliver us ; through the satisfaction of Thy Son our Lord, to whom, with Thee and the Holy
Ghost, be honour and glory, world without end.   Amen.*[2]

The Epistle.—S. Jude 17-25.
The Gospel.—S. Matt. xxv. 31-40.

Hora novissima, tempora pessima
   sunt, vigilemus !
Ecce ! minaciter imminet arbiter
   ille supremus.
	The world is very evil,
	   The times are waxing late ;
	Be sober and keep vigil,
	   The Judge is at the gate,—

---

[1] Third Sunday in Advent.　　[2] Fourth Sunday in Advent.

Imminet, imminet, ut mala ter-
    minet, æqua coronet,
Recta remuneret, anxia liberet,
    æthera donet.
      —Bernard of Morlaix, c. 1125;
        Moorsom, *Hist. Comp. to*
        Hys. Anc. and Mod.
	The Judge that comes in mercy,
	    The Judge that comes with might
	To terminate the evil,
	    To diadem the right.
	          —J. M. Neale.

"Jude, the servant of Jesus Christ, and brother of James, to
them that are sanctified by God the Father, and preserved in Jesus Christ, and called : mercy unto you, and
peace, and love, be multiplied."—S. Jude 1.

THRICE already—under S. Joseph, S. Jude the apostle,
and S. James the Lord's brother—we have had occasion
to anticipate the writer of the penultimate epistle of the New
Testament. Distinctly he calls himself "the brother of James";
he does not call himself an apostle, but alludes to the apostles
so as to suggest or imply that he was not one of them : " But,
beloved, remember ye the words which were spoken before of
the apostles of our Lord Jesus Christ "—ver. 17. This is the
Jude referred to in S. Matt. xiii. 55, "Is not this the carpenter's
son ? is not His mother called Mary ? and His brethren, James,
and Joses, and Simon, and Judas ?" From his place in the list
we may take Jude to be the youngest of the four, of whom two
—viz., James and Simon—were bishops of Jerusalem in succession, while Jude was a simple presbyter or travelling evangelist.
The brethren of Jesus, in their original unbelief, appear in the
Gospel of S. John vii. 3, 5 : " His brethren therefore said unto
Him, Depart hence, and go into Judea, that Thy disciples also
may see the works that Thou doest. . . . For neither did His
brethren believe in Him." This unbelief continued till our
Lord's resurrection, and prevented any of the four being chosen
as apostles among the twelve. After His resurrection our
Lord made a special appearance to James, 1 Cor. xv. 7, which
seems to have changed him and the rest ; for in Acts i. 14,
after the ascension and preceding Pentecost, we find the

brethren of Jesus meeting in company with the apostles and the female disciples. "These all continued with one accord in prayer and supplication, with the women, and Mary the mother of Jesus, and with His brethren." There is a clear trace of the activity of these "brethren of the Lord" in travelling to proclaim the Gospel and gather Christian congregations in 1 Cor. ix. 5, where, referring to his own method and that of Barnabas, S. Paul asks, "Have we not power to lead about a sister, a wife, as well as other apostles, and as the brethren of the Lord, and Cephas?" This was written by S. Paul about 57 A.D., and it must have been in the course of these Gospel journeys, when accompanied by his sister or wife, that Jude the presbyter came in contact with the depraved and perverse men afterwards known as Gnostic heretics and libertines, whom he so vehemently denounces in his·short epistle. His careful, devout, and even ascetic training, received in the well-regulated house of S. Joseph, would enable Jude the more quickly to make up his mind as to the hopelessly corrupt character and principles of these false teachers. And the same training would lead him to expose and denounce them without mercy as wretches fitted to wreck the Church of Christ at its· very start. His letter is thus not an epistle in the sense of those by Paul, Peter, or John, expounding Christian doctrine or exhorting to duty, but a Church defence circular warning believers against a set of villains—corrupt, greedy, and subtle —who were using the name of Christ as a covering to their wicked devices. Jude's own language of description is plain and strong, launched forth without any balancing or restraining phrases. "There are certain men crept in unawares, who were before of old ordained to this condemnation, ungodly men, turning the grace of our God into lasciviousness, and denying the only Lord God, and our Lord Jesus Christ. . . . Likewise also these filthy dreamers defile the flesh, despise dominion, and speak evil of dignities. . . . These are murmurers, complainers, walking after their own lusts ; and their mouth speaketh great swelling words, having men's persons in admiration because of advantage. . . . These be they who separate themselves, sensual, having not the Spirit."

This torrent of reproach is very strikingly reproduced in 2 Peter ii., and applied to the same wicked deceivers; and the one passage is transparently based on the other. Which is the original of the two is not difficult to settle; because Jude's version is the more vehement, while Peter's, though also vehement, bears marks of critical revision—changing the clouds without water (which is a mixed image and impossible in nature) into "wells without water." Jude's allusions to the dispute of Michael and Satan over the body of Moses, and also the Enoch prophecy, drawn from Jewish apocrypha and legend, are both omitted by S. Peter, who, as a higher authority in the Church, had stricter ideas of canonicity, and combated the heretics with more select and orthodox weapons than Jude in his tempestuous rage cared for. This priority of Jude over 2 Peter determines for us the date of Jude's epistle, that it must be before 67 A.D., and before 2 Timothy, as also before any of S. John's writings, which are the latest of all in the New Testament. The inclusion of Jude, as of James, in the Canon, throws some light on the principles of its structure; and in a minor degree the same applies to the three books of S. Mark and S. Luke. The latter were junior men, writing by inspiration, but under supervision of the two chief of the apostles. James and Jude, however, wrote under no apostolic supervision, nor were themselves apostles, but evidently got their place in the Canon as inspired men, honoured as "brethren of the Lord," and sons of the sainted foster-father of Jesus—the husband of the blessed Mary. Bishop James of Jerusalem was a greater power in the early Church than any except three of the twelve apostles. And Jude the presbyter owes his place in the Canon to his brothership with James, and his forceful leaflet against the foul and venomous enemies of the Gospel, who harassed the Church in the last quarter of the first century and the whole of the second. Moreover, the decision to include these two books by a bishop and presbyter of S. Joseph's family, shows an exercise of judgment and authority on the part of those ecclesiastics who framed the Canon which hardly coincides with the narrow views of ordinary Protestants as to the relation of the Bible to the Church in its Councils.

S. Michael and all Angels.

DAY, SEPTEMBER 29.

ORATIONES.—*Deus qui miro ordine angelorum ministeria hominumque dispensas, concede propitius : ut quibus tibi ministrantibus in cœlo semper assistitur, ab his in terra vita nostra muniatur.*

Beati Michaelis archangeli tui interventione suffulti, supplices te, Domine, deprecamur : ut quos honore prosequimur, contingamus et mente.

For the Epistle.—Rev. i. 5.
The Gospel.—S. Matt. xviii. 1-10.

COLLECT.—*O everlasting God, who hast ordained and constituted the services of angels and men in a wonderful order; Mercifully grant, that as Thy holy angels alway do Thee service in heaven, so by Thy appointment they may succour and defend us on earth ; through Jesus Christ our Lord.   Amen.*

For the Epistle.—Rev. xii. 7-12.
The Gospel.—S. Matt. xviii. 1-10.

Tibi Christe splendor Patris	Christ, the FATHER's mirrored
Vita ac virtus cordium	brightness, [art !
In conspectu angelorum	Life and strength of souls Thou
Votis voce psallimus	And to Thee before the angels
Alternantes concrepando	Sing we laud with voice and heart,
Melos damus vocibus.	In alternate modulation
	Bearing each our tuneful part.

Collandamus venerantes
Omnes cœli milites
Sed præcipue primatem
Cœlestis exercitus
Michaelem in virtute
Conterentem Zabulum.

Quo custode procul pellas
Rex Christe piissime
Omne nefas inimici
Mundo corde et corpore
Paradiso redde tuo
Nos sola clementia.
—*Anglo-Saxon Hymnarium*,
p. 114.

Praise we with meet veneration
 All the warriors of the sky;
Before all, the princely chieftain
 Of the heavenly chivalry,
Michael, who in battle victor,
 Hurled Abaddon from on high,

By his prowess all excelling,
 CHRIST, Thou King of boundless
 grace,
All the foes' assaults repelling,
 Pure in heart before Thy face,
Us in Paradise Thy dwelling,
 Of Thine only mercy place.
  —JOHN D. CHAMBERS
   (*in People's Hymnal*).

Christe sanctorum decus angel-
  orum
Autor humani generisque rector
Nobis æternum tribue benignum
  Scandere regnum.

O Christ! the beauty of the angel
  worlds!   [blest!
Of man the Maker and Redeemer
Grant us one day to reach those
  bright abodes
  And in Thy glory rest.

Angelum pacis Michael ad istam
Cœlitus mitti rogitamus aulam
Nobis ut crebro veniant et crescant
  Prospera cuncta.

Angel of peace! thou, Michael, from
  above,   [to dwell;
Come down, amid the homes of man
And banish wars with all their tears
  and blood,
  Back to their native Hell.

Angelus fortis Gabriel ut hostem
Pellat antiquuum volitet ab alto
Sæpius templum veniat et istud
  Visere nostrum.

Angel of strength! thou, Gabriel,
  cast out   [reign;
Thine ancient foes, usurpers of thy
The temples of thy triumph round
  the globe
  Revisit once again.

Angelum nobis medicum salutis
Mitte de cœlis Raphael ut omnes
Sanet ægrotos pariterque nostros
  Dirigat actus.

And Raphael, physician of the soul,
Let him descend from his pure halls
  of light,   [for us
To heal our sicknesses, and guide
  Each dubious course aright.

Hinc Dei nostri Genetrix Maria
Totus et nobis chorus angelorum
Semper assistat simul et beata
    Concio tota.
   —*Anglo-Saxon Hymnarium,*
     p. 116.

Thou too, fair virgin daughter of
    the skies!   [Peace, descend!
Mother of Light and Queen of
Bringing with thee the radiant
    Court of Heaven,
    To aid us and defend.
       —E. CASWALL.

Dear Angel! ever at my side
  How loving must thou be,
To leave thy home in Heaven to guard
  An erring child like me!

Thy beautiful and shining face
  I see not, though so near;
The sweetness of thy soft low voice
  I am too deaf to hear.

I cannot feel thee touch my hand,
  With pressure light and mild,
To check me as my mother did,
  In kindness to her child.

But I have felt thee in my thoughts
  Fighting with sin for me;
And when my heart loves God, I know
  The sweetness is from thee.

And when, dear Spirit! I kneel down
  Morning and night to prayer,
Something there is within my heart
  Which tells me thou art there.

Yes! when I pray, thou prayest too—
  Thy prayer is all for me!
But when I sleep, thou sleepest not,
  But watchest patiently.

But most of all I feel thee near,
  When from the good Priest's feet,
I go absolved in fearless love,
  Fresh toils and cares to meet.

And thou in life's last hour wilt bring
  A fresh supply of grace,
And afterwards wilt let me kiss
  Thy beautiful bright face.

Ah me ! how lovely they must be
Whom God has glorified !
Yet one of them, oh sweetest thought,
Is ever at my side.
—F. W. FABER.

"Ye are come unto Mount Sion, . . . and to an innumerable
company of angels."—HEB. xii. 22.
" And there was war in heaven : Michael and his angels fought
against the dragon ; and the dragon fought and his angels,
and prevailed not ; neither was their place found any
more in heaven."—REV. xii. 7.

ON the subject of angels it is peculiarly necessary to keep
close to Holy Scripture, for it is by revelation alone that we
have our knowledge of them. What we do know of them is
fitted to widen and heighten our conception of God's kingdom
and ways ; not only in checking the narrowness, coarseness,
and presumption associated with materialism, but also in giving
scope to the nobler part of our own nature which makes us
kindred to the angels, as it does also to God Himself, the
original and Father Spirit. And in truth, by carefully putting
together from the Bible into one view the various allusions
made to the world of angels, we know a great deal more regarding them than is commonly supposed. Our reward, moreover, for collecting and piecing together the many angel-texts
of Scripture, is not mere method improved, and increase of
knowledge by the study of a fresh province of being, but has
distinctly and largely an edifying side as regards man's own
heart and salvation ; because when the Bible speaks of angels,
it is mostly in connection with human virtue and grace, or in
connection with the plan of our redemption through the Son
of God, as will be very apparent in the sequel.

Our text in speaking of Michael and his angels reminds us
of Michaelmas on 29th September as a fixed and important
date in the Calendar, associated in England with quarterly
payments of rent and salary ; and most people, especially in

these mercantile days, are more ready to connect the season with money payable or receivable than with contemplation of the ministry of angels in heaven or on earth. The modern Calendar is more that of house and income than of the Church as it used to be in its blessed round of seasons and services.

Instead of beginning with S. Michael, it may be well to see first what the two Testaments of the Word of God tell us regarding angels generally; and thereafter we shall be better able to consider S. Michael in particular.

(1.) No sooner had Adam fallen and been condemned to eat bread in the sweat of his brow, than "the Lord drove out the man; and He placed at the east of the Garden of Eden cherubim, and a flaming sword which turned every way, to keep the way of the tree of life." We read nothing more of the work of angels till after the Flood: two angels came to Sodom at even as Lot sat at the gate of the city, and warned him to depart from the accursed place. And when Hagar fled from the face of her mistress Sarah, and she cast away her child to die in the wilderness of Beersheba, the angel of God called unto her from heaven, and bade her return home cheered with the promise of a son whose seed should be a mighty nation. When Abraham was about to slay his son Isaac, a willing sacrifice in the land of Moriah, "the angel of the Lord called unto him out of heaven" and bade him to stay his hand; and when he obeyed, his voice declared that in his seed all nations of the earth should be blessed. And, to take but a few out of the many instances of angels' ministry, we are told that Jacob, when fearful of his brother's anger he lay down to sleep on his way to Haran, "dreamed, and behold a ladder set up on the earth, and the top of it reached to heaven: and behold the angels of God ascending and descending on it. And, behold, the Lord stood above it." Again, when Jacob went away from Laban, "the angels of God met him. And when Jacob saw them, he said, This is God's host." It was God's angel, too, that stood in the way for an adversary against Balaam, when he went on his message with the servants of

Balak. "The angel of the Lord appeared to Gideon, and said unto him, The Lord is with thee, thou mighty man of valour," and gave him a sign from heaven by touching his sacrifice and consuming it with fire. An angel came from God to the wife of Manoah, Samson's mother, and told her of the future birth of a son, and went up again to heaven in the flame of the altar.

(2.) Not less explicit and historical is the New Testament in what it tells of angels, associated in the closest manner with the events most important in the Gospel. It was an angel that was sent to Zacharias with the promise of a son, the forerunner of our Lord, while he was burning incense in the Temple. It was the angel Gabriel that was sent from God to bear to the Blessed Virgin His gracious word of prophetic assurance, "Fear not, Mary; for thou hast found favour with God. And, behold, thou shalt conceive in thy womb, and bring forth a son, and thou shalt call his name Jesus." And it was a band and multitude of the heavenly host that suddenly appeared with the angel, praising God and saying, "Glory to God in the highest, and on earth peace, good will toward men." And when our blessed Saviour had been made flesh and dwelt among us, the ministry of angels was not withdrawn: when, in His infinite wisdom and for our sakes, He retired into the secret wilderness, there to prevail over the serpent in successful combat; when in the might of God's Word He had thrice repelled the tempter,—then "angels came and ministered unto Him." And in the garden of Gethsemane, hard by the Mount of Olives, when for us He bore the weight of His Father's anger, and as man drank to the dregs the bitter cup of human bodily suffering; when, in the intensity of His agony, "His sweat was as it were large drops of blood falling to the ground,"—there appeared an angel unto Him from heaven "strengthening Him." And when the victory over death and hell had been achieved, and our blessed Saviour rose triumphant from the grave, two men in white garments stood by the side of that faithful band who had early repaired to their Master's tomb, and bade them seek not the living among the dead. Nor did their ministry end here; for when a cloud had received the Lord out of the sight of His disciples, "behold two men stood by them in white apparel" who testified of the future coming of Christ in glory. The angel of the Lord, too, opened the prison doors and brought forth thence God's chosen apostles, and bade them go stand and speak in the Temple all the words of this life. Cornelius the centurion was warned by a holy angel to send for S. Peter and receive him into his house. And when the same apostle was thrown into prison and lay between two soldiers bound by two chains, the angel of the Lord came upon him, and raised him up, and struck from off his hands those heavy chains, and led him through the city gate. And lastly, when S. Paul and his companions were in danger of shipwreck on their way to Rome, there stood by him at night the angel of the Lord, saying, "Fear not, Paul; thou must be brought before Cæsar: and, lo, God hath given thee all them that sail with thee." [1]

All these cases, drawn from the Old and New Testaments, are instances connected with historic persons on earth where angels are associated with events and actions recorded of the same persons. It is these clear and strong cases of angelic contact with practical sacred history that render the doctrine of the Sadducees who denied the existence of angel and spirit so untenable, if we at all accept the Bible as from God.

There are two or three other classes of Scripture allusions to angels of which illustrations, although not lists, may be given. First is an unimportant class where the name is simply a figure of speech; and yet the figure rests on the belief of a reality to support it. Thus is manna called "angels' food" and "bread of heaven." The angels of the seven churches in Revelation are probably the bishops of these churches. Another class of allusions may possibly partake of the nature of personification of Divine Providence. "The angel of the Lord encampeth

---

[1] Two paragraphs from 'The Christian Seasons,' ii. 409-413.

round about them that fear Him, and delivereth them." "He shall give His angels charge over thee, to keep thee in all thy ways." "The Lord, before whom I walk, will send His angel with thee, and prosper thee," said Abraham to his servant. There is yet another class of angel allusions which cannot, without wilful wresting of Scripture, be disjoined from spiritual and heavenly beings, who are as characteristic of the skies as our own race is of this earth; and whom there is no more reason to cut off from connection with our world and its affairs, than there is to cut off mankind from interest in the affairs of heaven and deny to them the possibility of an inheritance and future home there.

Some idea of the frequency of allusion to angels in Scripture may be formed from the fact that "angel of the Lord" occurs in Scripture fifty-seven times; while the single book of the prophet Zechariah gives us twelve times the expression, "the angel that talked with me"; and the book of Revelation, in the course of its twenty-two chapters, mentions angels above sixty times.

But it is the angel texts that occur throughout the four gospels that are of special importance from a doctrinal point of view; for there we escape from the region of poetical figures of speech and prophetical visions, and are face to face with a revelation which shares in all the reality that pertains to the personal history and teaching of our blessed Lord, and bids defiance to Sadducees ancient and modern alike.

And we must remember that one whole class of our Lord's miracles—the healing of demoniacs—is a dealing with angels fallen and wicked; just as the first event after our Lord's baptism was His forty days of temptation in the wilderness, when He passed through a special struggle with the great enemy of God and man. S. John 1, iii. 8, expressly says, "For this purpose the Son of God was manifested, that He might destroy the works of the devil." And it is in this connection that we can best give meaning to at least three Gospel passages—viz. : " I beheld Satan as lightning fall from heaven."—Luke x. 18. " Now is the judgment of this world : now shall the prince of this world be cast out." —John xii. 31. " Of judgment, because the prince of this world is judged."—John xvi. 11. Moreover, a prominent feature of the Gospel descriptions and predictions of the day of judgment is the attendance of angels upon the Judge. " The Son of man shall come in the glory of His Father with His angels." " He shall send His angels with a great sound of a trumpet, and they shall gather together His elect from the four winds." " Of that day and hour knoweth no man, no, not the angels of heaven, but my Father only."

From these more general allusions we may now pass to specify several particulars regarding angels on which Scripture throws light. The name itself of angels, both in the Greek *angeloi* and Hebrew *milakim*, marks their office in one of its chief functions as the *messengers* of God. The other name of spirits in Hebrew, Greek, and Latin—*ruagh, pneuma, spiritus*—marks not office but nature, as beings invisible and incorporeal, regarding whom we help our conception by thinking of breath, wind, inspiration, and fire. A certain class of texts relates to the number of angels. " The chariots of God are twenty thousand, even thousands of angels." " I beheld till the thrones were cast down, and the Ancient of days did sit. . . . Thousand thousands ministered unto Him, and ten thousand times ten thousand stood before Him : the judgment was set, and the books were opened." " And suddenly there was with the angel a multitude of the heavenly host praising God." " Thinkest thou that I cannot now pray to my Father, and He shall presently give me more than twelve legions of angels ? " " Ye are come unto . . . the heavenly Jerusalem, and to an innumerable company of angels."

After numbering, naturally comes marshalling of this heavenly host or army. Gregory the Great has written on the Celestial Hierarchy in their grades or orders. They have commonly been set down as nine, in three groups of three—viz. : Seraphim, Cherubim, Thrones ; Dominations, Principalities, Powers ; Virtues, Archangels, Angels. But the safest and simplest course in the matter is to follow two texts of Scripture—Eph. i. 21 ; Col. i. 16 : " Far above all principality, and power, and might, and dominion (*arche, exousia, dunamis, kuriotes*), and every name that is named, not only in this world, but also in that which is to come." " For by him were all things created that are in heaven, and that are in earth, visible and invisible, whether they be thrones, or dominions, or principalities, or powers" (*thronos, kuriotes, arche, exousia*). In each list we have four names apparently of angelic dignity ; but as three are common to each list, the total number is only five; which, however, is quite enough to indicate gradation in the hierarchy, whether the apostle spoke by revelation on the point, or only gave a certain sanction to current Jewish ideas by the adoption of them.

Other characteristics of angels that rest on Scripture passages are as follows :—

Superior intelligence: " Of that day and that hour knoweth no man, no, not the angels which are in heaven."—Mark xiii. 32.

Superior power: " When the Lord Jesus shall be revealed from heaven with His mighty angels."—2 Thess. i. 7. " Whereas angels, which are greater in power and might."—2 Peter ii. 11.

Moral perfection: " In His own glory, and in His Father's, and of the holy angels."—Luke ix. 26.

Unmarked by age: " They saw a young man sitting on the right side, clothed in a long white garment."—Mark xvi. 5.

Sexless: " In the resurrection they neither marry, nor are given in marriage, but are as the angels of God in heaven."—Matt. xxii. 30.

Special worshippers of God: " When He bringeth in the first-begotten into the world, He saith, And let all the angels of God worship Him."—Heb. i. 6. " And one cried unto another, and said, Holy, holy, holy is the Lord of hosts: the whole earth is full of His glory."—Isa. vi. 3.

A special ministry to man: "Are they not all ministering spirits, sent forth to minister for them who shall be heirs of salvation?"—Heb. i. 14. "The angel of the Lord encampeth round about them that fear Him, and delivereth them."—Ps. xxxiv. 7.

Here comes in a question whether we should rest at the last particular, of angels as a class having a special ministry to man, or add the doctrine of each man being under the care of one appointed guardian angel. Besides the text last quoted, the Scripture support of this idea is pretty much limited to the text in Matt. xviii. 10: "Take heed that ye despise not one of these little ones; for I say unto you, That in heaven their angels do always behold the face of my Father which is in heaven." The idea was held of old by the Jews, as we see in the apocryphal book of Tobit. It was also held by the Greeks in their use of the word *dæmon*, as by the Romans in their word *genius*. It has been a uniform tradition of Christians from the beginning, occurring first in a very distinct form in the 'Shepherd of Hermas' of the middle of the second century, wherein is a short chapter on the two genii in each man, and how they influence him. "There are two genii with a man, one of equity and one of iniquity. The genius of equity is gentle and truthful, mild and peaceful. When he enters your heart, he talks to you of justice, modesty, chastity, kindness, forgiveness, love, and piety. Him believe and obey. Hear now of the works of the genius of evil. First he is bitter, wrathful, and foolish, and his works are hurtful and destroy God's servants. . . . Withdraw from all these works and don't believe him, because his works are evil and unbecoming a servant of God." It is observable that the doctrine of the guardian angel is only a development and extension to each member of our race of the more general doctrine above stated, and which is undoubtedly Scriptural. Thus in point of principle there is no obstacle to our accepting the more specific and complete form of the angelic care through guardian angels as expressed so tenderly in Father Faber's hymn, " Dear Angel! ever at my side."

Now we come to S. Michael the archangel. In the Bible he and Gabriel stand by themselves as known by name.[1] Gabriel, = strength of God, was the high messenger commissioned to the prophet Daniel and to the Virgin Mary; probably also to Zacharias and S. Joseph,—all messages directly relating to the Messiah. Michael, = who is like God? seems to be the angel more national and ecclesiastic. He is thrice mentioned in Daniel, x. 13, 21, xii. 1, each time as a prince. " At that time shall Michael stand up, the great prince which standeth for the children of thy people." He appears in S. Jude, " Yet Michael the archangel, when contending with the devil, he disputed about the body of Moses, durst not bring against him a railing accusation, but said, The Lord rebuke thee." And when he appears in Rev. xii. 7 it is in a war against Satan; and the war proceeds on the lines already pointed out in three Gospel passages, two of which are in S. John, as to the Saviour's victory over the prince of this world. While part of Rev. xii. is mysterious—as to the woman clothed with the sun, and the man-child, and the fleeing into the wilderness —there is no reasonable doubt as to the meaning of the central portion touching the victory of truth over error, and of Christ over Satan. " Now is come salvation, and strength, and the kingdom of our God, and the power of His Christ : for the accuser of our brethren is cast down, which accused them before our God day and night. And they overcame him by the blood of the Lamb, and by the word of their testimony ; and they loved not their lives unto the death. Therefore rejoice, ye heavens, and ye that dwell in them."

This issue of the war in heaven, and the prominent part acted therein by Michael and his angels, have been thankfully

---

[1] Other names of angel princes are—Raphael = healing of God, named in Tobit ; Uriel = light of God, in Book of Enoch ; Phanuel or Peniel = face of God ; angel of Penitence and Hope, in Book of Enoch.

recognised in all ages of the Church in the honour accorded
to this angel-prince, who is the Church's ally and its Lord's
champion.   And in no land has this been more distinctly or
largely recognised than in Scotland, where in old times so
many of our churches bore S. Michael's name; although, in
these latter days, the meaning of the old nomenclature has
too much passed out of sight in the struggle of sects and the
hunt for funds.   Here is a list drawn from my 'Handbook
of the Church of Scotland,' showing twenty-two churches
dedicated to S. Michael and all Angels, in every one of which
the old Michaelmas festival of 29th September would be a
red-letter day.   Six are called S. Michael's—viz., Linlithgow,
Dumfries, Musselburgh, Cupar, Crieff, Tolsta in Lewis.   Eight
are called Kirkmichael—viz., in Dumfriesshire, Strathardle
in Perthshire, in Resolis, Crossmichael in Galloway, in Camp-
belton, Rothesay Castle Chapel, Glencloy in Arran, South
Sannox in Arran.   Eight more are Michael dedications, as
proven by old church writs, although not embodied in the
parish name—viz., Gordon in Berwickshire, Mauchline in
Ayrshire, Dalgarven in Ayrshire, Covington in Lanarkshire,
Sprouston in Roxburghshire, Maxwell, part of Kelso, in
Roxburghshire, Kirkdale in Galloway, Balnacross in Galloway.
Besides these twenty-two churches and chapels of S. Michael,
there were many altarages of S. Michael in other churches.
A military order of Knights of S. Michael was instituted by
Louis II. at Amboise in 1469; S. Michael being an ancient
patron saint of France.   There is a famous S. Michael's
Mount with a splendid monastery on the coast of Brittany,
and another S. Michael's Mount in Cornwall.

Thus the doctrine of the holy angels and of Michael, as one
of the angel-princes, is a real part of Christianity, intimately
associated with scores of texts of Scripture, and which we
cannot neglect without loss to ourselves individually, and loss
to the Church, as a kingdom warring against evil, and helped
in the war by all the hosts of heaven.

We need not invoke in prayer any angel however exalted:

all prayer is alone to God ; and direct to God through Christ.
But let us remember that all angels are fellow-workers in the
same Gospel cause, and fellow-worshippers of the same divine
Head of the Church and Ruler of the universe. And surely
this remembrance will tend to spiritualise and intensify our
worship—to increase our trust in God's providence and grace
—to widen our view of Christ's kingdom—and to increase our
Christian hope by looking forward not only to citizenship in
heaven, but to fellow-citizenship with angels.

All Saints.

DAY, NOVEMBER 1.

ORATIO.—*Omnipotens sempiterne Deus, qui nos omnium
sanctorum merita sub una tribuisti celebritate venerari:
quæsumus ut desideratam tuæ propitiationis abundantiam
multiplicatis intercessionibus largiaris.*
> For the Epistle.—Rev. vii. 2-12.
> The Gospel.—S. Matt. v. 1-12.

COLLECT.—*O Almighty God, who hast knit together thine
elect in one communion and fellowship, in the mystical body of
Thy Son our Lord ; Grant us grace so to follow Thy blessed
saints in all virtuous and godly living, that we may come to
those unspeakable joys which Thou hast prepared for them that
unfeignedly love Thee ; through Jesus Christ our Lord. Amen.*
> For the Epistle.—Rev. vii. 2-12.
> The Gospel.—S. Matt. v. 1-12.

Christe Redemptor omnium,	O Christ, Redeemer of mankind,
Conserva tuos famulos :	Thy servants here protect and spare.
Beatæ semper virginis	Who hearest with a loving mind
Placatus sanctis precibus.	The Blessèd Virgin's holy prayer.

Beata quoque agmina
Cœlestium spirituum :
Præterita, præsentia,
Futura mala pellite,

May those glad hosts which see Thy
    face,
The spirits of the heavenly home,
Away from us all evils chase,
  Both past and present and to come.

Vates æterni Judicis,
Apostolique Domini :
Suppliciter exposcimus
Salvari vestris precibus.

The prophets of the Judge most High,
The twelve apostles of the Lord,
For us, with interceding cry,
Pray that Thou keep us in Thy ward.

Martyres Dei inclyti,
Confessoresque lucidi
Vestris orationibus
Nos ferte in cœlestibus.

God's martyrs, who have won renown,
His confessors, in bright array,
Ask that we too may win the crown
Which shines in everlasting day.

Chorus sanctarum virginum
Monachorumque omnium :
Simul cum sanctis omnibus
Consortes Christi facite.

The choir of virgins lily-white,
Thy priests and all Thy ministry,
With every saint in prayer unite
Till we be joined, O Christ, to Thee.

Gentem auferte perfidam
Credentium de finibus :
Ut Christo laudes debitas
Persolvamus alacriter.
    —*Anglo-Saxon Hymnarium.*[1]

Then purge away all unbelief
From every land where Christians
    dwell,
That unto Thee, our Victor chief,
Our thanks and praises we may tell.
    —F. R. (*in People's Hymnal*).

O beata beatorum
  Martyrum certamina
O devote recolenda
  Victorum solennia.

Blessèd feasts of blessèd martyrs,
  Holy days of holy men,
With affection's recollections
  Greet we your return again.

Digni dignis fulgent signis
  Et florent virtutibus,
Illos semper condecenter
  Veneremur laudibus.

Worthy deeds they wrought and
    wonders,
  Worthy of the Name they bore ;
We with meetest praise and sweetest
  Honour them for evermore.

Fide, voto, corde toto
  Adhæserunt Domino,
Et invicti sunt addicti
  Atroci martyrio.

Faith prevailing, hope unfailing,
  Jesus loved with single heart—
Thus they glorious and victorious
  Bravely bore the martyr's part.

---

[1] A hymn quite parallel to this is *Jesu salvator seculi*, in the Sarum
Breviary. It is recast in the Roman Breviary as *Placare, Christe,
servulis.*

Carcerati, trucidati,
   Tormentorum genera
Igne læsi, ferro cæsi,
   Pertulerunt plurima.

Racked with   torture, haled to
   slaughter,   [sword,
   Fire, and axe, and murderous
Chains and prison, foes' derision,
   They endured for Christ the Lord.

Dum sic torti cedunt morti
   Carnis per interitum,
Ut electi, sunt adepti
   Beatorum præmium.

So they passed through pain and
   sorrow,
   Till they sank in death to rest ;
Earth's rejected, God's elected,
   Gained a portion with the blest.

Per contemptum mundanorum
   Et per bella fortia
Meruerunt angelorum
   Victores consortia.

By contempt of worldly pleasures,
   And by deeds of valour done,
They have reached the land of angels,
   And with them are knit in one.

Ergo facti cohæredes
   Christi in cœlestibus
Apud Ipsum vota nostra
   Promovete precibus.

Made co-heirs with Christ in glory,
   His celestial bliss they share :
May they now before Him bending
   Help us onward by their prayer ;

Ut post finem hujus vitæ
   Et post transitoria
In perenni mereamur
   Exultare gloria.
      —German Author of
       14th century.

That, this weary life completed,
   And its fleeting trials past,
We may win eternal glory
   In our Father's home at last.
      —J. M. NEALE.

From sea to sea, from shore to shore,
Earth travails with her dead once more.
In one long endless filing crowd,
   Apostles, martyrs, saints, have gone,
Where behind yon screen of cloud
   The Master is upon His throne !
   Only we are left alone !—
Left in this waste and desert place,
   Far from our natural home ;
Left to complete our weary race,
   Until His kingdom come.
Alas for us that cannot be
Among that shining company !
But once a-year with solemn hand
   The Church withdraws the veil,
And there we see that other land,
   Far in the distance pale :

> While good church-bells are loudly ringing,
>   All on the earth below,
> And white-robed choirs with angels singing,
>   Where stately organs blow :
> And up and down each holy street
> Faith hears the tread of viewless feet,
> Such as in Salem walked when He
> Had gotten Himself the victory.
> So be it ever year by year,
> Until the Judge Himself be here !
> —FABER'S POEMS, *All Saints' Day.*

"Theirs is the kingdom of heaven."—S. MATT. v. 3.

ALL SAINTS' DAY is specially devoted to the commemoration of the whole number who have ever lived serving God faithfully to the end, and are now at rest with Him. After the most distinguished saints have been commemorated on special days, generally the anniversary of their death, called *Natalitia* as their birthday to glory, there are still hundreds of good historic names to which it is useless or impossible to assign days of commemoration; and after these again are thousands of most genuine saints who have lived and died in obscurity, and whose very names have perished from the earth. To these two classes pre-eminently does All Saints' Day belong. An idea of the extent of the subject may be formed from the fact that Alban Butler's 'Lives of the Saints' in 12 vols., which take the year month by month and day by day, deal with nearly 1600 names, and of course no Reformer or Protestant, however good or famous, is among them. Copious as Alban Butler's list is, there is a much fuller one, actually containing above 11,000 names, almost all good and historic (but still excluding all Protestants), at the end of vol. iii. pp. 927-1116 of Migne's 'Dictionnaire des Cérémonies et des Rites Sacrés.' This list is entitled, "Catalogue Général des Saints, Saintes, Martyrs, Confesseurs, Bienheureux, Vénérables, Anchorètes, Solitaires, Reclus et Recluses, honorés par les

Y

Chrétiens sur toute la surface de la terre." There is one field
of this wide domain specially interesting to us. Alban Butler
in an Appendix of Irish Saints gives names and days for no
fewer than 169 ; and in notes added at the end of each of the
monthly subdivisions of these, he gives names and days for 78
more, making in all 247. With good reason, therefore, was
Erin once styled the Isle of Saints, although now declined to
boycotters. Many of these Irish saints are as much ours as
theirs, as those who are acquainted with Bishop Forbes's
Kalendars of Scottish Saints well know. The race of men
and the form of Church in these days were the same in Scotland
and Ireland, the old Celtic Church being a branch of the
Eastern Church associated with the south and west of France,
and with Galatia in Asia, the original seat of the Gauls or
Kelts. The substance of Bishop Forbes's Kalendars is given
in my 'Handbook of the Church of Scotland,' where is a
catalogue of 120 Scottish saints, with biographical notes and
names of churches dedicated to the chief of them.

Another division of hagiology specially worthy of our
attention on local grounds is that which belongs to England.
In Cardinal Newman's 'Apologia'—edition of 1891, pp. 323-
338—is a catalogue of no fewer than 323 names of English
saints, presented in two classifications,—Calendar-ways, according to month and day of commemoration ; and chronologically,
extending from the second to the fifteenth century. Of these
saints, from thirty to forty are as much Scottish as English,
chiefly in the fifth, sixth, seventh, and eighth centuries, and
associated with Wales, Brittany, Mona, Lindisfarne, and
Hexham.

These names, 247 for Ireland, 120 for Scotland, and 323
for England, constitute a precious inheritance for the United
Kingdom. And the names that are common to each of the
three lists, instead of forming a drawback, furnish a noble
testimony to religious and missionary intercourse, when Wales,
Northumberland, Ireland, and Scotland had one Church of

Eastern origin, with a system of its own ; as so fully developed and demonstrated by Mr Warren in his splendid book on 'Liturgy and Ritual of the Celtic Church,' printed by the Clarendon Press in 1881.

Wheatley[1] gives this account of the day : "The feast of All Saints is not of very great antiquity in the Church. About the year of our Lord 610, the pantheon, or temple dedicated to all the gods, at the desire of Boniface IV., Bishop of Rome, was taken from the heathens by Phocas the emperor, and dedicated to the honour of all martyrs. Hence came the original of All Saints, which was then celebrated upon the 1st of May : afterwards, by an order of Gregory IV., it was removed to the 1st of November, A.D. 834, where it hath stood ever since. And our reformers having laid aside the celebration of a great many martyrs' days, which had grown too numerous and cumbersome to the Church, thought fit to retain this day, whereon the Church, by a general commemoration, returns her thanks to God for them all."

But although the final settlement of All Saints' Day on 1st November was comparatively late, the principle of commemoration in the case of individual martyrs is the earliest of all Christian memorials, with the exception of the observance of the Lord's Day, as a weekly memorial of Christ's resurrection. The death of S. Stephen is clearly traceable as a yearly Christian observance from the date of its occurrence ; and the same applies locally to all the chief martyrs who suffered at Rome, Vienne, Lyons, and elsewhere.

All Saints' Day stands in specially close relation to "The Communion of Saints" in the 9th Article of the Creed. The communion of saints embodies a great spiritual fact and principle, which presents to us one line of believers under different economies of God's kingdom and different branches of the Church, as all sharing in common the substance of the same hopes and privileges. And specially those who have laboured

---

[1] On the Book of Common Prayer, v. § 28, 10.

and suffered for Christ in past ages are entitled to grateful and honourable remembrance from all later and living Christians who are now enjoying the fruits of ancient work and warfare. According to the plan of this book, we are particularly concerned with the first line of saints whose names are enshrined in the New Testament Scriptures; and it is remarkable how numerous these are when they are presented in order, omitting those who have already been taken up biographically in the preceding pages.

I. Names in the Gospels.

Zacharias and Elizabeth	Luke i. 5.
Anna the prophetess	Luke ii. 36.
The Wise Men	Matt. ii. 1.
Bride and Bridegroom at Cana	John ii. 1.
Zebedee	Matt. iv. 21.
Woman of Samaria	John iv. 7.
Nobleman and his Son	John iv. 46.
Lame man at Bethesda	John v. 2.
Widow of Nain and her Son	Luke vii. 11.
Simon the Pharisee	Luke vii. 36.
Simon's Wife and her Mother	Matt. viii. 14.
Woman with the issue	Matt. ix. 20.
Jairus and his Daughter	Matt. ix. 23.
The Seventy Disciples	Luke x. i.
Alphæus	Matt. x. 3.
Syrophenician woman and daughter	Matt. xv. 28.
Bartimæus	Matt. x. 46.
Widow with the mite	Mark xii. 42.
Woman bowed down	Luke xiii. 11.
Lepers healed	Luke xvii. 11.
Greeks at the Feast	John xii. 20.
Simon the leper	Matt. xxvi. 6.
Penitent malefactor	Luke xxiii. 40.
Simon of Cyrene	Matt. xxvii. 32.
Centurion at the cross	Matt. xxvii. 54.
The ministering Women	Matt. xxvii. 56.
Two Emmaus Disciples	Luke xxiv. 13.
Cleophas and Mary	John xix. 25.

II. Names in the Acts.

III. Names in the Epistles.

Phebe	Rom. xvi. 1.
Epenetus. Mary	„ 5, 6.
Andronicus and Junia, Amplias	„ 7, 8.
Urbane and Stachys	„ 9.
Apelles, Aristobulus's household	„ 10.
Herodion, Narcissus' household	„ 11.
Tryphena and Tryphosa, Persis	„ 12.
Rufus and his mother	„ 13.
Asyncritus, Phlegon, Hermas, Patrobas, Hermes, and brethren	„ 14.
Philologus and Julia	„ 15.
Nereas and his sister	„ 15.
Olympas and saints with them	„ 15.
Lucius, Jason, Sosipater	„ 21.
Tertius, Quartus	„ 22, 23.
Sosthenes	1 Cor. i. 1.
Chloe, Crispus, Stephanas	1 Cor. i. 11, 14, 16.
Fortunatus and Achaicus	1 Cor. xvi. 17.
Epaphroditus	Philip. ii. 25.
Saints of Cæsar's household	Philip. iv. 22.
Epaphras	Col. i. 7.
Onesimus, Aristarchus	Col. iv. 9, 10.
Jesus Justus	Col. iv. 11.
Nymphas, Archippus	Col. iv. 15, 17.
Lois, Eunice, Onesiphorus	2 Tim. i. 5, 16.
Crescens, Carpus	2 Tim. iv. 10, 13.
Eubulus, Pudens, Linus, Claudia	2 Tim. iv. 21.
Artemas, Zenas	Titus iii. 12, 13.
Philemon, Apphia, Archippus	Philem. 1, 2.
Elect lady and her children	2 John 1.
Gaius, Demetrius	3 John 1, 12.
Antipas	Rev. ii. 13.

It is very little that we know of these saints, although the names of all have a place in the Word of God which endureth for ever. In several cases we have simply the name and the testimony of an apostle or evangelist that the bearer of the name was a believer. And yet each had his own spiritual history, and acted his part in the early Christian Church, and is now inheriting the promises.

In particular, how interesting a memorial is Rom. xvi. of the warmth of early Christian friendship and of the communion of living saints rejoicing in each other's welfare and in the progress of the Gospel, and sending greetings across the sea from Corinth to Rome. To the formal reader the whole chapter seems dry, as containing so many names of persons very little known. To the half-educated reader the long list of classic names is a severe trial in pronunciation. Even university-trained men, but whose place was in the tail-end of their classes, take a breath at certain syllables and try to evade pronouncing them definitely long or definitely short. The chapter has two distinct lists,—one of persons residing in Rome to whom salutations were sent; the other of Paul's companions and helpers at Corinth, who through him send salutations to the Roman Christians. This latter list contains eight names in all, and is comprised in three verses, 21-23, shut in between two amens— each of which at first had formed the end of the epistle : in fact the whole chapter is only a postscript following the benediction and amen which end chapter xv. The former list begins with an introduction or commendation of the deaconess who is the bearer of the letter, and then follow twenty-five persons named for salutation. Among the twenty-five salutations, three are of groups of Christians and two are of households— so that the salutations really number from thirty-five to forty, or even more. Regarding six of the names we have scraps of knowledge elsewhere—viz., Phebe, Aquila and Priscilla, Rufus, and the mother of Rufus and Hermas. Thus an epistle the greatest and most deliberate of all in Christian doctrine, is in its postscript the fullest of all the epistles in Christian courtesy and messages of love revealing the brotherhood of disciples and communion of saints.

CONCLUDING REFLECTIONS.

TAKING up New Testament biography and reading
impartially (besides Scripture itself) the literature of
various Churches on, *e.g.*, S. Matthew, the Blessed Virgin,
S. Peter, S. Stephen, or S. Michael, one soon becomes aware
of a marvellous difference of treatment arising out of difference of Church system. In one group of Churches the chief
biographies are provided with a definite place once a-year,
and put before Christian people for their edification, accompanied by suitable prayers and hymns. In another group
of Churches the same lives of God's saints, however high
in honour, are left to chance. A few of them may receive
a passing allusion in the course of a year, while it is quite
possible that not one of them may be made matter of distinct
meditation. A further chance tells against anything suitable
in prayer; and a far greater chance is against a suitable
hymn; for in some cases all the material used in divine
praise was written from five to ten centuries before the birth
of any apostle or evangelist; and in these circumstances the
flavour of personality must be infinitesimally small.

The difference of treatment thus traceable extends not
only to the saints of the New Testament, but to the life of
our Lord Himself, to the doctrines of the Christian faith, the
duties of the Christian life, and the reading of Holy Scripture.
The same group of Churches that deals methodically and
respectfully with the saints, observes a like order in regard

of the chief events in the life of Christ, as also with the chief doctrines and duties of the Gospel, and with the reading of God's Word ; whereas the other group of Churches leaves the whole of these most momentous matters to chance or private convenience.

This extraordinary diversity dates from the Reformation, and is associated therewith as one of its concomitants ; and yet not necessarily so, as the happy exceptional cases of the Church of England and the Lutheran Church show. The Reformation controversy might have been argued and gained by Protestants without involving any one of the four above-named matters; because the real points at issue were certain unscriptural doctrines and practices, corrupt lives of many clergy, and Papal supremacy. But having got set so far against Rome, they seem to have proceeded a great deal further, as if on the idea that differing from Rome was a good thing in itself; and the more the difference the purer the Church. This terrible mistake and ecclesiastical disease of contrariety to Rome is a curse that has sprung from the Reformation, and is tending to the self-destruction of large bodies of religionists, especially Scottish Dissent and English Nonconformity. Wherever churchly principle is low—*i.e.*, where there is ignorance of and contempt for the work and methods of Christian men all along the centuries—the real tendency of such diseased Protestantism is toward Socinianism and Secularism. On one side they thrash empty straw on the subject of evidences of Christianity, instead of directly dealing with the Gospel itself: they raise criticism as to the canon and inspiration of Scripture, instead of expounding it : they resist learning and taste and ancient usage, on the plea of an evangelism which glorifies tea - meetings, and foreigners, and peripatetics, and the rubbish of tract "literature," and drivelling religious magazines which make heroes from quacks. On another side such Churches largely cease to be places for the worship of God, and become religious shops struggling to raise yearly funds for self-support, and aiming at the destruction of all neighbours however good in the same field, partly by organised calumny, and mainly by political deceit and force, and alliance with revolutionary incendiaries. No small part of this destructive, degrading, and unchristian work is done through the agency of so-called religious journals and magazines, which sometimes daringly call themselves undenominational, but whose true character cannot be concealed. For persistent narrowness and unfairness conveyed in unctuous canting language, there is no printed matter of modern times to match a "denominational organ" or "church newspaper."

If the Reformed Church is to hold its ground, it must improve itself in several directions. For one thing, by uniting its ranks—*i.e.*, endeavouring to reduce the number of "religious bodies," which are the laughing-stock of all respectable Churches, as they are also of the children of Belial. For a second, by ceasing to speak and think of Roman Catholics as outside of Christianity, or judging them by the trash circulated by fanatic controversialists filled with abuse of what is really the largest and oldest branch of the Church, and than which no Church is more wisely and efficiently governed. For a third, by intelligently and reverently going back to the reconsideration and restoration of several features of the old Church system, which ought never to have been touched in their essence by any Reformation.

Under this last category come the four matters already referred to above, and which may be here articulately repeated, with a brief note on each to explain its bearing.

1. **Lectionary.**—The systematic and evenly reading of Holy Scripture is not only one of the most ancient of ecclesiastical usages, but a method which is of great practical utility. Justin Martyr, 140 A.D., speaks of "the memoirs of the apostles being read as long as the time permits." The Apostolic Constitutions, previous to 325 A.D., mention four lessons; two from the Old Testament and two from the New. S. Chrysostom, c. 400 A.D., says, "Tell me what prophet was read to-day,

what apostle." Cassian, in 424 A.D., tells that in Egypt the practice was, after the chanting of the psalms one lesson from the Old Testament and another from the New, except on Saturdays, Sundays, and the fifty days of Pentecost, when both lessons were from the New Testament, one from the Acts or epistles, and the other from the gospels. A fixed Lectionary was in use in the fourth century. The Book of Genesis was read in Lent, according to Chrysostom. According to S. Augustin, 398 A.D., some lessons were so connected with certain seasons that no others might be used instead—*e.g.*, between Easter and Pentecost came the Acts. S. Ambrose, 374 A.D., specifies Job and Jonah as read in Holy Week. The Gallican and Roman Lectionaries still extant date from the sixth or seventh century.

An orderly reading of Scripture is the only fair method of dealing with the Word of God so as to prevent a narrow-minded minister from giving pet books or pet chapters a monopoly, to the injury of others possibly more practical. It is also a guide to a wider range of exposition and preaching, so that the whole counsel of God is set before a congregation.

2. **The Christian Year,** or Calendar.—This is a further application of the same principle. While the Lectionary provides for the even distribution of inspired Scripture, the Church Calendar provides for a careful distribution of edifying subjects over the days, and especially the Sundays, of the year, and furnishes an additional protection to a congregation against the prejudices and partialities and vagaries of an individual minister, often very poorly equipped, and always more or less raw in his early years.

The ecclesiastical or sacred year has two great parts—the first from Advent to Trinity, and the second from Trinity to Advent. From Advent to Trinity are commemorated the leading events in our Lord's life,—Incarnation; Circumcision; Epiphany or manifestation to the Gentiles; Fasting and Temptations; Crucifixion; Resurrection; Ascension; Gift of Pentecost,—so that this part ends most fitly with the con-

summation of Christian doctrine in the commemoration of the
Blessed Trinity. This following of Christ from Sunday to
Sunday is entirely Scriptural, and surely it is infinitely prefer-
able to the haphazard of any individual minister's texts and
sermons, wherein all the above and all else within the boards
of the Bible may turn up at any time as by a cast of the dice
or a dip in a lucky-bag.

As the first half of the sacred year is devoted to setting
forth the great doctrines of the Christian religion, as these
turn on the birth, life, death, and ascension of Christ; so the
second half of the year is given to a deliberate arrangement of
practical duties to be taken up in selected Scriptures Sunday
by Sunday in a long series of twenty-five, sometimes even
twenty-seven, after Trinity. The old Sarum Missal (mainly
used in Scotland before the Reformation) has services for
twenty-four Sundays after Trinity, and one for the Sunday
next before Advent. In the case of more or less than twenty-
five Sundays being between Trinity and Advent, according to
the earliness or lateness of the movable Feast of Easter, an
extra service or services was to be drawn from a Sunday
omitted after Epiphany, or a service dropped from the after
Trinity series.

The subjects appointed for these Sundays after Trinity are
as follows: 1. Grace and obedience. 2. Fear and love.
3. The desire to pray. 4. Things temporal and things eternal.
5. Peace without and within. 6. God's love to man; and
man's love to God. 7. The Author and Giver of all good
things. 8. Divine Providence. 9. Grace prevenient and
co-operative. 10. Successful prayer. 11. God's power shown
in mercy. 12. God the Giver and Forgiver. 13. True
service. 14. Faith, hope, and charity. 15. God's keeping.
16. Within and without. 17. Good works. 18. The good fight.
19. Without God, no pleasing God. 20. Cheerful obedience.
21. Pardon and peace. 22. Continual godliness. 23. Faithful
asking; effectual obtaining. 24. The bondage of sin. 25.
Plenteous fruit; plenteous reward. These titles specially

denote the purport of each collect ; but the collect is generally founded on the epistle and gospel. And, as regards preaching, either the whole of each passage may form a text, or any sentence in the passage, or any kindred passage of Scripture ; so that there is no irksome restraint, but great help in preventing hesitation. And this selection of twenty-five subjects is eminently evangelical in the best sense of the term, and practical as well, with great variety.

Here, again, it is surely vastly better to have such a 'Directory of Public Worship' as regards the distribution and order of topics of prayer and preaching, rather than to leave everything to the individual clergyman, who might devote twenty consecutive Sundays to consecutive verses of Psa. cxix., or consecutive verses of S. Mark i. or Rom. i.

The feature characteristic of these two series of Sundays from Advent to Trinity, and from Trinity to Advent, is that in addition to daily Common Prayer and the Daily Portion of the Lectionary and Psalter, there is a special collect, epistle, and gospel for the day, as also for each of the appointed saints' days. It is a prejudice arising from ignorance that this arrangement is the invention and private property of the Churches of England or Rome. How little of invention in the matter pertains to the Church of England is at once apparent on turning to the Sarum Breviary, drawn up by S. Osmund of Salisbury, and used in England since 1085 ; and in Scotland since 1233, when introduced into Glasgow by Bishop Bondington. Nor has the Church of Rome itself any more patent-right than the Church of England in the arrangement of the sacred year in collects, epistles, and gospels for fast and feast days, because the arrangement existed both in England and Scotland in the Anglo-Saxon Church and in the Celtic Church previous to the acknowledgment of Papal supremacy ; and existed over Christendom at large at a date when Rome counted only as one of five patriarchates which were co-ordinate. The proof of all this lies in the ancient collection of epistles and gospels known as the " Comes " of S. Jerome + 420, and mentioned in a charter of 471 A.D. This " Comes," = Presbyter's Companion or Vade-mecum, has epistles and gospels for all the Sundays of the year, and for most of the festivals and other holidays.[1] Any branch of the Church may lawfully revise the Lectionary or the sacred year in matters of detail—and this has again and again been advantageously done alike by the Roman and English Church ; but to cut off both at one fell stroke is nothing short of ecclesiastical barbarism. The case is so clear on grounds of history and utility, that the ministers and members of a Presbyterian Church like that of Scotland act most unwisely by continuing in bondage to a demonstrable error and excess committed by their forefathers in the heat of the Reformation. Enough if we retain the substance of their good work, and, as soon as we can, restore that wherein their zeal carried them too far in change. The practicableness of this course needs no argument, for it has already in the main been carried out for years past by some of our more cultured clergy. But while our excessive freedom can be turned to this good account by some, by others it is turned toward wilfulness, vulgarity, and monotony.

3. A **Book of Common Prayer**, or Liturgy. —— Here the Church of Scotland stands on good ground of her own ; for Knox and his friends provided a Liturgy in 1560, and it continued in use down to 1647, when, without ever being voted against as objectionable, it was pushed aside and cozened out of use by the inferior things which we were foolish enough to adopt under Puritan influence at Westminster. It was a very naked Liturgy, much too original, being mainly Swiss-Scottish, with little or no recognition of the Christian year; but half a loaf is better than no bread. Happily we are not far off from the restoration of a Book of Common Prayer, and with it a Lectionary ; and soon thereafter, at least an outline of the Christian year suitable to our simpler forms of service. The desire of the restoration of these most ancient tokens of Christian

---

[1] For a detailed account of the Christian year see Evan Daniel, ' The Prayer Book : its History, Language, and Contents.'

wisdom is a sign of survival as contrasted with the descent of Dissent into Socinianism and Socialist politics (*facilis descensus Averno*), unless they retrace their steps so as to return to the historic methods of Christianity.

4. **Divine Praise.**—This part of the Church service received a violent twist at the Reformation from needless abandonment of chanting the prose Psalms, and taking refuge for contrariety in fearful rhyming doggerel. Chant music, that had stood the test of above ten centuries of Christians, might surely have been exempted from the sweep of reform. What harm had the Gregorian tones ever done that they should have suffered Protestant excommunication? Or what harm had the prose Psalms ever done to be cut or moulded into eights and sixes like candles, by Sternhold and Hopkins, Tate and Brady, Whittingham, Craig, Kethe, or Rous? A better course was adopted in Germany, where a few freer adaptations of psalms appeared as hymns, and other hymns distinctively Christian were composed, many of them based on Latin originals, freely rendered like the Psalm versions. The French Psalms of Clement Marot had a rugged strength, like those of Sternhold and Hopkins. But by far the best of the three was the German ; and the superiority arose from their better music, and greater originality in the Reformation movement as a whole.

In the matter of anthems, Presbyterians through an inveterate prejudice have never succeeded, and hardly wish to succeed. Unfortunately their predilection was for gloom— they revelled in fast-days and fault-finding ; but the dilation and spiritual joy and rapturous beauty of an anthem jarred upon them like the Sunday song of a thrush, which was supposed to be a case of " Sabbath-breaking," secretly prompted by the Prince of the power of the air, and not to be listened to by the elect.

However, upon the whole, in these latter days, after a struggle of twenty-five years, we are more Christian-like in hymns and music than in almost anything else ecclesiastical : for one thing, general timidity has ceased regarding either hymn or tune being composed by a Catholic, who for three centuries has been the *bête noire* of Scotsmen, although on most other points we are sane and shrewd. The Secession and Celtic talk about "human hymns" is now rarely heard; and "instrumental music" is a formidable watchword no longer in Zion benorth the Tweed.

5. **Church Orderliness.**—Several distinct matters may be grouped under this title, which is here used for convenience and not as a technical term.

It is unnecessary further to allude to clerical orders, already criticised under Stephen and Timothy, where it is shown that there are only two original orders of presbyter and deacon; that presbyter and episcopos denote the same office under different aspects; and that there is no harm but great benefit in recognising the fact of the later growth and development of a special governing section of presbyters whose origin is in utility and not in distinct apostolic appointment. A Church which has few or no positions of superior honour and emolument can never hold up its head socially, nor can it conduct its business efficiently through a swarm of manikins, each struggling for a bare subsistence and cultivating almost exclusively the demagogue arts of the popular preacher. Solid scholarship, legal knowledge, administrative talent, and a proportion of men of good birth, and with their birth some hereditary private means, are each of them required before the Church as a profession can be properly equipped. When studying the history of the Celtic Church some years ago, I was much impressed by observing how many of the old saints were men of good family, in not a few cases closely related to the Reguli or district kings.

A clamant need of the whole group of Protestant Churches, if they are to hold their ground in the future, is to lay less stress on the study of the history of particular Churches since the Reformation, and give vastly more attention to the whole course of the Church, especially from its commencement to the separation of East and West in 1053 A.D. It is mere self-delusion to pretend to go back at one bound from the Reformation to the time of the apostles. The Church has been a growth and development all on from the first; and to attempt to ignore fifteen centuries of the most fresh and instructive period of the history of the Church, is an insane piece of ecclesiastical Radicalism. Yet it is on this monstrous proceeding that modern sects are constructed and maintained. They see no harm in starting a new shop or company as often as a little group of them fall out over some paltry detail. But meanwhile, the old Church with its undoubted orders and its well-tried methods of ecclesiastical and pastoral government, and finance, and devotion, and missions, is rapidly gaining ground on the whole mob of sects and "bodies" and Churches. These latter, by their mutual intolerance, by departing from their own original standards, and by misdirected study in tearing the Holy Scriptures to tatters by their sham criticism, are really though unintentionally playing into the hands of the old Roman Church. In my native city of Glasgow, the strongest religious denomination numerically, as also by far the best organised and governed, is the Roman Catholic. The town of Greenock, which I know from six years' clerical residence and work, is very nearly in the same position. The same venerable Church is also a mighty force in Edinburgh and Dundee. This great success of Rome is only the well-earned reward of several generations of brave steady work, in spite of Presbyterian prejudice and worse, as is clearly shown in Dr Gordon's 'Catholic Church in Scotland, from the suppression of the Hierarchy to the present time.'

Episcopal Protestantism is alienating itself from Presbyterian Protestantism by theories of Orders, which are a huge laughing-stock to Catholic onlookers. As typical instances of how Catholics regard Anglican orders, reference may be made to Cardinal Wiseman's Essay of 1837 on "The High Church Theory of Dogmatic Authority," wherein from his own point of view he utterly demolishes the position of Mr Keble on the subject. The same is done even more severely by Cardinal Newman in 1865, in his 'Apologia' (pp. 339-342 of ed. of 1891), in a note on the Anglican Church, after he had left it. Knowing themselves so hardly hit by the oldest and largest branch of the Church, how reckless is it to try to assail *bona fide* Presbyterian orders that were once recognised by the Reformed Church of England, and that are still recognised by part of it! This folly and impertinence of Protestants un-churching one another is peculiarly impolitic at a time when Protestants holding Church principles in any fair degree have need to unite in self-defence against Dissent on the one hand moving towards infidelity, and against Catholicism, which is steadily increasing in strength and boldness.

The curious position of Scottish Dissent is apparent from two facts—viz., their recent summons of Yankee revivalists to help in the work which they should have been able to do them-selves, for their ministers are already too numerous in pro-portion to their people ; and their Gladstone idolatry, in hope of, through his cunning and unscrupulousness, getting rid of the Church of their covenanted forefathers, as a sweet morsel of revenge for their own Secession blunder of 1843. Thus are Presbyterians in internecine war, while Catholics are going steadily on with their quiet policy of zeal and unity in priestly duty. It is to Catholicism, with all the faults that attach to it, that we are mainly indebted for the transmission to this age of the chief doctrines and duties of the Gospel, and for the wisest system of regulations to give unity and efficiency to the Christian Church. But if Dissent and Nonconformity are to prevail over national Protestant Churches (which I consider very unlikely, as well as extremely undesirable)—if Dissent is to continue in its present course towards Unitarianism and de-structive politics, then the future of Scotland, and of England as well, is vastly safer, from a real Christian point of view, with Catholicism than with a disintegrated, degraded, and un-historic Christianity. This expression of opinion is purely personal to myself, as an independent presbyter of the national Church of Scotland. It commits no one else ; and my candid anticipation is that but few of my brethren will either agree with my view or thank me for expressing it. Yet I hold it, and will hold it in my heart of hearts, however solitary I remain.

A third matter that may come under the heading of Church Orderliness is Church architecture and fittings. Until of late years there were very few churches in Scotland to which one could point as correct in style : nine-tenths almost were square or oblong packing-boxes provided with a roof. It helped the packing-box idea that the thing was hardly reckoned complete without a horse-shoe gallery as a cheap method of accommodation. Invariably the pulpit was stuck in the middle of a wall, and was the one commanding feature of the interior ; a small-type edition of the pulpit being provided on an intermediate level for the precentor. Born and bred in these atrocities up to the age of twenty, it was a revelation, in a long series of Continental holidays of fifty or sixty days apiece, to visit on foot all the best churches in Rhineland, by the Moselle, the Neckar, and Elbe ; by the Loire, the Rhone, the Seine, and round the coast of Brittany. There and thus one can study the true and comparative anatomy of an ecclesiastical building, and see each of its parts in living and devout use. Beyond all doubt the place of honour in a church belongs to the Communion table, which ought to stand central in some sort of chancel, and to stand permanently in its place, and be put to no purpose save one, and be as well made as convenient, and not a deal board like a kitchen-table. The pulpit, according to Christian usage, should stand on one side, commanding diagonally the main body of the building. The choir should be accommodated in the chancel sideways, and similarly the organ. The placing of an organ behind a pulpit, or in the central line of a church, is profanely suggestive of a concert-room. A reading-desk may stand across the church opposite to the pulpit ; and the font should be placed rather towards the entrance door of the church or in a side aisle, than in the chancel or beside the pulpit. If a gallery is unavoidable, let it be single, and at the end remote from the chancel, and not too deep. In that way it will least disfigure or choke the building. So much the better if the building can have its central line from west to east. One of the most savage of modern fashions, especially in meeting-houses, is the substitution of a platform for a pulpit. There is surely a feeling of comfort, peace, and retreat from the world in thus having our places of worship distinctive and significant in shape, arrangement, and furniture. Moreover, a wise and reverent conservatism maintains the type that has descended as a Christian heritage from early ages, a type which genius and piety have laboured for many successive centuries to make convenient and seemly.

These reflections may be closed by presenting, in the order of the Christian year, first a list of the chief saints of the New Testament as commemorated in the Calendar; and second, a short list of later saints, chiefly British, also in the order of the Calendar.

I. The Chief Saints of the New Testament.

S. Andrew, Apostle	Nov. 30.
S. Thomas, Apostle	Dec. 21.
S. Stephen, Protomartyr	" 26.
S. John, Apostle and Evangelist	" 27.
Holy Innocents	" 28.
S. Paul, Conversion	Jan. 25.
Blessed Virgin Mary, Purification	Feb. 2.
S. Matthias, Apostle	" 24.
S. Joseph, husband of Blessed Virgin Mary	March 19.
Blessed Virgin Mary, Annunciation	" 25.
S. Mark, Evangelist	April 25.
S. Philip and S. James, Apostles	May 1.
S. Barnabas, Apostle	June 11.
S. John Baptist, Nativity	" 24.
S. Peter and S. Paul, Apostles	" 29.
S. Paul, the Apostle	" 30.
S. James, Apostle and Martyr	July 25.
S. Bartholomew, Apostle	Aug. 24.
S. John Baptist, beheaded	" 29.

S. Matthew, Apostle and Evangelist .	Sept. 21.
S. Michael and All Angels . .	„ 29.
S. Luke, Evangelist . . .	Oct. 18.
S. Simon and S. Jude, Apostles .	„ 28.
All Saints	Nov. 1.

II. SOME LATER SAINTS, CHIEFLY BRITISH.

S. Kentigern or Mungo . .	A.D. 603	Jan. 13.
S. Bridget or Bride . .	„ 523	Feb. 1.
S. David of Wales . .	„ 544	March 1.
S. Chad or Cedda . .	„ 673	„ 2.
S. Gregory, Pope . . .	„ 604	„ 12.
S. Patrick . . .	„ 493	„ 17.
S. Cuthbert . . .	„ 687	„ 20.
S. Celestine, Pope . .	„ 432	April 7.
S. George of Cappadocia . .	„ 290	„ 23.
S. Augustin of Canterbury .	„ 610	May 26.
Venerable Bede . . .	„ 742	„ 27.
S. Columba . . .	„ 597	June 9.
S. Margaret, Queen . .	„ 1093	„ 10.
S. Alban	„ 303	„ 17.
S. Lawrence, Deacon . .	„ 258	Aug. 10.
S. Mælrubius of Applecross .	„ 722	„ 27.
S. Ninian	„ 432	Sept. 16.
S. Jerome or Hieronymus .	„ 422	„ 30.
S. Martin of Tours . .	„ 397	Nov. 11.

Catalogue

of

Messrs Blackwood & Sons' Publications

PHILOSOPHICAL CLASSICS FOR ENGLISH READERS.

EDITED BY WILLIAM KNIGHT, LL.D.,

Professor of Moral Philosophy in the University of St Andrews.

In crown 8vo Volumes, with Portraits, price 3s. 6d.

Contents of the Series.

DESCARTES, by Professor Mahaffy, Dublin.—BUTLER, by Rev. W. Lucas Collins, M.A.—BERKELEY, by Professor Campbell Fraser.—FICHTE, by Professor Adamson, Owens College, Manchester. — KANT, by Professor Wallace, Oxford.—HAMILTON, by Professor Veitch, Glasgow. — HEGEL, by Professor Edward Caird, Glasgow.—LEIB-NIZ, by J. Theodore Merz.—VICO, by Professor Flint, Edinburgh.—HOBBES, by Professor Croom Robertson.—HUME, by the Editor.—SPINOZA, by the Very Rev. Principal Caird, Glasgow. — BACON: Part I. The Life, by Professor Nichol.—BACON: Part II. Philosophy, by the same Author. LOCKE, by Professor Campbell Fraser.

FOREIGN CLASSICS FOR ENGLISH READERS.

EDITED BY MRS OLIPHANT.

In crown 8vo, 2s. 6d.

Contents of the Series.

DANTE, by the Editor. — VOLTAIRE, by General Sir E. B. Hamley, K.C.B. —PASCAL, by Principal Tulloch. — PETRARCH, by Henry Reeve, C.B.—GOETHE, by A. Hayward, Q.C.—MOLIÈRE, by the Editor and F. Tarver, M.A.—MONTAIGNE, by Rev. W. L. Collins, M.A.—RABELAIS, by Walter Besant, M.A. — CALDERON, by E. J. Hasell. — SAINT SIMON, by Clifton W. Collins, M.A. — CERVANTES, by the Editor. — CORNEILLE AND RACINE, by Henry M. Trollope. — MADAME DE SÉVIGNÉ, by Miss Thackeray.—LA FONTAINE, AND OTHER FRENCH FABULISTS, by Rev. W. Lucas Collins, M.A.—SCHILLER, by James Sime, M.A., Author of 'Lessing, his Life and Writings.'—TASSO, by E. J. Hasell. — ROUSSEAU, by Henry Grey Graham. — ALFRED DE MUSSET, by C. F. Oliphant.

ANCIENT CLASSICS FOR ENGLISH READERS.

EDITED BY THE REV. W. LUCAS COLLINS, M.A.

Complete in 28 Vols. crown 8vo, cloth, price 2s. 6d. each. And may also be had in 14 Volumes, strongly and neatly bound, with calf or vellum back, £3, 10s.

Contents of the Series.

HOMER: THE ILIAD, by the Editor.—HOMER: THE ODYSSEY, by the Editor.—HERODOTUS, by George C. Swayne, M.A.—XENOPHON, by Sir Alexander Grant, Bart., LL.D. — EURIPIDES, by W. B. Donne.—ARISTOPHANES, by the Editor.—PLATO, by Clifton W. Collins, M.A.—LUCIAN, by the Editor.—ÆSCHYLUS, by the Right Rev. the Bishop of Colombo. — SOPHOCLES, by Clifton W. Collins, M.A.—HESIOD AND THEOGNIS, by the Rev. J. Davies, M.A.—GREEK ANTHOLOGY, by Lord Neaves.—VIRGIL, by the Editor.—HORACE, by Sir Theodore Martin, K.C.B.—JUVENAL, by Edward Walford, M.A.—PLAUTUS AND TERENCE, by the Editor—THE COMMENTARIES OF CÆSAR, by Anthony Trollope.—TACITUS, by W. B. Donne.—CICERO, by the Editor. — PLINY'S LETTERS, by the Rev. Alfred Church, M.A., and the Rev. W. J. Brodribb, M.A. — LIVY, by the Editor.—OVID, by the Rev. A. Church, M.A. — CATULLUS, TIBULLUS, AND PROPERTIUS, by the Rev. Jas. Davies, M.A. — DEMOSTHENES, by the Rev. W. J. Brodribb, M.A.—ARISTOTLE, by Sir Alexander Grant, Bart., LL.D.—THUCYDIDES, by the Editor. — LUCRETIUS, by W. H. Mallock, M.A.—PINDAR, by the Rev. F. D. Morice, M.A.

Saturday Review.—"It is difficult to estimate too highly the value of such a series as this in giving 'English readers' an insight, exact as far as it goes, into those olden times which are so remote, and yet to many of us so close."

CATALOGUE

OF

MESSRS BLACKWOOD & SONS'

PUBLICATIONS.

ALISON.

History of Europe. By Sir ARCHIBALD ALISON, Bart., D.C.L.

1. From the Commencement of the French Revolution to the Battle of Waterloo.
    LIBRARY EDITION, 14 vols., with Portraits. Demy 8vo, £10, 10s.
    ANOTHER EDITION, in 20 vols. crown 8vo, £6.
    PEOPLE'S EDITION, 13 vols. crown 8vo, £2, 11s.

2. Continuation to the Accession of Louis Napoleon.
    LIBRARY EDITION, 8 vols. 8vo, £6, 7s. 6d.
    PEOPLE'S EDITION, 8 vols. crown 8vo, 34s.

Epitome of Alison's History of Europe. Thirtieth Thousand, 7s. 6d.

Atlas to Alison's History of Europe. By A. Keith Johnston.
    LIBRARY EDITION, demy 4to, £3, 3s.
    PEOPLE'S EDITION, 31s. 6d.

Life of John Duke of Marlborough. With some Account of his Contemporaries, and of the War of the Succession. Third Edition. 2 vols. 8vo. Portraits and Maps, 30s.

Essays: Historical, Political, and Miscellaneous. 3 vols. demy 8vo, 45s.

ACROSS FRANCE IN A CARAVAN: BEING SOME ACCOUNT OF A JOURNEY FROM BORDEAUX TO GENOA IN THE "ESCARGOT," taken in the Winter 1889-90. By the Author of 'A Day of my Life at Eton.' With fifty Illustrations by John Wallace, after Sketches by the Author, and a Map. Demy 8vo, 15s.

ACTA SANCTORUM HIBERNIÆ; Ex Codice Salmanticensi. Nunc primum integre edita opera CAROLI DE SMEDT et JOSEPHI DE BACKER, e Soc. Jesu, Hagiographorum Bollandianorum; Auctore et Sumptus Largiente JOANNE PATRICIO MARCHIONE BOTHAE. In One handsome 4to Volume, bound in half roxburghe, £2, 2s.; in paper cover, 31s. 6d.

AGRICULTURAL HOLDINGS ACT, 1883. With Notes by a MEMBER OF THE HIGHLAND AND AGRICULTURAL SOCIETY. 8vo, 3s. 6d.

AIKMAN.

Manures and the Principles of Manuring. By C. M. AIKMAN, B.Sc., F.R.S.E., &c. Lecturer on Agricultural Chemistry, West of Scotland Technical College; Examiner in Chemistry, University of Glasgow. Crown 8vo.
[*Shortly.*

AIKMAN.
 Farmyard Manure : Its Nature, Composition, and Treatment. Crown 8vo, 1s. 6d.

AIRD. Poetical Works of Thomas Aird. Fifth Edition, with Memoir of the Author by the Rev. JARDINE WALLACE, and Portrait. Crown 8vo, 7s. 6d.

ALLARDYCE.
 The City of Sunshine. By ALEXANDER ALLARDYCE. Three vols. post 8vo, £1, 5s. 6d.

 Memoir of the Honourable George Keith Elphinstone, K.B., Viscount Keith of Stonehaven, Marischal, Admiral of the Red. 8vo, with Portrait, Illustrations, and Maps, 21s.

ALMOND. Sermons by a Lay Head-master. By HELY HUTCHINSON ALMOND, M.A. Oxon., Head-master of Loretto School. Crown 8vo, 5s.

ANCIENT CLASSICS FOR ENGLISH READERS. Edited by Rev. W. LUCAS COLLINS, M.A. Price 2s. 6d. each. *For List of Vols., see p. 2.*

ANNALS OF A FISHING VILLAGE. By "A SON OF THE MARSHES." *See page* 28.

AYTOUN.
 Lays of the Scottish Cavaliers, and other Poems. By W. EDMONDSTOUNE AYTOUN, D.C.L., Professor of Rhetoric and Belles-Lettres in the University of Edinburgh. New Edition. Fcap. 8vo, 3s. 6d.
  ANOTHER EDITION. Fcap. 8vo, 7s. 6d.
  CHEAP EDITION. 1s. Cloth, 1s. 3d.

 An Illustrated Edition of the Lays of the Scottish Cavaliers. From designs by Sir NOEL PATON. Small 4to, in gilt cloth, 21s.

 Bothwell : a Poem. Third Edition. Fcap., 7s. 6d.

 Poems and Ballads of Goethe. Translated by Professor AYTOUN and Sir THEODORE MARTIN, K.C.B. Third Edition. Fcap., 6s.

 Bon Gaultier's Book of Ballads. By the SAME. Fifteenth Edition. With Illustrations by Doyle, Leech, and Crowquill. Fcap. 8vo, 5s.

 The Ballads of Scotland. Edited by Professor AYTOUN. Fourth Edition. 2 vols. fcap. 8vo, 12s.

 Memoir of William E. Aytoun, D.C.L. By Sir THEODORE MARTIN, K.C.B. With Portrait. Post 8vo, 12s.

BACH.
 On Musical Education and Vocal Culture. By ALBERT B. BACH. Fourth Edition. 8vo, 7s. 6d.

 The Principles of Singing. A Practical Guide for Vocalists and Teachers. With Course of Vocal Exercises. Crown 8vo, 6s.

 The Art of Singing. With Musical Exercises for Young People. Crown 8vo, 3s.

 The Art Ballad : Loewe and Schubert. With Music Illustrations. With a Portrait of LOEWE. Third Edition. Small 4to, 5s.

BAIRD LECTURES.
 Theism. By Rev. Professor FLINT, D.D., Edinburgh. Eighth Edition. Crown 8vo, 7s. 6d.

 Anti-Theistic Theories. By Rev. Professor FLINT, D.D., Edinburgh. Fourth Edition. Crown 8vo, 10s. 6d.

BAIRD LECTURES.

The Early Religion of Israel. As set forth by Biblical Writers and modern Critical Historians. By Rev. Professor ROBERTSON, D.D., Glasgow. Third Edition. Crown 8vo, 10s. 6d.

The Inspiration of the Holy Scriptures. By Rev. ROBERT JAMIESON, D.D. Crown 8vo, 7s. 6d.

The Mysteries of Christianity. By Rev. Professor CRAWFORD, D.D. Crown 8vo, 7s. 6d.

Endowed Territorial Work : Its Supreme Importance to the Church and Country. By Rev. WILLIAM SMITH, D.D. Crown 8vo, 6s.

BALLADS AND POEMS. By MEMBERS OF THE GLASGOW BALLAD CLUB. Crown 8vo, 7s. 6d.

BANNATYNE. Handbook of Republican Institutions in the United States of America. Based upon Federal and State Laws, and other reliable sources of information. By DUGALD J. BANNATYNE, Scotch Solicitor, New York ; Member of the Faculty of Procurators, Glasgow. Crown 8vo, 7s. 6d.

BELLAIRS.

The Transvaal War, 1880-81. Edited by Lady BELLAIRS. With a Frontispiece and Map. 8vo, 15s.

Gossips with Girls and Maidens, Betrothed and Free. New Edition. Crown 8vo, 3s. 6d. Cloth, extra gilt edges, 5s.

BELLESHEIM. History of the Catholic Church of Scotland. From the Introduction of Christianity to the Present Day. By ALPHONS BELLESHEIM, D.D., Canon of Aix-la-Chapelle. Translated, with Notes and Additions, by D. OSWALD HUNTER BLAIR, O.S.B., Monk of Fort Augustus. Complete in 4 vols. demy 8vo, with Maps. Price 12s. 6d. each.

BENTINCK. Racing Life of Lord George Cavendish Bentinck, M.P., and other Reminiscences. By JOHN KENT, Private Trainer to the Goodwood Stable. Edited by the Hon. FRANCIS LAWLEY. With Twenty-three full-page Plates, and Facsimile Letter. Second Edition. Demy 8vo, 25s.

BESANT.

The Revolt of Man. By WALTER BESANT. Tenth Edition. Crown 8vo, 3s. 6d.

Readings in Rabelais. Crown 8vo, 7s. 6d.

BEVERIDGE.

Culross and Tulliallan ; or Perthshire on Forth. Its History and Antiquities. With Elucidations of Scottish Life and Character from the Burgh and Kirk-Session Records of that District. By DAVID BEVERIDGE. 2 vols. 8vo, with Illustrations, 42s.

Between the Ochils and the Forth ; or, From Stirling Bridge to Aberdour. Crown 8vo, 6s.

BIRCH.

Examples of Stables, Hunting-Boxes, Kennels, Racing Establishments, &c. By JOHN BIRCH, Architect, Author of 'Country Architecture,' &c. With 30 Plates. Royal 8vo, 7s.

Examples of Labourers' Cottages, &c. With Plans for Improving the Dwellings of the Poor in Large Towns. With 34 Plates. Royal 8vo, 7s.

Picturesque Lodges. A Series of Designs for Gate Lodges, Park Entrances, Keepers', Gardeners', Bailiffs', Grooms', Upper and Under Servants' Lodges, and other Rural Residences. With 16 Plates. 4to, 12s. 6d.

BLACK. Heligoland and the Islands of the North Sea. By WILLIAM GEORGE BLACK. Crown 8vo, 4s.

BLACKIE.

Lays and Legends of Ancient Greece. By JOHN STUART BLACKIE, Emeritus Professor of Greek in the University of Edinburgh. Second Edition. Fcap. 8vo, 5s.

The Wisdom of Goethe. Fcap. 8vo. Cloth, extra gilt, 6s.

Scottish Song: Its Wealth, Wisdom, and Social Significance. Crown 8vo. With Music. 7s. 6d.

A Song of Heroes. Crown 8vo, 6s.

BLACKMORE. **The Maid of Sker.** By R. D. BLACKMORE, Author of 'Lorna Doone,' &c. New Edition. Crown 8vo, 6s.

BLACKWOOD.

Blackwood's Magazine, from Commencement in 1817 to December 1892. Nos. 1 to 926, forming 152 Volumes.

Index to Blackwood's Magazine. Vols. 1 to 50. 8vo, 15s.

Tales from Blackwood. First Series. Price One Shilling each, in Paper Cover. Sold separately at all Railway Bookstalls. They may also be had bound in 12 vols., cloth, 18s. Half calf, richly gilt, 30s. Or the 12 vols. in 6, roxburghe, 21s. Half red morocco, 28s.

Tales from Blackwood. Second Series. Complete in Twenty-four Shilling Parts. Handsomely bound in 12 vols., cloth, 30s. In leather back, roxburghe style, 37s. 6d. Half calf, gilt, 52s. 6d. Half morocco, 55s.

Tales from Blackwood. Third Series. Complete in Twelve Shilling Parts. Handsomely bound in 6 vols., cloth, 15s.; and in 12 vols., cloth, 18s. The 6 vols. in roxburghe, 21s. Half calf, 25s. Half morocco, 28s.

Travel, Adventure, and Sport. From 'Blackwood's Magazine.' Uniform with 'Tales from Blackwood.' In Twelve Parts, each price 1s. Handsomely bound in 6 vols., cloth, 15s. And in half calf, 25s.

New Educational Series. *See separate Catalogue.*

New Uniform Series of Novels (Copyright). Crown 8vo, cloth. Price 3s. 6d. each. Now ready:—

KATIE STEWART, and other Stories. By Mrs Oliphant.	ALTIORA PETO. By Laurence Oliphant.
VALENTINE, AND HIS BROTHER. By the Same.	PICCADILLY. By the Same. With Illustrations.
SONS AND DAUGHTERS. By the Same.	THE REVOLT OF MAN. By Walter Besant.
MARMORNE. By P. G. Hamerton.	LADY BABY. By D. Gerard.
REATA. By E. D. Gerard.	THE BLACKSMITH OF VOE. By Paul Cushing.
BEGGAR MY NEIGHBOUR. By the Same.	THE DILEMMA. By the Author of 'The Battle of Dorking.'
THE WATERS OF HERCULES. By the Same.	
FAIR TO SEE. By L. W. M. Lockhart.	MY TRIVIAL LIFE AND MISFORTUNE. By A Plain Woman.
MINE IS THINE. By the Same.	
DOUBLES AND QUITS. By the Same.	POOR NELLIE. By the Same.
HURRISH. By the Hon. Emily Lawless.	

Others in preparation.

Standard Novels. Uniform in size and binding. Each complete in one Volume.

FLORIN SERIES, Illustrated Boards. Bound in Cloth, 2s. 6d.

TOM CRINGLE'S LOG. By Michael Scott.	PEN OWEN. By Dean Hook.
THE CRUISE OF THE MIDGE. By the Same.	ADAM BLAIR. By J. G. Lockhart.
CYRIL THORNTON. By Captain Hamilton.	LADY LEE'S WIDOWHOOD. By General Sir E. B. Hamley.
ANNALS OF THE PARISH. By John Galt.	
THE PROVOST, &c. By the Same.	SALEM CHAPEL. By Mrs Oliphant.
SIR ANDREW WYLIE. By the Same.	THE PERPETUAL CURATE. By the Same.
THE ENTAIL. By the Same.	MISS MARJORIBANKS. By the Same.
MISS MOLLY. By Beatrice May Butt.	JOHN: A Love Story. By the Same.
REGINALD DALTON. By J. G. Lockhart.	

BLACKWOOD.
Standard Novels.

SHILLING SERIES, Illustrated Cover. Bound in Cloth, 1s. 6d.

THE RECTOR, and THE DOCTOR'S FAMILY. By Mrs Oliphant.

THE LIFE OF MANSIE WAUCH. By D. M. Moir.

PENINSULAR SCENES AND SKETCHES. By F. Hardman.

SIR FRIZZLE PUMPKIN, NIGHTS AT MESS, &c.

THE SUBALTERN.

LIFE IN THE FAR WEST. By G. F. Ruxton.

VALERIUS: A Roman Story. By J. G. Lockhart.

BOLTON. Lord Wastwater. A Novel. By SIDNEY BOLTON. 2 vols. crown 8vo, 17s.

BON GAULTIER'S BOOK OF BALLADS. Fifteenth Edition. With Illustrations by Doyle, Leech, and Crowquill. Fcap. 8vo, 5s.

BONNAR. Biographical Sketch of George Meikle Kemp, Architect of the Scott Monument, Edinburgh. By THOMAS BONNAR, F.S.A. Scot., Author of 'The Present Art Revival,' 'The Past of Art in Scotland,' 'Suggestions for the Picturesque of Interiors,' &c. With Three Portraits and numerous Illustrations. Post 8vo, 7s. 6d.

BOSCOBEL TRACTS. Relating to the Escape of Charles the Second after the Battle of Worcester, and his subsequent Adventures. Edited by J. HUGHES, Esq., A.M. A New Edition, with additional Notes and Illustrations, including Communications from the Rev. R. H. BARHAM, Author of the 'Ingoldsby Legends.' 8vo, with Engravings, 16s.

BROUGHAM. Memoirs of the Life and Times of Henry Lord Brougham. Written by HIMSELF. 3 vols. 8vo, £2, 8s. The Volumes are sold separately, price 16s. each.

BROWN. A Manual of Botany, Anatomical and Physiological. For the Use of Students. By ROBERT BROWN, M.A., Ph.D. Crown 8vo, with numerous Illustrations, 12s. 6d.

BROWN. The Book of the Landed Estate. Containing Directions for the Management and Development of the Resources of Landed Property. By ROBERT E. BROWN, Factor and Estate Agent. Royal 8vo, with Illustrations, 21s.

BROWN. The Forester: A Practical Treatise on the Planting, Rearing, and General Management of Forest-trees. By JAMES BROWN, LL.D., Inspector of and Reporter on Woods and Forests. Fifth Edition, Revised and Enlarged. Royal 8vo, with Engravings, 36s.

BRUCE. In Clover and Heather. Poems by WALLACE BRUCE. New and Enlarged Edition. Crown 8vo, 4s. 6d.

A limited number of Copies of the First Edition, on large hand-made paper, 12s. 6d.

BRYDALL. Art in Scotland; its Origin and Progress. By ROBERT BRYDALL, Master of St George's Art School of Glasgow. 8vo, 12s. 6d.

BUCHAN. Introductory Text-Book of Meteorology. By ALEXANDER BUCHAN, LL.D., F.R.S.E., Secretary of the Scottish Meteorological Society, &c. Crown 8vo, with 8 Coloured Charts and Engravings, 4s. 6d.

BUCHANAN. The Shirè Highlands (East Central Africa). By JOHN BUCHANAN, Planter at Zomba. Crown 8vo, 5s.

BURBIDGE.
Domestic Floriculture, Window Gardening, and Floral Decorations. Being practical directions for the Propagation, Culture, and Arrangement of Plants and Flowers as Domestic Ornaments. By F. W. BURBIDGE. Second Edition. Crown 8vo, with numerous Illustrations, 7s. 6d.

Cultivated Plants: Their Propagation and Improvement. Including Natural and Artificial Hybridisation, Raising from Seed, Cuttings, and Layers, Grafting and Budding, as applied to the Families and Genera in Cultivation. Crown 8vo, with numerous Illustrations 12s 6d.

BURROWS. Commentaries on the History of England, from the Earliest Times to 1865. By MONTAGU BURROWS, Chichele Professor of Modern History in the University of Oxford; Captain R.N.; F.S.A., &c.; "Officier de l'Instruction Publique" of France. Crown 8vo, 7s. 6d.

BURTON.

The History of Scotland : From Agricola's Invasion to the Extinction of the last Jacobite Insurrection. By JOHN HILL BURTON, D.C.L., Historiographer-Royal for Scotland. New and Enlarged Edition, 8 vols., and Index. Crown 8vo, £3, 3s.

History of the British Empire during the Reign of Queen Anne. In 3 vols. 8vo. 30s.

The Scot Abroad. Third Edition. Crown 8vo, 10s. 6d.

The Book-Hunter. New Edition. With Portrait. Crown 8vo, 7s. 6d.

BUTE.

The Roman Breviary : Reformed by Order of the Holy Œcumenical Council of Trent; Published by Order of Pope St Pius V.; and Revised by Clement VIII. and Urban VIII.; together with the Offices since granted. Translated out of Latin into English by JOHN, Marquess of Bute, K.T. In 2 vols. crown 8vo, cloth boards, edges uncut. £2, 2s.

The Altus of St Columba. With a Prose Paraphrase and Notes. In paper cover, 2s. 6d.

BUTLER. Pompeii : Descriptive and Picturesque. By W. BUTLER. Post 8vo, 5s.

BUTT.

Miss Molly. By BEATRICE MAY BUTT. Cheap Edition, 2s.

Eugenie. Crown 8vo, 6s. 6d.

Elizabeth, and other Sketches. Crown 8vo, 6s.

Delicia. New Edition. Crown 8vo, 2s. 6d.

CAIRD.

Sermons. By JOHN CAIRD, D.D., Principal of the University of Glasgow. Sixteenth Thousand. Fcap. 8vo, 5s.

Religion in Common Life. A Sermon preached in Crathie Church, October 14, 1855, before Her Majesty the Queen and Prince Albert. Published by Her Majesty's Command. Cheap Edition, 3d.

CALDER. Chaucer's Canterbury Pilgrimage. Epitomised by WILLIAM CALDER. With Photogravure of the Pilgrimage Company, and other Illustrations, Glossary, &c. Crown 8vo, 4s.

CAMPBELL. Critical Studies in St Luke's Gospel : Its Demonology and Ebionitism. By COLIN CAMPBELL, D.D., Minister of the Parish of Dundee, formerly Scholar and Fellow of Glasgow University. Author of the 'Three First Gospels in Greek, arranged in parallel columns.' Post 8vo, 7s. 6d.

CAMPBELL. Sermons Preached before the Queen at Balmoral. By the Rev. A. A. CAMPBELL, Minister of Crathie. Published by Command of Her Majesty. Crown 8vo, 4s. 6d.

CAMPBELL. Records of Argyll. Legends, Traditions, and Recollections of Argyllshire Highlanders, collected chiefly from the Gaelic. With Notes on the Antiquity of the Dress, Clan Colours, or Tartans of the Highlanders. By Lord ARCHIBALD CAMPBELL. Illustrated with Nineteen full-page Etchings. 4to, printed on hand-made paper, £3, 3s.

CAMPBELL, W. D., AND V. K. ERSKINE. The Bailie M'Phee; A Curling Song. With Illustrations, and the Music to which it may be sung. Small 4to, 1s. 6d.

CANTON. A Lost Epic, and other Poems. By WILLIAM CANTON. Crown 8vo, 5s.

CARRICK. Koumiss; or, Fermented Mare's Milk: and its uses in the Treatment and Cure of Pulmonary Consumption, and other Wasting Diseases. With an Appendix on the best Methods of Fermenting Cow's Milk. By GEORGE L. CARRICK, M.D., L.R.C.S.E. and L.R.C.P.E., Physician to the British Embassy, St Petersburg, &c. Crown 8vo, 10s. 6d.

CARSTAIRS. British Work in India. By R. CARSTAIRS. Crown 8vo, 6s.

CAUVIN. A Treasury of the English and German Languages. Compiled from the best Authors and Lexicographers in both Languages. By JOSEPH CAUVIN, LL.D. and Ph.D., of the University of Göttingen, &c. Crown 8vo, 7s. 6d.

CAVE-BROWN. Lambeth Palace and its Associations. By J. CAVE-BROWN, M.A., Vicar of Detling, Kent, and for many years Curate of Lambeth Parish Church. With an Introduction by the Archbishop of Canterbury. Second Edition, containing an additional Chapter on Medieval Life in the Old Palaces. 8vo, with Illustrations, 21s.

CHARTERIS. Canonicity; or, Early Testimonies to the Existence and Use of the Books of the New Testament. Based on Kirchhoffer's 'Quellensammlung.' Edited by A. H. CHARTERIS, D.D., Professor of Biblical Criticism in the University of Edinburgh. 8vo, 18s.

CHRISTISON. Life of Sir Robert Christison, Bart., M.D., D.C.L. Oxon., Professor of Medical Jurisprudence in the University of Edinburgh. Edited by his Sons. In 2 vols. 8vo. Vol. I.—Autobiography. 16s. Vol. II.—Memoirs. 16s.

CHRONICLES OF STRATHEDEN. A Highland Parish of To-day. By a Resident. Crown 8vo, 5s.

CHRONICLES OF WESTERLY: A Provincial Sketch. By the Author of 'Culmshire Folk,' 'John Orlebar,' &c. 3 vols. crown 8vo, 25s. 6d.

CHURCH SERVICE SOCIETY.

A Book of Common Order: being Forms of Worship issued by the Church Service Society. Sixth Edition. Crown 8vo, 6s. Also in 2 vols. crown 8vo, 6s. 6d.

Order of Divine Service for Children. Issued by the Church Service Society. With Scottish Hymnal. Cloth, 3d.

CLELAND. Too Apt a Pupil. By ROBERT CLELAND, Author of 'Barbara Allan, the Provost's Daughter.' Crown 8vo, 6s.

CLOUSTON. Popular Tales and Fictions: their Migrations and Transformations. By W. A. CLOUSTON, Editor of 'Arabian Poetry for English Readers,' &c. 2 vols. post 8vo, roxburghe binding, 25s.

COCHRAN. A Handy Text-Book of Military Law. Compiled chiefly to assist Officers preparing for Examination; also for all Officers of the Regular and Auxiliary Forces. Comprising also a Synopsis of part of the Army Act. By Major F. COCHRAN, Hampshire Regiment Garrison Instructor, North British District. Crown 8vo, 7s. 6d.

COLQUHOUN. The Moor and the Loch. Containing Minute Instructions in all Highland Sports, with Wanderings over Crag and Corrie, Flood and Fell. By JOHN COLQUHOUN. Seventh Edition. With Illustrations. Demy 8vo, 21s.

CONSTITUTION AND LAW OF THE CHURCH OF SCOTLAND. With an Introductory Note by the late Principal Tulloch. New Edition, Revised and Enlarged. Crown 8vo, 3s. 6d.

CONSTITUTIONAL YEAR BOOK. Published annually. Paper cover, 1s.; cloth, 1s. 6d.

COTTERILL. Suggested Reforms in Public Schools. By C. C.
Cotterill, M.A. Crown 8vo, 3s. 6d.

CRANSTOUN.

The Elegies of Albius Tibullus. Translated into English
Verse, with Life of the Poet, and Illustrative Notes. By James Cranstoun,
LL.D., Author of a Translation of 'Catullus.' Crown 8vo, 6s. 6d.

The Elegies of Sextus Propertius. Translated into English
Verse, with Life of the Poet, and Illustrative Notes. Crown 8vo, 7s. 6d.

CRAWFORD. An Atonement of East London, and other Poems.
By Howard Crawford, M.A. Crown 8vo, 5s.

CRAWFORD. Saracinesca. By F. Marion Crawford, Author
of 'Mr Isaacs,' &c. &c. Sixth Edition. Crown 8vo, 6s.

CRAWFORD.

The Doctrine of Holy Scripture respecting the Atonement.
By the late Thomas J. Crawford, D.D., Professor of Divinity in the University
of Edinburgh. Fifth Edition. 8vo, 12s.

The Fatherhood of God, Considered in its General and Special
Aspects. Third Edition, Revised and Enlarged. 8vo, 9s.

The Preaching of the Cross, and other Sermons. 8vo, 7s. 6d.

The Mysteries of Christianity. Crown 8vo, 7s. 6d.

CROSS. Impressions of Dante, and of the New World ; with a
Few Words on Bimetallism. By J. W. Cross, Editor of 'George Eliot's Life, as
related in her Letters and Journals.' Post 8vo. [*Immediately.*

CUSHING.

The Blacksmith of Voe. By Paul Cushing, Author of 'The
Bull i' th' Thorn,' 'Cut with his own Diamond.' Cheap Edition. Crown 8vo, 3s. 6d.

DAVIES.

Norfolk Broads and Rivers ; or, The Waterways, Lagoons,
and Decoys of East Anglia. By G. Christopher Davies. Illustrated with
Seven full-page Plates. New and Cheaper Edition. Crown 8vo, 6s.

Our Home in Aveyron. Sketches of Peasant Life in Aveyron
and the Lot. By G. Christopher Davies and Mrs Broughall. Illustrated
with full-page Illustrations. 8vo, 15s. Cheap Edition, 7s. 6d.

DE LA WARR. An Eastern Cruise in the 'Edeline.' By the
Countess De La Warr. In Illustrated Cover. 2s.

DESCARTES. The Method, Meditations, and Principles of Philo-
sophy of Descartes. Translated from the Original French and Latin. With a
New Introductory Essay, Historical and Critical, on the Cartesian Philosophy.
By Professor Veitch, LL.D., Glasgow University. Tenth Edition. 6s. 6d.

DEWAR. Voyage of the "Nyanza," R.N.Y.C. Being the Record
of a Three Years' Cruise in a Schooner Yacht in the Atlantic and Pacific, and her
subsequent Shipwreck. By J. Cumming Dewar, late Captain King's Dragoon
Guards and 11th Prince Albert's Hussars. With Two Autogravures, numerous
Illustrations, and a Map. Demy 8vo, 21s.

DICKSON. Gleanings from Japan. By W. G. Dickson, Author
of 'Japan: Being a Sketch of its History, Government, and Officers of the
Empire.' With Illustrations. 8vo, 16s.

DILEMMA, The. By the Author of 'The Battle of Dorking.'
New Edition. Crown 8vo, 3s. 6d.

DOGS, OUR DOMESTICATED: Their Treatment in reference
to Food, Diseases, Habits, Punishment, Accomplishments. By 'Magenta.'
Crown 8vo, 2s. 6d.

DOMESTIC EXPERIMENT, A. By the Author of 'Ideala: A
Study from Life.' Crown 8vo, 6s.

DOUGLAS. Chinese Stories. By ROBERT K. DOUGLAS. With
numerous Illustrations by Parkinson, Forestier, and others. Small demy 8vo,
12s. 6d.

DU CANE. The Odyssey of Homer, Books I.-XII. Translated
into English Verse. By Sir CHARLES DU CANE, K.C.M.G. 8vo, 10s. 6d.

DUDGEON. History of the Edinburgh or Queen's Regiment
Light Infantry Militia, now 3rd Battalion The Royal Scots; with an Account of
the Origin and Progress of the Militia, and a Brief Sketch of the Old Royal
Scots. By Major R. C. DUDGEON, Adjutant 3rd Battalion the Royal Scots.
Post 8vo, with Illustrations, 10s. 6d.

DUNCAN. Manual of the General Acts of Parliament relating
to the Salmon Fisheries of Scotland from 1828 to 1882. By J. BARKER DUNCAN.
Crown 8vo, 5s.

DUNSMORE. Manual of the Law of Scotland as to the Relations between Agricultural Tenants and the Landlords, Servants, Merchants, and
Bowers. By W. DUNSMORE. 8vo, 7s. 6d.

DUPRÈ. Thoughts on Art, and Autobiographical Memoirs of
Giovanni Duprè. Translated from the Italian by E. M. PERUZZI, with the
permission of the Author. New Edition. With an Introduction by W. W.
STORY. Crown 8vo, 10s. 6d.

ELIOT.

George Eliot's Life, Related in Her Letters and Journals.
Arranged and Edited by her husband, J. W. CROSS. With Portrait and other
Illustrations. Third Edition. 3 vols. post 8vo, 42s.

George Eliot's Life. (Cabinet Edition.) With Portrait and
other Illustrations. 3 vols. crown 8vo, 15s.

George Eliot's Life. With Portrait and other Illustrations.
New Edition, in one volume. Crown 8vo, 7s. 6d.

Works of George Eliot (Cabinet Edition). 21 volumes,
crown 8vo, price £5, 5s. Also to be had handsomely bound in half and full calf.
The Volumes are sold separately, bound in cloth, price 5s. each—viz. :
Romola. 2 vols.—Silas Marner, The Lifted Veil, Brother Jacob. 1 vol.—
Adam Bede. 2 vols.—Scenes of Clerical Life. 2 vols.—The Mill on the Floss.
2 vols.—Felix Holt. 2 vols.—Middlemarch. 3 vols.—Daniel Deronda. 3
vols.—The Spanish Gypsy. 1 vol.—Jubal, and other Poems, Old and New.
1 vol.—Theophrastus Such. 1 vol.—Essays. 1 vol.

Novels by George Eliot. Cheap Edition.
Adam Bede. Illustrated. 3s. 6d., cloth.—The Mill on the Floss. Illus-
trated. 3s. 6d., cloth.—Scenes of Clerical Life. Illustrated. 3s., cloth.—
Silas Marner: the Weaver of Raveloe. Illustrated. 2s. 6d., cloth.—Felix
Holt, the Radical. Illustrated. 3s. 6d., cloth.—Romola. With Vignette.
3s. 6d., cloth.

Middlemarch. Crown 8vo, 7s. 6d.

Daniel Deronda. Crown 8vo, 7s. 6d.

Essays. New Edition. Crown 8vo, 5s.

Impressions of Theophrastus Such. New Edition. Crown
8vo, 5s.

The Spanish Gypsy. New Edition. Crown 8vo, 5s.

The Legend of Jubal, and other Poems, Old and New.
New Edition. Crown 8vo, 5s.

Wise, Witty, and Tender Sayings, in Prose and Verse. Selected
from the Works of GEORGE ELIOT. Eighth Edition. Fcap. 8vo, 6s.

ELIOT.
> The George Eliot Birthday Book. Printed on fine paper, with red border, and handsomely bound in cloth, gilt. Fcap. 8vo, 3s. 6d. And in French morocco or Russia, 5s.

ESSAYS ON SOCIAL SUBJECTS. Originally published in the 'Saturday Review.' New Edition. First and Second Series. 2 vols. crown 8vo, 6s. each.

FAITHS OF THE WORLD, The. A Concise History of the Great Religious Systems of the World. By various Authors. Crown 8vo, 5s.

FARRER. A Tour in Greece in 1880. By RICHARD RIDLEY FARRER. With Twenty-seven full-page Illustrations by Lord WINDSOR. Royal 8vo, with a Map, 21s.

FERRIER.
> Philosophical Works of the Late James F. Ferrier, B.A. Oxon., Professor of Moral Philosophy and Political Economy, St Andrews. New Edition. Edited by Sir ALEXANDER GRANT, Bart., D.C.L., and Professor LUSHINGTON. 3 vols. crown 8vo, 34s. 6d.

> Institutes of Metaphysic. Third Edition. 10s. 6d.

> Lectures on the Early Greek Philosophy. 4th Edition. 10s. 6d.

> Philosophical Remains, including the Lectures on Early Greek Philosophy. New Edition. 2 vols., 24s.

FITZROY. Dogma and the Church of England. By A. I. FITZROY. Post 8vo, 7s. 6d.

FLINT.
> The Philosophy of History in Europe. By ROBERT FLINT, D.D., LL.D., Professor of Divinity, University of Edinburgh. 3 vols. 8vo.
> *[New Edition in preparation. Vol. I.—*FRANCE. *Immediately.*

> Agnosticism. Being the Croall Lecture for 1887-88.
> *[In the press.*

> Theism. Being the Baird Lecture for 1876. Eighth Edition, Revised. Crown 8vo, 7s. 6d.

> Anti-Theistic Theories. Being the Baird Lecture for 1877. Fourth Edition. Crown 8vo, 10s. 6d.

FORBES. Insulinde : Experiences of a Naturalist's Wife in the Eastern Archipelago. By Mrs H. O. FORBES. Crown 8vo, with a Map. 4s. 6d.

FOREIGN CLASSICS FOR ENGLISH READERS. Edited by Mrs OLIPHANT. Price 2s. 6d. *For List of Volumes published, see page 2.*

FOSTER. The Fallen City, and other Poems. By WILL FOSTER. Crown 8vo, 6s.

FRANCILLON. Gods and Heroes ; or, The Kingdom of Jupiter. By R. E. FRANCILLON. With 8 Illustrations. Crown 8vo, 5s.

FULLARTON. Merlin : A Dramatic Poem. By RALPH MAC-LEOD FULLARTON. Crown 8vo, 5s.

GALT. Novels by JOHN GALT. Fcap. 8vo, boards, each 2s. ; cloth, 2s. 6d.
ANNALS OF THE PARISH.—THE PROVOST.—SIR ANDREW WYLIE.—THE ENTAIL.

GENERAL ASSEMBLY OF THE CHURCH OF SCOTLAND.
Scottish Hymnal, With Appendix Incorporated. Published for use in Churches by Authority of the General Assembly. 1. Large type, cloth, red edges, 2s. 6d.; French morocco, 4s. 2. Bourgeois type, limp cloth, 1s.; French morocco, 2s. 3. Nonpareil type, cloth, red edges, 6d.; French morocco, 1s. 4d. 4. Paper covers, 3d. 5. Sunday-School Edition, paper covers, 1d., cloth, 2d. No. 1, bound with the Psalms and Paraphrases, French morocco, 8s. No. 2, bound with the Psalms and Paraphrases, cloth, 2s.; French morocco, 3s.

Prayers for Social and Family Worship. Prepared by a Special Committee of the General Assembly of the Church of Scotland. Entirely New Edition, Revised and Enlarged. Fcap. 8vo, red edges, 2s.

Prayers for Family Worship. A Selection of Four Weeks' Prayers. New Edition. Authorised by the General Assembly of the Church of Scotland. Fcap. 8vo, red edges, 1s. 6d.

GERARD.
Reata : What's in a Name. By E. D. GERARD. Cheap Edition. Crown 8vo, 3s. 6d.

Beggar my Neighbour. Cheap Edition. Crown 8vo, 3s. 6d.

The Waters of Hercules. Cheap Edition. Crown 8vo, 3s. 6d.

GERARD.
The Land beyond the Forest. Facts, Figures, and Fancies from Transylvania. By E. GERARD. With Maps and Illustrations. 2 vols. post 8vo, 25s.

Bis : Some Tales Retold. Crown 8vo, 6s.

A Secret Mission. 2 vols. crown 8vo, 17s.

GERARD.
Lady Baby. By DOROTHEA GERARD. Cheap Edition. Crown 8vo, 3s. 6d.

Recha. Second Edition. Crown 8vo, 6s.

GERARD. Stonyhurst Latin Grammar. By Rev. JOHN GERARD. Second Edition. Fcap. 8vo, 3s.

GILL.
Free Trade : an Inquiry into the Nature of its Operation. By RICHARD GILL. Crown 8vo, 7s. 6d.

Free Trade under Protection. Crown 8vo, 7s. 6d.

GOETHE. Poems and Ballads of Goethe. Translated by Professor AYTOUN and Sir THEODORE MARTIN, K.C.B. Third Edition. Fcap. 8vo, 6s.

GOETHE'S FAUST. Translated into English Verse by Sir THEODORE MARTIN, K.C.B. Part I. Second Edition, post 8vo, 6s. Ninth Edition, fcap., 3s. 6d. Part II. Second Edition, Revised. Fcap. 8vo, 6s.

GORDON CUMMING.
At Home in Fiji. By C. F. GORDON CUMMING. Fourth Edition, post 8vo. With Illustrations and Map. 7s. 6d.

A Lady's Cruise in a French Man-of-War. New and Cheaper Edition. 8vo. With Illustrations and Map. 12s. 6d.

Fire-Fountains. The Kingdom of Hawaii : Its Volcanoes, and the History of its Missions. With Map and Illustrations. 2 vols. 8vo, 25s.

Wanderings in China. New and Cheaper Edition. 8vo, with Illustrations, 10s.

Granite Crags : The Yō-semité Region of California. Illustrated with 8 Engravings. New and Cheaper Edition. 8vo, 8s. 6d.

GRAHAM. The Life and Work of Syed Ahmed Khan, C.S.I. By Lieut.-Colonel G. F. I. GRAHAM, B.S.C. 8vo, 14s.

GRAHAM. Manual of the Elections (Scot.) (Corrupt and Illegal Practices) Act, 1890. With Analysis, Relative Act of Sederunt, Appendix containing the Corrupt Practices Acts of 1883 and 1885, and Copious Index. By J. EDWARD GRAHAM, Advocate. 8vo, 4s. 6d.

GRANT. Bush-Life in Queensland. By A. C. GRANT. New Edition. Crown 8vo, 6s.

GUTHRIE-SMITH. Crispus: A Drama. By H. GUTHRIE-SMITH. Fcap. 4to, 5s.

HAINES. Unless! A Romance. By RANDOLPH HAINES. Crown 8vo, 6s.

HALDANE. Subtropical Cultivations and Climates. A Handy Book for Planters, Colonists, and Settlers. By R. C. HALDANE. Post 8vo, 9s.

HALLETT. A Thousand Miles on an Elephant in the Shan States. By HOLT S. HALLETT, M. Inst. C.E., F.R.G.S., M.R.A.S., Hon. Member Manchester and Tyneside Geographical Societies. 8vo, with Maps and numerous Illustrations, 21s.

HAMERTON.

Wenderholme: A Story of Lancashire and Yorkshire Life. By P. G. HAMERTON, Author of 'A Painter's Camp.' Crown 8vo, 6s.

Marmorne. New Edition. Crown 8vo, 3s. 6d.

HAMILTON.

Lectures on Metaphysics. By Sir WILLIAM HAMILTON, Bart., Professor of Logic and Metaphysics in the University of Edinburgh. Edited by the Rev. H. L. MANSEL, B.D., LL.D., Dean of St Paul's; and JOHN VEITCH, M.A., LL.D., Professor of Logic and Rhetoric, Glasgow. Seventh Edition. 2 vols. 8vo, 24s.

Lectures on Logic. Edited by the SAME. Third Edition, Revised. 2 vols., 24s.

Discussions on Philosophy and Literature, Education and University Reform. Third Edition. 8vo, 21s.

Memoir of Sir William Hamilton, Bart., Professor of Logic and Metaphysics in the University of Edinburgh. By Professor VEITCH, of the University of Glasgow. 8vo, with Portrait, 18s.

Sir William Hamilton: The Man and his Philosophy. Two Lectures delivered before the Edinburgh Philosophical Institution, January and February 1883. By Professor VEITCH. Crown 8vo, 2s.

HAMLEY.

The Operations of War Explained and Illustrated. By General Sir EDWARD BRUCE HAMLEY, K.C.B., K.C.M.G. Fifth Edition, Revised throughout. 4to, with numerous Illustrations, 30s.

National Defence; Articles and Speeches. Post 8vo, 6s.

Shakespeare's Funeral, and other Papers. Post 8vo, 7s. 6d.

Thomas Carlyle: An Essay. Second Edition. Crown 8vo, 2s. 6d.

On Outposts. Second Edition. 8vo, 2s.

Wellington's Career; A Military and Political Summary. Crown 8vo, 2s.

Lady Lee's Widowhood. Crown 8vo, 2s. 6d.

Our Poor Relations. A Philozoic Essay. With Illustrations, chiefly by Ernest Griset. Crown 8vo, cloth gilt, 3s. 6d.

HAMLEY. Guilty, or Not Guilty? A Tale. By Major-General
W. G. HAMLEY, late of the Royal Engineers. New Edition. Crown 8vo, 3s. 6d.

HARRISON. The Scot in Ulster. The Story of the Scottish
Settlement in Ulster. By JOHN HARRISON, Author of 'Oure Tounis Colledge.'
Crown 8vo, 2s. 6d.

HASELL.
Bible Partings. By E. J. HASELL. Crown 8vo, 6s.
Short Family Prayers. Cloth, 1s.

HAY. Arakan: Past—Present—Future. A Resumé of Two
Campaigns for its Development. By JOHN OGILVY HAY, J.P. ('Old Arakan'),
Formerly Honorary Magistrate of the town of Akyab, Author of 'Indo-Burmah-
China Railway Connections a Pressing Necessity.' With a Map. Demy 8vo, 4s. 6d.

HAY. The Works of the Right Rev. Dr George Hay, Bishop of
Edinburgh. Edited under the Supervision of the Right Rev. Bishop STRAIN.
With Memoir and Portrait of the Author. 5 vols. crown 8vo, bound in extra
cloth, £1, 1s. The following Volumes may be had separately—viz.:
The Devout Christian Instructed in the Law of Christ from the Written
Word. 2 vols., 8s.—The Pious Christian Instructed in the Nature and Practice
of the Principal Exercises of Piety. 1 vol., 3s.

HEATLEY.
The Horse-Owner's Safeguard. A Handy Medical Guide for
every Man who owns a Horse. By G. S. HEATLEY, M.R.C.V.S. Crown 8vo, 5s.

The Stock-Owner's Guide. A Handy Medical Treatise for
every Man who owns an Ox or a Cow. Crown 8vo, 4s. 6d.

HEDDERWICK.
Lays of Middle Age; and other Poems. By JAMES HEDDER-
WICK, LL.D. Price 3s. 6d.

Backward Glances; or, Some Personal Recollections. With
a Portrait. Post 8vo, 7s. 6d.

HEMANS.
The Poetical Works of Mrs Hemans. Copyright Editions.
Royal 8vo, 5s. The Same with Engravings, cloth, gilt edges, 7s. 6d.

Select Poems of Mrs Hemans. Fcap., cloth, gilt edges, 3s.

HERKLESS. Cardinal Beaton: Priest and Politician. By
JOHN HERKLESS, Minister of Tannadice. With a Portrait. Post 8vo, 7s. 6d.

HOME PRAYERS. By Ministers of the Church of Scotland
and Members of the Church Service Society. Second Edition. Fcap. 8vo, 3s.

HOMER.
The Odyssey. Translated into English Verse in the Spenserian Stanza. By PHILIP STANHOPE WORSLEY. 3d Edition. 2 vols. fcap., 12s.

The Iliad. Translated by P. S. WORSLEY and Professor CON-
INGTON. 2 vols. crown 8vo, 21s.

HUTCHINSON. Hints on the Game of Golf. By HORACE G.
HUTCHINSON. Seventh Edition, Enlarged. Fcap. 8vo, cloth, 1s.

IDDESLEIGH.
Lectures and Essays. By the late EARL of IDDESLEIGH,
G.C.B., D.C.L., &c. 8vo, 16s.

Life, Letters, and Diaries of Sir Stafford Northcote, First
Earl of Iddesleigh. By ANDREW LANG. With Three Portraits and a View of
Pynes. Third Edition. 2 vols. post 8vo, 31s. 6d.
POPULAR EDITION. With Portrait and View of Pynes. Post 8vo, 7s. 6d.

INDEX GEOGRAPHICUS: Being a List, alphabetically arranged, of the Principal Places on the Globe, with the Countries and Subdivisions of the Countries in which they are situated, and their Latitudes and Longitudes. Imperial 8vo, pp. 676, 21s.

JEAN JAMBON. Our Trip to Blunderland; or, Grand Excursion to Blundertown and Back. By JEAN JAMBON. With Sixty Illustrations designed by CHARLES DOYLE, engraved by DALZIEL. Fourth Thousand. Cloth, gilt edges, 6s. 6d. Cheap Edition, cloth, 3s. 6d. Boards, 2s. 6d.

JENNINGS. Mr Gladstone: A Study. By LOUIS J. JENNINGS, M.P., Author of 'Republican Government in the United States,' 'The Croker Memoirs,' &c. Popular Edition. Crown 8vo, 1s.

JERNINGHAM.

Reminiscences of an Attaché. By HUBERT E. H. JERNINGHAM. Second Edition. Crown 8vo, 5s.

Diane de Breteuille. A Love Story. Crown 8vo, 2s. 6d.

JOHNSTON.

The Chemistry of Common Life. By Professor J. F. W. JOHNSTON. New Edition, Revised. By ARTHUR HERBERT CHURCH, M.A. Oxon.; Author of 'Food: its Sources, Constituents, and Uses,' &c. With Maps and 102 Engravings. Crown 8vo, 7s. 6d.

Elements of Agricultural Chemistry. An entirely New Edition from the Edition by Sir CHARLES A. CAMERON, M.D., F.R.C.S.I., &c. Revised and brought down to date by C. M. AIKMAN, M.A., B.Sc., F.R.S.E., Lecturer on Agricultural Chemistry, West of Scotland Technical College. Fcap. 8vo.   [*In preparation.*

Catechism of Agricultural Chemistry. An entirely New Edition from the Edition by Sir CHARLES A. CAMERON. Revised and Enlarged by C. M. AIKMAN, M.A., &c. 92d Thousand. With numerous Illustrations. Crown 8vo, 1s.

JOHNSTON. Patrick Hamilton: a Tragedy of the Reformation in Scotland, 1528. By T. P. JOHNSTON. Crown 8vo, with Two Etchings. 5s.

JOHNSTON. Agricultural Holdings (Scotland) Acts, 1883 and 1889; and the Ground Game Act, 1880. With Notes, and Summary of Procedure, &c. By CHRISTOPHER N. JOHNSTON, M.A., Advocate. Demy 8vo, 5s.

KEBBEL. The Old and the New: English Country Life. By T. E. KEBBEL, M.A., Author of 'The Agricultural Labourers,' 'Essays in History and Politics,' 'Life of Lord Beaconsfield.' Crown 8vo, 5s.

KENNEDY. Sport, Travel, and Adventure in Newfoundland and the West Indies. By Captain W. R. KENNEDY, R.N. With Illustrations by the Author. Post 8vo, 14s.

KING. The Metamorphoses of Ovid. Translated in English Blank Verse. By HENRY KING, M.A., Fellow of Wadham College, Oxford, and of the Inner Temple, Barrister-at-Law. Crown 8vo, 10s. 6d.

KINGLAKE.

History of the Invasion of the Crimea. By A. W. KINGLAKE. Cabinet Edition, Revised. With an Index to the Complete Work. Illustrated with Maps and Plans. Complete in 9 vols., crown 8vo, at 6s. each.

History of the Invasion of the Crimea. Demy 8vo. Vol. VI. Winter Troubles. With a Map, 16s. Vols. VII. and VIII. From the Morrow of Inkerman to the Death of Lord Raglan. With an Index to the Whole Work. With Maps and Plans. 28s.

Eothen. A New Edition, uniform with the Cabinet Edition of the 'History of the Invasion of the Crimea.' 6s.

KNEIPP. My Water-Cure. As Tested through more than
Thirty Years, and Described for the Healing of Diseases and the Preservation of
Health. By SEBASTIAN KNEIPP, Parish Priest of Wörishofen (Bavaria). With a
Portrait and other Illustrations. Authorised English Translation from the
Thirtieth German Edition, by A. de F. Crown 8vo, 5s.

KNOLLYS. The Elements of Field-Artillery. Designed for
the Use of Infantry and Cavalry Officers. By HENRY KNOLLYS, Captain Royal
Artillery; Author of 'From Sedan to Saarbrück,' Editor of 'Incidents in the
Sepoy War,' &c. With Engravings. Crown 8vo, 7s. 6d.

LAMINGTON. In the Days of the Dandies. By the late Lord
LAMINGTON. Crown 8vo. Illustrated cover, 1s.; cloth, 1s. 6d.

LANG. Life, Letters, and Diaries of Sir Stafford Northcote,
First Earl of Iddesleigh. By ANDREW LANG. With Three Portraits and a View
of Pynes. Third Edition. 2 vols. post 8vo, 31s. 6d.
POPULAR EDITION. With Portrait and View of Pynes. Post 8vo, 7s. 6d.

LAWLESS. Hurrish: A Study. By the Hon. EMILY LAWLESS,
Author of 'A Chelsea Householder,' &c. Fourth Edition. Crown 8vo, 3s. 6d.

LEES. A Handbook of the Sheriff and Justice of Peace Small
Debt Courts. With Notes, References, and Forms. By J. M. Lees, Advocate,
Sheriff-Substitute of Lanarkshire. 8vo, 7s. 6d.

LIGHTFOOT. Studies in Philosophy. By the REV. J. LIGHT-
FOOT, M.A., D.Sc.; Vicar of Cross Stone, Todmorden. Crown 8vo, 4s. 6d.

LINDSAY. The Progressiveness of Modern Christian Thought.
By the Rev. JAMES LINDSAY, M.A., B.D., B.Sc., F.R.S.E., F.G.S., Minister of
the Parish of St Andrews, Kilmarnock. Crown 8vo, 6s.

LLOYD. Ireland under the Land League. A Narrative of
Personal Experiences. By CLIFFORD LLOYD, Special Resident Magistrate.
Post 8vo, 6s.

LOCKHART.
Doubles and Quits. By LAURENCE W. M. LOCKHART. New
Edition. Crown 8vo, 3s. 6d.
Fair to See. New Edition. Crown 8vo, 3s. 6d.
Mine is Thine. New Edition. Crown 8vo, 3s. 6d.

LOCKHART. The Church of Scotland in the Thirteenth Century. The Life and Times of David de Bernham of St Andrews (Bishop), A.D.
1239 to 1253. With List of Churches dedicated by him, and Dates. By WILLIAM
LOCKHART, A.M., F.S.A. Scot., Minister of Colinton Parish. 2d Edition 8vo, 6s.

LORIMER.
The Institutes of Law: A Treatise of the Principles of Juris-
prudence as determined by Nature. By the late JAMES LORIMER, Professor of
Public Law and of the Law of Nature and Nations in the University of Edin-
burgh. New Edition, Revised and much Enlarged. 8vo, 18s.
The Institutes of the Law of Nations. A Treatise of the
Jural Relation of Separate Political Communities. In 2 vols. 8vo. Volume I.,
price 16s. Volume II., price 20s.

LOVE. Scottish Church Music. Its Composers and Sources.
With Musical Illustrations. By JAMES LOVE. Post 8vo, 7s. 6d.

M'COMBIE. Cattle and Cattle-Breeders. By WILLIAM M'COMBIE,
Tillyfour. New Edition, Enlarged, with Memoir of the Author by JAMES
MACDONALD, of the 'Farming World.' Crown 8vo, 3s. 6d.

M'CRIE.
Works of the Rev. Thomas M'Crie, D.D. Uniform Edition.
4 vols. crown 8vo, 24s.

M'CRIE.
Life of John Knox.   Crown 8vo, 6s.   Another Edition, 3s. 6d.
Life of Andrew Melville.   Crown 8vo, 6s.
History of the Progress and Suppression of the Reformation
in Italy in the Sixteenth Century.   Crown 8vo, 4s.
History of the Progress and Suppression of the Reformation
in Spain in the Sixteenth Century.   Crown 8vo, 3s. 6d.
Lectures on the Book of Esther.   Fcap. 8vo, 5s.

M'CRIE.   The Public Worship of Presbyterian Scotland.   Histori-
cally treated.   With copious Notes, Appendices, and Index.   The Fourteenth
Series of the Cunningham Lectures.   By the Rev. CHARLES G. M'CRIE.   Demy
8vo, 10s. 6d.

MACDONALD.   A Manual of the Criminal Law (Scotland) Procedure Act, 1887.   By NORMAN DORAN MACDONALD.   Revised by the LORD
JUSTICE-CLERK.   8vo, 10s. 6d.

MACDONALD.
History of Polled Aberdeen and Angus Cattle.   Giving an
Account of the Origin, Improvement, and Characteristics of the Breed.   By JAMES
MACDONALD and JAMES SINCLAIR, Sub-Editor 'Irish Farmer's Gazette.'   Illus-
trated with numerous Animal Portraits.   Post 8vo, 12s. 6d.
Stephens Book of the Farm.   Fourth Edition.   Revised and
in great part Rewritten by JAMES MACDONALD of the 'Farming World.'
Complete in 3 vols., bound with leather back, gilt top, £3, 3s.   In Six Divisions,
bound in cloth, each 10s. 6d.
Pringle's Live Stock of the Farm.   Third Edition.   Revised
and Edited by JAMES MACDONALD.   Crown 8vo, 7s. 6d.
M'Combie's Cattle and Cattle-Breeders.   New Edition,
Enlarged, with Memoir of the Author by JAMES MACDONALD.   Crown 8vo, 3s. 6d.

MACGREGOR.   Life and Opinions of Major-General Sir Charles
MacGregor K.C.B., C.S.I., C.I.E., Quartermaster-General of India.   From his
Letters and Diaries.   Edited by Lady MACGREGOR.   With Portraits and Maps to
illustrate Campaigns in which he was engaged.   2 vols. 8vo, 35s.

M'INTOSH.   The Book of the Garden.   By CHARLES M'INTOSH,
formerly Curator of the Royal Gardens of his Majesty the King of the Belgians,
and lately of those of his Grace the Duke of Buccleuch, K.G., at Dalkeith Palace.
2 vols. royal 8vo, with 1350 Engravings.   £4, 7s. 6d.   Vol. I.   On the Formation
of Gardens and Construction of Garden Edifices, £2, 10s.   Vol. II.   Practical
Gardening, £1, 17s. 6d.

MACINTYRE.   Hindu-Koh: Wanderings and Wild Sports on
and beyond the Himalayas.   By Major-General DONALD MACINTYRE, V.C., late
Prince of Wales' Own Goorkhas, F.R.G.S.   *Dedicated to H.R.H. The Prince of
Wales.*   New and Cheaper Edition, Revised, with numerous Illustrations.   Post
8vo, 7s. 6d.

MACKAY.   A Sketch of the History of Fife and Kinross.   A
Study of Scottish History and Character.   By Æ. J. G. MACKAY, Sheriff of these
Counties.   Crown 8vo, 6s.

MACKAY.
A Manual of Modern Geography; Mathematical, Physical,
and Political.   By the Rev. ALEXANDER MACKAY, LL.D., F.R.G.S.   11th
Thousand, Revised to the present time.   Crown 8vo, pp. 688, 7s. 6d.
Elements of Modern Geography.   55th Thousand, Revised to
the present time.   Crown 8vo, pp. 300, 3s.
The Intermediate Geography.   Intended as an Intermediate
Book between the Author's 'Outlines of Geography' and 'Elements of Geo-
graphy.'   Seventeenth Edition, Revised.   Crown 8vo, pp. 238, 2s.

MACKAY.

Outlines of Modern Geography. 188th Thousand, Revised to the present time. 18mo, pp. 118, 1s.

First Steps in Geography. 105th Thousand. 18mo, pp. 56. Sewed, 4d. ; cloth, 6d.

Elements of Physiography and Physical Geography. With Express Reference to the Instructions issued by the Science and Art Department. 30th Thousand, Revised. Crown 8vo, 1s. 6d.

Facts and Dates ; or, The Leading Events in Sacred and Profane History, and the Principal Facts in the various Physical Sciences. For Schools and Private Reference. New Edition. Crown 8vo, 3s. 6d.

MACKAY. An Old Scots Brigade. Being the History of Mackay's Regiment, now incorporated with the Royal Scots. With an Appendix containing many Original Documents connected with the History of the Regiment. By JOHN MACKAY (late) OF HERRIESDALE. Crown 8vo, 5s.

MACKENZIE. Studies in Roman Law. With Comparative Views of the Laws of France, England, and Scotland. By Lord MACKENZIE, one of the Judges of the Court of Session in Scotland. Sixth Edition, Edited by JOHN KIRKPATRICK, M.A., LL.B., Advocate, Professor of History in the University of Edinburgh. 8vo, 12s.

MACPHERSON. Glimpses of Church and Social Life in the Highlands in the Olden Times. By ALEXANDER MACPHERSON, F.S.A. Scot. With Illustrations. In one volume. Small 4to. [*In the press.*

M'PHERSON.

Summer Sundays in a Strathmore Parish. By J. GORDON M'PHERSON, Ph.D., F.R.S.E., Minister of Ruthven. Crown 8vo, 5s.

Golf and Golfers. Past and Present. With an Introduction by the Right Hon. A. J. BALFOUR, and a Portrait of the Author. Fcap. 8vo, 1s. 6d.

MACRAE. A Handbook of Deer-Stalking. By ALEXANDER MACRAE, late Forester to Lord Henry Bentinck. With Introduction by Horatio Ross, Esq. Fcap. 8vo, with two Photographs from Life. 3s. 6d.

MAIN. Three Hundred English Sonnets. Chosen and Edited by DAVID M. MAIN. Fcap. 8vo, 6s.

MAIR. A Digest of Laws and Decisions, Ecclesiastical and Civil, relating to the Constitution, Practice, and Affairs of the Church of Scotland. With Notes and Forms of Procedure. By the Rev. WILLIAM MAIR, D.D., Minister of the Parish of Earlston. Crown 8vo. With Supplements. 8s.

MARSHALL.

French Home Life. By FREDERICK MARSHALL, Author of 'Claire Brandon.' Second Edition. 5s.

It Happened Yesterday. A Novel. Crown 8vo, 6s.

MARSHMAN. History of India. From the Earliest Period to the Close of the India Company's Government; with an Epitome of Subsequent Events. By JOHN CLARK MARSHMAN, C.S.I. Abridged from the Author's larger work. Second Edition, Revised. Crown 8vo, with Map, 6s. 6d.

MARTIN.

Goethe's Faust. Part I. Translated by Sir THEODORE MARTIN, K.C.B. Second Edition, crown 8vo, 6s. Ninth Edition, fcap. 8vo, 3s. 6d.

Goethe's Faust. Part II. Translated into English Verse. Second Edition, Revised. Fcap. 8vo, 6s.

The Works of Horace. Translated into English Verse, with Life and Notes. 2 vols. New Edition, crown 8vo, 21s.

Poems and Ballads of Heinrich Heine. Done into English Verse. Second Edition. Printed on *papier vergé*, crown 8vo, 8s.

MARTIN.

The Song of the Bell, and other Translations from Schiller, Goethe, Uhland, and Others. Crown 8vo, 7s. 6d.

Catullus. With Life and Notes. Second Edition, Revised and Corrected. Post 8vo, 7s. 6d.

Aladdin: A Dramatic Poem. By ADAM OEHLENSCHLAEGER. Fcap. 8vo, 5s.

Correggio: A Tragedy. By OEHLENSCHLAEGER. With Notes. Fcap. 8vo, 3s.

King Rene's Daughter: A Danish Lyrical Drama. By HENRIK HERTZ. Second Edition, fcap., 2s. 6d.

MARTIN. On some of Shakespeare's Female Characters. In a Series of Letters. By HELENA FAUCIT, Lady MARTIN. Dedicated by permission to Her Most Gracious Majesty the Queen. New Edition, Enlarged. 8vo, with Portrait by Lane, 7s. 6d. Bound in cloth, gilt edges, 8s. 6d.

MARWICK. Observations on the Law and Practice in regard to Municipal Elections and the Conduct of the Business of Town Councils and Commissioners of Police in Scotland. By Sir JAMES D. MARWICK, LL.D., Town-Clerk of Glasgow. Royal 8vo, 30s.

MATHESON.

Can the Old Faith Live with the New ? or, The Problem of Evolution and Revelation. By the Rev. GEORGE MATHESON, D.D. Third Edition. Crown 8vo, 7s. 6d.

The Psalmist and the Scientist ; or, Modern Value of the Religious Sentiment. New and Cheaper Edition. Crown 8vo, 5s.

Spiritual Development of St Paul. Third Edition. Cr. 8vo, 5s.

The Distinctive Messages of the Old Religions. Cr. 8vo, 5s.

Sacred Songs. New and Cheaper Edition. Crown 8vo, 2s. 6d.

MAURICE. The Balance of Military Power in Europe. An Examination of the War Resources of Great Britain and the Continental States. By Colonel MAURICE, R.A., Professor of Military Art and History at the Royal Staff College. Crown 8vo, with a Map, 6s.

MAXWELL. Meridiana: Noontide Essays. By Sir HERBERT MAXWELL, Bart., M.P., F.S.A., &c., Author of 'Passages in the Life of Sir Lucian Elphin,' &c. Post 8vo, 7s. 6d.

MEREDYTH. The Brief for the Government, 1886-92. A Handbook for Conservative and Unionist Writers, Speakers, &c. Second Edition. By W. H. MEREDYTH. Crown 8vo, 2s. 6d.

MICHEL. A Critical Inquiry into the Scottish Language. With the view of Illustrating the Rise and Progress of Civilisation in Scotland. By FRANCISQUE-MICHEL, F.S.A. Lond. and Scot. Correspondant de l'Institut de France, &c. 4to, printed on hand-made paper, and bound in roxburghe, 66s.

MICHIE.

The Larch: Being a Practical Treatise on its Culture and General Management. By CHRISTOPHER Y. MICHIE, Forester, Cullen House. Crown 8vo, with Illustrations. New and Cheaper Edition, Enlarged, 5s.

The Practice of Forestry. Crown 8vo, with Illustrations. 6s.

MIDDLETON. The Story of Alastair Bhan Comyn ; or, The Tragedy of Dunphail. A Tale of Tradition and Romance. By the Lady MIDDLETON. Square 8vo, 10s. Cheaper Edition, 5s.

MILLER. Landscape Geology. A Plea for the Study of Geology by Landscape Painters. By HUGH MILLER, of H.M. Geological Survey. Crown 8vo, 3s. Cheap Edition, paper cover, 1s.

MILNE-HOME. Mamma's Black Nurse Stories. West Indian Folk-lore. By MARY PAMELA MILNE-HOME. With six full-page tinted Illustrations. Small 4to, 5s.

MINTO.

A Manual of English Prose Literature, Biographical and Critical: designed mainly to show Characteristics of Style. By W. MINTO, M.A., Professor of Logic in the University of Aberdeen. Third Edition, Revised. Crown 8vo, 7s. 6d.

Characteristics of English Poets, from Chaucer to Shirley. New Edition, Revised. Crown 8vo, 7s. 6d.

MOIR. Life of Mansie Wauch, Tailor in Dalkeith. By D. M. MOIR. With 8 Illustrations on Steel, by the late GEORGE CRUIKSHANK. Crown 8vo, 3s. 6d. Another Edition, fcap. 8vo, 1s. 6d.

MOMERIE.

Defects of Modern Christianity, and other Sermons. By ALFRED WILLIAMS MOMERIE, M.A., D.Sc., LL.D. Fourth Edition. Crown 8vo, 5s.

The Basis of Religion. Being an Examination of Natural Religion. Third Edition. Crown 8vo, 2s. 6d.

The Origin of Evil, and other Sermons. Seventh Edition, Enlarged. Crown 8vo, 5s.

Personality. The Beginning and End of Metaphysics, and a Necessary Assumption in all Positive Philosophy. Fourth Edition, Revised Crown 8vo, 3s.

Agnosticism. Fourth Edition, Revised. Crown 8vo, 5s.

Preaching and Hearing ; and other Sermons. Third Edition, Enlarged. Crown 8vo, 5s.

Belief in God. Third Edition. Crown 8vo, 3s.

Inspiration ; and other Sermons. Second Edition, Enlarged. Crown 8vo, 5s.

Church and Creed. Second Edition. Crown 8vo, 4s. 6d.

MONTAGUE. Campaigning in South Africa. Reminiscences of an Officer in 1879. By Captain W. E. MONTAGUE, 94th Regiment, Author of 'Claude Meadowleigh,' &c. 8vo, 10s. 6d.

MONTALEMBERT. Memoir of Count de Montalembert. A Chapter of Recent French History. By Mrs OLIPHANT, Author of the 'Life of Edward Irving,' &c. 2 vols. crown 8vo, £1, 4s.

MORISON.

Æolus. A Romance in Lyrics. By JEANIE MORISON. Crown 8vo, 3s.

There as Here. Crown 8vo, 3s.

*** A limited impression on hand-made paper, bound in vellum, 7s. 6d.*

Selections from Poems. Crown 8vo, 4s. 6d.

Sordello. An Outline Analysis of Mr Browning's Poem. Crown 8vo, 3s.

Of "Fifine at the Fair," "Christmas Eve and Easter Day," and other of Mr Browning's Poems. Crown 8vo, 3s.

The Purpose of the Ages. Crown 8vo, 9s.

Gordon : An Our-day Idyll. Crown 8vo, 3s.

Saint Isadora, and other Poems. Crown 8vo, 1s. 6d.

Snatches of Song. Paper, 1s. 6d. ; Cloth, 3s.

MORISON.
Pontius Pilate.   Paper, 1s. 6d. ; Cloth, 3s.
Mill o' Forres.   Crown 8vo, 1s.
Ane Booke of Ballades.   Fcap. 4to, 1s.

MOZLEY.   Essays from 'Blackwood.'   By the late ANNE
Mozley, Author of 'Essays on Social Subjects'; Editor of 'The Letters and
Correspondence of Cardinal Newman,' 'Letters of the Rev. J. B. Mozley,' &c.
With a Memoir by her Sister, FANNY MOZLEY.   Post 8vo, 7s. 6d.

MUNRO.   On Valuation of Property.   By WILLIAM MUNRO,
M.A., Her Majesty's Assessor of Railways and Canals for Scotland.   Second
Edition, Revised and Enlarged.   8vo, 3s. 6d.

MURDOCH.   Manual of the Law of Insolvency and Bankruptcy:
Comprehending a Summary of the Law of Insolvency, Notour Bankruptcy,
Composition - contracts, Trust - deeds, Cessios, and Sequestrations; and the
Winding-up of Joint-Stock Companies in Scotland; with Annotations on the
various Insolvency and Bankruptcy Statutes; and with Forms of Procedure
applicable to these Subjects.   By JAMES MURDOCH, Member of the Faculty of
Procurators in Glasgow.   Fifth Edition, Revised and Enlarged.   8vo, £1, 10s.

MY TRIVIAL LIFE AND MISFORTUNE: A Gossip with
no Plot in Particular.   By A PLAIN WOMAN.   Cheap Edition.   Crown 8vo, 3s. 6d.

By the SAME AUTHOR.
POOR NELLIE.   Cheap Edition.   Crown 8vo, 3s. 6d.

NAPIER.   The Construction of the Wonderful Canon of Loga-
rithms.   By JOHN NAPIER of Merchiston.   Translated, with Notes, and a
Catalogue of Napier's Works, by WILLIAM RAE MACDONALD.   Small 4to, 15s.
A few large-paper copies on Whatman paper, 30s.

NEAVES.
Songs and Verses, Social and Scientific.   By An Old Con-
tributor to 'Maga.'   By the Hon. Lord NEAVES.   Fifth Edition.   Fcap. 8vo, 4s.
The Greek Anthology.   Being Vol. XX. of 'Ancient Classics
for English Readers.'   Crown 8vo, 2s. 6d.

NICHOLSON.
A Manual of Zoology, for the use of Students.   With a
General Introduction on the Principles of Zoology.   By HENRY ALLEYNE
NICHOLSON, M.D., D.Sc., F.L.S., F.G.S., Regius Professor of Natural History in
the University of Aberdeen.   Seventh Edition, Rewritten and Enlarged.   Post
8vo, pp. 956, with 555 Engravings on Wood, 18s.

Text-Book of Zoology, for the use of Schools.   Fourth Edition, Enlarged.   Crown 8vo, with 188 Engravings on Wood, 7s. 6d.

Introductory Text-Book of Zoology, for the use of Junior
Classes.   Sixth Edition, Revised and Enlarged, with 166 Engravings, 3s.

Outlines of Natural History, for Beginners : being Descriptions of a Progressive Series of Zoological Types.   Third Edition, with
Engravings, 1s. 6d.

A Manual of Palæontology, for the use of Students.   With a
General Introduction on the Principles of Palæontology.   By Professor H.
ALLEYNE NICHOLSON and RICHARD LYDEKKER, B.A.   Third Edition, entirely
Rewritten and greatly Enlarged.   2 vols. 8vo, £3, 3s.

The Ancient Life-History of the Earth.   An Outline of the
Principles and Leading Facts of Palæontological Science.   Crown 8vo, with 276
Engravings, 10s. 6d.

On the "Tabulate Corals" of the Palæozoic Period, with
Critical Descriptions of Illustrative Species.   Illustrated with 15 Lithographed
Plates and numerous Engravings.   Super-royal 8vo, 21s.

NICHOLSON.
Synopsis of the Classification of the Animal Kingdom. 8vo, with 106 Illustrations, 6s.

On the Structure and Affinities of the Genus Monticulipora and its Sub-Genera, with Critical Descriptions of Illustrative Species. Illustrated with numerous Engravings on Wood and Lithographed Plates. Super-royal 8vo, 18s.

NICHOLSON.
Communion with Heaven, and other Sermons. By the late MAXWELL NICHOLSON, D.D., Minister of St Stephen's, Edinburgh. Crown 8vo, 5s. 6d.

Rest in Jesus. Sixth Edition. Fcap. 8vo, 4s. 6d.

NICHOLSON.
A Treatise on Money, and Essays on Present Monetary Problems. By JOSEPH SHIELD NICHOLSON, M.A., D.Sc., Professor of Commercial and Political Economy and Mercantile Law in the University of Edinburgh. 8vo, 10s. 6d.

Thoth. A Romance. Third Edition. Crown 8vo, 4s. 6d.

A Dreamer of Dreams. A Modern Romance. Second Edition. Crown 8vo, 6s.

NICOLSON AND MURE. A Handbook to the Local Government (Scotland) Act, 1889. With Introduction, Explanatory Notes, and Index. By J. BADENACH NICOLSON, Advocate, Counsel to the Scotch Education Department, and W. J. MURE, Advocate, Legal Secretary to the Lord Advocate for Scotland. Ninth Reprint. 8vo, 5s.

OLIPHANT.
Masollam : A Problem of the Period. A Novel. By LAURENCE OLIPHANT. 3 vols. post 8vo, 25s. 6d.

Scientific Religion ; or, Higher Possibilities of Life and Practice through the Operation of Natural Forces. Second Edition. 8vo, 16s.

Altiora Peto. Cheap Edition. Crown 8vo, boards, 2s. 6d. ; cloth, 3s. 6d. Illustrated Edition. Crown 8vo, cloth, 6s.

Piccadilly. With Illustrations by Richard Doyle. New Edition, 3s. 6d. Cheap Edition, boards, 2s. 6d.

Traits and Travesties ; Social and Political. Post 8vo, 10s. 6d.

Episodes in a Life of Adventure ; or, Moss from a Rolling Stone. Fifth Edition. Post 8vo, 6s.

Haifa : Life in Modern Palestine. Second Edition. 8vo, 7s. 6d.

The Land of Gilead. With Excursions in the Lebanon. With Illustrations and Maps. Demy 8vo, 21s.

Memoir of the Life of Laurence Oliphant, and of Alice Oliphant, his Wife. By Mrs M. O. W. OLIPHANT. Seventh Edition. 2 vols. post 8vo, with Portraits. 21s.
POPULAR EDITION. With a New Preface. Post 8vo, with Portraits. 7s. 6d.

OLIPHANT.
Katie Stewart. By Mrs OLIPHANT. Illustrated boards, 2s. 6d.

Katie Stewart, and other Stories. New Edition. Crown 8vo, cloth, 3s. 6d.

Valentine and his Brother. New Edition. Crown 8vo, 3s. 6d.

Sons and Daughters. Crown 8vo, 3s. 6d.

OLIPHANT.
Diana Trelawny : The History of a Great Mistake. 2 vols.
crown 8vo, 17s.

Two Stories of the Seen and the Unseen. The Open Door
—Old Lady Mary. Paper covers, 1s.

OLIPHANT. Notes of a Pilgrimage to Jerusalem and the Holy
Land. By F. R. OLIPHANT. Crown 8vo, 3s. 6d.

ON SURREY HILLS. By "A SON OF THE MARSHES."
See page 28.

OSSIAN. The Poems of Ossian in the Original Gaelic. With
a Literal Translation into English, and a Dissertation on the Authenticity of the
Poems. By the Rev. ARCHIBALD CLERK. 2 vols. imperial 8vo, £1, 11s. 6d.

OSWALD. By Fell and Fjord ; or, Scenes and Studies in Ice-
land. By E. J. OSWALD. Post 8vo, with Illustrations. 7s. 6d.

PAGE.
Introductory Text-Book of Geology. By DAVID PAGE, LL.D.,
Professor of Geology in the Durham University of Physical Science, Newcastle,
and Professor LAPWORTH of Mason Science College, Birmingham. With Engravings and Glossarial Index. Twelfth Edition, Revised and Enlarged. 3s. 6d.

Advanced Text-Book of Geology, Descriptive and Industrial.
With Engravings, and Glossary of Scientific Terms. Sixth Edition, Revised and
Enlarged. 7s. 6d.

Introductory Text-Book of Physical Geography. With Sketch-
Maps and Illustrations. Edited by Professor LAPWORTH, LL.D., F.G.S., &c.,
Mason Science College, Birmingham. Twelfth Edition, Revised. 2s. 6d.

Advanced Text-Book of Physical Geography. Third Edition,
Revised and Enlarged by Professor LAPWORTH. With Engravings. 5s.

PATON.
Spindrift. By Sir J. NOEL PATON. Fcap., cloth, 5s.

Poems by a Painter. Fcap., cloth, 5s.

PATON. Body and Soul. A Romance in Transcendental Path-
ology. By FREDERICK NOEL PATON. Third Edition. Crown 8vo, 1s.

PATRICK. The Apology of Origen in Reply to Celsus. A
Chapter in the History of Apologetics. By the Rev. J. PATRICK, B.D. Post 8vo,
7s. 6d.

PATTERSON.
Essays in History and Art. By R. HOGARTH PATTERSON.
8vo, 12s.

The New Golden Age, and Influence of the Precious Metals
upon the World. 2 vols. 8vo, 31s. 6d.

PAUL. History of the Royal Company of Archers, the Queen's
Body-Guard for Scotland. By JAMES BALFOUR PAUL, Advocate of the Scottish
Bar. Crown 4to, with Portraits and other Illustrations. £2, 2s.

PEILE. Lawn Tennis as a Game of Skill. With latest revised
Laws as played by the Best Clubs. By Captain S. C. F. PEILE, B.S.C. Cheaper
Edition. Fcap., cloth, 1s.

PETTIGREW. The Handy Book of Bees, and their Profitable
Management. By A. PETTIGREW. Fifth Edition, Enlarged, with Engravings.
Crown 8vo, 3s. 6d.

PHILIP. The Function of Labour in the Production of Wealth.
By ALEXANDER PHILIP, LL.B., Edinburgh. Crown 8vo, 3s. 6d.

PHILOSOPHICAL CLASSICS FOR ENGLISH READERS.

Edited by WILLIAM KNIGHT, LL.D., Professor of Moral Philosophy, University of St Andrews. In crown 8vo volumes, with Portraits, price 3s. 6d.

[For list of Volumes published, see page 2.

POLLOK. The Course of Time : A Poem. By ROBERT POLLOK, A.M. Cottage Edition, 32mo, 8d. The Same, cloth, gilt edges, 1s. 6d. Another Edition, with Illustrations by Birket Foster and others, fcap., cloth, 3s. 6d., or with edges gilt, 4s.

PORT ROYAL LOGIC. Translated from the French ; with Introduction, Notes, and Appendix. By THOMAS SPENCER BAYNES, LL.D., Professor in the University of St Andrews. Tenth Edition, 12mo, 4s.

POTTS AND DARNELL.

Aditus Faciliores : An Easy Latin Construing Book, with Complete Vocabulary. By A. W. POTTS, M.A., LL.D., and the Rev. C. DARNELL, M.A., Head-Master of Cargilfield Preparatory School, Edinburgh. Tenth Edition, fcap. 8vo, 3s. 6d.

Aditus Faciliores Graeci. An Easy Greek Construing Book, with Complete Vocabulary. Fifth Edition, Revised. Fcap. 8vo, 3s.

POTTS. School Sermons. By the late ALEXANDER WM. POTTS. LL.D., First Head-Master of Fettes College. With a Memoir and Portrait. Crown 8vo, 7s. 6d.

PRINGLE. The Live - Stock of the Farm. By ROBERT O. PRINGLE. Third Edition. Revised and Edited by JAMES MACDONALD. Crown 8vo, 7s. 6d.

PUBLIC GENERAL STATUTES AFFECTING SCOTLAND from 1707 to 1847, with Chronological Table and Index. 3 vols. large 8vo, £3, 3s.

PUBLIC GENERAL STATUTES AFFECTING SCOTLAND, COLLECTION OF. Published Annually, with General Index.

RADICAL CURE FOR IRELAND, The. A Letter to the People of England and Scotland concerning a new Plantation. With 2 Maps. 8vo, 7s. 6d.

RAE. The Syrian Church in India. By GEORGE MILNE RAE, M.A., Fellow of the University of Madras ; late Professor in the Madras Christian College. With 6 full-page Illustrations. Post 8vo, 10s. 6d.

RAMSAY. Scotland and Scotsmen in the Eighteenth Century. Edited from the MSS. of JOHN RAMSAY, Esq. of Ochtertyre, by ALEXANDER ALLARDYCE, Author of 'Memoir of Admiral Lord Keith, K.B.,' &c. 2 vols. 8vo, 31s. 6d.

RANKIN.

A Handbook of the Church of Scotland. By JAMES RANKIN, D.D., Minister of Muthill ; Author of 'Character Studies in the Old Testament,' &c. An entirely New and much Enlarged Edition. Crown 8vo, with 2 Maps, 7s. 6d.

The Creed in Scotland. An Exposition of the Apostles' Creed. With Extracts from Archbishop Hamilton's Catechism of 1552, John Calvin's Catechism of 1556, and a Catena of Ancient Latin and other Hymns. Post 8vo, 7s. 6d.

The Worthy Communicant. A Guide to the Devout Observance of the Lord's Supper. Limp cloth, 1s. 3d.

The Young Churchman. Lessons on the Creed, the Commandments, the Means of Grace, and the Church. Limp cloth, 1s. 3d.

First Communion Lessons. 23d Edition. Paper Cover, 2d.

RECORDS OF THE TERCENTENARY FESTIVAL OF THE
UNIVERSITY OF EDINBURGH. Celebrated in April 1884. Published under
the Sanction of the Senatus Academicus. Large 4to, £2, 12s. 6d.

ROBERTSON. The Early Religion of Israel. As set forth by
Biblical Writers and Modern Critical Historians. Being the Baird Lecture for
1888-89. By JAMES ROBERTSON, D.D., Professor of Oriental Languages in the
University of Glasgow. Third Edition. Crown 8vo, 10s. 6d.

ROBERTSON. Orellana, and other Poems. By J. LOGIE
ROBERTSON, M.A. Fcap. 8vo. Printed on hand-made paper. 6s.

ROBERTSON. Our Holiday among the Hills. By JAMES and
JANET LOGIE ROBERTSON. Fcap. 8vo, 3s. 6d.

ROBERTSON. Essays and Sermons. By the late W. ROBERT-
son, B.D., Minister of the Parish of Sprouston. With a Memoir and Portrait.
Crown 8vo, 5s. 6d.

RODGER. Aberdeen Doctors at Home and Abroad. The Story
of a Medical School. By ELLA HILL BURTON RODGER. In one volume, demy
8vo. [*In the press.*

ROSCOE. Rambles with a Fishing-rod. By E. S. ROSCOE.
Crown 8vo, 4s. 6d.

ROSS. Old Scottish Regimental Colours. By ANDREW ROSS,
S.S.C., Hon. Secretary Old Scottish Regimental Colours Committee. Dedicated
by Special Permission to Her Majesty the Queen. Folio. £2, 12s. 6d.

RUSSELL. The Haigs of Bemersyde. A Family History. By
JOHN RUSSELL. Large 8vo, with Illustrations. 21s.

RUSSELL. Fragments from Many Tables. Being the Recollections of some Wise and Witty Men and Women. By GEORGE RUSSELL.
Crown 8vo, 4s. 6d.

RUTLAND.

Notes of an Irish Tour in 1846. By the DUKE OF RUTLAND,
G.C.B. (Lord JOHN MANNERS). New Edition. Crown 8vo, 2s. 6d.

Correspondence between the Right Honble. William Pitt
and Charles Duke of Rutland, Lord-Lieutenant of Ireland, 1781-1787. With
Introductory Note by JOHN DUKE OF RUTLAND. 8vo, 7s. 6d.

RUTLAND.

Gems of German Poetry. Translated by the DUCHESS OF
RUTLAND (Lady JOHN MANNERS). [*New Edition in preparation.*

Impressions of Bad-Homburg. Comprising a Short Account
of the Women's Associations of Germany under the Red Cross. Crown 8vo, 1s. 6d

Some Personal Recollections of the Later Years of the Earl
of Beaconsfield, K.G. Sixth Edition, 6d.

Employment of Women in the Public Service. 6d.

Some of the Advantages of Easily Accessible Reading and
Recreation Rooms, and Free Libraries. With Remarks on Starting and Maintaining them. Second Edition. Crown 8vo, 1s.

A Sequel to Rich Men's Dwellings, and other Occasional
Papers. Crown 8vo, 2s. 6d.

Encouraging Experiences of Reading and Recreation Rooms,
Aims of Guilds, Nottingham Social Guide, Existing Institutions, &c., &c.
Crown 8vo, 1s.

SCHILLER. Wallenstein. A Dramatic Poem. By FRIEDRICH
VON SCHILLER. Translated by C. G. N. LOCKHART. Fcap. 8vo, 7s. 6d.

SCOTCH LOCH FISHING. By "BLACK PALMER." Crown 8vo, interleaved with blank pages, 4s.

SCOUGAL. Prisons and their Inmates; or, Scenes from a Silent World. By FRANCIS SCOUGAL. Crown 8vo, boards, 2s.

SELLAR. Manual of the Education Acts for Scotland. By the late ALEXANDER CRAIG SELLAR, M.P. Eighth Edition. Revised and in great part rewritten by J. EDWARD GRAHAM, B.A. Oxon., Advocate. With Rules for the conduct of Elections, with Notes and Cases. 8vo.
[*New Edition in preparation.*
[SUPPLEMENT TO SELLAR's MANUAL. Being the Acts of 1889 in so far as affecting the Education Acts. 8vo, 2s.]

SETH.
    Scottish Philosophy. A Comparison of the Scottish and German Answers to Hume. Balfour Philosophical Lectures, University of Edinburgh. By ANDREW SETH, M.A., Professor of Logic and Metaphysics in Edinburgh University. Second Edition. Crown 8vo, 5s.

    Hegelianism and Personality. Balfour Philosophical Lectures. Second Series. Crown 8vo, 5s.

SETH. Freedom as Ethical Postulate. By JAMES SETH, M.A., Brown University, Providence, Rhode Island. 8vo, 1s.

SHADWELL. The Life of Colin Campbell, Lord Clyde. Illustrated by Extracts from his Diary and Correspondence. By Lieutenant-General SHADWELL, C.B. With Portrait, Maps, and Plans. 2 vols. 8vo. 36s.

SHAND.
    Half a Century; or, Changes in Men and Manners. By ALEX. INNES SHAND, Author of 'Against Time,' &c. Second Edition. 8vo, 12s. 6d.

    Letters from the West of Ireland. Reprinted from the 'Times.' Crown 8vo, 5s.

    Kilcarra. A Novel. 3 vols. crown 8vo, 25s. 6d.

SHARPE. Letters from and to Charles Kirkpatrick Sharpe. Edited by ALEXANDER ALLARDYCE, Author of 'Memoir of Admiral Lord Keith, K.B.,' &c. With a Memoir by the Rev. W. K. R. BEDFORD. In 2 vols. 8vo. Illustrated with Etchings and other Engravings. £2, 12s. 6d.

SIM. Margaret Sim's Cookery. With an Introduction by L. B. WALFORD, Author of 'Mr Smith: A Part of his Life,' &c. Crown 8vo, 5s.

SKELTON.
    Maitland of Lethington; and the Scotland of Mary Stuart. A History. By JOHN SKELTON, C.B., LL.D., Author of 'The Essays of Shirley.' Demy 8vo, 2 vols., 28s.

    The Handbook of Public Health. A Complete Edition of the Public Health and other Sanitary Acts relating to Scotland. Annotated, and with the Rules, Instructions, and Decisions of the Board of Supervision brought up to date with relative forms. Second Edition. With Introduction, containing the Administration of the Public Health Act in Counties. 8vo, 8s. 6d.

    The Local Government (Scotland) Act in Relation to Public Health. A Handy Guide for County and District Councillors, Medical Officers, Sanitary Inspectors, and Members of Parochial Boards. Second Edition. With a new Preface on appointment of Sanitary Officers. Crown 8vo, 2s.

SKRINE. Columba: A Drama. By JOHN HUNTLEY SKRINE, Warden of Glenalmond; Author of 'A Memory of Edward Thring. Fcap. 4to.
[*Immediately.*

SMITH. For God and Humanity. A Romance of Mount Carmel. By HASKETT SMITH, Author of 'The Divine Epiphany,' &c. 3 vols. post 8vo, 25s. 6d.

SMITH.
Thorndale ; or, The Conflict of Opinions. By WILLIAM SMITH, Author of 'A Discourse on Ethics,' &c. New Edition. Crown 8vo, 10s. 6d.

Gravenhurst ; or, Thoughts on Good and Evil. Second Edition. With Memoir and Portrait of the Author. Crown 8vo, 8s.

The Story of William and Lucy Smith. Edited by GEORGE MERRIAM. Large post 8vo, 12s. 6d.

SMITH. Memoir of the Families of M'Combie and Thoms, originally M'Intosh and M'Thomas. Compiled from History and Tradition. By WILLIAM M'COMBIE SMITH. With Illustrations. 8vo, 7s. 6d.

SMITH. Greek Testament Lessons for Colleges, Schools, and Private Students, consisting chiefly of the Sermon on the Mount and the Parables of our Lord. With Notes and Essays. By the Rev. J. HUNTER SMITH, M.A., King Edward's School, Birmingham. Crown 8vo, 6s.

SMITH. Writings by the Way. By JOHN CAMPBELL SMITH, M.A., Sheriff-Substitute. Crown 8vo, 9s.

SMITH. The Secretary for Scotland. Being a Statement of the Powers and Duties of the new Scottish Office. With a Short Historical Introduction and numerous references to important Administrative Documents. By W. C. SMITH, LL.B., Advocate. 8vo, 6s.

"SON OF THE MARSHES, A."
Within an Hour of London Town : Among Wild Birds and their Haunts. By "A SON OF THE MARSHES." Edited by J. A. OWEN. Second Edition. Crown 8vo, 6s.

On Surrey Hills. Third Edition. Crown 8vo, 6s.

Annals of a Fishing Village. New and Cheaper Edition. Crown 8vo, 5s. Illustrated Edition. Crown 8vo, 7s. 6d.

SORLEY. The Ethics of Naturalism. Being the Shaw Fellowship Lectures, 1884. By W. R. SORLEY, M.A., Fellow of Trinity College, Cambridge, Professor of Logic and Philosophy in University College of South Wales. Crown 8vo, 6s.

SPEEDY. Sport in the Highlands and Lowlands of Scotland with Rod and Gun. By TOM SPEEDY. Second Edition, Revised and Enlarged. With Illustrations by Lieut.-General Hope Crealocke, C.B., C.M.G., and others. 8vo, 15s.

SPROTT. The Worship and Offices of the Church of Scotland. By GEORGE W. SPROTT, D.D., Minister of North Berwick. Crown 8vo, 6s.

STARFORTH. Villa Residences and Farm Architecture : A Series of Designs. By JOHN STARFORTH, Architect. 102 Engravings. Second Edition. Medium 4to, £2, 17s. 6d.

STATISTICAL ACCOUNT OF SCOTLAND. Complete, with Index. 15 vols. 8vo, £16, 16s.

STEPHENS.
Book of the Farm ; detailing the Labours of the Farmer, Farm-Steward, Ploughman, Shepherd, Hedger, Farm-Labourer, Field-Worker, and Cattle-man. Illustrated with numerous Portraits of Animals and Engravings of Implements, and Plans of Farm Buildings. Fourth Edition. Revised, and in great part Rewritten by JAMES MACDONALD, of the 'Farming World,' &c. Complete in Six Divisional Volumes, bound in cloth, each 10s. 6d., or handsomely bound, in 3 volumes, with leather back and gilt top, £3, 3s.

The Book of Farm Implements and Machines. By J. SLIGHT and R. SCOTT BURN, Engineers. Edited by HENRY STEPHENS. Large 8vo, £2, 2s.

Catechism of Agriculture.   [*New Edition in preparation.*

STEVENSON. British Fungi. (Hymenomycetes). By Rev.
JOHN STEVENSON, Author of 'Mycologia Scotia,' Hon. Sec. Cryptogamic Society
of Scotland. Vols. I. and II., post 8vo, with Illustrations, price 12s. 6d. net each.

STEWART.
Advice to Purchasers of Horses. By JOHN STEWART, V.S.
New Edition. 2s. 6d.

Stable Economy. A Treatise on the Management of Horses
in relation to Stabling, Grooming, Feeding, Watering, and Working. Seventh
Edition. Fcap. 8vo, 6s. 6d.

STEWART. A Hebrew Grammar, with the Pronunciation, Syl-
labic Division and Tone of the Words, and Quantity of the Vowels. By Rev.
DUNCAN STEWART, D.D. Fourth Edition. 8vo, 3s. 6d.

STEWART. Boethius: An Essay. By HUGH FRASER STEWART,
M.A., Trinity College, Cambridge. Crown 8vo, 7s. 6d.

STODDART. Angling Songs. By THOMAS TOD STODDART.
New Edition, with a Memoir by ANNA M. STODDART. Crown 8vo, 7s. 6d.

STORMONTH.
Etymological and Pronouncing Dictionary of the English
Language. Including a very Copious Selection of Scientific Terms. For use in
Schools and Colleges, and as a Book of General Reference. By the Rev. JAMES
STORMONTH. The Pronunciation carefully revised by the Rev. P. H. PHELP, M.A.
Cantab. Eleventh Edition, Revised throughout, with Supplement. Crown 8vo,
pp. 800. 7s. 6d.

Dictionary of the English Language, Pronouncing, Etymological, and Explanatory. Revised by the Rev. P. H. PHELP. Library Edition.
Imperial 8vo, handsomely bound in half morocco, 31s. 6d.

The School Etymological Dictionary and Word-Book. Fourth
Edition. Fcap. 8vo, pp. 254. 2s.

STORY.
Nero; A Historical Play. By W. W. STORY, Author of
'Roba di Roma.' Fcap. 8vo, 6s.

Vallombrosa. Post 8vo, 5s.

Poems. 2 vols., 7s. 6d.

Fiammetta. A Summer Idyl. Crown 8vo, 7s. 6d.

Conversations in a Studio. 2 vols. crown 8vo, 12s. 6d.

Excursions in Art and Letters. Crown 8vo, 7s. 6d.

STRICKLAND. Life of Agnes Strickland. By her SISTER.
Post 8vo, with Portrait engraved on Steel, 12s. 6d.

STURGIS.
John-a-Dreams. A Tale. By JULIAN STURGIS. New Edition. Crown 8vo, 3s. 6d.

Little Comedies, Old and New. Crown 8vo, 7s. 6d.

SUTHERLAND (DUCHESS OF). How I Spent my Twentieth
Year. Being a Record of a Tour Round the World, 1886-87. By the DUCHESS
OF SUTHERLAND (MARCHIONESS OF STAFFORD). With Illustrations. Crown 8vo,
7s. 6d.

SUTHERLAND. Handbook of Hardy Herbaceous and Alpine
Flowers, for General Garden Decoration. Containing Descriptions of upwards
of 1000 Species of Ornamental Hardy Perennial and Alpine Plants; along with
Concise and Plain Instructions for their Propagation and Culture. By WILLIAM
SUTHERLAND, Landscape Gardener; formerly Manager of the Herbaceous Depart-
ment at Kew. Crown 8vo, 7s. 6d.

TAYLOR. The Story of my Life. By the late Colonel MEADOWS TAYLOR, Author of 'The Confessions of a Thug,' &c., &c. Edited by his Daughter. New and Cheaper Edition, being the Fourth. Crown 8vo, 6s.

THOLUCK. Hours of Christian Devotion. Translated from the German of A. Tholuck, D.D., Professor of Theology in the University of Halle. By the Rev. ROBERT MENZIES, D.D. With a Preface written for this Translation by the Author. Second Edition. Crown 8vo, 7s. 6d.

THOMSON. A History of the Fife Light Horse. By Colonel ANSTRUTHER THOMSON. With numerous Portraits. Small 4to. 21s.

THOMSON.

Handy Book of the Flower-Garden : being Practical Directions for the Propagation, Culture, and Arrangement of Plants in Flower-Gardens all the year round. With Engraved Plans. By DAVID THOMSON, Gardener to his Grace the Duke of Buccleuch, K.T., at Drumlanrig. Fourth and Cheaper Edition. Crown 8vo, 5s.

The Handy Book of Fruit-Culture under Glass : being a series of Elaborate Practical Treatises on the Cultivation and Forcing of Pines, Vines, Peaches, Figs, Melons, Strawberries, and Cucumbers. With Engravings of Hothouses, &c. Second Edition, Revised and Enlarged. Crown 8vo, 7s. 6d.

THOMSON. A Practical Treatise on the Cultivation of the Grape Vine. By WILLIAM THOMSON, Tweed Vineyards. Tenth Edition. 8vo, 5s.

THOMSON. Cookery for the Sick and Convalescent. With Directions for the Preparation of Poultices, Fomentations, &c. By BARBARA THOMSON. Fcap. 8vo, 1s. 6d.

THORNTON. Opposites. A Series of Essays on the Unpopular Sides of Popular Questions. By LEWIS THORNTON. 8vo, 12s. 6d.

TOM CRINGLE'S LOG. A New Edition, with Illustrations. Crown 8vo, cloth gilt, 5s. Cheap Edition, 2s.

TRANSACTIONS OF THE HIGHLAND AND AGRICUL-TURAL SOCIETY OF SCOTLAND. Published annually, price 5s.

TRAVEL, ADVENTURE, AND SPORT. From 'Blackwood's Magazine.' Uniform with 'Tales from Blackwood.' In 12 Parts, each price 1s. Handsomely bound in 6 vols., cloth, 15s. ; half calf, 25s.

TRAVERS. Mona Maclean, Medical Student. A Novel. By GRAHAM TRAVERS. 3 vols. crown 8vo, 25s. 6d.

TULLOCH.

Rational Theology and Christian Philosophy in England in the Seventeenth Century. By JOHN TULLOCH, D.D., Principal of St Mary's College in the University of St Andrews ; and one of her Majesty's Chaplains in Ordinary in Scotland. Second Edition. 2 vols. 8vo, 16s.

Modern Theories in Philosophy and Religion. 8vo, 15s.

Luther, and other Leaders of the Reformation. Third Edition, Enlarged. Crown 8vo, 3s. 6d.

Memoir of Principal Tulloch, D.D., LL.D. By Mrs OLIPHANT, Author of 'Life of Edward Irving.' Third and Cheaper Edition. 8vo, with Portrait, 7s. 6d.

TURNBULL. Othello : A Critical Study. By W. R. TURNBULL. Demy 8vo, 15s.

TWEEDIE. The Arabian Horse : his Country and People. With Portraits of Typical or Famous Arabians, and numerous other Illustrations ; also a Map of the Country of the Arabian Horse, and a descriptive Glossary of Arabic words and proper names. By Colonel W. TWEEDIE, C.S.I., Bengal Staff Corps, H.B.M.'s Consul-General, Baghdad, and Political Resident for the Government of India in Turkish Arabia. *[In the press.*

VEITCH.
Institutes of Logic. By JOHN VEITCH, LL.D., Professor of Logic and Rhetoric in the University of Glasgow. Post 8vo, 12s. 6d.

History and Poetry of the Scottish Border. In One Volume. Demy 8vo. [*In the press.*

The Feeling for Nature in Scottish Poetry. From the Earliest Times to the Present Day. 2 vols. fcap. 8vo, in roxburghe binding, 15s.

Merlin and other Poems. Fcap. 8vo. 4s. 6d.

Knowing and Being. Essays in Philosophy. First Series. Crown 8vo, 5s.

VIRGIL. The Æneid of Virgil. Translated in English Blank Verse by G. K. RICKARDS, M.A., and Lord RAVENSWORTH. 2 vols. fcap. 8vo, 10s.

WACE. The Christian Faith and Recent Agnostic Attacks. By the Rev. HENRY WACE, D.D., Principal of King's College, London ; Preacher of Lincoln's Inn ; Chaplain to the Queen. In one vol. post 8vo. [*Shortly.*

WALFORD. Four Biographies from 'Blackwood': Jane Taylor, Hannah More, Elizabeth Fry, Mary Somerville. By L. B. WALFORD. Crown 8vo, 5s.

WARREN'S (SAMUEL) WORKS :—
Diary of a Late Physician. Cloth, 2s. 6d. ; boards, 2s.

Ten Thousand A-Year. Cloth, 3s. 6d. ; boards, 2s. 6d.

Now and Then. The Lily and the Bee. Intellectual and Moral Development of the Present Age. 4s. 6d.

Essays : Critical, Imaginative, and Juridical. 5s.

WARREN. The Five Books of the Psalms. With Marginal Notes. By Rev. SAMUEL L. WARREN, Rector of Esher, Surrey ; late Fellow, Dean, and Divinity Lecturer, Wadham College, Oxford. Crown 8vo, 5s.

WEBSTER. The Angler and the Loop - Rod. By DAVID WEBSTER. Crown 8vo, with Illustrations, 7s. 6d.

WELLINGTON. Wellington Prize Essays on "the System of Field Manœuvres best adapted for enabling our Troops to meet a Continental Army." Edited by General Sir EDWARD BRUCE HAMLEY, K.C.B., K.C.M.G. 8vo, 12s. 6d.

WENLEY. Socrates and Christ : A Study in the Philosophy of Religion. By R. M. WENLEY, M.A., Lecturer on Mental and Moral Philosophy in Queen Margaret College, Glasgow ; Examiner in Philosophy in the University of Glasgow. Crown 8vo, 6s.

WERNER. A Visit to Stanley's Rear-Guard at Major Barttelot's Camp on the Aruhwimi. With an Account of River-Life on the Congo. By J. R. WERNER, F.R.G.S., Engineer, late in the Service of the Etat Independant du Congo. With Maps, Portraits, and other Illustrations. 8vo, 16s.

WESTMINSTER ASSEMBLY. Minutes of the Westminster Assembly, while engaged in preparing their Directory for Church Government, Confession of Faith, and Catechisms (November 1644 to March 1649). Edited by the Rev. Professor ALEX. T. MITCHELL, of St Andrews, and the Rev. JOHN STRUTHERS, LL.D. With a Historical and Critical Introduction by Professor Mitchell. 8vo, 15s.

WHITE.
The Eighteen Christian Centuries. By the REV. JAMES WHITE. Seventh Edition, post 8vo, with Index, 6s.

History of France, from the Earliest Times. Sixth Thousand. Post 8vo, with Index, 6s.

WHITE.
  Archæological Sketches in Scotland—Kintyre and Knapdale.
  By Colonel T. P. WHITE, R.E., of the Ordnance Survey. With numerous Illustrations. 2 vols. folio, £4, 4s. Vol. I., Kintyre, sold separately, £2, 2s.

  The Ordnance Survey of the United Kingdom. A Popular Account. Crown 8vo, 5s.

WILLIAMSON. The Horticultural Exhibitor's Handbook. A Treatise on Cultivating, Exhibiting, and Judging Plants, Flowers, Fruits, and Vegetables. By W. WILLIAMSON, Gardener. Revised by MALCOLM DUNN, Gardener to his Grace the Duke of Buccleuch and Queensberry, Dalkeith Park. Crown 8vo, 3s. 6d.

WILLIAMSON. Poems of Nature and Life. By DAVID R. WILLIAMSON, Minister of Kirkmaiden. Fcap. 8vo, 3s.

WILLIAMSON. Light from Eastern Lands on the Lives of Abraham, Joseph, and Moses. By the Rev. ALEX. WILLIAMSON, Author of 'The Missionary Heroes of the Pacific,' 'Sure and Comfortable Words,' 'Ask and Receive,' &c. Crown 8vo, 3s. 6d.

WILLS AND GREENE. Drawing-room Dramas for Children. By W. G. WILLS and the Hon. Mrs GREENE. Crown 8vo, 6s.

WILSON.
  Works of Professor Wilson. Edited by his Son-in-Law, Professor FERRIER. 12 vols. crown 8vo, £2, 8s.

  Christopher in his Sporting-Jacket. 2 vols., 8s.

  Isle of Palms, City of the Plague, and other Poems. 4s.

  Lights and Shadows of Scottish Life, and other Tales, 4s.

  Essays, Critical and Imaginative. 4 vols., 16s.

  The Noctes Ambrosianæ. 4 vols., 16s.

  Homer and his Translators, and the Greek Drama. Crown 8vo, 4s.

WITHIN AN HOUR OF LONDON TOWN. Among Wild Birds and their Haunts. By "A SON OF THE MARSHES," *See page* 28.

WORSLEY.
  Poems and Translations. By PHILIP STANHOPE WORSLEY, M.A. Edited by EDWARD WORSLEY. Second Edition, Enlarged. Fcap. 8vo, 6s.

  Homer's Odyssey. Translated into English Verse in Spenserian Stanza. By P. S. Worsley. Third Edition. 2 vols. fcap., 12s.

  Homer's Iliad. Translated by P. S. Worsley and Prof. Conington. 2 vols. Crown 8vo, 21s.

YATE. England and Russia Face to Face in Asia. A Record of Travel with the Afghan Boundary Commission. By Captain A. C. YATE, Bombay Staff Corps. 8vo, with Maps and Illustrations, 21s.

YATE. Northern Afghanistan; or, Letters from the Afghan Boundary Commission. By Major C. E. YATE, C.S.I., C.M.G. Bombay Staff Corps, F.R.G.S. 8vo, with Maps, 18s.

YOUNG. A Story of Active Service in Foreign Lands. Compiled from letters sent home from South Africa, India, and China, 1856-1882. By Surgeon-General A. GRAHAM YOUNG, Author of 'Crimean Cracks.' Crown 8vo, Illustrated, 7s. 6d.

YULE. Fortification: For the use of Officers in the Army, and Readers of Military History. By Colonel YULE, Bengal Engineers. 8vo, with Numerous Illustrations, 10s. 6d.

11/92.